ENTERTAINING WITH

GOOD HOUSEKEEPING

Sundial

CONTENTS

NOTES

All recipes serve 4 unless otherwise stated
All eggs are grade 3, 4, 5 (standard)
Plain flour and granulated sugar are used unless otherwise stated
All spoon measures are level unless otherwise stated
Ovens should be preheated to the specified temperature

The copyright in this book is
the property of:

© National Magazine Company Ltd. 1979
ISBN 0 904230 87 2

First published in 1979 by Sundial Books Limited
59 Grosvenor Street, London W.1.

Third impression, 1980

Produced by
Mandarin Publishers Limited Hong Kong

INTRODUCTION

Parties of all sorts can be great fun and enormously rewarding but no hostess gets by on inspiration alone. It needs careful arrangements for looking after your guests and a bit of hard work in the kitchen beforehand if you're to avoid driving yourself and the family into a frenzy. Work things out ahead, follow a few basic rules and everything on the day will be fine.

Menu Planning

Always plan a menu that has plenty of variety and keep within the limitations of your skill and circumstances. If timing worries you choose a casserole dish as a main course, accompanied by oven baked potatoes and a salad. It sounds obvious to say don't try anything new on the night – but don't. An old favourite perfectly served is far, far better than an experiment which flops. You wouldn't of course serve a quiche followed by steak and kidney pudding and then a fruit pie – three pastry dishes – but beware also of serving three rather sloppy courses. A general principle is 'wet' followed by 'dry', so soup with a crisp tasting main course followed by a soufflé is a good choice. Be careful with flavours too and don't paralyse the palate with curried soup before serving a delicately flavoured fish or chicken dish.

Serve foods in season when you can; for example, if melons or strawberries are plentiful choose these instead of making an elaborate dessert. Don't dismiss the possibility of serving convenience foods, especially at a buffet party. There are some excellent quiches, pâtés and cold meats available but buy them only from a tried and tested source. Try not to leave shopping until the last minute; always make a list. Remember, too, if you need to have a joint or chicken boned give the butcher as much notice as you can.

Laying the Table

This is one of the pleasanter pre-tasks of entertaining. Don't overdo it though. China, glasses and cutlery provide a lot of detail and too much decoration can look fussy. What is important is to have everything sparklingly clean. Tablecloths for buffet and informal meals need to be freshly ironed and paper table napkins chosen in subtle colours to match the cloth or mats. The cutlery should be placed neatly, knife blades pointing inwards and always on the right in the order in which they will be used, with forks to match on the left. The dessert spoon and fork may be laid nearest the plate or across the top in neat alignment with the spoon handle to the right and fork handle to the left.

Flower arrangements should be low and not overpoweringly scented. The photographs in the following chapters give ideas of how flowers can complement food. On a buffet table use taller arrangements in candlestick holders to keep the flowers above the food. Candlelight is more flattering than electric light but if you must have the latter have it casting light on the food and not faces.

Choosing Wine

There are no rules about wines to be served with food. It is very much a personal choice. It is generally accepted, however, that dry wines should come before sweet ones and light before the full bodied ones, for the good reason that the reverse order turns the dry wine bitter and the light wine insipid. It is also commonsense to serve dry white wine with fish and white meats rather than to obliterate their delicate flavour with heavier reds. Red meats and game, however, need the stronger company of a full red wine. Sweet desserts need sweet wine for a partner. Two wines are usually considered enough for entertaining at home though many a dinner party gets by very happily with one – chosen to go with the main course. For buffet parties and informal suppers a sparkling wine is often a good choice, with a light red table wine as an alternative. Seek the advice of your local wine merchant if you are not sure what to buy but at the same time don't despise wine from the better chain stores and supermarkets which is often explicitly labelled to help your choice. Play safe and buy a bottle to try before the party. Always serve wine correctly. All white wines should be served chilled but not iced. One to two hours in the refrigerator should be enough. Most red wines should be served at room temperature so let them stand in a room at about 15°-18°C (60°-65°F) for a few hours and uncork them at least an hour before serving. Wine glasses should be clear, colourless and thin, preferably with a bowl curving in towards the rim so as to hold the wine's bouquet. The glass should be stemmed – long or short. A 162-175 ml (5½-6 fl oz) glass is a good all purpose size. Never fill the glass more than half to two-thirds full.

Streamlining the Work

Having the right equipment does wonders for one's kitchen morale. Most of us can't change the cooker just because we've decided to entertain but if you happen to be buying one choose a model with two ovens, a large grill, good plate warming facilities and a reliable simmering hot plate or burner. If you have to make do with a small cooker, consider buying a plug-in electric frypan, casserole or grill to give extra cooking facilities.

For food preparation sharp knives, a pair of kitchen scissors and cooking tongs for lifting food from a frying pan, are all indispensable. An electric blender can halve the time it takes to make soups, pâtés and puréed desserts, while a mixer for whipping and beating and an attachment for shredding and slicing are invaluable when cooking for numbers. A pop-up toaster solves the problem of last minute hot toast to serve with pâtés and an electric coffee maker – the filter or percolator type – can be left to make coffee on its own. Use a vacuum flask to keep the milk hot.

A plug-in hot plate on the sideboard will ensure that food is kept hot and the plates warm. A trolley is also an asset for bringing the food into the dining room and for whisking the unattractive remains quickly away.

How A Freezer Can Help

A freezer can help as much as anything in the preparation of a party. Many cooked dishes can be made in advance, put in the freezer and brought out to thaw the day before the party. Casseroles and quiches can be put straight into the oven for reheating. The tables on pages 184-5 give an idea of what freezes well, how to wrap food for the freezer and how long foods take to thaw. Unless you have a microwave oven, there is nothing much that can be safely done to speed the process of thawing, so get food out of the freezer in good time. As a general rule it's best to allow most foods to thaw overnight in the refrigerator. Don't wrap and freeze food in very large portions. For instance, it's much better to make two pâtés for six to eight people than one huge one for twelve or more.

If you want to serve pâté in slices, cut it when it is nearly frozen and wrap the slices, interleaved with cling film or waxed paper. Write the number of slices on the label and place back in the freezer, fully wrapped, to finish freezing. The same can be done with cream filled cakes. It helps on the day and the slices look neat and even.

Don't forget to label everything. It's so easy to forget which package is which and it's not funny to find you've taken a loaf of bread out of the freezer instead of a pie when it is too late to do anything about it.

INFORMAL SUPPER PARTIES

Even informal meals need careful thought. These menus have been planned so that most of the preparation can be done beforehand and all but the finishing touches completed before the guests arrive. Cold dishes complement hot ones and this means departures to the kitchen for progress checks can be kept to a minimum once the party has started.

The meals cover a wide variety of informal occasions and are for a varying number of guests. The dishes are easy to prepare and include such things as soups, quiches and pies which do not need elaborate last minute dishing up. Table settings can be just as informal as the food. Use a plug-in electric hot plate, if you have one, to keep food and plates warm on the serving table. To drink, choose litre bottles of table wine or dry cider and have soft drinks available.

SOUPS AND SALADS FOR TEN

Lentil broth, Toasted flapovers/Smoked sausage and cheese salad, Beef salad niçoise/Apricot orange flan, Almond cream

BEFOREHAND

Make the soup. Shape the flapovers. Complete the sausage and beef salads. Refrigerate, covered.

Apricot orange flan
The custard-filled bases can be completed the day before and kept, loosely covered, in a cool place – not the refrigerator.

Almond cream
Whip up the ingredients, except the almonds, up to 2 hours ahead and refrigerate.

LENTIL BROTH

Metric	Imperial
50 g butter	2 oz butter
100 g smoked bacon rashers, rinds removed, diced	4 oz smoked bacon rashers, rinds removed, diced
225 g onions, peeled and chopped	8 oz onions, peeled and chopped
225 g carrots, peeled and chopped	8 oz carrots, peeled and chopped
225 g celery, trimmed and chopped	8 oz celery, trimmed and chopped
350 g lentils	12 oz lentils
3.5 litres light stock	6¼ pints light stock
4 cloves	4 cloves
1 bay leaf	1 bay leaf
1 x 5 ml spoon dried oregano	1 teaspoon dried oregano
1 x 5 ml spoon dried thyme	1 teaspoon dried thyme
Salt	Salt
Freshly ground black pepper	Freshly ground black pepper

Melt the butter in a large saucepan. Add the bacon, onions, carrots and celery and fry for 5 minutes. Add the remaining ingredients with salt and pepper to taste and bring to the boil. Reduce the heat, cover and simmer for 1½ hours.

Remove the cloves and bay leaf. Purée the soup in an electric blender. Reheat, and adjust the seasoning.

TOASTED FLAPOVERS

Cut the crusts from a small, thinly sliced white loaf. Spread each slice liberally with softened butter. Fold over the two opposite corners to the centre and thread the flapover on a skewer. Repeat, using all the slices. Lightly dust the flapovers with mild curry powder. Cover with kitchen foil or cling film, or keep in a plastic bag until needed. Grill until crisp and golden on both sides.

Right: Lentil broth. Far right: Smoked sausage and cheese salad; Toasted flapovers.

SMOKED SAUSAGE AND CHEESE SALAD

Metric	Imperial
100 g onion, peeled and chopped	4 oz onion, peeled and chopped
4 x 15 ml spoons chopped fresh parsley	4 tablespoons chopped fresh parsley
4 x 15 ml spoons salad oil	4 tablespoons salad oil
2 x 15 ml spoons wine vinegar	2 tablespoons wine vinegar
4 x 5 ml spoons French mustard	4 teaspoons French mustard
Salt	Salt
Freshly ground black pepper	Freshly ground black pepper
500 g smoked pork sausage, cut into 3 mm thick slices	1 lb smoked pork sausage, cut into ⅛ inch thick slices
350 g Gouda cheese, cut into 1 cm cubes	12 oz Gouda cheese, cut into ½ inch cubes

Combine the onion, parsley, oil, vinegar, mustard and salt and pepper to taste in a screwtop jar. Shake them well together.

Put the sausage and cheese in a serving bowl and pour over the dressing. Toss well to mix. Cover and leave to infuse the flavours for about 1 hour. Serve lightly chilled.

Beef salad niçoise.

BEEF SALAD NIÇOISE

Metric	**Imperial**
275 g pasta bows	10 oz pasta bows
Salt	Salt
20 black olives	20 black olives
225 g cooked brisket, thinly sliced and cut into strips	8 oz cooked brisket, thinly sliced and cut into strips
5 anchovy fillets, chopped	5 anchovy fillets, chopped
5 tomatoes, skinned, seeded and cut into strips	5 tomatoes, skinned, seeded and cut into strips
7.5 cm piece cucumber	3 inch piece cucumber
For the dressing:	**For the dressing:**
150 ml thick mayonnaise	¼ pint thick mayonnaise
4 x 15 ml spoons salad oil	4 tablespoons salad oil
2 x 15 ml spoons garlic vinegar	2 tablespoons garlic vinegar
1 x 2.5 ml spoon salt	½ teaspoon salt
Freshly ground black pepper	Freshly ground black pepper

Cook the pasta in boiling salted water until tender – about 10 minutes. Drain and refresh in cold water. Drain thoroughly. Leave to cool.

Combine the olives, beef, anchovies, tomatoes and pasta in a bowl.

Place the dressing ingredients with pepper to taste in a screwtop jar. Shake well, then add to the bowl and toss lightly.

Run the prongs of a fork down the skin of the cucumber. Cut into thin slices and arrange, overlapping, around the edge of a dish to give a scalloped effect. Spoon in the salad. Cover and chill for about 1 hour before serving.

APRICOT ORANGE FLAN

Metric	**Imperial**
275 g plain flour	10 oz plain flour
2 oranges	2 oranges
150 g butter	5 oz butter
300 ml soured cream	½ pint soured cream
2 eggs, separated	2 eggs, separated
2 x 15 ml spoons sugar	2 tablespoons sugar
2 x 822 g cans apricot halves	2 x 1 lb 13 oz cans apricot halves
1 x 15 ml spoon arrowroot	1 tablespoon arrowroot
2 x 15 ml spoons water	2 tablespoons water
Pistachio nuts, blanched and halved	Pistachio nuts, blanched and halved

Sift the flour into a bowl. Grate the rind from one orange into the flour. Thinly pare the rind from the other orange and cut it into julienne strips. Set aside. Squeeze the juice from both oranges and set aside. Rub the butter into the flour until the mixture resembles fine breadcrumbs. Add enough of the orange juice to knit the dough together – about 3 x 15 ml spoons (3 tablespoons). Chill for 1 hour.

Divide the dough into two and roll out each piece to line a 23.5 cm (9¼ inch) French fluted flan tin. Bake blind in a preheated moderately hot oven (200°C/400°F, Gas Mark 6) for 20 minutes. Remove the paper lining and bake for 10 minutes more. Remove from the oven and allow to cool.

Mix the soured cream with the egg yolks and sugar. Beat the whites until stiff and fold through the soured cream mixture. Divide equally between the pastry cases and spread evenly. Return to the oven and bake for 10 minutes. Leave to cool.

Drain the apricots. Arrange, hollow sides up, over the filling. Put the apricot can syrup, the rest of the orange juice and the orange rind strips in a saucepan and bring to the boil. Boil until reduced by half. Dissolve the arrowroot in the water. Pour into the pan and cook, stirring, until clear. Cool. Use to glaze the fruit. Decorate with halved pistachio nuts.

ALMOND CREAM

Metric	**Imperial**
150 ml soured cream	¼ pint soured cream
150 ml single cream	¼ pint single cream
150 ml double cream	¼ pint double cream
2 x 5 ml spoons caster sugar	2 teaspoons caster sugar
1 egg white	1 egg white
50 g flaked almonds, toasted	2 oz flaked almonds, toasted

Whisk the creams and sugar together until frothy and lightly thickened. Beat the egg white until stiff and fold into the cream mixture. Chill. Fold in the almonds just before serving.

Apricot orange flan; Almond cream.

Harvest Home for Eight

Cole slaw appetiser/Crackers and pretzels/Harvest pie, Tomatoes with lemon/Almond-stuffed apples, Butterscotch sauce

BEFOREHAND

Cole slaw appetiser

Shred the cabbage, chop the celery and onion and mix together in a lidded bowl. Combine the walnuts and raisins, but store separately. All the slaw ingredients can be combined several hours ahead of the meal and then spooned into dishes 1 hour ahead; cover with cling film.

Harvest pie

Make the pie filling and refrigerate. Keep the reserved onion in cling film. Rub margarine into self-raising flour for the topping mixture. (Add milk just before cooking.)

Tomatoes with lemon

Skin the tomatoes and refrigerate, covered.

Almond-stuffed apples with Butterscotch sauce

Up to 1 hour ahead, arrange the apples ready for cooking and brush with butter. (Time the cooking so that they're nearly ready when supper begins, then reduce the heat and keep them warm.) Make the sauce. (Reheat later in a double saucepan or in a heatproof bowl over a pan of simmering water.)

Tomatoes with lemon.

TOMATOES WITH LEMON

Metric	Imperial
75 g butter	3 oz butter
1 garlic clove, crushed	1 garlic clove, crushed
Finely grated rind of $\frac{1}{2}$ lemon	Finely grated rind of $\frac{1}{2}$ lemon
1 x 15 ml spoon lemon juice	1 tablespoon lemon juice
1 x 2.5 ml spoon salt	$\frac{1}{2}$ teaspoon salt
Freshly ground black pepper	Freshly ground black pepper
2 x 15 ml spoons chopped parsley	2 tablespoons chopped parsley
1 x 5 ml spoon caster sugar	1 teaspoon caster sugar
8 large tomatoes, skinned	8 large tomatoes, skinned

Melt the butter in a frying pan. Add the garlic, lemon rind, lemon juice, salt, pepper to taste, parsley and sugar and stir well. Heat very gently for about 3 minutes, for the flavours to blend. Add the tomatoes and cook for 5 minutes, turning frequently to baste.

COLE SLAW APPETISER

Metric	Imperial
225 g white cabbage, cored and finely shredded	8 oz white cabbage, cored and finely shredded
75 g celery, trimmed and finely chopped	3 oz celery, trimmed and finely chopped
75 g onion, peeled and finely chopped	3 oz onion, peeled and finely chopped
75 g walnuts, roughly chopped	3 oz walnuts, roughly chopped
75 g seedless raisins, cleaned	3 oz seedless raisins, cleaned
Grated rind and juice of 1 small lemon	Grated rind and juice of 1 small lemon
150 ml thick mayonnaise	$\frac{1}{4}$ pint thick mayonnaise
2 x 15 ml spoons oil	2 tablespoons oil
1 x 15 ml spoon vinegar	1 tablespoon vinegar
1 x 5 ml spoon dry mustard	1 teaspoon dry mustard
Salt	Salt
Freshly ground black pepper	Freshly ground black pepper
Paprika for garnish	Paprika for garnish

Put the cabbage, celery, onion, walnuts and raisins in a bowl. Combine the lemon rind and juice with the mayonnaise, oil, vinegar and mustard. Adjust the seasoning to taste. Fold the mayonnaise dressing through the vegetables. Serve on individual dishes, garnished with a dusting of paprika. Accompany with crackers and pretzels.

Cole slaw appetiser.

HARVEST PIE

Metric	Imperial
1 x 1.5 kg lean collar joint of bacon	1 x 3 lb lean collar joint of bacon
500 g carrots, peeled and diced	1 lb carrots, peeled and diced
Salt	Salt
50 g butter	2 oz butter
500 g onions, peeled and thinly sliced	1 lb onions, peeled and thinly sliced
50 g plain flour	2 oz plain flour
1 x 326 g can sweetcorn kernels	1 x 11½ oz can sweetcorn kernels
Milk	Milk
Freshly ground black pepper	Freshly ground black pepper
Oil	Oil
For the topping:	**For the topping:**
350 g self-raising flour	12 oz self-raising flour
1 x 2.5 ml spoon salt	½ teaspoon salt
75 g margarine	3 oz margarine
Milk	Milk

Put the bacon in a saucepan and cover with cold water. Bring slowly to the boil. Simmer for about 1 hour 35 minutes. Drain and cool. Cut into cubes. Meanwhile, cook the carrots in boiling salted water until tender. Drain.

Melt the butter in a saucepan. Reserve 16 slices of onion and add the rest to the butter. Cook gently until soft. Stir in the flour and cook, stirring, for 1 to 2 minutes.

Drain the sweetcorn and make the can liquid up to 900 ml (1½ pints) with milk. Add the liquid to the pan, and bring to the boil, stirring. Simmer until thickened, then remove from the heat. Fold in the carrots, corn and bacon. Season to taste. Divide between two shallow 1.7 litre (3 pint) ovenproof dishes.

To make the topping, sift the flour and salt into a bowl. Rub the margarine into the flour, then add enough milk to give a light scone dough. Roll out to 1 cm (½ inch) thick. Cut out sixteen 5 cm (2 inch) rounds with a plain cutter. Lay an onion slice on each, and arrange, overlapping, over the bacon and vegetables in the dishes. Brush with oil. Bake in a preheated very hot oven (240°C/450°F, Gas Mark 8) for about 25 minutes, or until the topping is risen and golden brown.

Harvest pie.

Almond-stuffed apples; Butterscotch sauce.

ALMOND-STUFFED APPLES

Metric	Imperial
8 large cooking apples	8 large cooking apples
100 g marzipan	4 oz marzipan
8 walnut halves	8 walnut halves
50 g butter, melted	2 oz butter, melted

Wipe the apples and core with an apple corer. With a pointed knife, make a slit around the middle circumference of each apple. On the top half make 5 to 6 slits down to the middle. Place the apples in a roasting tin.

Cut the marzipan into eight long sticks and insert one into each core cavity. Top with a walnut half. Brush all over with melted butter and cover with foil. Bake in the bottom of a preheated very hot oven (240°C/450°F, Gas Mark 8) for 25 minutes. Lower the oven temperature to moderate (180°C/350°F, Gas Mark 4), remove the foil and bake in the centre of the oven for a further 30 to 40 minutes or until soft but not floppy. Serve with Butterscotch sauce and pouring cream.

BUTTERSCOTCH SAUCE

Metric	Imperial
100 g butter	4 oz butter
50 g cane or golden syrup	2 oz cane or golden syrup
225 g soft brown sugar	8 oz soft brown sugar
300 ml single cream	½ pint single cream
2 x 15 ml spoons lemon juice	2 tablespoons lemon juice

Melt the butter in a saucepan. Add the syrup and sugar and heat slowly, stirring until dissolved. Stir in the remaining ingredients. Bring to the boil. Keep at a 'rolling boil' for 5 minutes, stirring occasionally. Allow to cool. Serve warm.

PASTA PARTY FOR TWELVE

Cannelloni with chicken and ham or Macaroni and smoked cod with soured cream sauce/Wholewheat and ale loaves/Orange bavarois

---

BEFOREHAND

Cannelloni with chicken and ham
Complete preparation, but do not bake; cover with foil and refrigerate.
Macaroni and smoked cod with soured cream sauce
Poach the fish and use to make the sauce; store, covered, in the refrigerator. Hard-boil the eggs.
Wholewheat and ale loaves
Bake the day before, cool and foil-wrap, ready to refresh when required.
Orange bavarois
Make the day before and keep in the refrigerator.

CANNELLONI WITH CHICKEN AND HAM

Metric	Imperial
750 g onions, peeled and sliced	1½ lb onions, peeled and sliced
150 g butter	6 oz butter
225 g lean cooked ham, minced	8 oz lean cooked ham, minced
500 g cold cooked chicken meat, chopped	1 lb cold cooked chicken meat, chopped
225 g mushrooms, finely chopped	8 oz mushrooms, finely chopped
250 g fresh white breadcrumbs	9 oz fresh white breadcrumbs
6 x 15 ml spoons chopped fresh parsley	6 tablespoons chopped fresh parsley
1 x 5 ml spoon dried sage	1 teaspoon dried sage
Salt	Salt
Freshly ground black pepper	Freshly ground black pepper
2 eggs, beaten	2 eggs, beaten
24 cannelloni tubes	24 cannelloni tubes
75 g plain flour	3 oz plain flour
1.4 litres milk	2½ pints milk
500 g tomatoes, skinned, seeded and sliced	1 lb tomatoes, skinned, seeded and sliced

Finely chop 225 g (8 oz) of the onions. Melt 50 g (2 oz) of the butter in a frying pan and fry the chopped onions until soft. Stir in the ham and chicken and fry for 5 minutes. Add the mushrooms and stir well. Remove from the heat.

In a large bowl, combine 225 g (8 oz) of the breadcrumbs, the parsley, sage, chicken mixture and plenty of seasoning. Bind with the eggs. Use to stuff the cannelloni.

Melt 75 g (3 oz) of the remaining butter in a saucepan. Add the rest of the onions, sliced, and soften without colouring – about 10 minutes. Stir in the flour and cook for 1 minute. Off the heat, stir in the milk, then bring to the boil, stirring, and simmer for 5 minutes. Season well. Spoon some of the onion sauce onto the bottom of two shallow ovenproof serving dishes, each large enough to take half the cannelloni in a single layer.

Divide the cannelloni between the two dishes. Pour over the rest of the sauce. Sprinkle with the rest of the breadcrumbs and bake in a preheated moderate oven (180°C/350°F, Gas Mark 4) for 40 to 45 minutes or until the top is browned.

Meanwhile, melt the remaining butter in the cleaned-out frying pan. Add the tomatoes and fry for 2 to 3 minutes, turning to coat with the butter. Garnish the dishes of cannelloni with the tomato slices and sprinkle with plenty of black pepper.

WHOLEWHEAT AND ALE LOAVES

Metric	Imperial
1 x 15 ml spoon dried yeast	1 tablespoon dried yeast
450 ml brown ale	¾ pint brown ale
25 g butter	1 oz butter
450 g plain wholewheat flour	1 lb plain wholewheat flour
225 g strong plain flour, sifted	8 oz strong plain flour, sifted
2 x 5 ml spoons salt	2 teaspoons salt
50 g Cheddar cheese, grated	2 oz Cheddar cheese, grated

Dissolve the dried yeast in 6 x 15 ml spoons (6 tablespoons) of the brown ale and leave in a warm place until frothy. Put the remaining ale and the butter in a saucepan and bring to the boil. Cool until lukewarm.

Mix the flours and salt together in a large bowl. Add the warm ale mixture and the yeast liquid and work to a dough. Turn onto a floured surface and knead for about 10 minutes, until smooth and elastic. Shape into a ball and place in a lightly oiled polythene bag. Leave to rise in a warm place until doubled in size.

Turn the dough onto a floured surface and knead for 2 to 3 minutes. Shape into 12 even-sized balls and place in a 25 by 20 cm (10 by 8 inch) oblong roasting tin. Cover lightly and leave to rise for 30 to 35 minutes, until doubled in size.

Sprinkle the cheese over the tops and bake in a preheated moderately hot oven (200°C/400°F, Gas Mark 6) for about 30 minutes. Cool on a wire rack. Break apart into small loaves for eating.
Makes 12

Cannelloni with chicken and ham.

MACARONI AND SMOKED COD WITH SOURED CREAM SAUCE

Metric	Imperial
500 g wholewheat short-style macaroni	1¼ lb wholewheat short-style macaroni
Salt	Salt
1.25 kg smoked cod fillets	2½ lb smoked cod fillets
1.2 litres milk	2 pints milk
1 slice of onion	1 slice of onion
1 slice of carrot	1 slice of carrot
6 peppercorns	6 peppercorns
1 bay leaf	1 bay leaf
50 g butter	2 oz butter
4 x 15 ml spoons plain flour	4 tablespoons plain flour
300 ml soured cream	½ pint soured cream
2 eggs, hard-boiled and chopped	2 eggs, hard-boiled and chopped
Freshly ground black pepper	Freshly ground black pepper
Snipped fresh chives to garnish	Snipped fresh chives to garnish

Cook the macaroni in plenty of boiling salted water as directed on the packet. Drain and cool under cold running water.

Place the fish in a roasting tin with the milk, onion, carrot, peppercorns and bay leaf. Cover and cook in a preheated moderate oven (180°C/350°F, Gas Mark 4) for about 20 minutes or until the fish flakes when forked. Strain off the milk and reserve. Flake the fish, removing any skin and bones. Increase the oven temperature to moderately hot (200°C/400°F, Gas Mark 6).

Melt the butter in a large saucepan. Stir in the flour and cook, stirring, for 1 minute. Off the heat, stir in the reserved milk from the fish. Bring to the boil, stirring, and simmer for 2 minutes. Stir in the soured cream, flaked fish and the hard-boiled eggs. Season well.

Fold the cooked macaroni into the fish mixture, combining well to coat the pasta. Adjust the seasoning. Divide between two lightly buttered casserole dishes. Cover and cook in the oven for about 25 minutes until piping hot. Stir well to loosen the pasta and garnish with snipped chives.

Above: Orange bavarois. Right: Macaroni and smoked cod with soured cream sauce; Green salad.

ORANGE BAVAROIS

Make three

Metric	Imperial
3 oranges	3 oranges
300 ml milk	½ pint milk
1 x 142 g lemon jelly tablet	1 x 5 oz lemon jelly tablet
1 x 15 ml spoon lemon juice	1 tablespoon lemon juice
1 x 15 ml spoon custard powder	1 tablespoon custard powder
2 x 5 ml spoons castor sugar	2 teaspoons castor sugar
150 ml double cream	¼ pint double cream
To decorate:	**To decorate:**
Whipped cream	Whipped cream
Orange slices	Orange slices

Finely grate the rind from one orange into the milk. Using a serrated knife, pare all the oranges, removing all traces of white pith. Remove the fleshy segments free of white pith over a measure – to catch any juice. Squeeze out any juice from the remaining membrane. Divide the jelly tablet in half. Place one half in the measure with the lemon juice and make up to 300 ml (½ pint) with boiling water. Stand the measure in hot water and stir to dissolve the jelly. When dissolved leave in a cold place until set to the consistency of unbeaten egg white. Fold the orange segments into the half-set jelly and spoon into a 900 ml (1½ pint) jelly mould. Leave to set.

Make a thin custard with the milk, custard powder and sugar. While the custard is still hot, add the rest of the jelly tablet, broken up, and stir until it is dissolved. Cool, stirring occasionally to prevent a skin forming. Whip the cream to the consistency of the custard and fold it into the custard mixture. Spoon over the jelly base. Leave overnight to set. Unmould onto a serving dish and decorate with cream and orange slices.

Wholewheat and ale loaves.

CUT AND COME AGAIN QUICHE PARTY FOR SIX

Mushroom cream flan or Bacon, celery and cream cheese quiche, Tossed green salad, Tomato cole slaw/
Frozen cranberry meringue ring

BEFOREHAND

Make the flans (heat just before serving). Make the slaw, omitting the apple; add this just before serving. Make the sweet. Prepare the salad ingredients; toss shortly before serving.

MUSHROOM CREAM FLAN

Metric	Imperial
For the pastry:	**For the pastry:**
125 g wholemeal flour	4 oz wholemeal flour
125 g plain flour, sifted	4 oz plain flour, sifted
1 x 2.5 ml spoon salt	½ teaspoon salt
125 g block margarine	4 oz block margarine
For the filling:	**For the filling:**
25 g butter or margarine	1 oz butter or margarine
225 g button mushrooms, quartered	8 oz button mushrooms, quartered
2 eggs	2 eggs
1 egg yolk	1 egg yolk
150 ml unsweetened natural yogurt	¼ pint unsweetened natural yogurt
6 x 15 ml spoons single cream	6 tablespoons single cream
Salt	Salt
Freshly ground black pepper	Freshly ground black pepper
2 x 15 ml spoons snipped fresh chives	2 tablespoons snipped fresh chives

Put the flours and salt into a mixing bowl and rub in the margarine until the mixture resembles breadcrumbs. Mix in enough water to bind to a dough. Roll out and use to line a 23 cm (9 inch) loose-bottomed flan tin. Bake blind in a preheated moderately hot oven (190°C/375°F, Gas Mark 5) for 15 minutes or until dry and just beginning to colour.

Meanwhile, melt the butter or margarine for the filling in a frying pan. Add the mushrooms and fry for 2 minutes. Drain. Whisk the whole eggs, egg yolk, yogurt, cream, seasoning and chives together. Scatter the mushrooms over the bottom of the flan case and pour over the yogurt mixture. Return to the moderately hot oven and bake for about 30 minutes, or until just set and golden brown. Serve hot or cold.

BACON, CELERY AND CREAM CHEESE QUICHE

Metric	Imperial
For the pastry:	**For the pastry:**
150 g butter or margarine	5 oz butter or margarine
300 g plain flour, sifted	10 oz plain flour, sifted
175 g Cheddar cheese, grated	6 oz Cheddar cheese, grated
2 egg yolks	2 egg yolks
For the filling:	**For the filling:**
350 g streaky bacon rashers, rinds removed, diced	12 oz streaky bacon rashers, rinds removed, diced
175 g celery, trimmed and thinly sliced	6 oz celery, trimmed and thinly sliced
4 eggs, beaten	4 eggs, beaten
175 g cream cheese	6 oz cream cheese
300 ml milk	½ pint milk
Freshly ground black pepper	Freshly ground black pepper

Rub the butter or margarine into the flour until it resembles fine breadcrumbs. Stir in the Cheddar cheese, egg yolks and just enough cold water to bind together. Knead lightly. Roll out the dough and use to line two 20 cm (8 inch) fluted flan rings, placed on a baking sheet. Bake blind in a preheated hot oven (220°C/425°F, Gas Mark 7) for 10 minutes.

Fry the bacon in its own fat until crisp and golden. Add the celery and cook gently for 2 to 3 minutes. Drain. Beat the eggs into the cream cheese and stir in the milk. Season with black pepper.

Fill the flan cases with the bacon and celery and pour over the egg mixture. Return the flans to the oven to bake for a further 10 minutes, then reduce the heat to moderately hot (190°C/375°F, Gas Mark 5). Bake for a further 15 to 20 minutes. Serve hot or cold.

TOMATO COLE SLAW

Metric	Imperial
500 g crisp green eating apples, cored and diced	1 lb crisp green eating apples, cored and diced
Juice of 1 lemon	Juice of 1 lemon
500 g white cabbage, cored and finely shredded	1 lb white cabbage, cored and finely shredded
75 g seedless raisins, cleaned	3 oz seedless raisins, cleaned
300 ml thick mayonnaise	½ pint thick mayonnaise
Salt	Salt
Freshly ground black pepper	Freshly ground black pepper
500 g tomatoes, sliced	1 lb tomatoes, sliced

Put the apples in a bowl with the lemon juice and toss lightly to coat the pieces with the juice.

In a large bowl, combine the cabbage with the raisins, mayonnaise and drained apple. Season well. Place two-thirds of the cabbage mixture in a deep serving dish, levelling the surface. Season the tomato slices and place most in a layer over the slaw. Cover with the remaining cabbage mixture, piling up in the centre. Arrange the remaining tomato slices around the top edge. Keep in a cool place.

Left: Mushroom cream flan.

FROZEN CRANBERRY MERINGUE RING

Metric
350 g whole cranberries
60 g granulated sugar
200 ml water
3 x 15 ml spoons cornflour
300 ml skimmed milk
60 g soft margarine
60 g icing sugar
75 g meringue shells, roughly
  broken up
A few meringue pieces for
  decoration

Imperial
12 oz whole cranberries
2½ oz granulated sugar
⅓ pint water
3 tablespoons cornflour
½ pint skimmed milk
2½ oz soft margarine
2½ oz icing sugar
3 oz meringue shells, roughly
  broken up
A few meringue pieces for
  decoration

Place the cranberries, granulated sugar and water in a pan and cook gently until the fruit pops and softens. Cool.

Mix the cornflour with a little of the milk to a smooth paste. Bring the remaining milk to the boil and pour onto the cornflour, stirring. Return this mixture to the pan and bring to the boil, still stirring. Cover and leave to cool.

Blend the margarine, cornflour mixture, sifted icing sugar and half the cranberry mixture in an electric blender until smooth. Fold together the meringue pieces, puréed mixture, and nearly all the remaining whole cranberry mixture (reserve a few cranberries for decoration). Turn into a lightly oiled 900 ml (1½ pint) non-stick ring mould. Cover and freeze until firm. To serve, unmould and decorate with extra broken meringue and the reserved whole cranberries.

Below: Bacon, celery and cream cheese quiche; Green salad; Tomato cole slaw; Frozen cranberry meringue ring.

ONE-POT SUPPER FOR SIX

Avocado-stuffed tomatoes/Lamb bourguignon, Fluffy boiled rice, Glazed carrots (oven-cooked)/Chocolate and orange ice cream

BEFOREHAND

Avocado-stuffed tomatoes
Stuff the tomatoes. Store, covered with cling film, in the refrigerator for not more than 2 hours.
Lamb bourguignon
Prepare the meat, blanch the onions and fry the mushrooms. The lamb can be cooked completely in advance and then reheated in a preheated moderate oven (160°C/325°F, Gas Mark 3) for 1 hour.
Chocolate and orange ice cream
Chill the evaporated milk. Make the ice cream and freeze.

AVOCADO-STUFFED TOMATOES

Metric	Imperial
1 avocado, peeled, stoned and diced	1 avocado, peeled, stoned and diced
2 x 5 ml spoons lemon juice	2 teaspoons lemon juice
1 x 15 ml spoon mayonnaise	1 tablespoon mayonnaise
100 g cream cheese	4 oz cream cheese
1 x 5 ml spoon snipped fresh chives	1 teaspoon snipped fresh chives
Salt	Salt
Freshly ground black pepper	Freshly ground black pepper
6 large ripe tomatoes	6 large ripe tomatoes

Push the avocado flesh through a nylon sieve and beat in the lemon juice, mayonnaise, cream cheese and chives. When smooth, turn into a bowl and adjust the seasoning.

Cut the tops from the tomatoes, scoop out the seeds and membrane, and fill with the avocado mixture. Chill before serving.

LAMB BOURGUIGNON

Metric	Imperial
1.25 kg boned lean leg of lamb (boned weight)	2½ lb boned lean leg of lamb (boned weight)
225 g small onions	8 oz small onions
3 x 15 ml spoons corn oil	3 tablespoons corn oil
50 g margarine	2 oz margarine
225 g button mushrooms	8 oz button mushrooms
225 ml red wine	8 fl oz red wine
300 ml brown stock	½ pint brown stock
1 x 2.5 ml spoon salt	½ teaspoon salt
Freshly ground black pepper	Freshly ground black pepper
1 x 15 ml spoon arrowroot	1 tablespoon arrowroot
1 x 15 ml spoon water	1 tablespoon water
Chopped fresh parsley and fried croûtons to garnish	Chopped fresh parsley and fried croûtons to garnish

Discard all skin and fat from the lamb. Cut into large fork-size pieces. Blanch the onions in boiling water for 2 minutes, then drain and peel them.

Heat the oil in a deep frying pan. Add the margarine and, when frothing, put in the meat to seal on all sides. Remove the meat cubes from the pan as they brown. Add the onions and brown evenly. Drain and add to the meat. Finally, lightly fry the mushrooms.

Replace the meat and vegetables in the pan and stir in the wine, stock and seasoning. Bring to the boil, then transfer to a flameproof casserole. Cover and cook in a preheated moderate oven (160°C/325°F, Gas Mark 3) for about 1½ hours or until the meat is tender.

Dissolve the arrowroot in the water. When the lamb is cooked, put the casserole on top of the cooker and stir in the arrowroot. Cook until clear and thickened – about 2 minutes. Serve the lamb garnished with parsley and croûtons.

Avocado-stuffed tomatoes.

Lamb bourguignon; Glazed carrots; Rice.

GLAZED CARROTS

Metric	**Imperial**
1 kg carrots, peeled and cut into thin strips	2 lb carrots, peeled and cut into thin strips
300 ml water	$\frac{1}{2}$ pint water
50 g butter	2 oz butter
4 x 15 ml spoons demerara sugar	4 tablespoons demerara sugar

Put the carrots in an ovenproof dish with the water, butter and sugar. Cover loosely with foil and cook in a preheated moderate oven (160°C/325°F, Gas Mark 3) for 1$\frac{1}{2}$ hours, with the Lamb bourguigon.

CHOCOLATE AND ORANGE ICE CREAM

Metric	**Imperial**
1 small can evaporated milk, chilled	1 small can evaporated milk, chilled
150 ml double cream	$\frac{1}{4}$ pint double cream
75 g plain chocolate-flavoured cake covering, finely grated	3 oz plain chocolate-flavoured cake covering, finely grated
Finely grated rind and juice of 1 large orange	Finely grated rind and juice of 1 large orange
1 x 15 ml spoon orange-flavoured liqueur	1 tablespoon orange-flavoured liqueur
3 x 15 ml spoons icing sugar	3 tablespoons icing sugar
Ice cream wafers to serve	Ice cream wafers to serve

Whip the evaporated milk as thickly as possible. Whip the cream to the same consistency and fold into the evaporated milk. Fold in the grated chocolate and orange rind, strained orange juice and liqueur.

Sift in the icing sugar. Stir well to mix. Pour into a rigid container and freeze until mushy. Remove from the freezer and whisk with a fork to break down any ice crystals. Freeze until firm. Allow to come to cool room temperature before serving with ice cream wafers.

Chocolate and orange ice cream.

23

SIMPLE DINNER PARTIES

The subtle flavours belie the simplicity of preparation of these dinners for six, and the main courses are chosen to avoid last minute attention. The Southern Beef and Bean Pot is a wonderfully warming dish for a chilly evening and will not spoil if your guests are late arriving. Sage and Bacon Stuffed Pork can be kept waiting, too. Summer calls for lighter but equally flavourful fare, using fresh fruit and vegetables. You can add an extra-delicious touch to the new potatoes by grinding coarse sea salt over them at the table.

WINTER DINNER PARTY FOR SIX

Prawn cauliflower salad, Brown bread and butter / Sage and bacon stuffed pork, Baked jacket potatoes, Brussels sprouts with Brazil nuts / Mandarin vacherin

BEFOREHAND

Prawn cauliflower salad
In the morning, prepare, cover and refrigerate. Prepare bread and butter, cling-wrap and refrigerate.
Sage and bacon stuffed pork
In the morning, open out the joint, stuff and tie; refrigerate.
Brussels sprouts with Brazil nuts
Prepare sprouts, breadcrumbs and nuts and keep in separate polythene bags in refrigerator.
Mandarin vacherin
Make the meringue well ahead – several days if convenient – and keep in airtight tin, unfilled.

BRUSSELS SPROUTS WITH BRAZIL NUTS

Metric	Imperial
750 g Brussels sprouts	1½ lb Brussels sprouts
75 g butter	3 oz butter
100 g Brazil nuts, shelled and chopped	4 oz Brazil nuts, shelled and chopped
75 g fresh white breadcrumbs	3 oz fresh white breadcrumbs
Salt	Salt
Freshly ground black pepper	Freshly ground black pepper

Trim the Brussels sprouts and cut a cross in the base of each. Cook in boiling salted water for 10 to 15 minutes until tender. Drain.

Melt the butter in a pan, add the Brazil nuts and cook over a gentle heat until golden. Add the breadcrumbs and continue cooking until they have absorbed the butter and are crisp and golden. Add the Brussels sprouts and salt and pepper to taste. Heat through, stirring.

PRAWN CAULIFLOWER SALAD

Metric	Imperial
6 x 15 ml spoons thick mayonnaise	6 tablespoons thick mayonnaise
1 x 15 ml spoon tomato paste	1 tablespoon tomato paste
1 x 15 ml spoon medium sherry	1 tablespoon medium sherry
2 x 15 ml spoons lemon juice	2 tablespoons lemon juice
Salt	Salt
Freshly ground black pepper	Freshly ground black pepper
1 small cauliflower, about 500 g trimmed weight, broken into tiny florets	1 small cauliflower, about 1 lb trimmed weight, broken into tiny florets
100 g cucumber, diced	4 oz cucumber, diced
100 g frozen shelled prawns, thawed	4 oz frozen shelled prawns, thawed
1 small endive, broken into leaves	1 small endive, broken into leaves
Chopped fresh parsley to garnish	Chopped fresh parsley to garnish

In a large bowl, mix the mayonnaise with the tomato paste, sherry, lemon juice and seasoning. Blanch the cauliflower florets in boiling salted water for 2 to 3 minutes, then drain them well. While warm, stir into the mayonnaise mixture and allow to cool.

Sprinkle the cucumber dice lightly with salt and leave for about 20 minutes. Drain. Fold through the cauliflower with the prawns. Cover and chill.

To serve, line six natural scallop shells or small dishes with endive leaves. Pile on the cauliflower mixture and garnish with parsley.

SAGE AND BACON STUFFED PORK

Metric	Imperial
1 kg boned loin of pork, well scored	2¼ lb boned loin of pork, well scored
225 g back bacon rashers, rinds removed	8 oz back bacon rashers, rinds removed
12 fresh or dried sage leaves	12 fresh or dried sage leaves
Cooking oil and salt	Cooking oil and salt

Ask the butcher to bone the pork and score the rind deeply and evenly. Place the joint on a flat surface, fat side down, and cut the flesh at intervals to open it out a little. Lay the rashers over the flesh and place the sage leaves at intervals. Roll up carefully and secure firmly with string, parcel fashion. Put in a roasting tin. Rub the rind well with oil and salt and roast in a preheated moderately hot oven (190°C/375°F, Gas Mark 5) for about 2 hours. Remove the strings and place the meat on a serving dish.

Prawn cauliflower salad.

Sage and bacon stuffed pork; Brussels sprouts with Brazil nuts; Mandarin vacherin.

MANDARIN VACHERIN

Metric
For the meringues:
3 egg whites
175 g caster sugar
75 g toasted ground hazelnuts
For the filling:
300 ml double cream
Icing sugar
2 x 312 g cans mandarins,
    drained

Imperial
For the meringues:
3 egg whites
6 oz caster sugar
3 oz toasted ground hazelnuts
For the filling:
½ pint double cream
Icing sugar
2 x 11 oz cans mandarins, drained

To make the meringues, beat the egg whites until stiff. Gradually beat in the sugar, keeping the mixture stiff. Fold in the ground nuts. Draw two 20 cm (8 inch) circles on non-stick paper. Divide one into six wedge shapes. Pipe a good half of the mixture onto the plain circle, using a 1 cm (½ inch) plain nozzle. Pipe the remaining mixture into six separated triangles within the circle area on the other sheet of paper, allowing room between them for spreading. Bake in a preheated moderately hot oven (190°C/375°F, Gas Mark 5) for 30 to 35 minutes or until crisp and golden. Cool, then peel off the paper.

To complete the vacherin, stiffly whip the cream with icing sugar to taste. Reserve a few mandarins for the decoration. Fold the remaining mandarins into half the cream and pile onto the meringue circle. Place the wedges on top. Decorate with the rest of the whipped cream. Just before serving, dust with icing sugar and add the reserved mandarins.

Winter Dinner Party for Six

Artichoke and pepper gratin/Southern beef and bean pot, Jacket potatoes, Chicory, tomato and chive salad/Apple fig snow

BEFOREHAND

Artichoke and pepper gratin
Complete, but do not cook, on the morning of the party.
Southern beef and bean pot
This can be made a day ahead and reheated in a preheated moderate oven (180°C/350°F, Gas Mark 4) for 1 hour when required. But remember that the beans must be soaked overnight before you use them.
Jacket potatoes
Scrub the day before.
Chicory, tomato and chive salad
Make just before the party.
Apple fig snow
Make on the morning of the party. (The apples can be stewed, and then the figs added, on the day before.)

ARTICHOKE AND PEPPER GRATIN

Metric	Imperial
25 g margarine	1 oz margarine
50 g onion, peeled and finely chopped	2 oz onion, peeled and finely chopped
1 medium green pepper, cored, seeded and finely chopped	1 medium green pepper, cored, seeded and finely chopped
2 x 312 g cans artichoke fronds, drained	2 x 11 oz cans artichoke fronds, drained
50 g Edam cheese, grated	2 oz Edam cheese, grated
50 g fresh white breadcrumbs	2 oz fresh white breadcrumbs
1 x 2.5 ml spoon paprika	½ teaspoon paprika

Above: Artichoke and pepper gratin. Right: Southern beef and bean pot; Chicory, tomato and chive salad; Apple fig snow.

Melt the margarine in a frying pan. Add the onion and green pepper and fry until softened. Place 2 or 3 artichoke fronds in six well-greased individual ovenproof dishes and pile the pepper mixture on top. Combine the cheese, breadcrumbs and paprika and scatter a little over each serving. Bake in a preheated very hot oven (230°C/450°F, Gas Mark 8) for 10 minutes.

SOUTHERN BEEF AND BEAN POT

Metric	Imperial
1 kg lean chuck steak	2 lb lean chuck steak
3 x 15 ml spoons seasoned flour	3 tablespoons seasoned flour
3 x 15 ml spoons corn oil	3 tablespoons corn oil
175 g onions, peeled and sliced	6 oz onions, peeled and sliced
450 ml beef stock	¾ pint beef stock
100 g dried red kidney beans, soaked overnight and drained	4 oz dried red kidney beans, soaked overnight and drained
8 juniper berries	8 juniper berries
1 bay leaf	1 bay leaf
Thinly pared rind of ½ orange	Thinly pared rind of ½ orange
Salt	Salt
Freshly ground black pepper	Freshly ground black pepper
Parsley sprigs to garnish	Parsley sprigs to garnish

Trim all fat from the meat and cut it into large fork-size pieces. Coat in the seasoned flour. Heat the oil in a saucepan and fry the meat with the onions until evenly browned, stirring occasionally. Add the stock, beans and berries. Tie the bay leaf and orange rind in a piece of muslin and add. Season and bring to the boil. Cover, reduce the heat and simmer for 2 to 2½ hours, stirring from time to time. Alternatively, place in a casserole and cook in the bottom of a preheated moderate oven (180°C/350°F, Gas Mark 4) for 2 to 2½ hours. Stir occasionally and add more stock if necessary. Discard the orange rind and bay leaf. Serve garnished with parsley.

APPLE FIG SNOW

Metric	Imperial
1 kg cooking apples, peeled, cored and sliced	2 lb cooking apples, peeled, cored and sliced
Grated rind and juice of 1 lemon	Grated rind and juice of 1 lemon
3 x 15 ml spoons water	3 tablespoons water
25 g margarine	1 oz margarine
25 g soft brown sugar	1 oz soft brown sugar
75 g honeyed dessert figs, finely chopped	3 oz honeyed dessert figs, finely chopped
3 egg whites	3 egg whites

Put the apple slices, lemon rind and juice, water, margarine and sugar in a saucepan. Cover and stew gently until really soft, being careful that the fruit does not stick and burn in the pan.

Remove the pan from the heat and beat the apple mixture until smooth. Then, while still warm, add the figs. Leave to cool.

Whisk the egg whites until stiff. Beat 2 x 15 ml spoons (2 tablespoons) into the apple to lighten the mixture, then fold in the rest carefully. Pile into a glass dish and chill well. Serve decorated with a piece of fresh fig, if available.

SUMMER DINNER PARTY FOR SIX

Mushroom quiches/Veal escalopes with tomatoes and cucumber, New potatoes in their jackets, Buttered mange-tout/
Gooseberry almond crush

BEFOREHAND

Mushroom quiches
Make the pastry the day before. Line the tins, cover tightly and keep in a cool place. On the morning of the dinner, soak the anchovies in milk and slice and fry the mushrooms. Cool. Start baking the unfilled pastry cases about 45 minutes before dinner. Finish the quiche mixture.

Veal escalopes with tomatoes and cucumber
The escalopes can be beaten out on the day before; keep them in the refrigerator, loosely covered. Prepare the vegetables on the morning of the dinner; keep covered. Reduce the wine if wished.

Potatoes and mange-tout
Wash and store – separately – in polythene bags in refrigerator.

Gooseberry almond crush
Prepare this on the morning of the dinner party.

MUSHROOM QUICHES

Metric	Imperial
6 anchovy fillets, drained	6 anchovy fillets, drained
Milk	Milk
100 g plain flour	4 oz plain flour
1 x 2.5 ml spoon salt	½ teaspoon salt
1 x 1.25 ml spoon paprika	¼ teaspoon paprika
75 g block margarine	3 oz block margarine
25 g mature Cheddar cheese, finely grated	1 oz mature Cheddar cheese, finely grated
About 1 x 15 ml spoon water	About 1 tablespoon water
25 g butter	1 oz butter
175 g button mushrooms, sliced	6 oz button mushrooms, sliced
2 small eggs, beaten	2 small eggs, beaten
200 ml single cream	⅓ pint single cream
Freshly ground black pepper	Freshly ground black pepper

Soak the anchovies in a little milk for about 1 hour.

Sift together the flour, salt and half the paprika. Rub in the margarine until the mixture resembles breadcrumbs. Stir in the cheese and enough water to bind. Knead lightly and roll out thinly

Mushroom quiches.

on a floured surface. Cut out six circles with a 12.5 cm (5 inch) cutter – use a saucer or a saucepan lid – and press gently into six 11.5 cm (4½ inch) individual loose-bottomed flan tins. Prick the bottoms and bake blind in a preheated moderately hot oven (200°/400°F, Gas Mark 6) for 10 minutes.

Melt the butter in a frying pan and quickly fry the mushrooms. Divide between the cases. Drain the anchovies and pound to a paste in a small bowl. Beat in the eggs and cream, and season with black pepper. Spoon into the pastry cases. Dust lightly with the remaining paprika and return to the oven to bake for a further 20 minutes or until lightly set and slightly browned on top. Serve at once.

VEAL ESCALOPES WITH TOMATOES AND CUCUMBER

Metric	Imperial
6 veal escalopes, about 75 g each	6 veal escalopes, about 3 oz each
Salt	Salt
Freshly ground black pepper	Freshly ground black pepper
25 g butter	1 oz butter
2 x 15 ml spoons corn oil	2 tablespoons corn oil
100 g onion, peeled and sliced	4 oz onion, peeled and sliced
1 garlic clove, crushed	1 garlic clove, crushed
150 ml dry white wine	¼ pint dry white wine
½ cucumber, peeled, halved, seeded and sliced	½ cucumber, peeled, halved, seeded and sliced
500 g firm tomatoes, skinned, quartered and seeded	1 lb firm tomatoes, skinned, quartered and seeded
1 x 15 ml spoon lemon juice	1 tablespoon lemon juice
4 x 15 ml spoons finely chopped fresh parsley	4 tablespoons finely chopped fresh parsley

Trim the escalopes and bat them out between sheets of non-stick paper, then season. Heat the butter and oil in a large frying pan and brown the escalopes, two at a time. Keep on one side. Add the onion and fry until golden. Stir in the garlic, wine and seasoning. Replace the veal, with any juices, in the pan and simmer gently, uncovered, for 10 minutes. Arrange the escalopes in a large warmed serving dish and keep warm.

Boil the liquid in the frying pan to reduce to 4 x 15 ml spoons (4 tablespoons). Add the cucumber and cook, stirring, for 5 minutes. Add the tomatoes and lemon juice, stir gently and adjust the seasoning. Cook for 2 minutes. Spoon over the escalopes and garnish with the parsley.

Note: To give more depth of flavour to the wine for cooking, start with 300 ml (½ pint) and boil to reduce by half in an open pan.

NEW POTATOES IN THEIR JACKETS

Metric	Imperial
1 kg walnut-sized new potatoes	2 lb walnut-sized new potatoes
Salt	Salt
50 g butter	2 oz butter
Freshly ground black pepper	Freshly ground black pepper

Wash the potatoes carefully, put into cold salted water and bring to the boil. Cover and simmer for 15 to 20 minutes or until just tender. Drain well and return to the pan. Add the butter and plenty of pepper. Stir over a low heat until the potatoes are covered with melted butter. Transfer to a serving dish and serve hot.

Veal escalopes with tomatoes and cucumber; Buttered mange-tout; New potatoes in their jackets.

BUTTERED MANGE-TOUT
(SUGAR PEAS)

Metric	Imperial
750 g mange-tout, topped and tailed	1½ lb mange-tout, topped and tailed
Salt	Salt
25 g butter	1 oz butter
Freshly ground black pepper	Freshly ground black pepper

Put the mange-tout in a pan containing 1 cm (½ inch) boiling salted water. Bring back to the boil, cover and simmer for 5 minutes or until just tender. Drain well and toss in the butter, adding plenty of freshly ground pepper.

GOOSEBERRY ALMOND CRUSH

Metric	Imperial
500 g gooseberries, topped and tailed	1 lb gooseberries, topped and tailed
2 x 15 ml spoons water	2 tablespoons water
100-125 g caster sugar	4 oz caster sugar
2 x 15 ml spoons Kirsch	2 tablespoons Kirsch
100 g French almond macaroons, crumbled	4 oz French almond macaroons, crumbled
150 ml whipping cream	¼ pint whipping cream
3 macaroons to decorate	3 macaroons to decorate

Cook the gooseberries with the water and sugar until the fruit is soft and well reduced, then sieve it. Stir in the Kirsch. Arrange the macaroon crumbs and gooseberry purée in alternate layers in six tall glasses. Leave in a cool place for several hours.

Whip the cream until it barely holds its shape. Spoon some of the soft cream over each serving and top each with a halved macaroon.

Gooseberry almond crush.

EXOTIC DINNER PARTIES

If you want to give an unusual and enjoyable party without putting too much of a strain on the budget, organise a meal with an exotic flavour. There are several here, all adapted when necessary to the foods available in this country.

Follow the specific menus through with a careful choice of drinks and table settings. Serve the Chinese food, for example, the Chinese way, from small bowls grouped in the centre of the table. Provide chop-sticks; even though you and your guests may not be very good at eating with them, you'll enjoy having a try.

Before the Indian dinner party, serve hot samosas as appetisers with pre-dinner drinks. Serve them with segmented limes for squeezing over them (lemons make an acceptable substitute if limes aren't available). With the curries, serve poppadums and a few side dishes such as desiccated coconut, raisins, sliced tomatoes, diced cucumber, mango chutney and sliced bananas (prepared just before they are needed).

CHINESE PARTY FOR SIX

Almond soup/Chicken with cashews, Crispy noodles with pork and water chestnuts, Prawns with bean sprouts, Boiled rice, Prawn crackers/Canned litchis in syrup, or Fruit-filled melon

BEFOREHAND

Almond soup
Make this early in the day and reheat in pan when needed.

Chicken with cashews
The day before, cube the chicken and cut up the vegetables. Keep the chicken and vegetables covered (separately) in the refrigerator. Fry the cashews. One hour before required, mix the ingredients for the sauce and make the sauce; keep it warm, preferably in a double saucepan. Fry the chicken and vegetables and keep warm, having removed them from the pan. When required, return to the pan, pour over the sauce and complete preparation.

Crispy noodles with pork and water chestnuts
The day before, boil and drain the noodles. Refrigerate, covered. Dice the pork; refrigerate. Prepare the vegetables; keep in polythene bag in refrigerator.

Prawns with bean sprouts
In the morning of the party, soak the prawns.

Fruit-filled melon
Prepare early in the day. Chill thoroughly in the refrigerator.

Rice
Boil the day before and heat when required, as indicated in the recipe.

ALMOND SOUP

Metric	Imperial
3 x 15 ml spoons olive oil	3 tablespoons olive oil
175 g blanched almonds, finely chopped	6 oz blanched almonds, finely chopped
1.5 x 15 ml spoons chopped onion	1½ tablespoons chopped onion
1 x 5 ml spoon crushed garlic	1 teaspoon crushed garlic
1.5 x 5 ml spoons chopped fresh parsley	1½ teaspoons chopped fresh parsley
10 x 15 ml spoons fresh white breadcrumbs	10 tablespoons fresh white breadcrumbs
1.8 litres chicken stock	3 pints chicken stock
Salt	Salt
Freshly ground black pepper	Freshly ground black pepper
Spring onion fans to garnish	Spring onion fans to garnish

Heat the oil in a saucepan and gently cook the almonds, onion, garlic and parsley, stirring all the time. Do not brown. Stir in the breadcrumbs and cook slowly for a further 3 minutes. Pour on the stock, season and cover. Simmer for 15 minutes. Serve garnished with spring onion fans.

Almond soup.

34

Chicken with cashews; Crispy noodles with pork and water chestnuts; Rice.

CHICKEN WITH CASHEWS

Metric
4 x 15 ml spoons cooking oil
100 g cashews, blanched
1 onion, peeled and chopped
350 g chicken meat, cut into
 small cubes
50 g mushrooms, chopped
1 green pepper, cored, seeded
 and chopped
1 carrot, peeled and sliced
1 canned bamboo shoot,
 chopped
Salt
2 x 5 ml spoons cornflour
2 x 5 ml spoons sugar
1 x 15 ml spoon soy sauce
2 x 5 ml spoons dry sherry
300 ml water

Imperial
4 tablespoons cooking oil
4 oz cashews, blanched
1 onion, peeled and chopped
12 oz chicken meat, cut into
 small cubes
2 oz mushrooms, chopped
1 green pepper, cored, seeded
 and chopped
1 carrot, peeled and sliced
1 canned bamboo shoot,
 chopped
Salt
2 teaspoons cornflour
2 teaspoons sugar
1 tablespoon soy sauce
2 teaspoons dry sherry
½ pint water

Heat 1 x 15 ml spoon (1 tablespoon) of the oil in a frying pan and fry the cashews until golden brown. Remove from the pan. Add 2 x 15 ml spoons (2 tablespoons) of the oil to the pan. Heat and fry the onion until it is transparent. Remove it from the pan. Fry the chicken until it begins to brown. Add the remaining oil, the vegetables, including the onion, and salt to taste and cook, stirring occasionally, for 5 to 6 minutes.

Mix together the cornflour, a little salt, the sugar, soy sauce, sherry and water in a saucepan. Bring to the boil, stirring all the time, and pour over the chicken. Add the nuts and cook until very hot. Serve at once in warmed bowls.

CRISPY NOODLES WITH PORK AND WATER CHESTNUTS

Metric
175 g packet Chinese egg
 noodles
Oil for deep frying
100 g boneless pork, finely diced
Salt
Freshly ground black pepper
50 g canned water chestnuts,
 shredded
50 g mushrooms, finely chopped
50 g onion, peeled and finely
 chopped
175 g bean sprouts
1 x 5 ml spoon cornflour
2 x 5 ml spoons soy sauce
Few drops of sesame oil
 (optional)

Imperial
6 oz packet Chinese egg noodles
Oil for deep frying
4 oz boneless pork, finely diced
Salt
Freshly ground black pepper
2 oz canned water chestnuts,
 shredded
2 oz mushrooms, finely chopped
2 oz onion, peeled and finely
 chopped
6 oz bean sprouts
1 teaspoon cornflour
2 teaspoons soy sauce
Few drops of sesame oil
 (optional)

Cook the noodles in boiling water for 5 minutes, then rinse under cold running water and drain. Heat the oil to 190°C/375°F. Arrange the noodles in a frying basket in the shape of six nests and deep fry for 5 minutes, until crisp and golden.

Oil a large frying pan and heat it. Fry the pork for 2 minutes, stirring. Season to taste. Add the vegetables and cook for 2 minutes. Dissolve the cornflour in the soy sauce and enough water to make a thin paste. Add to the pan and cook for 1 minute. Sprinkle with the sesame oil, if used, and serve in the noodle nests.

PRAWNS WITH BEAN SPROUTS

Metric	Imperial
500 g shelled prawns	1 lb shelled prawns
120 ml dry sherry	4 fl oz dry sherry
150 ml oil	$\frac{1}{4}$ pint oil
1.5 x 5 ml spoons salt	1$\frac{1}{2}$ teaspoons salt
500 g bean sprouts	1 lb bean sprouts
4.5 x 15 ml spoons light soy sauce	4$\frac{1}{2}$ tablespoons light soy sauce
1.5 x 5 ml spoons sugar	1$\frac{1}{2}$ teaspoons sugar

Soak the prawns in the sherry for 1$\frac{1}{2}$ hours. Drain. Heat the oil in a large saucepan or frying pan. Add the prawns and salt and fry for 2 minutes. Add the bean sprouts and fry for 2 minutes. Add the soy sauce and sugar and mix well. Heat thoroughly. Serve in warmed bowls.

BOILED RICE

Metric	Imperial
350 g long-grain rice	12 oz long-grain rice
1.5 x 5 ml spoons salt	1$\frac{1}{2}$ teaspoons salt
25 g butter	1 oz butter

Cook the rice in boiling salted water for 11 minutes. Drain, rinse and drain again thoroughly. Place in a lightly greased baking dish, dot with butter and cover with foil. Reheat when required in a preheated moderate oven (180°C/350°F, Gas Mark 4) for 30 to 40 minutes.

Fruit-filled melon.

Prawns with bean sprouts.

FRUIT-FILLED MELON

Metric	Imperial
1 medium firm ripe watermelon	1 medium firm ripe watermelon
Canned litchis, loquats, kumquats and/or Chinese gooseberries as available, drained	Canned litchis, loquats, kumquats and/or Chinese gooseberries as available, drained

Cut the melon in half crossways. Scoop out the pulp with a melon baller or scoop into balls. Discard the seeds. Alternatively cut the pulp into cubes with a knife. Mix with the rest of the fruit and spoon back into the watermelon shells. Chill thoroughly.

Note: Canned drained apricots, orange sections, apple wedges and/or canned or fresh pineapple wedges can be added to or substituted for the fruits mentioned.

INDIAN DINNER PARTY FOR EIGHT

Samosas (deep-fried savoury pastries) /Lamb biryani or Fish curry, Rice, Avial (vegetable curry), Chappatis, Raita /Fresh fruit

BEFOREHAND

Samosas
Make these the day before, or on the morning of the party, and reheat them later. Or prepare them, without frying, and complete this process 30 minutes before your guests are due. Keep them warm.

Lamb biryani
Make the day before, then, when required, reheat it in a preheated moderate oven (180°C/350°F, Gas Mark 4) for 1 hour. Sauté the almonds and sultanas for the garnish while the biryani is reheating.

Fish curry
Make the sauce the day before. One hour before the curry is required, reheat it gently in a large pan. When it is simmering, add the fish. Put into a casserole and cook in a preheated moderate oven (180°C/350°F, Gas Mark 4) for 45 minutes or until the fish is tender. (Or cook on top of the stove as indicated in the recipe.)

Avial
Prepare the vegetables and keep in a covered container in the refrigerator until needed. (They can be prepared the day before or early on the day of the party.)

Rice
Measure and place in dish ready for the addition of water when required.

Chappatis
Cook earlier in the day and reheat when required.

Raita
Make during the afternoon and keep chilled.

These deep-fried pastries contain a spicy filling which can be meat or vegetable; they are delicious as appetizers or snacks.

Sift the flour and salt into a bowl, then rub in the butter until the mixture resembles breadcrumbs. Mix in enough water to bind to a dough. Knead for about 5 minutes or until smooth and elastic. Leave covered with a damp cloth while you make the filling.

Melt the butter in a frying pan and gently fry the onion, garlic, chilli and ginger for 5 minutes. Stir in the seasonings and the meat and fry for 15 minutes longer. Remove from the heat and allow to cool while shaping the dough.

Divide the dough into 15 equal pieces. Roll each piece out to form a 10 cm (4 inch) round. Cut each round in half and lightly dampen the edges of the semi-circles. Shape each to form a cone and fill each with some of the filling. Seal the edges well and set aside in a cool place for 30 minutes.

Heat the oil in a deep-frying pan to 190°C/375°F. Deep-fry the samosas, a few at a time, for 2 to 3 minutes or until golden brown. Drain and serve hot. Makes 30

SAMOSAS

Metric
For the pastry:
225 g plain flour
1 x 2.5 ml spoon salt
25 g butter
4-6 x 15 ml spoons water
Oil for deep frying
For the filling:
25 g butter
1 onion, peeled and finely chopped
2 garlic cloves, crushed
1 green chilli, seeded and finely chopped
2.5 cm piece of fresh root ginger, peeled and chopped
1 x 2.5 ml spoon ground turmeric
1 x 2.5 ml spoon mild chilli powder
1 x 5 ml spoon salt
2 x 5 ml spoons garam masala
350 g lean minced meat

Imperial
For the pastry:
8 oz plain flour
½ teaspoon salt
1 oz butter
4-6 tablespoons water
Oil for deep frying
For the filling:
1 oz butter
1 onion, peeled and finely chopped
2 garlic cloves, crushed
1 green chilli, seeded and finely chopped
1 inch piece of fresh root ginger, peeled and chopped
½ teaspoon ground turmeric
½ teaspoon mild chilli powder
1 teaspoon salt
2 teaspoons garam masala
12 oz lean minced meat

Right: Samosas.

LAMB BIRYANI

Metric
700 g long-grain rice
2 x 5 ml spoons saffron fronds or
  1.56 grain packet of saffron
  powder
120 ml hot water
120 ml oil
4 garlic cloves, crushed
5 cm piece of fresh root ginger,
  peeled and chopped
1.5 kg boned lean lamb, cubed
1 x 2.5 ml spoon cayenne pepper
2 x 5 ml spoons ground cumin
2 x 5 ml spoons ground
  coriander
2 x 5 ml spoons ground cloves
2 x 5 ml spoons ground
  cinnamon
2 x 5 ml spoons salt
2 x 5 ml spoons freshly ground
  black pepper
600 ml unsweetened natural
  yogurt
4 onions, peeled and thinly
  sliced
50 g flaked almonds
50 g sultanas, cleaned
50 g butter

Imperial
1½ lb long-grain rice
2 teaspoons saffron fronds or
  1.56 grain packet of saffron
  powder
4 fl oz hot water
4 fl oz oil
4 garlic cloves, crushed
2 inch piece of fresh root ginger,
  peeled and chopped
3 lb boned lean lamb, cubed
½ teaspoon cayenne pepper
2 teaspoons ground cumin
2 teaspoons ground coriander
2 teaspoons ground cloves
2 teaspoons ground cinnamon
2 teaspoons salt
2 teaspoons freshly ground black
  pepper
1 pint unsweetened natural
  yogurt
4 onions, peeled and thinly
  sliced
2 oz flaked almonds
2 oz sultanas, cleaned
2 oz butter

This dish from the Moglai area traditionally layers rice with spiced meat and onions. It was originally made with lamb, but chicken pieces can equally well be used. Biryani can also be served without the meat as a vegetable dish.

Soak the rice in cold water to cover for 30 minutes. Put the saffron to soak in the hot water for 30 minutes (powdered saffron does not need soaking). Meanwhile, heat the oil in a frying pan and lightly fry the garlic and ginger. Add the meat and fry for 5 minutes. Stir in the spices and seasoning and the yogurt. Mix well together and simmer for about 35 minutes.

Bring a large saucepan of lightly salted water to the boil. Drain the rice and plunge it into the boiling water. Bring back to the boil and boil for 2 minutes. Drain well and divide the rice into three portions. Place one portion of rice in a 2.75 litre (5 pint) casserole dish. Soak another portion of rice in the saffron water to colour it yellow. Place half of the lamb mixture on top of the rice in the casserole and top with half the onions. Add the drained saffron rice. Cover with the rest of the lamb, then onions, then third portion of rice as the top layer. Cover the casserole with aluminium foil and then the lid and bake in a preheated moderate oven (180°C/350°F, Gas Mark 4) for 1 hour.

Sauté the almonds and sultanas in the butter and sprinkle on top of the biryani to garnish.

Below: Fish curry; Lamb biryani; Avial.

FISH CURRY

Metric	Imperial
50 g butter	2 oz butter
2 large onions, peeled and chopped	2 large onions, peeled and chopped
2 x 15 ml spoons curry powder	2 tablespoons curry powder
50 g plain flour	2 oz plain flour
600 ml chicken stock	1 pint chicken stock
600 ml milk	1 pint milk
2 small apples, peeled, cored and chopped	2 small apples, peeled, cored and chopped
4 tomatoes, skinned and chopped	4 tomatoes, skinned and chopped
50-100 g sultanas	2-4 oz sultanas
Salt	Salt
Freshly ground black pepper	Freshly ground black pepper
1.5 kg filleted cod, haddock, or similar white fish, skinned and cut into 2.5 cm cubes	3 lb filleted cod, haddock, or similar white fish, skinned and cut into 1 inch cubes

Melt the butter in a saucepan and fry the onions gently for 5 minutes without browning. Stir in the curry powder and fry it for 2 to 3 minutes, then add the flour and cook for a further 2 to 3 minutes. Remove the pan from the heat and gradually stir in the stock and milk. Bring to the boil, stirring, and simmer until the sauce thickens.

Add the apples, tomatoes, sultanas and salt and pepper to taste. Cover and simmer for 15 minutes. Add the fish, stir well and simmer for a further 10 minutes or until the fish is tender. Add more salt and pepper if necessary and serve with boiled rice. (For oven-cooking, see "Beforehand".)

AVIAL

Metric	Imperial
4 x 15 ml spoons oil	4 tablespoons oil
1 x 5 ml spoon mustard seeds	1 teaspoon mustard seeds
1 onion, peeled and finely chopped	1 onion, peeled and finely chopped
1 green chilli, seeded and finely chopped	1 green chilli, seeded and finely chopped
1 x 5 ml spoon ground turmeric	1 teaspoon ground turmeric
1 x 15 ml spoon ground coriander	1 tablespoon ground coriander
500 g mixed vegetables, prepared and sliced – choose from aubergine, carrots, beans, cauliflower, green pepper, okra, potatoes and tomatoes	1 lb mixed vegetables, prepared and sliced – choose from aubergine, carrots, beans, cauliflower, green pepper, okra, potatoes and tomatoes
1 x 5 ml spoon salt	1 teaspoon salt
100 g grated fresh coconut	4 oz grated fresh coconut
120 ml unsweetened natural yogurt	4 fl oz unsweetened natural yogurt
25 g butter, melted	1 oz butter, melted

A mild vegetable curry with coconut and yogurt, this includes a variety of vegetables. Indians include okra ('ladies' fingers') in this and other vegetable dishes whenever possible.

Heat the oil in a saucepan and gently fry the mustard seeds, onion, chilli and spices. Toss in the prepared vegetables. Season with the salt, and simmer with just enough water to keep the vegetables moist until they are cooked through but still crunchy. (The time will depend on the choice of vegetables used; those needing a little longer cooking can be started first.)

Stir in the coconut and simmer for a further 5 minutes. Remove from the heat, stir in the yogurt and melted butter and serve.

RICE (OVEN-COOKED)

Metric	Imperial
350 g long-grain rice	12 oz long-grain rice
900 ml water	1½ pints water
1.5 x 5 ml spoons salt	1½ teaspoons salt

Put the rice in an ovenproof dish. Bring the water to the boil with the salt, pour it over the rice and stir well. Cover tightly with a lid or with foil. Bake in a preheated moderate oven (180°C/350°F, Gas Mark 4) for 35 to 40 minutes or until the grains are just soft and the cooking liquid has all been absorbed by the rice.

Chappatis; Raita.

CHAPPATIS

Metric	Imperial
350 g plain wholewheat flour	12 oz plain wholewheat flour
1 x 5 ml spoon salt	1 teaspoon salt
200-300 ml water	7-10 fl oz water

Sift the flour and salt into a bowl. Add enough of the water to make a soft dough and knit together with your fingertips. Knead well for 10 minutes. Leave, covered with a damp cloth, for at least 1 hour.

Knead well again, then divide into eight pieces. Roll out each piece on a generously floured surface to make 10 to 12 cm (4 to 5 inch) rounds. Heat a very lightly greased griddle or a heavy based frying pan. Cook two chappatis at a time until pale brown on each side. Serve hot, brushed with butter, as an accompaniment to the main dishes. Makes 8

RAITA

Metric	Imperial
1 cucumber (about 500 g), finely diced	1 cucumber (about 1 lb), finely diced
2 onions, peeled and finely chopped	2 onions, peeled and finely chopped
2 garlic cloves, crushed	2 garlic cloves, crushed
600 ml unsweetened natural yogurt	1 pint unsweetened natural yogurt
1 x 5 ml spoon salt	1 teaspoon salt
1 x 2.5 ml spoon freshly ground black pepper	½ teaspoon freshly ground black pepper

A cool, fresh-tasting accompaniment to Indian dishes, Raita can be made from a variety of fresh raw vegetables. Combine all the ingredients and chill for 1 hour before serving.

ITALIAN DINNER FOR SIX

Pasta hors d'oeuvre/Saltimbocca alla romana, Courgettes with tomatoes, Green salad/Fresh peaches in wine

BEFOREHAND

Pasta hors d'oeuvre
The day before, cook the pasta shells and refrigerate them, covered. Make the mayonnaise. Cut the meats into strips; keep covered in refrigerator. Chop the parsley and keep in refrigerator. Cube the bread for croûtons.

Saltimbocca alla romana
Early in the day, prepare the veal rolls; keep, covered, in the refrigerator. Cube the bread for croûtons.

Courgettes with tomatoes
Early in the day, skin and chop the tomatoes. Chop the parsley and crush the garlic; keep wrapped until required. Slice the courgettes and sprinkle with salt an hour before cooking. (Drain before cooking.)

Green salad
The day before, prepare the vegetables and refrigerate in polythene bags. Make the dressing.

Fresh peaches in wine
Prepare an hour beforehand and chill thoroughly.

PASTA HORS D'OEUVRE

Metric	Imperial
175 g pasta shells	6 oz pasta shells
100 g garlic sausage, cut into strips	4 oz garlic sausage, cut into strips
100 g cooked tongue, cut into strips	4 oz cooked tongue, cut into strips
225 g crisp green apples, cored and finely diced	8 oz crisp green apples, cored and finely diced
1 egg yolk	1 egg yolk
Pinch of sugar	Pinch of sugar
1 x 2.5 ml spoon dry mustard	½ teaspoon dry mustard
Salt	Salt
Freshly ground black pepper	Freshly ground black pepper
225 ml corn oil	7½ fl oz corn oil
1.5 x 15 ml spoons vinegar	1½ tablespoons vinegar
1 x 15 ml spoon top of the milk	1 tablespoon top of the milk
50 g onion, peeled and finely chopped	2 oz onion, peeled and finely chopped
2 x 5 ml spoons tomato paste	2 teaspoons tomato paste
Chopped fresh parsley to garnish	Chopped fresh parsley to garnish

Cook the pasta shells in boiling salted water until tender. Drain and rinse under cold running water. Add the garlic sausage, tongue and apples to the pasta shells and toss together.

Put the egg yolk, sugar, mustard and salt and pepper to taste in a bowl and mix well. Gradually add the oil in drops, whisking well. When half the oil is incorporated, the remainder may be added in a thin stream. If the mayonnaise becomes too thick to work, add a little of the vinegar. Mix in the top of the milk, onion, tomato paste and remaining vinegar.

Fork the mayonnaise through the pasta mixture. Serve on individual plates garnished with chopped parsley.

SALTIMBOCCA ALLA ROMANA

Metric	Imperial
12 thin slices of veal	12 thin slices of veal
Lemon juice	Lemon juice
Freshly ground black pepper	Freshly ground black pepper
12 fresh sage or basil leaves or 2 x 5 ml spoons dried marjoram	12 fresh sage or basil leaves or 2 teaspoons dried majoram
12 thin slices of prosciutto or boiled ham	12 thin slices of prosciutto or boiled ham
75 g butter	3 oz butter
3 x 15 ml spoons Marsala	3 tablespoons Marsala
1 cm squares day-old bread, fried as croûtons	½ inch squares day-old bread, fried as croûtons

Ask the butcher to bat out the veal to pieces about 10 x 12.5 cm (4 x 5 inches). Season with lemon juice and pepper. Place a sage or basil leaf or a little marjoram in the centre of each slice of veal and cover with a slice of ham. Roll up and fix firmly with a wooden cocktail stick.

Melt the butter in a frying pan just large enough to take the rolls in a single layer, packed fairly tightly to keep the rolls a good shape. Gently fry the veal rolls until golden brown. Do not overheat the butter. Add the Marsala. Bring to simmering point, cover the pan and simmer gently until the veal rolls are tender. Serve hot, garnished with fried croûtons.

Left: Pasta hors d'oeuvre.

Above: Saltimbocca alla romana; Green salad; Courgettes with tomatoes. Below: Fresh peaches in wine.

COURGETTES WITH TOMATOES

Metric
750 g courgettes, cut into 1 cm
 slices
Salt
100 g butter
225 g tomatoes, skinned and
 chopped
4 x 15 ml spoons chopped fresh
 parsley
1 small garlic clove, crushed
Freshly ground black pepper
1 x 5 ml spoon sugar

Imperial
1½ lb courgettes, cut into ½ inch
 slices
Salt
4 oz butter
8 oz tomatoes, skinned and
 chopped
4 tablespoons chopped fresh
 parsley
1 small garlic clove, crushed
Freshly ground black pepper
1 teaspoon sugar

Put the courgette slices into a colander, sprinkle them with salt and allow to drain for about 1 hour. Dry them well. Melt 75 g (3 oz) of the butter in a frying pan. Add the courgettes and cook them gently until soft and slightly transparent. Put in a serving dish; keep warm.

Melt the remaining butter in the pan and cook the tomatoes, the parsley, the garlic, pepper to taste and sugar until a thickish purée forms. Adjust the seasoning if necessary and pour the purée over the courgettes in the serving dish.

FRESH PEACHES IN WINE

Metric
6 ripe yellow peaches, peeled
6 x 5 ml spoons caster sugar
175 ml sweet white wine
 (such as Orvieto)

Imperial
6 ripe yellow peaches, peeled
6 teaspoons caster sugar
6 fl oz sweet white wine
 (such as Orvieto)

Put one peach into each of six wine glasses and sprinkle with the sugar. Pour over the wine. Chill. The peach is eaten first, then the wine is drunk.

American Party for Eight

Tomato jelly rings, Bread sticks/Chilli con carne, Baked jacket potatoes with soured cream and chives, Tossed green salad/Baked Alaska

Beforehand

Tomato jelly rings
Make the day before.
Chilli con carne
Prepare and cook the day before, except for the beans. Cool before putting in the refrigerator. On the day, bring back to the boil, stirring, before adding the beans.
Potatoes
Scrub the day before.
Tossed green salad
Prepare the ingredients the day before and keep in separate polythene bags in the refrigerator.
Baked Alaska
The day before make or buy the sponge cake for the base.

Above: Chilli con carne; Green salad; Baked potatoes.
Right: Baked Alaska.

Tomato Jelly Rings

Metric	Imperial
1 kg firm ripe tomatoes, skinned and quartered	2 lb firm ripe tomatoes, skinned and quartered
4 small onions, peeled and chopped	4 small onions, peeled and chopped
2 small garlic cloves, crushed	2 small garlic cloves, crushed
2 x 5 ml spoons sugar	2 teaspoons sugar
1 x 5 ml spoon salt	1 teaspoon salt
Pinch of celery salt	Pinch of celery salt
Pinch of grated nutmeg	Pinch of grated nutmeg
2 bay leaves	2 bay leaves
2 x 5 ml spoons peppercorns	2 teaspoons peppercorns
2 x 15 ml spoons powdered gelatine	2 tablespoons powdered gelatine
4 x 15 ml spoons water	4 tablespoons water
2 x 15 ml spoons tarragon vinegar	2 tablespoons tarragon vinegar
6 x 15 ml spoons lemon juice	6 tablespoons lemon juice
Watercress to garnish	Watercress to garnish

Remove the centres from the tomatoes if they are tough. Put the tomatoes, onions, garlic, sugar, salts and nutmeg in a saucepan. Add the bay leaves and peppercorns, tied in muslin, and cook over a low heat until the onion is tender. Remove the muslin bag.

Dissolve the gelatine in the water in a small heatproof bowl over hot water. Purée the tomato mixture in an electric blender, then rub it through a sieve and pour it into a measuring jug. Add the vinegar and lemon juice and, if necessary, make up to 1 litre (1¾ pints) with water. Stir in the dissolved gelatine. Pour into eight dampened individual ring moulds and leave to set. To serve, turn out of the moulds and garnish with watercress.

Chilli Con Carne

Metric	Imperial
1.5 kg minced beef	3 lb minced beef
2 x 15 ml spoons fat or oil	2 tablespoons fat or oil
2 large onions, peeled and chopped	2 large onions, peeled and chopped
2 green peppers, cored, seeded and chopped (optional)	2 green peppers, cored, seeded and chopped (optional)
1 x 900 g can tomatoes	1 x 30 oz can tomatoes
Salt	Salt
Freshly ground black pepper	Freshly ground black pepper
2 x 15 ml spoons chilli powder	2 tablespoons chilli powder
2 x 15 ml spoons vinegar	2 tablespoons vinegar
2 x 5 ml spoons sugar	2 teaspoons sugar
4 x 15 ml spoons tomato paste	4 tablespoons tomato paste
2 x 425 g cans red kidney beans, drained	2 x 15 oz cans red kidney beans, drained

Fry the beef in the fat or oil in a saucepan until lightly browned. Add the onions and peppers, if using, and fry for 5 minutes or until soft. Drain off any excess fat. Stir in the tomatoes. Mix together seasoning, the chilli powder, vinegar, sugar and tomato paste and add to the pan. Mix well. Cover and simmer for 30 to 40 minutes. Ten minutes before the cooking time is completed, add the kidney beans.
Note: Add the chilli powder very judiciously; some of it is very hot. American chilli powder is usually a milder, pre-mixed seasoning, based on ground Mexican chilli peppers, so look for this kind.

Tomato jelly rings.

BAKED ALASKA

Metric
1 x 22.5 cm round sponge cake
1 x 566 g can fruit, e.g.
    raspberries, drained (syrup
    reserved)
1 litre block vanilla ice cream
6 egg whites
275 g caster sugar

Imperial
1 x 9 inch round sponge cake
1 x 20 oz can fruit, e.g.
    raspberries, drained (syrup
    reserved)
35¼ fl oz block vanilla ice cream
6 egg whites
10 oz caster sugar

Put the sponge cake on a flat ovenproof dish and spoon over just enough fruit syrup to moisten it. Put the ice cream in the centre of the cake and pile the fruit on top. Whisk the egg whites until stiff. Whisk in half the sugar, then fold in the remaining sugar. Pile this meringue mixture on the cake, covering the cake, ice cream and fruit completely, and taking the meringue down to the dish. Bake in a preheated very hot oven (230°C/450°F, Gas Mark 8) for 2 to 3 minutes, or until the outside of the meringue just begins to brown. Serve at once.

Variations: Use fresh crushed fruit, e.g. strawberries, when in season. Or sprinkle 2 to 4 x 15 ml spoons (2 to 4 tablespoons) sherry or rum over the cake before the ice cream is added.

CELEBRATION DINNER PARTIES

Get out your best linen and china; dress up the table with a centrepiece of flowers, set low so that you can see your guests as well as hear them, and light the candles. Both these menus are perfect for a special celebration, whether for a summer or winter occasion.

Vermouth, used for the chicken in the winter menu, is a valuable cookery ingredient at any time of the year; keep it in the refrigerator and use it, if possible, within a month. This recipe also calls for tarragon. Use fresh tarragon if you can; if not use dried tarragon (half the quantity) but make sure it's a fresh supply and not something that's been crumbling away for months in the kitchen cupboard.

Make the most of summer foods in the second menu with a dinner party planned around a spectacular stuffed crown roast of lamb. Order the lamb a few days ahead and ask the butcher to prepare it. Make these celebration parties a memorable occasion by choosing special wines to go with them.

WINTER DINNER PARTY FOR SIX

Marinated kipper fillets, Toast triangles/Chicken with vermouth and mushrooms, Potato and chicory duchesse, Green peas/ Pineapple sorbet, Almond tuiles/Coffee, Peppermint creams

BEFOREHAND

Marinated kipper fillets
Prepare and marinate overnight.
Chicken with vermouth and mushrooms
Wipe and trim chicken; keep in the refrigerator. Prepare mushrooms and watercress; refrigerate in polythene bags.
Potato and chicory duchesse
Prepare chicory; refrigerate in polythene bags. Peel potatoes; keep covered with water.
Pineapple sorbet
Can be made a week ahead and kept in freezer.
Almond tuiles
Make one day ahead; store in airtight tin.
Peppermint creams
Can be made several days ahead; store as indicated in recipe.

Marinated kipper fillets.

MARINATED KIPPER FILLETS

Metric	Imperial
500 g kipper fillets, skinned and cut into very thin strips	1 lb kipper fillets, skinned and cut into very thin strips
75 g onion, peeled and thinly sliced	3 oz onion, peeled and thinly sliced
100 g celery heart, thinly sliced	4 oz celery heart, thinly sliced
150 ml white wine vinegar	$\frac{1}{4}$ pint white wine vinegar
5 x 15 ml spoons soft brown sugar	5 tablespoons soft brown sugar
1 x 15 ml spoon snipped fresh or 1 x 5 ml spoon dried chives	1 tablespoon snipped fresh or 1 teaspoon dried chives
Freshly ground black pepper	Freshly ground black pepper
Tomato wedges and lettuce to garnish	Tomato wedges and lettuce to garnish

Layer the fish strips, onion and celery heart in a shallow serving dish. Mix the vinegar, sugar, chives and pepper to taste together and spoon over the fish. Cover the dish tightly and leave to marinate in the refrigerator for at least 12 hours, longer if possible. Remove from the refrigerator about 30 minutes before serving with fingers of toast. Garnish the fish with tomato wedges and lettuce.

POTATO AND CHICORY DUCHESSE

Metric	Imperial
225 g chicory	8 oz chicory
1 kg potatoes, peeled	2 lb potatoes, peeled
50 g butter	2 oz butter
1 garlic clove, crushed	1 garlic clove, crushed
6 x 15 ml spoons double cream	6 tablespoons double cream
3 eggs, separated	3 eggs, separated
Salt	Salt
Freshly ground black pepper	Freshly ground black pepper

Remove any damaged leaves from the chicory. Halve lengthways, then slice across into thin strips. Cook the potatoes in boiling water. Meanwhile, melt half of the butter in a frying pan. Add the garlic and chicory and cook gently for 10 minutes.

Drain the potatoes and mash until smooth. Beat in the chicory mixture, cream, egg yolks and seasoning. Beat the egg whites until stiff and fold into the potato mixture. Spoon into a well-buttered shallow oval ovenproof dish, and rough up with a fork. Dot with pieces of the remaining butter and bake in a preheated moderate oven (180°C/350°F, Gas Mark 4) for 35 to 40 minutes or until well risen and golden brown. Serve as soon as possible. If necessary, keep warm in a low oven.

CHICKEN WITH VERMOUTH AND MUSHROOMS

Metric
6 x 275 g chicken wing portions
25 g butter
2 x 15 ml spoons vegetable oil
6 x 15 ml spoons dry vermouth
450 ml chicken stock
1 x 15 ml spoon chopped fresh or
    1 x 5 ml spoon dried tarragon
Salt
Freshly ground black pepper
350 g small button mushrooms
3 x 15 ml spoons cornflour
4 x 15 ml spoons water
Watercress sprigs to garnish

Imperial
6 x 10 oz chicken wing portions
1 oz butter
2 tablespoons vegetable oil
6 tablespoons dry vermouth
¾ pint chicken stock
1 tablespoon chopped fresh or
    1 teaspoon dried tarragon
Salt
Freshly ground black pepper
12 oz small button mushrooms
3 tablespoons cornflour
4 tablespoons water
Watercress sprigs to garnish

Wipe and trim the joints (remove the skin, if you wish). Melt the butter with the oil in a flameproof casserole. Add the chicken joints and fry for 15 minutes or until browned all over. Warm the vermouth, pour into the casserole and set alight. Shake the pan gently until the flames subside. Stir in the stock, tarragon and seasoning and bring to the boil. Cover tightly and transfer to a preheated moderate oven (180°C/350°F, Gas Mark 4). Cook for about 40 minutes.

Add the mushrooms to the casserole, pushing them under the surface of the liquid. Cover and cook for a further 10 minutes, or until clear liquid runs from the joints when pierced with a skewer.

Remove the chicken from the casserole and place on a large warmed serving platter. Cover with foil and keep warm. Dissolve the cornflour in the water. Stir into the casserole juices and simmer on top of the stove for a few minutes, stirring until thickened. Spoon a little sauce over the chicken and pour the rest into a warmed sauceboat. Garnish the chicken with watercress sprigs and serve.

Chicken with vermouth and mushrooms; Potato and chicory duchesse.

Peppermint creams; Pineapple sorbet; Almond tuiles.

PINEAPPLE SORBET

Metric	Imperial
1 x 375 g can pineapple rings or chunks	1 x 13 oz can pineapple rings or chunks
50 g sugar	2 oz sugar
3 x 15 ml spoons lemon juice	3 tablespoons lemon juice
1 egg white	1 egg white

Put the undrained pineapple, sugar and lemon juice in an electric blender goblet and blend until a smooth purée. Pour into a freezer container and freeze until mushy.

Turn the pineapple mixture into a chilled bowl and beat well until the ice crystals are broken down. Whisk the egg white until stiff and fold into the pineapple mixture. Spoon into six freezerproof serving dishes, cover and freeze.

Allow to 'come to' for 15 minutes in the refrigerator before serving with Almond tuiles.

ALMOND TUILES

Metric	Imperial
3 egg whites	3 egg whites
175 g caster sugar	6 oz caster sugar
75 g plain flour	3 oz plain flour
75 g flaked or nibbed almonds	3 oz flaked or nibbed almonds
75 g butter, melted	3 oz butter, melted

Using a rotary whisk and a large bowl, whisk the egg whites until stiff. Fold in the caster sugar, sifted flour and almonds. Mix well. Fold in the cooled melted butter. Place very small spoonsful of the mixture on a baking sheet lined with non-stick paper, keeping them well apart. Smooth each one out thinly with the back of the spoon, retaining the circular shape. Bake in a preheated moderately hot oven (190°C/375°F, Gas Mark 5) for 8 to 10 minutes or until lightly browned.

Use a palette knife to lift each biscuit from the baking sheet and place it over the handle of a wooden spoon so that it sets in a curled shape. Allow a moment or two for the biscuit to harden, then remove it to a wire rack to cool. Store in an airtight tin. Makes about 30

PEPPERMINT CREAMS

Metric	Imperial
225 g icing sugar, sifted	8 oz icing sugar, sifted
1 x 15 ml spoon beaten egg white (approx)	1 tablespoon beaten egg white (approx)
Few drops of peppermint essence	Few drops of peppermint essence
25 g plain chocolate, melted (optional)	1 oz plain chocolate, melted (optional)

In a bowl, mix the icing sugar to a stiff paste with the egg white. Add a few drops of peppermint essence to taste. Roll out the peppermint dough to 6 mm (¼ inch) thick between sheets of non-stick kitchen or wax paper. Stamp out 2.5 cm (1 inch) rounds with a plain cutter. Leave for at least 24 hours to firm. Coat half the peppermint creams with melted chocolate, to give a fifty-fifty effect. Place on wax paper to dry.

Store both plain and chocolate creams in an airtight container, with paper between each of the layers. Makes about 28

Summer Dinner Party for Six

Cream of prawn soup or Croûtes aux tomates/Stuffed crown roast of lamb, Château potatoes, Carrots in orange butter/Strawberry and orange mousse, Meringue twists

Beforehand

Cream of prawn soup
This can be made earlier in the day, but don't add the prawns until you reheat the soup for serving.

Stuffed crown roast of lamb
A few days ahead, order the lamb – most butchers will prepare a crown roast and may also supply the cutlet frills. The day before, make the stuffing and stuff the lamb; weigh the completed joint in order to calculate cooking time. Refrigerate, covered. Make sure you have redcurrant jelly in the storecupboard.

Potatoes
Scrape and keep covered in cold water.

Carrots
Trim and scrub and keep refrigerated in a polythene bag.

Strawberry and orange mousse
Make the day before (even earlier if you have a freezer).

Meringue twists
Make several days ahead; store in an airtight tin.

Croûtes aux tomates
Prepare the rounds of bread, grate the cheese, and skin and slice the tomatoes several hours ahead; keep refrigerated, separately, in polythene bags or containers. Fry the croûtes about 2 hours before the meal; add toppings and leave on a baking sheet ready for the oven.

Melt the margarine in a heavy-based pan. Add the vegetables and cook gently, covered, for about 15 minutes or until they are soft. Stir in the flour and cook for 1 minute. Remove from the heat and stir in the milk and stock.

Return to the heat and bring to the boil, stirring. Add seasoning and the bay leaf. Cover and simmer gently for 30 minutes, stirring occasionally. Cool slightly, then remove the bay leaf and liquidise the soup. Return to the rinsed-out pan and reheat.

Reserve a few prawns for garnish and roughly chop the rest. Add the chopped prawns to the soup and heat through gently. Adjust the seasoning and garnish with chives and the reserved prawns.

Croûtes aux Tomates

Metric	Imperial
2 large slices of medium cut bread	2 large slices of medium cut bread
Oil for frying	Oil for frying
25 g Gruyère cheese, finely grated	1 oz Gruyère cheese, finely grated
2 medium tomatoes, skinned and sliced	2 medium tomatoes, skinned and sliced
1 x 275 g can asparagus tips, drained	1 x 10 oz can asparagus tips, drained

Using a 3 cm (1½ inch) plain round or oval cutter, stamp out six rounds or ovals from the bread. Fry in a little oil until golden brown on both sides. Remove and drain on absorbent kitchen paper, then arrange on a baking sheet. Top each croûte with a little cheese, using half of it, and a tomato slice. Cut the asparagus tips to fit the croûtes. (The remaining stalks can be used for a soup or casserole.) Arrange the asparagus tips on top of the tomatoes in pairs. Sprinkle the remaining cheese over the stalk ends of the asparagus.

Bake in a preheated moderately hot oven (190°C/375°F, Gas Mark 5) at the lowest shelf position, for 20 minutes. Transfer to a warmed serving dish and serve immediately.

Note: If fresh asparagus is available and not too expensive, cook it and use instead of the canned asparagus. These croûtes may also be served as a savoury.

Cream of prawn soup.

Cream of Prawn Soup

Metric	Imperial
75 g margarine	3 oz margarine
175 g onions, peeled and thinly sliced	6 oz onions, peeled and thinly sliced
175 g celery, trimmed and thinly sliced	6 oz celery, trimmed and thinly sliced
5 x 15 ml spoons plain flour	5 tablespoons plain flour
900 ml milk	1½ pints milk
450 ml light stock	¾ pint light stock
Salt	Salt
Freshly ground black pepper	Freshly ground black pepper
1 bay leaf	1 bay leaf
175 g frozen shelled prawns, thawed	6 oz frozen shelled prawns, thawed
Snipped fresh chives to garnish	Snipped fresh chives to garnish

Croûtes aux tomates.

STUFFED CROWN ROAST OF LAMB

Metric
50 g butter or margarine
100 g onion, peeled and chopped
100 g streaky bacon rashers,
   rinds removed, diced
225 g dessert apples, peeled,
   cored and finely chopped
225 g celery, trimmed and
   chopped
Finely grated rind and juice of
   1 lemon
50 g walnuts, chopped
2 x 15 ml spoons chopped fresh
   parsley
225 g fresh white breadcrumbs
Salt
Freshly ground black pepper
Beaten egg, to bind
1 x 12-bone crown roast of lamb
Lard or dripping for roasting
Parsley sprigs to garnish

Imperial
2 oz butter or margarine
4 oz onion, peeled and chopped
4 oz streaky bacon rashers, rinds
   removed, diced
8 oz dessert apples, peeled, cored
   and finely chopped
8 oz celery, trimmed and
   chopped
Finely grated rind and juice of
   1 lemon
2 oz walnuts, chopped
2 tablespoons chopped fresh
   parsley
8 oz fresh white breadcrumbs
Salt
Freshly ground black pepper
Beaten egg, to bind
1 x 12-bone crown roast of lamb
Lard or dripping for roasting
Parsley sprigs to garnish

The 'crown' is formed by joining two best ends of neck, and is stuffed with a savoury filling. Melt the butter or margarine and lightly brown the onion and bacon. Remove from the heat and mix in the apples, celery, lemon rind and juice, walnuts, parsley, breadcrumbs and seasoning. Add sufficient beaten egg to bind.

Place the crown roast in a roasting tin greased with lard or dripping and spoon the stuffing into the hollow. (If there is too much stuffing, form the excess into balls and place around the meat.) Weigh the roast. Wrap foil around the tips of the bones to prevent them burning. Roast in a preheated moderate oven (180°C/350°F, Gas Mark 4), allowing 30 minutes per 450 g (1 lb) plus 30 minutes over.

Remove the foil for serving and replace with small cutlet frills. Garnish with parsley. Serve with gravy made from the pan drippings and redcurrant jelly.

CHÂTEAU POTATOES

Metric
75 g butter
1 kg new potatoes, scraped
Salt
Freshly ground black pepper
Fresh parsley sprigs to garnish

Imperial
3 oz butter
2 lb new potatoes, scraped
Salt
Freshly ground black pepper
Fresh parsley sprigs to garnish

Melt the butter in a frying pan and add the potatoes. Cover and cook over a gentle heat, shaking the pan occasionally, for 15 to 20 minutes, until golden brown.

If the potatoes are fairly large, pour the butter and potatoes into an ovenproof dish, cover and cook in the oven with the crown roast (in a preheated moderate oven 180°C/350°F, Gas Mark 4) for 20 to 25 minutes, until cooked. Season well and serve garnished with parsley.

Below: Stuffed crown roast of lamb; Château potatoes; Carrots in orange butter.

CARROTS IN ORANGE BUTTER

Metric	Imperial
1 kg new carrots, scrubbed or scraped	2 lb new carrots, scrubbed or scraped
Salt	Salt
50 g butter	2 oz butter
4 x 15 ml spoons brown sugar	4 tablespoons brown sugar
Grated rind and juice of 2 oranges	Grated rind and juice of 2 oranges
Orange slices to garnish	Orange slices to garnish

Cook the carrots in boiling salted water for 10 minutes until just tender but still crisp. Drain well. Return the carrots to the saucepan and stir in the butter, sugar and orange rind and juice. Heat gently to dissolve the sugar and melt the butter, then bring to the boil and simmer gently for 5 minutes. Turn into a warmed serving dish and garnish with orange slices.

STRAWBERRY AND ORANGE MOUSSE

Metric	Imperial
500 g ripe strawberries, hulled and sliced	1 lb ripe strawberries, hulled and sliced
5 x 15 ml spoons icing sugar	5 tablespoons icing sugar
2 x 15 ml spoons orange-flavoured liqueur	2 tablespoons orange-flavoured liqueur
Finely grated rind of 1 orange	Finely grated rind of 1 orange
1 small can evaporated milk	1 small can evaporated milk
4 x 5 ml spoons powdered gelatine	4 teaspoons powdered gelatine
	4 tablespoons orange juice
4 x 15 ml spoons orange juice	4 fl oz double cream, whipped
120 ml double cream, whipped	1 egg white
1 egg white	Red food colouring (optional)
Red food colouring (optional)	

Strawberry and orange mousse; Meringue twists.

Put the strawberries into a shallow dish and spoon on the sugar, liqueur and orange rind. Marinate for several hours, covered. Mix with the evaporated milk and rub through a nylon sieve, or use an electric blender, to form a purée.

Sprinkle the gelatine over the orange juice in a small heatproof bowl. When the juice is absorbed, dissolve the gelatine by standing the bowl in a pan of simmering water. Stir into the fruit purée with the cream. Beat the egg white until stiff, then fold into the fruit mixture with food colouring, if used.

Turn into a well-oiled 1 litre (1¾ pint) non-stick brioche tin and refrigerate until set. Turn out when required and decorate with meringue twists. (If using a metal tin, turn out the mousse as soon as it has set in order to prevent metallic tainting.)

MERINGUE TWISTS

Metric	Imperial
1 egg white	1 egg white
50 g caster sugar	2 oz caster sugar

Whisk the egg white until it is fairly stiff and looks like cottonwool. Whisk in half the sugar until the texture is smooth and close and the meringue stands in stiff peaks when the whisk is lifted. Lightly but evenly fold in the remaining sugar.

Pipe the meringue into small figures of eight on non-stick paper and dry in a preheated very cool oven (120°C/250°F, Gas Mark ½) for about 1 hour.

CHILDREN'S PARTIES

Lots of colour, lots of individual, tasty mouthfuls – savoury and sweet – make a children's party fun for the guests and help to guarantee success for the hostess. Young children like easy-to-eat food that looks inviting, such as savoury sandwiches with familiar fillings but cut in fancy shapes, for instance. Slightly older children love bridge rolls topped with savoury spreads. All children enjoy little sausages, crisps and cheesy savouries.

Pipe initials or names, in icing, on little iced cakes or biscuits and use them as place markers. Jellies and ice creams in individual waxed containers are always popular.

For young children, unbreakable or disposable tableware is advisable. You can get delightful coordinated sets of plates, cups, dishes, serviettes and cloths.

Keep the party happily short rather than boringly long; specify exact times of arrival and departure on the invitations.

Decorate the room with balloons to be given to the guests when they go. Have a list of games ready and be sure that everyone gets a prize at the end.

PARTY FOR 8 TO 12 GUESTS, 4 TO 6 YEARS OLD

Chocolate train, Cheese shorties, Sausage kebabs, Crisps, Jammy faces, Traffic lights

BEFOREHAND

Chocolate train
Make the slab cake several days ahead, the Swiss roll two days ahead. Two days ahead cut the cakes as shown in the diagram, and as described in the recipe. The day before, continue construction of the cake and decorate it.

Cheese shorties
These can be made one or two days ahead, stored in an airtight tin and refreshed in the oven when needed.

Sausage kebabs
Roll up the bacon, twist the sausages, and cut up the cheese the day before; keep in polythene bags in the refrigerator. About 1 hour before serving, cook the kebabs and finish making the arrangement.

Jammy faces and Traffic lights
Make the biscuits several days ahead and keep in airtight tins. Put together with jam the day before the party.

Coating the cake sections with glacé icing.

CHOCOLATE TRAIN

Metric	Imperial
For the slab cake:	**For the slab cake:**
275 g butter	10 oz butter
275 g caster sugar	10 oz caster sugar
5 eggs	5 eggs
275 g self-raising flour	10 oz self-raising flour
For the Swiss roll:	**For the Swiss roll:**
3 eggs	3 eggs
100 g caster sugar	4 oz caster sugar
100 g plain flour	4 oz plain flour
1 x 15 ml spoon hot water	1 tablespoon hot water
Caster sugar to dredge	Caster sugar to dredge
Warmed raspberry jam	Warmed raspberry jam
For the glacé icing:	**For the glacé icing:**
175 g plain chocolate or chocolate dots	6 oz plain chocolate or chocolate dots
About 150 ml water	About $\frac{1}{4}$ pint water
15 g butter	$\frac{1}{2}$ oz butter
450 g icing sugar, sifted	1 lb icing sugar, sifted
Vanilla essence	Vanilla essence
For the buttercream:	**For the buttercream:**
100 g butter	4 oz butter
225 g icing sugar, sifted	8 oz icing sugar, sifted
Cottonwool, small candles and 1 box of Smarties to decorate	Cottonwool, small candles and 1 box of Smarties to decorate

Spread the making of the cake over several days.

For the slab cake, grease and line a 30 by 25 cm (12 by 10 inch) baking tin. Cream the butter and sugar together until pale and fluffy. Add the eggs a little at a time, beating well after each addition. Fold in half the sifted flour using a metal spoon, then fold in the rest. Place the mixture in the tin and level it with a knife. Bake in the centre of a preheated moderate oven (180°C/350°F, Gas Mark 4) for 40 to 50 minutes. Cool on a wire rack.

To make the Swiss roll, line a 30 by 23 cm (12 by 9 inch) Swiss roll tin with non-stick paper. Put the eggs and sugar in a large heatproof bowl placed over a pan of hot water and whisk until light and creamy; the mixture should be stiff enough to retain the impression of the whisk for a few seconds. Remove the bowl from the heat and whisk until cool. Sift half the flour over the mixture and fold in very lightly, using a metal spoon. Add the remaining flour in the same way, then lightly stir in the hot water. Pour the mixture into the prepared tin.

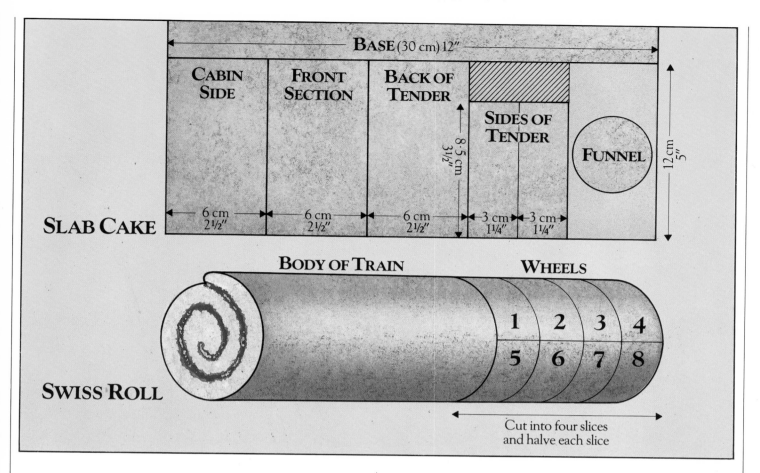

SLAB CAKE

BASE (30 cm) 12"

| CABIN SIDE | FRONT SECTION | BACK OF TENDER | | SIDES OF TENDER | FUNNEL |

6 cm 2½" 6 cm 2½" 6 cm 2½" 3 cm 1¼" 3 cm 1¼"

8·5 cm 3½"

12 cm 5"

SWISS ROLL

BODY OF TRAIN   WHEELS

| 1 | 2 | 3 | 4 |
| 5 | 6 | 7 | 8 |

Cut into four slices and halve each slice

Tilt the tin backwards and forwards so the mixture spreads over the whole surface. Bake in a preheated hot oven (220°C/425°F, Gas Mark 7) for 7 to 9 minutes or until golden brown and well risen.

Meanwhile, sprinkle a sheet of greaseproof paper liberally with caster sugar. To help make the sponge pliable, place the paper on a teatowel lightly wrung out in hot water.

Turn the cake quickly out onto the paper. Trim off the crusty edges with a sharp knife and spread the surface with warmed jam. Roll up with the aid of the paper. Make the first turn firmly so that the whole cake will roll evenly and have a good shape when finished, but roll more lightly after this turn. Cool on a wire rack.

To make the rich chocolate glacé icing, cut the chocolate into small pieces and put them in a pan with the water. Melt slowly over a gentle heat. Remove from the heat and allow to cool slightly, then beat in the butter. Gradually add the icing sugar, with a little vanilla essence, and beat until the mixture is glossy. If necessary, add more tepid water or more sifted icing sugar to give the correct consistency. If the icing contains many air bubbles after it has been beaten, warm it slightly and stir very gently.

For the buttercream, cream the butter until soft, then gradually beat in the icing sugar.

To assemble the cake, two days ahead, cut the slab cake in half lengthways and cut the pieces from one-half as shown in the diagram. Cut up the Swiss roll as shown. Split the cabin side and the front section to make four pieces. Cut a strip 3.5 cm (1½ inches) deep from either the top or the bottom of the tender sides. From the remaining section cut out a round funnel. Coat all these cut sections, including the other half of the slab cake (the train's base), with the rich chocolate glacé icing and leave to set on a wire rack.

The day before, cover an oblong board or a piece of thick card measuring 36 by 15 cm (14 by 6 inches) with kitchen foil. Place the large base, iced side uppermost, on the board. Spread a little buttercream on the underside of the body of the train and place it on the base. Spread more buttercream over the cabin end of the body and join one of the front sections in an upright position to this. Spread buttercream over the narrow ends and top of the front sections and fix the cabin sides to it, supported on the board. Use the other front sections as a roof.

To make the tender, cover the back section lengthways. Buttercream one long edge and end of each side and place in position on top of the base. Fix the wheels and funnel with buttercream.

Give the funnel a plume of cottonwool steam. Pipe with buttercream. Fill the tender with Smarties and insert the candles at the back of the tender.

The finished Chocolate train.

55

CHEESE SHORTIES

Metric	Imperial
175 g plain flour	6 oz plain flour
Salt	Salt
Freshly ground pepper	Freshly ground pepper
175 g Cheddar cheese, grated	6 oz Cheddar cheese, grated
175 g butter	6 oz butter
2 x 15 ml spoons top of the milk	2 tablespoons top of the milk

Sift the flour and a little salt and pepper into a mixing bowl. Stir in the cheese, then work in the butter and milk by kneading and squeezing the butter and flour with the fingers. When the mixture has formed a smooth dough, roll out to 6 mm (¼ inch) thick on a lightly floured surface. Stamp out shapes with fancy cutters and place on a lightly greased baking sheet. Bake in a preheated moderately hot oven (190°C/375°F, Gas Mark 5) for about 15 minutes, until golden. Cool and serve piled on a plate.

SAUSAGE KEBABS

Metric	Imperial
500 g pork chipolatas	1 lb pork chipolatas
500 g streaky bacon rashers, rinds removed	1 lb streaky bacon rashers, rinds removed
500 g Cheddar cheese, cubed	1 lb Cheddar cheese, cubed

Twist each sausage in half and cut into two small sausages. Place these in a baking tin and cook in a preheated moderately hot oven (200°C/400°F, Gas Mark 6) for about 30 minutes.

Meanwhile, stretch the rashers on a flat surface with the back of a knife. Cut each in half crossways and form into rolls. Place in a tin and cook in the oven with the sausages until beginning to colour.

Spear the cheese cubes on cocktail sticks. Spear the sausages and bacon rolls on sticks. Stick all the cheese cubes, sausages and bacon rolls into a cabbage, large apples or a long French loaf. The sausages and bacon are best eaten just warm. Surround the cabbage, apples or loaf with potato crisps.

SHREWSBURY BISCUITS

Metric	Imperial
125 g butter or margarine	4 oz butter or margarine
150 g caster sugar	5 oz caster sugar
1 egg yolk	1 egg yolk
225 g plain flour	8 oz plain flour
Grated rind of 1 lemon	Grated rind of 1 lemon

Cream the fat and sugar together until pale and fluffy. Add the egg yolk and beat well. Stir in the sifted flour and lemon rind and mix to a fairly firm dough. Knead lightly and roll out to about 6 mm (¼ inch) thick on a lightly floured surface. Cut into rounds with a 6 cm (2½ inch) fluted cutter and put on greased baking sheets. Bake in a preheated moderate oven (180°C/350°F, Gas Mark 4) for about 15 minutes, until firm and a very light brown colour.
Makes 20 to 24

Jammy faces
Roll out the Shrewsbury biscuit mixture and cut it into 6 cm (2½ inch) rounds with a plain or fluted cutter. From half the biscuits remove two holes with a small round cutter, to represent eyes, and make a slit to represent a mouth. Bake. When the biscuits are cool, spread the plain rounds with jam and cover with the 'faces.'
Makes 10 to 12

Traffic lights
Roll out the Shrewsbury biscuit mixture and cut it into fingers. Using a small round cutter, cut out three holes, one above the other, from half the fingers. Bake. When the biscuits are cool, place a little raspberry, apricot and greengage jam on each of the plain biscuits and cover with the others, dredged with icing sugar. (Apricot jam, tinted with a little green food colouring, can be used instead of greengage jam.) Makes 12

Below: Traffic lights; Jammy faces; Cheese shorties; Sausage kebabs.

PARTY FOR 8 TO 12 GUESTS, 6 TO 8 YEARS OLD

Clock birthday cake, Chicken puffs, Egg boats, Pinwheel sandwiches, Lollipop biscuits, Banana and honey ice cream

BEFOREHAND

Clock birthday cake
Can be made and iced two or three days ahead.
Chicken puffs
Prepare and cook the day before the party. Just before tea, reheat them in a preheated moderate oven (180°C/350°F, Gas Mark 4) for about 15 minutes.
Egg boats
Hard-boil the eggs.
Pinwheel sandwiches
Make these on the morning of the party and refrigerate, wrapped in polythene or foil. Cut across in slices just before serving.
Lollipop biscuits
Bake these several days ahead. Complete, with icing, the day before the party.
Banana and honey ice cream
Make several days ahead. Keep in the freezer compartment of the refrigerator, but remove it 1 hour before serving and allow it to 'come to' in the refrigerator.

CLOCK BIRTHDAY CAKE

Metric	Imperial
225 g margarine	8 oz margarine
225 g caster sugar	8 oz caster sugar
4 eggs, beaten	4 eggs, beaten
225 g self-raising flour	8 oz self-raising flour
For the buttercream:	**For the buttercream:**
50 g butter or margarine	2 oz butter or margarine
75 g icing sugar	3 oz icing sugar
25 g cocoa powder	1 oz cocoa powder
Little milk	Little milk
For the glacé icing and decoration:	**For the glacé icing and decoration:**
250 g icing sugar	9 oz icing sugar
2 x 5 ml spoons cocoa powder	2 teaspoons cocoa powder
100 g almond paste (bought or see page 77)	4 oz almond paste (bought or see page 77)
Edible flower decorations	Edible flower decorations
Candles	Candles

Grease and bottom line two 20.5 to 23 cm (8 to 9 inch) sandwich tins. Cream the margarine and sugar together until fluffy. Beat in the eggs a little at a time, then sift in the flour. Fold in lightly and divide the mixture between the tins. Smooth the tops and bake in a preheated moderate oven (180°C/350°F, Gas Mark 4) for 25 to 30 minutes. Cool, then split each cake into two layers.

To make the buttercream, cream together the butter or margarine and sifted icing sugar until soft. Gradually beat in the cocoa, adding a little milk if necessary. Use the buttercream to sandwich the cake layers together. Place the cake on a 25 to 28 cm (10 to 11 inch) cake board.

Add enough warm water to the icing sugar to make a smooth glacé icing. Use to coat the cake. Allow to set.

Knead the cocoa powder into the almond paste to make chocolate coloured paste. Cut or shape two-thirds of it into rabbits and place round the side of the cake, securing with a little icing. Between them place the edible flowers. Roll out the remaining paste and cut out the numerals for the clock face. Place around the top of the cake. From the trimmings, cut out clock hands and place them to show the child's age, adding the correct number of candles opposite the age.

As an alternative use chocolate rabbits round the edge and pipe chocolate icing numbers and hands on the cake.

Below: Clock birthday cake.

CHICKEN PUFFS

Metric	Imperial
50 g butter or margarine	2 oz butter or margarine
100 g onion, peeled and finely chopped	4 oz onion, peeled and finely chopped
50 g plain flour	2 oz plain flour
300 ml milk	½ pint milk
450 g cooked chicken meat, cut into 1 cm pieces	1 lb cooked chicken meat, cut into ½ inch pieces
Lemon juice	Lemon juice
Salt	Salt
Freshly ground black pepper	Freshly ground black pepper
1 x 368 g packet frozen puff pastry, thawed	1 x 13 oz packet frozen puff pastry, thawed
Beaten egg to glaze	Beaten egg to glaze

Melt the butter or margarine in a saucepan. Add the onion and fry until soft but not coloured. Stir in the flour and cook for 2 minutes. Off the heat add the milk, stirring. Bring to the boil, stirring, then reduce the heat and cook for 3 minutes. Add the chicken, lemon juice and seasoning. Turn into a bowl, cover closely with damp greaseproof paper and leave to cool.

Roll out the dough very thinly, then cut out twenty-four 10 cm (4 inch) rounds. Brush the edge of each with egg. Put a small spoonful of the chicken mixture in the centre of each, fold over the dough, seal and glaze with egg. Bake on a baking sheet in a preheated moderately hot oven (200°C/400°F, Gas Mark 6) for about 20 minutes until puffed and golden. Serve warm, not hot. Makes 24

EGG BOATS

Metric	Imperial
12 small bread rolls	12 small bread rolls
3 eggs, hard-boiled and chopped	3 eggs, hard-boiled and chopped
1.5 x 15 ml spoons mayonnaise	1½ tablespoons mayonnaise
Butter	Butter
3 medium tomatoes, quartered and seeded	3 medium tomatoes, quartered and seeded

Left: Pinwheel sandwiches; Chicken puffs; Egg boats; Lollipop biscuits. Above: Banana and honey ice cream.

Cut the tops off the bread rolls and scoop out some of the crumb. Mix with the chopped hard-boiled eggs and mayonnaise. Butter the rolls and fill with the egg mixture. Push a cocktail stick through each tomato quarter and use to represent a sail. Makes 12

PINWHEEL SANDWICHES

Metric	Imperial
1 large uncut sandwich loaf	1 large uncut sandwich loaf
175-225 g butter, softened	6-8 oz butter, softened
Marmite	Marmite
Cream cheese and chopped tomatoes	Cream cheese and chopped tomatoes

Cut the loaf into slices lengthways and trim off the crusts. Butter right to the edges. Spread one slice with Marmite. Roll up like a Swiss roll. Spread another slice with cream cheese and chopped tomatoes and roll up. Cover the remaining slices in this way. Wrap the rolls in cling film or aluminium foil and put in a cool place or refrigerator for several hours. Just before serving, cut across in slices.

LOLLIPOP BISCUITS

Metric	Imperial
175 g block margarine	6 oz block margarine
Grated rind of 1 lemon	Grated rind of 1 lemon
175 g caster sugar	6 oz caster sugar
1 egg, beaten	1 egg, beaten
175 g plain flour	6 oz plain flour
50 g rice flour	2 oz rice flour
Smarties and iced lolly sticks to decorate	Smarties and iced lolly sticks to decorate
Lemon glacé icing:	**Lemon glacé icing:**
225 g icing sugar, sifted	8 oz icing sugar, sifted
2 x 15 ml spoons lemon juice	2 tablespoons lemon juice

Cream together the margarine, lemon rind and sugar, then beat in the egg gradually. Sift in the flours and mix evenly. Knead lightly to a smooth mixture. Roll out to about 3 mm (⅛ inch) thick on a well-floured surface. Stamp out into rounds, using a 5 cm (2 inch) plain cutter. Re-roll the trimmings as necessary. Bake in rotation on greased baking sheets in a preheated moderate oven (180°C/350°F, Gas Mark 4) for 10 to 15 minutes. Cool for a few minutes on the sheets, then transfer to wire racks.

Mix together the icing sugar and lemon juice for the icing and use to sandwich together pairs of biscuits. Decorate with coloured Smarties held in place with a little icing, or thicken the icing, using more icing sugar, and pipe a child's name on each lollipop. Insert an iced lolly stick between the two biscuits. Makes about 35

BANANA AND HONEY ICE CREAM

Metric	Imperial
500 g bananas	1 lb bananas
150 ml double cream	¼ pint double cream
150 ml unsweetened natural yogurt	¼ pint unsweetened natural yogurt
Juice of 1 large lemon	Juice of 1 large lemon
5 x 15 ml spoons thick honey	5 tablespoons thick honey
2 egg whites	2 egg whites

Mash the bananas in a large bowl using a fork. Add the unwhipped cream, yogurt, lemon juice and honey. Beat well to combine. Turn into a rigid plastic container – not too deep. Cover and half-freeze, to the mushy stage.

Whisk the egg whites until stiff. Fold them into the banana mixture and finish freezing. Allow to 'come to' in the refrigerator for 1 hour before serving with fan wafers.

PARTY FOR 8 TO 12 GUESTS, 6 TO 8 YEARS OLD

Birthday house, Cheese scones with butter, Windmill thins with butter and Marmite, Cheese and sausage toasts, Twiglets, salted nuts, various crisps, Fairy fingers, Orange fizz

BEFOREHAND

Birthday house
Make the cakes several days ahead; store in airtight containers. Make up the house and decorate it the day before the party.
Cheese scones
Make on the morning of the party.
Windmill thins
Make a day or two before; keep in an airtight container.
Cheese and sausage toasts
Can be made up the day before and browned when needed.
Fairy fingers
Make several days ahead and store in an airtight tin.
Orange fizz
Make this on the morning of the party, without the addition of the lemonade, cucumber and orange slices; add these just before serving.

BIRTHDAY HOUSE

Metric	Imperial
550 g butter or margarine	1¼ lb butter or margarine
550 g caster sugar	1¼ lb caster sugar
10 eggs, beaten	10 eggs, beaten
550 g self-raising flour	1¼ lb self-raising flour
2 x 15 ml spoons cocoa powder	2 tablespoons cocoa powder
5 x 15 ml spoons water	5 tablespoons water
Cochineal	Cochineal
For the buttercream:	**For the buttercream:**
175 g butter	6 oz butter
350 g icing sugar, sifted	12 oz icing sugar, sifted
For the decoration:	**For the decoration:**
1 x 30.5 cm square cake board	1 x 12 inch square cake board
700 g royal icing, made with 700 g icing sugar (see page 77)	1½ lb royal icing, made with 1½ lb icing sugar (see page 77)
Green food colouring	Green food colouring
Coffee essence	Coffee essence
225 g milk chocolate finger biscuits	8 oz milk chocolate finger biscuits
17 chocolate sticks	17 chocolate sticks
Ice cream wafers	Ice cream wafers
1 packet jelly sweets	1 packet jelly sweets
1 piece of nougat	1 piece of nougat
Polka dots	Polka dots
2 round ice cream cones	2 round ice cream cones

Grease and line two 20.5 x 15 cm (8 x 6 inch) cake tins that are 10 cm (4 inches) deep. Cream the butter or margarine and sugar together, then beat in the eggs one at a time. Fold in the flour. Halve the mixture. Dissolve the cocoa in the water and beat it into one half of the cake mixture. Turn it into one of the tins. Colour the other half of the mixture pink with cochineal and turn it into the second tin. Bake in the centre of a preheated moderate oven (180°C/350°F, Gas Mark 4) for about 70 minutes. Turn out and cool on a wire rack.

When cold, level off the cakes and split each into two layers.

To make the buttercream, cream the butter and icing sugar together. Using one pink cake layer as a base, sandwich alternate coloured layers with the buttercream.

Make up the royal icing to the "peak" stage. Colour about 1 x 15 ml spoon (1 tablespoon) icing green and put it in a paper icing bag without a nozzle. Keep 4 x 15 ml spoons (4 tablespoons) of the remaining icing white and colour the rest to resemble stone with coffee essence.

Cut away two wedges from the top quarter of the cake and use these to make the point of the roof. Cover the whole house with the stone-coloured icing. Tile the roof with finger biscuits. Spread 2 x 15 ml spoons (2 tablespoons) of the white icing over the board and rough up with a palette knife. Place the cake on the board.

From the cake trimmings cut out a door, doorstep and lintel. Place on the long side of cake. Using whole and halved chocolate sticks, make one large window on the same side as the door, two windows, one above the other, on each of the two ends and one window on the back wall. Keep 2 chocolate sticks for the chimney. Cut the wafers to fit the windows for shutters and place round the roof. Fix jelly sweets on the door with a little icing, and use the rest to decorate the front and back of the cake.

Attach the piece of nougat to the side of the roof with a little white icing. Cut each remaining chocolate stick in half. Stick two halves together with a little icing and place on the nougat, as chimneys, with a little icing. Use white icing on the roof to resemble snow.

Make a pathway with polka dots. Cover the two ice cream cones with the green icing and rough up to resemble trees. Place on the board to each side of the path. Attach to the board with a little icing.

Birthday house.

60

CHEESE SCONES

Metric	Imperial
450 g self-raising flour	1 lb self-raising flour
Pinch of salt	Pinch of salt
2 x 5 ml spoons dry mustard	2 teaspoons dry mustard
150-200 g Cheddar cheese, grated	6-8 oz Cheddar cheese, grated
6 x 15 ml spoons corn oil	6 tablespoons corn oil
About 200 ml cold milk	About 8 fl oz cold milk

Sift together the flour, salt and mustard. Stir in the remaining ingredients and knead lightly to a manageable dough. On a lightly floured board, roll out the dough to 2 cm (¾ inch) thick and stamp out 5 cm (2 inch) diameter rounds. Place on a lightly greased baking sheet. Bake in a preheated hot oven (220°C/425°F, Gas Mark 7) for about 10 minutes. Cool on a wire rack. Makes 16

WINDMILL THINS

Metric	Imperial
225 g plain flour	8 oz plain flour
1 x 2.5 ml spoon salt	½ teaspoon salt
1 x 5 ml spoon baking powder	1 teaspoon baking powder
50 g butter or block margarine	2 oz butter or block margarine
5-6 x 15 ml spoons water	5-6 tablespoons water
Beaten egg to glaze	Beaten egg to glaze
Rock salt	Rock salt

Sift the flour, salt and baking powder into a bowl. Rub in the fat until the mixture resembles fine crumbs. Bind to a soft but manageable dough with cold water. Roll out *very* thinly and stamp out 7.5 cm (3 inch) plain rounds. Prick well with a fork. Place on a greased baking sheet. Brush with beaten egg and sprinkle with salt. Bake in a preheated moderate oven (180°C/350°F, Gas Mark 4) for 15 to 20 minutes until golden. Cool on a wire rack. Spread these crisp salted savoury crackers with butter and Marmite to serve. Makes about 20

CHEESE AND SAUSAGE TOASTS

Metric	Imperial
24 small squares of toast	24 small squares of toast
Butter	Butter
French mustard	French mustard
6 cooked sausages, thinly sliced	6 cooked sausages, thinly sliced
100 g cheese, finely grated	4 oz cheese, finely grated

Spread the toast squares with butter and a thin layer of mustard. Top each with a few slices of sausage, then sprinkle with grated cheese. Either brown in a preheated moderate oven (180°C/350°F, Gas Mark 4) or under the grill. (The toasts can be made in advance and browned when needed.) Makes 24

Cheese scones; Windmill thins; Cheese and sausage toasts.

Fairy fingers; Orange fizz.

FAIRY FINGERS

Metric	Imperial
50 g butter	2 oz butter
40 g caster sugar	1½ oz caster sugar
2 x 15 ml spoons single cream	2 tablespoons single cream
50 g plain flour	2 oz plain flour
2 x 15 ml spoons cornflour	2 tablespoons cornflour
1 x 2.5 ml spoon baking powder	½ teaspoon baking powder

These are bite-size, crisp and not too sweet. Cream the butter and sugar together until soft. Beat in the cream. Sift the flour, cornflour and baking powder over the creamed ingredients and mix well together. Place the mixture in a piping bag fitted with a 1 cm (½ inch) plain nozzle. Pipe into 5 cm (2 inch) fingers on non-stick paper-lined baking sheets, leaving room for the biscuits to spread. Bake in a preheated moderate oven (190°C/375°F, Gas Mark 5) for about 12 minutes, or until firm to the touch and golden brown around the edges. Cool on a wire rack and store in an airtight tin. Serve dredged with icing sugar, if you like. Makes about 20

ORANGE FIZZ

Metric	Imperial
2 x 190 ml cans frozen orange juice, thawed	2 x 6½ fl oz cans frozen orange juice, thawed
150 ml blackcurrant syrup	¼ pint blackcurrant syrup
2 x 700 ml bottles fizzy lemonade	2 x 25 fl oz bottles fizzy lemonade
Cucumber slices	Cucumber slices
Orange slices	Orange slices

Make up the concentrated orange juice to 1.2 litres (2 pints) with water and add the blackcurrant syrup. Just before serving, stir in the lemonade and cucumber and orange slices. Serve in glasses, with straws. Makes about 2 litres (3½ pints)

THE YOUNG SET

Lots of food, plenty of soft drinks and enough room to enjoy both the food and the music – those are necessary ingredients for a successful teenage party. Here are lots of ideas which are calculated to make it go with a swing. The youngsters may not feel up to coping with *all* the preparations, but they can help to prepare some of the dishes. If you have an attic or spare room which can house the party, the young people will enjoy decorating it for the occasion. If there aren't enough chairs, provide cushions and nobody will mind as long as there's enough food to eat. For safety's sake, ban candles but see the lights are dim by using low wattage bulbs. The menus include a panic-free party for ten, French farmhouse style, with everything prepared the day before. Provide sturdy rustic pottery and bright cloths and table napkins. Choose warmer fare for colder days like the hot punch and pancakes party, served in the kitchen on a 'come-and-get-it-while-it's-hot' basis.

PÂTÉ AND POT LUCK FOR TEN

Sardine and anchovy pâté, Toast/Beef and bean pot, Tomato and cucumber salad/Iced lemon pie

BEFOREHAND

Sardine and anchovy pâté
Make two or three days ahead and refrigerate. (Or make the day before and keep in a cool place.) Make the toast for the pâté just before serving.

Beef and bean pot
Cook the day before; cool quickly and refrigerate.

Tomato and cucumber salad
Put dressing ingredients in a lidded container – avoid a metal lid. Put the salad together 1 hour before serving.

Iced lemon pie
The day before, make as far as the lemon filling stage and freeze. On the day, add the ice cream topping and return to the freezer compartment for about 1 hour. (Or freeze the finished pie, uncovered, in the freezer and take out a short time before serving. If to be left for more than a day in the freezer, keep in a freezer bag.)

SARDINE AND ANCHOVY PÂTÉ

Metric	Imperial
3 x 140 g cans sardines in tomato sauce	3 x 4⅞ oz cans sardines in tomato sauce
225 g curd or cream cheese	8 oz curd or cream cheese
50 g butter, melted	2 oz butter, melted
1 x 15 ml spoon lemon juice	1 tablespoon lemon juice
2 x 15 ml spoons anchovy essence	2 tablespoons anchovy essence
Freshly ground black pepper	Freshly ground black pepper
10 lemon slices	10 lemon slices

Put the sardines, cheese, butter, lemon juice and anchovy essence in a bowl and beat with an electric mixer until smooth and creamy. Season to taste with pepper. Divide between ten individual ramekin dishes and fork up the tops. Place a lemon slice on top of each. Cover and chill for at least 30 minutes before serving with toast.

BEEF AND BEAN POT

Metric	Imperial
1.5 kg lean minced beef	3 lb lean minced beef
2 eggs	2 eggs
50 g fresh white breadcrumbs	2 oz fresh white breadcrumbs
50 g onion, peeled and finely chopped	2 oz onion, peeled and finely chopped
Salt	Salt
Freshly ground black pepper	Freshly ground black pepper
2 x 15 ml spoons oil	2 tablespoons oil
3 x 432 g cans red kidney beans	3 x 15¼ oz cans red kidney beans
2 x 400 g cans tomatoes	2 x 14 oz cans tomatoes
300 ml beef stock	½ pint beef stock
1 x 141 g can tomato paste	1 x 5 oz can tomato paste
2 garlic cloves, crushed	2 garlic cloves, crushed
3 x 15 ml spoons chilli seasoning	3 tablespoons chilli seasoning

In a bowl, combine the minced beef, eggs, breadcrumbs, onion, 1 x 5 ml spoon (1 teaspoon) salt and pepper to taste. Shape into about 100 small balls the size of a walnut, with floured hands.

Heat the oil in a frying pan. Add a single layer of beef balls and cook over medium heat for 5 minutes until browned on all sides to seal the surface. Repeat until all the meatballs are browned. Drain well on absorbent kitchen paper.

In a large saucepan or flameproof casserole, combine the rest of the ingredients, including the bean can juices. Season with salt and pepper. Add the meat balls. Cover and cook over medium heat for 30 minutes. Uncover and continue to cook for a further 30 minutes, until the juices have thickened. Stir occasionally to prevent burning on the bottom.

Left: Sardine and anchovy pâté.

Beef and bean pot; Iced lemon pie; Tomato and cucumber salad.

TOMATO AND CUCUMBER SALAD

Metric
8 large tomatoes, sliced
2 cucumbers, sliced
225 g onions, peeled and cut into rings
For the dressing:
150 ml salad oil
4 x 15 ml spoons garlic vinegar
1 x 2.5 ml spoon salt
1 x 2.5 ml spoon sugar
1 x 2.5 ml spoon dry mustard
Freshly ground black pepper

Imperial
8 large tomatoes, sliced
2 cucumbers, sliced
8 oz onions, peeled and cut into rings
For the dressing:
¼ pint salad oil
4 tablespoons garlic vinegar
½ teaspoon salt
½ teaspoon sugar
½ teaspoon dry mustard
Freshly ground black pepper

Arrange alternate layers of tomato slices, cucumber slices and onion rings on a serving plate.

Shake the dressing ingredients together with pepper to taste in a screwtop jar. Pour evenly over the salad. Leave to marinate for at least 2 hours to infuse the flavours.

ICED LEMON PIE

Metric
100 g butter
225 g digestive biscuits, crushed
25 g demerara sugar
3 eggs, separated
200 ml condensed milk
Grated rind of 2 lemons
9 x 15 ml spoons lemon juice
4 x 15 ml spoons caster sugar
2.3 litres vanilla ice cream
Lemon slices to garnish

Imperial
4 oz butter
8 oz digestive biscuits, crushed
1 oz demerara sugar
3 eggs, separated
⅓ pint condensed milk
Grated rind of 2 lemons
9 tablespoons lemon juice
4 tablespoons caster sugar
½ gallon vanilla ice cream
Lemon slices to garnish

Melt the butter in a saucepan and add the biscuits and demerara sugar. Mix well. Divide the crumb mixture between two 20 cm (8 inch) pie plates, reserving about 3 x 15 ml spoons (3 tablespoons) crumbs. Press the crumbs onto the bottoms and sides of the pans.

Beat the egg yolks until thick and creamy. Stir in the condensed milk, lemon rind and juice and continue stirring until thick. Whisk the egg whites until stiff, then whisk in the sugar until the mixture stands in peaks. Fold into the lemon mixture and divide between the crumb cases. Freeze until firm.

Scoop out small balls of ice cream and arrange on top of the pies. Decorate with the reserved crumb mixture. Freeze for about 1 hour. Allow a short while to 'come to' before serving. Garnish with halved lemon slices. Makes 2 pies, each to serve 5 to 6

HOT PUNCH AND PANCAKES FOR EIGHT TO TEN

Non-alcoholic punch (see pages 180-1), Salted twisters and Cheese crescents/Curried beef pancakes, Gouda cheese and prawn pancakes/Hazelnut meringues, Chocolate fudge sauce

BEFOREHAND

Salted twisters and Cheese crescents
Bake the day before and when cold store in an airtight tin. Refresh in the oven when needed for about 10 minutes, along with the reheated pancakes.

Pancakes
Make the day before and layer up in packs of 10 with greaseproof paper between each. Foil-wrap and refrigerate. Make the fillings; store in covered containers in the refrigerator. Fill the pancakes early on the day of the party, ready for reheating.

Hazelnut meringues with Chocolate fudge sauce
Make the meringues several days ahead and keep in airtight containers. Make the sauce the day before the party.

SALTED TWISTERS AND CHEESE CRESCENTS

Metric	Imperial
1 x 368 g packet frozen puff pastry, thawed	1 x 13 oz packet frozen puff pastry, thawed
Beaten egg	Beaten egg
Coarse sea salt	Coarse sea salt
25 g cheese, finely grated	1 oz cheese, finely grated
Poppy seeds	Poppy seeds

Divide the pastry dough in half. For the twisters, roll out one portion to a rectangle about 38 by 12.5 cm (15 by 5 inches). Cut into 1 cm (½ inch) strips along the length, and cut each strip into two, widthways. To shape, wrap the end of a dough strip round the loop end of a plain round skewer, but do not take in the loop itself. Press the dough to secure, then continue to spiral the strip around the skewer, leaving a space between each turn. Place join side down on a baking sheet. Twist each strip of dough in the same way. Brush with beaten egg and sprinkle lightly with salt. Bake in a preheated moderately hot oven (200°C/400°F, Gas Mark 6) for 10 to 15 minutes. Remove from the skewers while warm.

For the crescents, roll out the rest of the dough to an oblong 40 by 20 cm (16 by 8 inches). Cut into eight equal sized squares. Cut each square in half diagonally to make 16 triangles. Brush with beaten egg. Scatter with cheese. Roll up from the long edges and shape into crescents. Brush again with egg and sprinkle with poppy seeds. Bake as for the twisters. Serve warm. Makes 20 twisters and 16 crescents

CURRIED BEEF PANCAKES

Metric	Imperial
For the pancakes:	**For the pancakes:**
175 g plain flour	6 oz plain flour
Pinch of salt	Pinch of salt
2 eggs	2 eggs
450 ml milk	¾ pint milk
Oil for frying	Oil for frying
For the filling:	**For the filling:**
100 g butter	4 oz butter
350 g onions, peeled and chopped	12 oz onions, peeled and chopped
225 g cooking apples, peeled, cored and chopped	8 oz cooking apples, peeled, cored and chopped
1 x 15 ml spoon mild curry powder	1 tablespoon mild curry powder
75 g plain flour	3 oz plain flour
1 x 350 g can corned beef, chopped	1 x 12 oz can corned beef, chopped
1 x 198 g can corned beef, chopped	1 x 7 oz can corned beef, chopped
300 ml beef stock	½ pint beef stock
2 x 5 ml spoons lemon juice	2 teaspoons lemon juice
Salt	Salt
Freshly ground black pepper	Freshly ground black pepper
Flaked almonds and strips of canned pimiento to garnish	Flaked almonds and strips of canned pimiento to garnish

Sift the flour and salt into a bowl. Make a well in the centre and add the eggs and half the milk. Mix well until smooth, then beat in the remaining milk. Pour this batter into a jug. Heat a little oil in an 18 cm (7 inch) diameter frying pan. Pour in a little batter, just enough to cover the bottom of the pan. Fry until the underside of the pancake is golden brown, then, with the help of a palette knife, turn it and brown the other side. Turn out onto kitchen paper. Make 15 pancakes stacking them with greaseproof paper between them.

For the filling, melt 75 g (3 oz) of the butter in a large saucepan and fry the onions and apples until golden. Stir in the curry powder and flour and cook for 2 minutes. Add the corned beef and stock and bring to the boil, stirring. Reduce the heat, cover and simmer for 30 minutes. Season with lemon juice, salt and pepper.

Divide the filling between the pancakes and roll up. Place side by side in an ovenproof dish. Garnish with almonds and pimiento and brush with the remaining butter, melted. Reheat in a preheated moderate oven (160°C/325°F, Gas Mark 3) for 20 minutes. Makes 15
Note: Stuffed pancakes take about 1 hour to reheat from cold.

Left: Salted twisters; Cheese crescents.

Hazelnut meringues, Chocolate fudge sauce.

Melt the butter in a saucepan. Add the flour and cook, stirring, for 1 minute. Remove from the heat and gradually stir in the milk. Return to the heat and bring to the boil, stirring constantly. Simmer until thickened, then stir in the nutmeg, chives, salt and pepper to taste and the lemon juice.

Remove from the heat and stir in the eggs and 175 g (6 oz) of the cheese. Continue stirring until the cheese has melted. Stir in the prawns.

Divide the filling between the pancakes and roll up. Place side by side in an ovenproof dish. Sprinkle with the remaining cheese and reheat in a preheated moderate oven (160°C/325°F, Gas Mark 3) for about 20 minutes. Makes 15

HAZELNUT MERINGUES

Metric	Imperial
4 egg whites	4 egg whites
225 g caster sugar	8 oz caster sugar
50 g hazelnuts, ground or grated	2 oz hazelnuts, ground or grated

Whisk the egg whites until stiff. Whisk in the sugar, 1 x 15 ml spoon (1 tablespoon) at a time, until the meringue is really thick and white. Fold in the hazelnuts. Turn the meringue mixture into a large forcing bag fitted with a large star vegetable nozzle. Pipe 10 small baskets on baking sheets lined with non-stick paper. Bake in the coolest part of a preheated very cool oven (130°C/250°F, Gas Mark ½) for about 2 hours until well dried out. Cool on a wire rack. Serve filled with chocolate ice cream and with chocolate fudge sauce. Makes 10

CHOCOLATE FUDGE SAUCE

Metric	Imperial
225 ml evaporated milk	8 fl oz evaporated milk
1 x 100 g packet chocolate drops	1 x 4 oz packet chocolate drops
1 x 150 g packet marshmallows	1 x 5 oz packet marshmallows

Put all the ingredients in a heatproof bowl over simmering water and melt gently, stirring to combine. When the sauce is smooth, serve.

If making the sauce ahead of time and refrigerating overnight, it may be too thick. In this case, gently beat in a little more evaporated milk until the sauce is the right consistency.

Below: Curried beef pancakes; Gouda cheese and prawn pancakes.

GOUDA CHEESE AND PRAWN PANCAKES

Metric	Imperial
50 g butter	2 oz butter
50 g plain flour	2 oz plain flour
600 ml milk	1 pint milk
1 x 1.25 ml spoon grated nutmeg	¼ teaspoon grated nutmeg
3 x 15 ml spoons chopped fresh chives	3 tablespoons chopped fresh chives
Salt	Salt
Freshly ground black pepper	Freshly ground black pepper
4 x 5 ml spoons lemon juice	4 teaspoons lemon juice
3 eggs, hard-boiled and chopped	3 eggs, hard-boiled and chopped
225 g Gouda cheese, grated	8 oz Gouda cheese, grated
500 g frozen shelled prawns, thawed and drained	1 lb frozen shelled prawns, thawed and drained
15 x 18 cm pancakes (see Curried beef pancakes above)	15 x 7 inch pancakes (see Curried beef pancakes above)

FARMHOUSE PIE PARTY FOR TWELVE

Veal and ham farmhouse pie, Tomato and onion salad, French sticks (small French loaves), Golden slaw/Coffee refrigerator cake

BEFOREHAND

Veal and ham farmhouse pie
Leave preparation and cooking until the day of the party.
Tomato and onion salad
Make on the day of the party from quartered tomatoes and chopped onion and French dressing (see page 91).
Golden slaw
Prepare the cabbage bowl and thinly slice the cabbage heart. Keep, polythene wrapped, in the refrigerator until required.
Coffee refrigerator cake
Layer the soaked boudoir biscuits and cream the day before and leave, covered, in the refrigerator. Whip the rest of the cream and complete the cake about 3 hours before the party.

VEAL AND HAM FARMHOUSE PIE

Metric	Imperial
1.25 kg stewing veal, cut into 2.5 cm cubes	2½ lb stewing veal, cut into 1 inch cubes
500 g boneless bacon joint, cut into 2.5 cm cubes	1 lb boneless bacon joint, cut into 1 inch cubes
350 g button onions, peeled	12 oz button onions, peeled
Finely grated rind of 1 lemon	Finely grated rind of 1 lemon
6 x 15 ml spoons plain flour	6 tablespoons plain flour
8 x 15 ml spoons chopped parsley	8 tablespoons chopped parsley
8 x 15 ml spoons mango chutney, chopped	8 tablespoons mango chutney, chopped
Salt	Salt
Freshly ground black pepper	Freshly ground black pepper
450 ml light stock	¾ pint light stock
350 g plain wholemeal flour	12 oz plain wholemeal flour
175 g shredded suet	6 oz shredded suet
About 250 ml water	About 9 fl oz water
Beaten egg to glaze	Beaten egg to glaze

Above: Tomato and onion salad; Golden slaw; Veal and ham farmhouse pie. Right: Coffee refrigerator cake.

Mix together the meats, onions, lemon rind, plain flour, parsley, chutney and seasoning. Divide between two 1.2 litre (2 pint) pie dishes, with a pie funnel in each. Pour in the stock.

Mix the wholemeal flour and suet and bind to a soft dough with the water. Divide the dough in half. Roll out each piece and use to cover the pie dishes, sealing the edges well. Decorate with dough trimmings. Glaze with beaten egg and bake in a preheated moderately hot oven (200°C/400°F, Gas Mark 6) until golden – about 35 minutes. Lower the heat to moderate (160°C/325°F, Gas Mark 3). Lay a piece of foil on top of each pie and bake for a further hour. Makes 2 pies, each to serve 6

GOLDEN SLAW

Metric	Imperial
1 large Savoy cabbage	1 large Savoy cabbage
225-350 g Gruyère cheese, cut in thin strips	8-12 oz Gruyère cheese, cut in thin strips
500 g red-skinned apples, cored and chopped	1 lb red-skinned apples, cored and chopped
300 ml mayonnaise	½ pint mayonnaise
2 x 15 ml spoons prepared mustard	2 tablespoons prepared mustard
2 x 5 ml spoons sugar	2 teaspoons sugar
Salt	Salt
Freshly ground black pepper	Freshly ground black pepper

Wash the cabbage well. Curl back the outer leaves, cut around the base of the heart and scoop out the heart, leaving a 'bowl'. Finely shred the cabbage heart and put in a bowl with the cheese and apples. Combine the mayonnaise with the mustard, sugar and seasoning and toss the salad in this dressing until the ingredients are well coated. Serve in the scooped-out cabbage 'bowl'.

COFFEE REFRIGERATOR CAKE

Make two

Metric	Imperial
2-3 x 15 ml spoons brandy	2-3 tablespoons brandy
150 ml strong black coffee	¼ pint strong black coffee
28 boudoir biscuits	28 boudoir biscuits
300 ml double cream, chilled	½ pint double cream, chilled
2 x 15 ml spoons milk	2 tablespoons milk
Pistachio nuts, blanched and halved, or chocolate fingers	Pistachio nuts, blanched and halved, or chocolate fingers

Mix the brandy with the coffee in a shallow dish. Dip the boudoir biscuits one at a time into the coffee. Arrange seven biscuits side by side on a serving plate. Whip half the chilled cream and 1 x 15 ml spoon (1 tablespoon) milk together until it just holds its shape. Use a little to spread over the seven biscuits. Repeat with the remaining biscuits, using seven for each layer, all the coffee mixture and the cream. Chill, covered, for several hours.

Whip the remaining cream and milk together until it holds its shape and spread a little over the top of the layered biscuits. Turn the remainder of the cream into a fabric piping bag, fitted with a star vegetable nozzle. Use this to pipe cream shells across the top. Decorate with halved pistachio nuts or chocolate fingers. Chill until required. Serves 6

Pasta Party for Twelve

Curried chicken lasagne, or Spaghetti with bacon ragu, Tossed green salad, Blue cheese dressing, Country herb soda bread/Fruit and hazelnut shortcake

BEFOREHAND

Curried chicken lasagne
Prepare completely the day before, but do not bake; keep refrigerated, lightly covered. Reheat in a preheated moderate oven (180°C/350°F, Gas Mark 4) for 1 to 1½ hours when needed.

Bacon ragu
Prepare and cook the ragu the day before; keep refrigerated, lightly covered. Reheat thoroughly on the top of the stove over a low heat, stirring occasionally to prevent sticking.

Salad and dressing
The day before, choose salad ingredients in season; prepare, put in polythene bags and refrigerate. Crumble enough blue cheese into French dressing for personal taste.

Country herb soda bread
Make completely the day before; when cold, foil-wrap. Refresh next day.

Fruit and hazelnut shortcake
Make the shortcake bases the day before; when cold store in airtight container.

CURRIED CHICKEN LASAGNE

Metric	Imperial
2 x 2 kg oven-ready chickens, skinned	2 x 4½ lb oven-ready chickens, skinned
100 g butter	4 oz butter
4 x 15 ml spoons plain flour	4 tablespoons plain flour
6 x 15 ml spoons hot (Madras) curry powder	6 tablespoons hot (Madras) curry powder
2.4 litres milk	4 pints milk
Salt	Salt
Freshly ground black pepper	Freshly ground black pepper
75 g desiccated coconut	3 oz desiccated coconut
750 g lasagne	1½ lb lasagne
2 x 15 ml spoons fresh breadcrumbs	2 tablespoons fresh breadcrumbs

Remove all the meat from the chicken carcasses with a small sharp knife. Trim off any fat and cut the meat into 1 cm (½ inch) chunks.

Melt the butter in a large heavy-based saucepan. Stir in the flour and curry powder and cook for 2 minutes. Off the heat, gradually stir in the milk and seasoning, then bring to the boil, stirring all the time. Simmer for 5 minutes, then stir in 50 g (2 oz) of the coconut. Spoon some of the sauce over the bottoms of two 2.3 litre (4 pint) shallow ovenproof dishes. Layer the lasagne and the chicken in the ovenproof dishes, spooning a little sauce over each layer. Finish with a layer of lasagne, covered with the remaining sauce. Sprinkle over the remaining coconut and the breadcrumbs. Bake in a preheated moderate oven (180°C/350°F, Gas Mark 4) for 1 to 1¼ hours until the lasagne is tender and the top browned. Serve with chutney, chopped hard-boiled egg and cucumber, etc. Makes 2 batches, each to serve 6
Note: The lasagne sheets are not first cooked in boiling water as they cook very well in the made-up dish with the sauce to moisten them.

SPAGHETTI WITH BACON RAGU

Metric	Imperial
120 ml oil	4 fl oz oil
500 g onions, peeled and sliced	1 lb onions, peeled and sliced
2 garlic cloves, crushed	2 garlic cloves, crushed
1.5 kg lean collar bacon, very finely chopped	3 lb lean collar bacon, very finely chopped
4 x 15 ml spoons plain flour	4 tablespoons plain flour
1 x 142 g can concentrated tomato purée	1 x 5 oz can concentrated tomato purée
1 x 15 ml spoon dried sage	1 tablespoon dried sage
1 kg tomatoes, skinned, seeded and quartered	2 lb tomatoes, skinned, seeded and quartered
120 ml dry white wine	4 fl oz dry white wine
900 ml unseasoned stock	1½ pints unseasoned stock
Freshly ground black pepper	Freshly ground black pepper
750 g spaghetti	1½ lb spaghetti
Salt	Salt
50 g butter, melted	2 oz butter, melted
Grated Parmesan cheese to serve	Grated Parmesan cheese to serve

Heat the oil in a large heavy-based saucepan. Add the onions and fry until golden brown. Add the garlic and cook for a further 1 minute. Stir in the bacon and fry, stirring, for 5 minutes.

Sprinkle over the flour and cook, stirring, for 1 minute. Add the tomato purée, sage and tomatoes and mix well, then stir in the wine and stock. Bring to the boil, stirring. Season well with pepper and simmer, uncovered, for about 1¼ hours or until the mixture is reduced by half and the meat is tender.

Fifteen minutes before the ragu is ready, cook the spaghetti in plenty of boiling salted water until it is just tender. Drain well and return to the saucepan. Add the melted butter and toss until all the spaghetti strands are coated.

Pile the spaghetti in a warmed serving dish and pour over the bacon ragu. Serve sprinkled with grated Parmesan.

Left: Curried chicken lasagne. Right: Country herb soda bread; Spaghetti with bacon ragu.

COUNTRY HERB SODA BREAD

Metric	Imperial
225 g plain flour	8 oz plain flour
225 g plain wholemeal flour	8 oz plain wholemeal flour
1.5 x 5 ml spoons salt	1½ teaspoons salt
1 x 5 ml spoon bicarbonate of soda	1 teaspoon bicarbonate of soda
25 g butter	1 oz butter
225 g onions, peeled and minced	8 oz onions, peeled and minced
100 g celery, trimmed and minced	4 oz celery, trimmed and minced
1 x 2.5 ml spoon dried mixed herbs	½ teaspoon dried mixed herbs
2 x 15 ml spoons chopped parsley	2 tablespoons chopped parsley
175 ml milk	6 fl oz milk
2 x 5 ml spoons lemon juice	2 teaspoons lemon juice
Milk to glaze	Milk to glaze
50 g mature Cheddar cheese, grated	2 oz mature Cheddar cheese, grated

Place the flours, salt and bicarbonate of soda in a large bowl and mix well together. Rub in the butter. Stir in the onions, celery and herbs. Mix the milk and lemon juice together and stir into the dry ingredients. Knead lightly on a floured surface to a smooth dough. Pat out to a 23 cm (9 inch) round on a floured baking sheet. Brush with milk and sprinkle with the grated cheese. Score the top into 12 portions and bake in a preheated moderately hot oven (200°C/400°F, Gas Mark 6) for about 35 minutes, or until golden brown. Serve warm or cold.

FRUIT AND HAZELNUT SHORTCAKE

Metric	Imperial
225 g shelled hazelnuts	8 oz shelled hazelnuts
300 g butter, softened	10 oz butter, softened
175 g caster sugar	6 oz caster sugar
350 g plain flour	12 oz plain flour
600 ml whipping cream, lightly whipped	1 pint whipping cream, lightly whipped
3 x 412 g cans guavas or passion fruit, drained	3 x 14½ oz cans guavas or passion fruit, drained
Icing sugar	Icing sugar

Fruit and hazelnut shortcake.

Roast the hazelnuts in a preheated hot oven (220°C/425°F, Gas Mark 7) until dark, then rub in a cloth to remove the skins. Grind. Cream the butter and sugar together until light and fluffy and work in the sifted flour and ground nuts. Knead lightly to form a dough and leave to rest for 15 minutes.

Divide the dough into six equal pieces. Shape each piece into a 20 cm (8 inch) round in a flan ring on a non-stick paper-lined baking sheet. Press the dough into the shape of the ring, then remove the ring and roll the surface of the round lightly with a rolling pin to smooth it. Bake each round in rotation in a preheated moderate oven (180°C/350°F, Gas Mark 4) for 12 to 15 minutes or until pale golden. Cut two of the rounds into 12 sections each and leave on the sheets to become crisp – about 5 minutes. Transfer to wire racks to cool.

About 2 hours before they are needed, assemble the two cakes, sandwiching two lots of rounds together with half the cream and fruit. Spoon the rest of the cream on the tops and arrange the cut triangles on their edges. Slice the remaining fruit and pile in the centre. Sift icing sugar over the cakes just before serving.
Makes 2 cakes, each to serve 6

SEASONAL
CELEBRATIONS

Appropriate decorations can help to create the right atmosphere for a seasonal celebration, but something special in the way of food is needed, too. Christmas and Easter aren't the only occasions for traditional fare; events such as those commemorating Guy Fawkes and Hallowe'en for instance, coming at rather bleak times of the year, provide good excuses for celebrations and special food.

When seasonal celebrations are also family get-togethers, it's important to cater for the very young and very old too, providing them with something familiar and not too elaborate in the way of traditional fare.

Although winter parties call for warming food, cool starters and puddings provide a refreshing balance; it often makes life easier for the hostess if there's only one hot course to dish up and serve. While chilled soup is an ideal starter for a summer party, lashings of hot coffee, in good-sized cups, will be more than welcome as the evening grows cooler.

CHRISTMAS DINNER FOR SIX TO EIGHT

Roast turkey, Chestnut stuffing, Sausagemeat stuffing, Chipolatas, Bacon rolls, Bread sauce, Cranberry sauce, Pickled prunes, Roast potatoes, Brussels sprouts, Parsnips/Brandy butter, Apricot mincemeat flan, Christmas pudding, Light Christmas cake

BEFOREHAND

Weeks ahead
Make the Christmas cake, the pudding and preserves.

Early in December
Decide on the meat and/or poultry you're going to have and order it, if necessary. When ordering a turkey, allow about 350 g (12 oz) oven-ready weight per person; a good, fleshy 4.5 to 5.4 kg (10 to 12 lb) oven-ready bird should give 6 to 8 hot helpings, 8 cold cut helpings and some leftover.

Mid-December
Almond-paste the cake. Royal ice the cake one week before Christmas. Make and refrigerate brandy butter.

December 23
Prepare crumbs for bread sauce. Make dry stuffing mix; store in the refrigerator. Prepare the giblet stock for the gravy: simmer the giblets – gizzard, heart and neck – with 1.2 litres (2 pints) water, seasoning, flavouring vegetables and a few bacon rinds for about 2 hours. Cook the liver separately; mince. Refrigerate.

Christmas Eve
If you're having a bacon joint, soak it and cook it. Prepare the potatoes and leave in cold water. Trim the sprouts, put into polythene bags and store in a cool place. Have the giblet gravy ready, a little thicker than required, so that it will take the de-fatted turkey juices. Make the Apricot mincemeat flan.

Christmas Day
Times based on a 4.5 to 5.4 kg (10 to 12 lb) stuffed turkey in foil, fast roasting method. For other times, see chart.

Three and a half hours before: switch on oven; stuff and truss the bird.

Three hours before: put pudding to steam.

Two and a half hours before: lay the table; put out the cranberry sauce and prepare the wines. Put the bread sauce to infuse.

One and a half hours before: boil potatoes for roasting in salted water for 7 minutes; drain. Heat 2.5 cm (1 inch) dripping in a baking tin; put the potatoes in the hot fat, spoon it over and place it in the oven.

One hour before: grill the chipolatas and bacon rolls, turning them to brown evenly; cover with foil to keep warm. Cook the Brussels sprouts and gravy. Finish the gravy, having poured off into it the juices from the bird. Add the liver.

Just before required, simmer the bread sauce for 5 minutes; remove the onion and add 25 g (1 oz) butter. Drain the sprouts and dish them. Turn out the pudding; leave the upturned basin over it to keep it warm. When the bird is cooked, remove the trussing and dish up on a serving platter.

CHOOSING AND COOKING THE TURKEY

Approx thawing times at room temp 21°C/70°F	Weight	Quick method: 230°C/450°F, Gas Mark 8	Slow method: 160°C/325°F, Gas Mark 3
12 hrs	2.7-3.6 kg (6-8 lb)	2¼-2½ hrs	3-3½ hrs
14 hrs	3.6-4.5 kg (8-10 lb)	2½-2¾ hrs	3½-3¾ hrs
15-17 hrs	4.5-5.4 kg (10-12 lb)	2¾-2 hrs 50 mins	3¾-4 hrs
17 hrs	5.4-6.4 kg (12-14 lb)	2 hrs 50 mins-3 hrs	4-4¼ hrs
17-20 hrs	6.4-7.2 kg (14-16 lb)	3-3¼ hrs	4¼-4½ hrs
24 hrs	7.2-8.1 kg (16-18 lb)	3¼-3½ hrs	4½-4 hrs 50 mins

PICKLED PRUNES

Metric
1 kg prunes, soaked overnight
   and drained
450 g sugar
450 ml vinegar
Thinly pared rind of ¼ lemon
2 whole cloves
1 x 15 ml spoon whole allspice
Small piece of root ginger
Piece of cinnamon stick

Imperial
2 lb prunes, soaked overnight
   and drained
1 lb sugar
¾ pint vinegar
Thinly pared rind of ¼ lemon
2 whole cloves
1 tablespoon whole allspice
Small piece of root ginger
Piece of cinnamon stick

These are delicious with roast pork or turkey. Prick the skins of the prunes with a pin. Dissolve the sugar in the vinegar in a saucepan, then add the flavouring ingredients. Add the prunes and boil gently for about 15 minutes.

Pack the prunes into hot jars. Discard the flavourings from the vinegar mixture and boil until syrupy. Pour over the prunes to fill the jars. Seal at once with vinegar-proof preserving skin. If jars with cork stoppers are used, cover the base and sides of the stoppers with cling film.

CHESTNUT STUFFING

Metric
50 g bacon, rinds removed,
   chopped
100 g fresh white breadcrumbs
1 x 5 ml spoon chopped parsley
25 g butter, melted
Grated rind of 1 lemon
225 g chestnut purée (see note)
Salt
Freshly ground black pepper
1 egg, beaten

Imperial
2 oz bacon, rinds removed,
   chopped
4 oz fresh white breadcrumbs
1 teaspoon chopped parsley
1 oz butter, melted
Grated rind of 1 lemon
8 oz chestnut purée (see note)
Salt
Freshly ground black pepper
1 egg, beaten

Pickled prunes.

Fry the bacon gently in its own fat for 3 to 5 minutes, until crisp. Drain and add the rest of the ingredients, binding with the beaten egg. Makes enough for a 4.5 kg (10 lb) oven-ready turkey.
Note: Chestnut purée may be made from fresh, canned or dried chestnuts – or use unsweetened canned chestnut purée. If using fresh chestnuts, snip or cut the brown outer skins across the top with a pair of scissors or a sharp knife. Blanch the chestnuts in boiling water for 3 to 5 minutes. Lift them out, a few at a time, and peel off both the brown and inner skins. To cook, simmer them gently in a little chicken stock until tender; they will take 35 to 40 minutes. 450 g (1 lb) fresh chestnuts gives 350 g (12 oz) peeled. When cooked and puréed the yield is about 400 g (14 oz) unsweetened purée.

Whole canned, unsweetened chestnuts may be used as fresh cooked chestnuts and puréed for this stuffing.

Dried chestnuts should be soaked overnight in cold water. Drain and simmer in stock or milk until tender – about 40 minutes. 450 g (1 lb) dried chestnuts gives 900 g (2 lb) whole chestnuts, which may be used as fresh cooked chestnuts.

SAUSAGE MEAT STUFFING

Metric
1 large onion, peeled and
   chopped
500 g pork sausage meat
2 x 5 ml spoons chopped parsley
1 x 5 ml spoon dried mixed herbs
25 g fresh white breadcrumbs
Salt
Freshly ground black pepper

Imperial
1 large onion, peeled and
   chopped
1 lb pork sausage meat
2 teaspoons chopped parsley
1 teaspoon dried mixed herbs
1 oz fresh white breadcrumbs
Salt
Freshly ground black pepper

Ingredients for stuffings.

Mix all the ingredients together. Use with chicken or turkey, adapting the quantities as necessary.
Enough for a 4 to 4.5 kg (9 to 10 lb) oven-ready turkey

BREAD SAUCE

Metric	Imperial
2 cloves	2 cloves
1 medium onion, peeled	1 medium onion, peeled
450 ml milk	¾ pint milk
Salt	Salt
Few peppercorns	Few peppercorns
½ small bay leaf	½ small bay leaf
Knob of butter	Knob of butter
75 g fresh white breadcrumbs	3 oz fresh white breadcrumbs

Stick the cloves into the onion and put it in a saucepan with the milk, salt, peppercorns and bay leaf. Bring almost to boiling point, then remove from the heat and leave in a warm place for about 20 minutes to infuse.

Remove the peppercorns and bay leaf. Add the butter and breadcrumbs. Mix well and allow to cook very gently for about 15 minutes. Remove the onion.

If you prefer, remove the onion before adding the breadcrumbs; however, a better flavour is obtained by cooking it with the crumbs, as this allows the taste of the onion to penetrate them.
Makes about 600 ml (1 pint)

APRICOT MINCEMEAT FLAN

Metric	Imperial
For the pastry:	**For the pastry:**
175 g plain flour	6 oz plain flour
Pinch of salt	Pinch of salt
2 x 5 ml spoons caster sugar	2 teaspoons caster sugar
100 g butter or block margarine	4 oz butter or block margarine
1 egg yolk	1 egg yolk
1 x 15 ml spoon water	1 tablespoon water
For the filling:	**For the filling:**
50 g dried apricots, soaked overnight, drained and chopped	2 oz dried apricots, soaked overnight, drained and chopped
1 x 410 g jar mincemeat	1 x 14½ oz jar mincemeat
100 g ground almonds	4 oz ground almonds
75 g caster sugar	3 oz caster sugar
2 egg whites	2 egg whites
Few drops of almond essence	Few drops of almond essence
To decorate:	**To decorate:**
Icing sugar	Icing sugar
Glacé cherries	Glacé cherries
Candied angelica	Candied angelica

Apricot mincemeat flan.

Christmas pudding.

Sift the flour and salt into a bowl. Stir in the sugar, then rub in the fat until the mixture resembles breadcrumbs. Bind to a dough with the egg yolk and water. Roll out and use to line a 23 cm (9 inch) fluted flan tin. Prick and chill for 20 minutes, then bake blind in a preheated moderately hot oven (190°C/375°F, Gas Mark 5) for about 20 minutes. Cool in the tin.

Mix together the apricots and mincemeat and spoon into the flan case. Sift together the ground almonds and caster sugar. Whisk the egg whites until stiff, then fold in the almond mixture with the essence. Using a large star vegetable nozzle, pipe the mixture onto the mincemeat mixture, leaving a star shape uncovered in the centre. Bake in a preheated moderate oven (180°C/350°F, Gas Mark 4) for 30 to 40 minutes. Dust with icing sugar and decorate with glacé cherries and angelica while hot. Serve slightly warm or cold.
Serves 6 to 8

BRANDY BUTTER

Metric	Imperial
175 g butter	6 oz butter
175 g caster sugar	6 oz caster sugar
4-6 x 15 ml spoons brandy	4-6 tablespoons brandy

Cream the butter until pale and soft. Beat in the sugar gradually and add the brandy a few drops at a time, taking care not to allow the mixture to curdle. The finished sauce should be pale and frothy. Pile it up in a small dish and leave to harden before serving.

For a less granular texture, use sifted icing sugar, or half icing and half caster sugar. Serves 8

CHRISTMAS PUDDING

Metric	Imperial
450 g fresh white breadcrumbs	1 lb fresh white breadcrumbs
1 x 5 ml spoon ground ginger	1 teaspoon ground ginger
1 x 5 ml spoon mixed spice	1 teaspoon mixed spice
1 x 5 ml spoon salt	1 teaspoon salt
225 g shredded suet	8 oz shredded suet
225 g soft brown sugar	8 oz soft brown sugar
100 g chopped mixed peel	4 oz chopped mixed peel
100 g currants, cleaned	4 oz currants, cleaned
100 g sultanas, cleaned	4 oz sultanas, cleaned
450 g seedless raisins, cleaned	1 lb seedless raisins, cleaned
75 g carrots, peeled and grated	3 oz carrots, peeled and grated
5 x 15 ml spoons milk	5 tablespoons milk
2 x 15 ml spoons golden syrup	2 tablespoons golden syrup

This is a light-textured pudding, delicious served with brandy or orange-flavoured chilled whipped cream, brandy butter, rum butter or dairy ice cream.

Grease two 1.2 litre (2 pint) pudding basins. Mix together all the dry ingredients. Mix the milk and syrup together and stir into the dry ingredients. Let the mixture stand for 1 hour.

Stir again and divide between the basins. Cover with greased greaseproof paper and then kitchen foil and secure with string. Steam for 8 hours, topping up the pan with water as necessary.

Take the puddings from the pan and allow to cool. Remove the covering and replace with fresh greaseproof paper. Store in a cool dry place for at least 1 month. To use, steam for a further 2 to 3 hours. Makes 2 puddings, each to serve 6 to 8

LIGHT CHRISTMAS CAKE

Metric	Imperial
125 g glacé cherries	4 oz glacé cherries
50 g glacé pineapple, diced	2 oz glacé pineapple, diced
225 g currants, cleaned	8 oz currants, cleaned
225 g sultanas, cleaned	8 oz sultanas, cleaned
125 g chopped mixed peel	4 oz chopped mixed peel
125 g plain flour, sifted	4 oz plain flour, sifted
225 g butter or block margarine	8 oz butter or block margarine
Finely grated rind of 1 lemon	Finely grated rind of 1 lemon
Finely grated rind of 1 orange	Finely grated rind of 1 orange
225 g light soft brown sugar	8 oz light soft brown sugar
50 g ground almonds	2 oz ground almonds
4 eggs, beaten	4 eggs, beaten
100 g self-raising flour, sifted	4 oz self-raising flour, sifted
2 x 15 ml spoons lemon juice	2 tablespoons lemon juice
3 x 15 ml spoons brandy	3 tablespoons brandy

Wash the cherries if syrupy and dry them well, then quarter. Mix all the fruit well together with 3 x 15 ml spoons (3 tablespoons) of the plain flour. Cream the fat with the lemon and orange rinds, then add the sugar and continue to cream until light and fluffy. Stir in the almonds. Beat in the eggs little by little and lastly fold in the remaining plain flour, the self-raising flour, fruit, strained lemon juice and brandy. Turn into a greased and lined 20 cm (8 inch) round cake tin.

Bake in a preheated moderate oven (160°C/325°F, Gas Mark 3) for 2½ to 3 hours, covering with double greaseproof paper after 2 hours if necessary. Cool in the tin.

You will need 550 g (1¼ lb) Almond paste and 750 g (1½ lb) Royal icing to finish the cake. Makes a 20 cm (8 inch) cake

Light Christmas cake.

ALMOND PASTE

Metric	Imperial
225 g icing sugar	8 oz icing sugar
225 g caster sugar	8 oz caster sugar
450 g ground almonds	1 lb ground almonds
1 x 5 ml spoon vanilla essence	1 teaspoon vanilla essence
2 standard eggs, lightly beaten	2 standard eggs, lightly beaten
Lemon juice	Lemon juice

Sift the icing sugar into a bowl and mix with the caster sugar and almonds. Add the essence, with sufficient egg and lemon juice to mix to a stiff dough. Form into a ball and knead lightly.

Any almond paste left over after covering the cake can be used for stuffing dates and making other marzipan sweets. Makes 900 g (2 lb)

ROYAL ICING

Metric	Imperial
900 g icing sugar	2 lb icing sugar
4 egg whites	4 egg whites
1 x 15 ml spoon glycerine (optional)	1 tablespoon glycerine (optional)

Sift the sugar twice. Put the egg whites in a bowl and stir slightly – just sufficiently to break up the albumen, but without causing too many air bubbles. Add half the icing sugar and stir until well mixed, using a wooden spoon. Beat for about 5 to 10 minutes, or until the icing is smooth, glossy and white. Cover the bowl with a damp cloth or dampened greaseproof paper and leave for at least 30 minutes to allow any air bubbles to rise to the surface.

Gradually add the remaining icing sugar until the required consistency is obtained. When the icing is intended for flat work, stand a wooden spoon upright in it – if the consistency is correct it will fall slowly to one side. For rough icing, the mixture should be stiff enough for peaks to be easily formed on the surface when you 'pull' it up with the spoon. Add any desired colouring and the glycerine for a softer texture. If possible, leave the icing overnight in an airtight container in a cool place before use.

To obtain a really smooth result, just before using the icing, remove 1 x 15 ml spoon (1 tablespoon) of it and mix to a coating consistency with water. Return it to the rest and mix until smooth. Makes 900 g (2 lb) quantity

GUY FAWKES OR HALLOWE'EN PARTY FOR EIGHT

Curried chicken pilaf, Sambals/or Lamb and cider hotpot/Cauliflower with fried walnuts/Baked fruit flambé

Curried chicken pilaf, sambals of bananas, cucumber and salted peanuts.

BEFOREHAND

Curried chicken pilaf
Prepare ingredients (and keep in polythene bags or containers in the refrigerator) on the day before. Don't cook until the evening of the party.

Lamb and cider hotpot
Make a day ahead, then cool quickly and store in refrigerator. Reheat for about 1 hour in a preheated moderate oven (180°C/350°F, Gas Mark 4).

Baked fruit flambé
Prepare the fruit and arrange in the ovenproof dish, with the syrup poured over (but don't bake).

CURRIED CHICKEN PILAF

Metric	Imperial
4 x 15 ml spoons chicken fat	4 tablespoons chicken fat
350 g onions, peeled and sliced	12 oz onions, peeled and sliced
350 g leeks, trimmed and sliced	12 oz leeks, trimmed and sliced
2 x 15 ml spoons hot (Madras) curry powder	2 tablespoons hot (Madras) curry powder
450 g long-grain rice	1 lb long-grain rice
1.2 litres chicken stock	2 pints chicken stock
50 g sultanas, cleaned	2 oz sultanas, cleaned
Salt	Salt
Freshly ground black pepper	Freshly ground black pepper
1 kg cooked chicken meat, chopped	2 lb cooked chicken meat, chopped
Chopped parsley to garnish	Chopped parsley to garnish

Heat the fat in a flameproof casserole or heavy pan and fry the onions and leeks with the curry powder for 1 minute. Add the rice and cook gently for 2 minutes, stirring. Gradually add the stock, then the sultanas and seasoning. Bring to the boil, cover and simmer for 10 minutes.

Add the chicken and simmer for another 5 minutes or until the rice is cooked and the liquid is absorbed. Adjust the seasoning and serve sprinkled with parsley.

LAMB AND CIDER HOTPOT

Metric	Imperial
2 kg shoulder of lamb, boned and cut into 5 cm pieces	4 lb shoulder of lamb, boned and cut into 2 inch pieces
50 g plain flour	2 oz plain flour
90 g butter	3½ oz butter
6 x 15 ml spoons vegetable oil	6 tablespoons vegetable oil
225 g onions, peeled and sliced	8 oz onions, peeled and sliced
350 g celery, trimmed and sliced	12 oz celery, trimmed and sliced
500 g cooking apples, peeled, cored and sliced	1 lb cooking apples, peeled, cored and sliced
600 ml light stock	1 pint light stock
300 ml cider	½ pint cider
Salt	Salt
Freshly ground black pepper	Freshly ground black pepper
750 g potatoes, peeled and thinly sliced	1½ lb potatoes, peeled and thinly sliced

Toss the meat in the flour. Melt 50 g (2 oz) of the butter with the oil in a frying pan and brown the meat on all sides. Drain and put in a 3 litre (5 pint) capacity pie dish. Sprinkle in any excess flour.

Add the onions, celery and apples to the frying pan and brown lightly. Spoon on top of the meat. Pour in the stock and cider and add plenty of seasoning. Top with the sliced potatoes and dot with the remaining butter. Stand the dish on a baking sheet and bake in a preheated moderate oven (180°C/350°F, Gas Mark 4) for about 1½ hours or until the meat is tender and the potatoes crisp.

Left: Lamb and cider hotpot. Right: Baked fruit flambé.

BAKED FRUIT FLAMBÉ

Metric
1 small fresh pineapple
4 x 15 ml spoons thick honey
1 x 2.5 ml spoon ground
    cinnamon
50 g butter
150 ml water
4 oranges, peeled and
    segmented
350 g fresh apricots, halved and
    stoned (see note)
4 x 15 ml spoons rum or vodka

Imperial
1 small fresh pineapple
4 tablespoons thick honey
½ teaspoon ground cinnamon
2 oz butter
¼ pint water
4 oranges, peeled and
    segmented
12 oz fresh apricots, halved and
    stoned (see note)
4 tablespoons rum or vodka

Trim off both ends of the pineapple, then cut it into 1 cm (½ inch) slices. Remove the skin with a sharp knife and the centre core with an apple corer. Cut the rings into 6 to 8 segments each.

Heat the honey, cinnamon, butter and water until well mixed. Arrange the fruit in a shallow ovenproof dish and pour over the honey mixture. Cover and bake in a preheated moderate oven (180°C/350°F, Gas Mark 4) for 50 minutes, until the apricots are tender. Transfer to a pre-heated chafing dish, over a lighted burner.

Heat the rum or vodka in a small pan. Pour it over the fruit, set alight and serve immediately, flaming. Serve with thick pouring cream.

Note: Instead of fresh apricots, a drained 439 g (15 oz) can of apricot halves can be used. Cook for 25 minutes only.

EASTER PARTY FOR SIX

Coloured Easter eggs/Egg and watercress mousse/Barbecued shoulder of lamb, Roast potatoes, Broccoli amandine/Sherry trifle

BEFOREHAND

Coloured Easter eggs
Any children in the house might like to do these for themselves.
Egg and watercress mousse
Make the day before; keep in the refrigerator.
Barbecued shoulder of lamb
Prepare the sauce ingredients the day before.
Roast potatoes
Peel the potatoes and keep in water.
Sherry trifle
Prepare the day before up to the addition of cream; keep in the refrigerator, covered with cling film. Decorate with cream, cherries, etc. just before serving.

COLOURED EASTER EGGS

You can decorate hard-boiled eggs with wax crayons, non-toxic felt-tipped pens, vegetable dyes, water colours or oil paints – but it's more fun if you colour them as they cook.

Only use white-shelled eggs. Hard-boiled with onion or shallot skins tied around them with brown cotton, you'll get a mottled orangey-brown effect.

Stick narrow strips of masking tape onto eggs and add a few drops of vegetable dye or food colouring to the water. This will produce a white design on a coloured background – even initials can be produced in this way. Lightly brush with glue and roll in glitter for a frosted effect or stick on sequins with a touch of glue.

Once the eggs have been hard-boiled they can be polished with a little olive oil.

EGG AND WATERCRESS MOUSSE

Metric	Imperial
1 large bunch of watercress, trimmed	1 large bunch of watercress, trimmed
4 eggs, hard-boiled and finely chopped	4 eggs, hard-boiled and finely chopped
300 ml mayonnaise	½ pint mayonnaise
1 x 15 ml spoon powdered gelatine	1 tablespoon powdered gelatine
1 x 15 ml spoon lemon juice	1 tablespoon lemon juice
2 x 15 ml spoons water	2 tablespoons water
Salt	Salt
Freshly ground black pepper	Freshly ground black pepper
1 egg white	1 egg white

A light, creamy cool starter, this has a refreshing taste of watercress.

Reserve about six tiny watercress sprigs for the garnish and finely chop the remainder. Mix the chopped watercress with the eggs and mayonnaise.

Sprinkle the gelatine over the lemon juice and water in a small heatproof bowl. Dissolve by standing the bowl in a pan of simmering water. Cool a little, then fold into the other ingredients with seasoning to taste.

Whisk the egg white until stiff and fold it into the watercress mixture. Turn into a 1.2 litre (2 pint) soufflé dish (or six individual ones). Cover and refrigerate until set.

Serve well chilled, garnished with the reserved watercress sprigs and accompanied by crispbread.

Note: The watercress and eggs can be chopped together in the blender with the mayonnaise; put half the ingredients at a time into the goblet.

BARBECUED SHOULDER OF LAMB

Metric	Imperial
1 x 1.75 kg shoulder of lamb	1 x 3½ lb shoulder of lamb
1 x 5 ml spoon dry mustard	1 teaspoon dry mustard
1 x 5 ml spoon ground ginger	1 teaspoon ground ginger
1 x 5 ml spoon salt	1 teaspoon salt
1 x 5 ml spoon freshly ground black pepper	1 teaspoon freshly ground black pepper
2 garlic cloves, crushed	2 garlic cloves, crushed
Plain flour	Plain flour
For the barbecue sauce:	**For the barbecue sauce:**
4 x 15 ml spoons Worcestershire sauce	4 tablespoons Worcestershire sauce
4 x 15 ml spoons brown table sauce	4 tablespoons brown table sauce
4 x 15 ml spoons mushroom ketchup	4 tablespoons mushroom ketchup
2 x 5 ml spoons sugar	2 teaspoons sugar
1 x 15 ml spoon malt or white vinegar	1 tablespoon malt or white vinegar
3 x 15 ml spoons melted butter	3 tablespoons melted butter
Cayenne pepper	Cayenne pepper
Salt	Salt
150 ml water	¼ pint water
1 small onion, peeled and thinly sliced	1 small onion, peeled and thinly sliced

Trim off any excess fat from the shoulder of lamb. Score the skin in diamonds. Mix the mustard, ginger, salt, pepper and garlic well together and rub into the surface of the meat. Sprinkle the meat with flour and put it in a roasting tin.

Mix the sauce ingredients well together, adding the sliced onion last, and pour over the meat. Cook in a preheated hot oven (220°C/425°F, Gas Mark 7) for 30 minutes, then lower the heat to moderate (180°C/350°F, Gas Mark 4) and continue to cook for a further 1 hour 35 minutes. Baste the joint with the sauce two or three times during the cooking, adding a little more water to the sauce if needed.

BROCCOLI AMANDINE

Metric	Imperial
1 kg broccoli, trimmed	2 lb broccoli, trimmed
Salt	Salt
50 g butter	2 oz butter
50 g flaked almonds	2 oz flaked almonds
2 x 15 ml spoons lemon juice	2 tablespoons lemon juice
Freshly ground black pepper	Freshly ground black pepper

Cook the broccoli in boiling salted water for 10 to 15 minutes. Meanwhile, melt the butter in another pan. Add the almonds and cook over a gentle heat for about 5 minutes until golden brown. Stir in the lemon juice and seasoning.

Drain the broccoli well and turn into a warmed serving dish. Spoon over the almond mixture.

Below: Barbecued shoulder of lamb; Broccoli amandine; Egg and watercress mousse; Sherry trifle. Below left: Coloured Easter eggs.

SHERRY TRIFLE

Metric	Imperial
8 trifle sponge cakes	8 trifle sponge cakes
Jam	Jam
150 ml medium sherry	$\frac{1}{4}$ pint medium sherry
6 macaroons, crushed	6 macaroons, crushed
450 ml custard	$\frac{3}{4}$ pint custard
300 ml double cream, whipped	$\frac{1}{2}$ pint double cream, whipped
Sugar	Sugar
Flavouring	Flavouring
Glacé cherries and ratafias to decorate	Glacé cherries and ratafias to decorate

Split the sponge cakes in half. Spread them with jam and arrange them in a glass dish. Pour the sherry over and leave to soak for 30 minutes. Sprinkle the macaroons over the sponge cakes and pour on the warm, not hot, custard. Cover the dish with a plate to prevent a skin forming and leave until cold.

Sweeten and flavour the whipped cream to taste and spread most of it over the custard. Decorate with the rest of the cream, piped, the cherries and ratafias (or with angelica, almonds, etc.). Fruit juice, such as orange juice, may replace some or all of the sherry.

MIDSUMMER'S EVE PARTY FOR EIGHT

Chilled summer soup/Lemon-stuffed roast veal, or Chicken à la grecque, Avocado apple mayonnaise, crusty French bread/Syllabub trifle/Cheese board and crackers

BEFOREHAND

The day before:
Make the soup and cook the chicken; refrigerate. Prepare the fruit for the trifle and layer in the dish, topped with a single layer of macaroons; cling-film cover.

The morning of the party:
Prepare the veal, ready for cooking.

The afternoon of the party:
Complete the trifle without the decoration (of cream-filled ratafias and berries). Prepare the Avocado apple mayonnaise and cover with polythene; chill. Garnish just before serving.

CHILLED SUMMER SOUP

Metric	Imperial
1 large bunch of watercress, trimmed	1 large bunch of watercress, trimmed
75 g butter or margarine	3 oz butter or margarine
175 g onions, peeled and thinly sliced	6 oz onions, peeled and thinly sliced
1.8 litres milk	3 pints milk
1.5 kg peas, podded or 750 g frozen peas	3 lb peas, podded or 1½ lb frozen peas
Salt	Salt
Freshly ground black pepper	Freshly ground black pepper
225 ml single cream	8 fl oz single cream

Reserve a few watercress sprigs for the garnish and chop the remainder. Melt the fat in a saucepan. Add the chopped watercress and onions and cover. Cook gently for about 15 minutes, without browning. Off the heat, stir in the milk, peas and seasoning. Bring to the boil, stirring.

Cover and simmer gently for about 30 minutes, or until the peas are really soft. Cool slightly, then purée. Pour into a large bowl. Adjust the seasoning. Cool. Stir in the cream and chill well before serving, garnished with the reserved watercress sprigs.

LEMON-STUFFED ROAST VEAL

Metric	Imperial
1 x 1.5 kg boned breast of veal	1 x 3 lb boned breast of veal
Salt	Salt
Freshly ground black pepper	Freshly ground black pepper
3 x 15 ml spoons lemon juice	3 tablespoons lemon juice
25 g fresh white breadcrumbs, toasted	1 oz fresh white breadcrumbs, toasted
1 x 5 ml spoon dried rosemary	1 teaspoon dried rosemary
1 x 15 ml spoon chopped parsley	1 tablespoon chopped parsley
1 garlic clove, crushed	1 garlic clove, crushed
25 g butter, melted	1 oz butter, melted
1 egg, beaten	1 egg, beaten
4 thin lemon slices	4 thin lemon slices
4 streaky bacon rashers, rinds removed	4 streaky bacon rashers, rinds removed
1 x 15 ml spoon cooking oil	1 tablespoon cooking oil
Watercress and lemon wedges to garnish	Watercress and lemon wedges to garnish

Flatten out the meat and season with salt, pepper and 1 x 15 ml spoon (1 tablespoon) of the lemon juice. In a bowl, combine the breadcrumbs, rosemary, parsley, garlic, melted butter, 1 x 1.25 ml spoon (¼ teaspoon) salt, black pepper to taste and the egg. Using a palette knife, fill the pocket in the meat with this stuffing and spread any remaining stuffing over the meat. With scissors, remove the rind from the lemon slices and arrange them down the centre. Roll up the meat and secure it with string at intervals. Lay the bacon across the meat.

Put the oil and the rest of the lemon juice on the bottom of a casserole just large enough to take the joint. Place the meat on top, cover and roast in a preheated moderate oven (180°C/350°F, Gas Mark 4) for about 3½ hours, until tender. Baste occasionally.

Serve garnished with watercress and lemon wedges.

AVOCADO APPLE MAYONNAISE

Metric	Imperial
500 g green-skinned eating apples, cored and sliced	1 lb green-skinned eating apples, cored and sliced
3 x 15 ml spoons lemon juice	3 tablespoons lemon juice
200 ml mayonnaise	⅓ pint mayonnaise
4 x 15 ml spoons single cream	4 tablespoons single cream
Salt	Salt
Freshly ground black pepper	Freshly ground black pepper
2 large ripe avocados	2 large ripe avocados

Sprinkle one of the sliced apples with 1 x 15 ml spoon (1 tablespoon) of the lemon juice and reserve. Mix the mayonnaise with the remaining lemon juice and the cream. Season well. Halve the avocados and remove the stones. Peel off the skin, slice the flesh and fold through the mayonnaise immediately. Fold in the apple slices and adjust the seasoning to taste. Cover and chill well before piling into a salad bowl for serving. Garnish with the reserved apple slices. *Note:* Polish the apples with a clean dry cloth before slicing.

Left: Chilled summer soup.

Lemon-stuffed roast veal; Chicken à la grecque; Avocado apple mayonnaise.

CHICKEN À LA GRECQUE

Metric
50 g butter
2 x 1.5 kg oven-ready chickens
450 ml chicken stock
150 ml vegetable oil
2 x 15 ml spoons wine vinegar
4 x 5 ml spoons tomato paste
1 large garlic clove, crushed
1 x 15 ml spoon chopped fresh
  thyme or basil, or 1 x 5 ml
  spoon dried thyme or basil
Salt
Freshly ground black pepper
350 g small button onions,
  peeled
2 x 5 ml spoons caster sugar
500 g button mushrooms, halved
  or quartered

Imperial
2 oz butter
2 x 3 lb oven-ready chickens
¾ pint chicken stock
¼ pint vegetable oil
2 tablespoons wine vinegar
4 teaspoons tomato paste
1 large garlic clove, crushed
1 tablespoon chopped fresh
  thyme or basil, or 1 teaspoon
  dried thyme or basil
Salt
Freshly ground black pepper
12 oz small button onions,
  peeled
2 teaspoons caster sugar
1 lb button mushrooms, halved
  or quartered

Spread the butter over the chickens and place them in a roasting tin. Pour around the stock and roast in a preheated moderately hot oven (200°C/400°F, Gas Mark 6) for about 1¼ hours, basting frequently.

Meanwhile, mix 6 x 15 ml spoons (6 tablespoons) of the oil with the vinegar, tomato paste, garlic, herbs and seasoning. Blanch the onions in boiling water for 5 minutes. Drain them well, then fry in the remaining oil, sprinkled with the sugar. Add the mushrooms and toss over a high heat for a few seconds. Tip the contents of the pan into the dressing.

Joint each hot chicken into eight pieces and spoon the vegetables and dressing over them. Allow to cool, then chill well.

Syllabub trifle.

SYLLABUB TRIFLE

Metric
500 g strawberries, hulled and
   halved
225 g green grapes, halved and
   pipped
175 g macaroons
3 egg whites
175 g caster sugar
150 ml dry white wine
Juice of ½ lemon
2 x 15 ml spoons brandy
300 ml double cream
Miniature ratafias to decorate

Imperial
1 lb strawberries, hulled and
   halved
8 oz green grapes, halved and
   pipped
6 oz macaroons
3 egg whites
6 oz caster sugar
¼ pint dry white wine
Juice of ½ lemon
2 tablespoons brandy
½ pint double cream
Miniature ratafias to decorate

Arrange the strawberries and grapes alternately round the bottom of a glass dish. Cover with a single layer of macaroons. Layer with the remaining fruit and macaroons, reserving 10 strawberries and grape halves for decoration.

Whisk the egg whites until stiff. Gradually add half the sugar and continue whisking until the meringue holds its shape. Fold in the remaining sugar. Pour the wine, lemon juice and brandy over and fold the liquids into the egg whites.

Whip the cream until it just holds its shape. Use a little to sandwich pairs of the ratafias and fold the remainder through the frothy meringue mixture. Pour over the fruit and allow to stand for several hours in a cool place, to let the macaroons become moistened. Just before serving, place the cream-filled ratafias and reserved strawberries and grapes on top.

New Year's Eve Party for Six

Dubonnet almond punch (or see pages 176-81) /Cock-a-leekie soup, Oatcakes /Spiced silverside, Bashed neeps and chappit tatties /Old English egg nog pie. Instead of the silverside, you could serve haggis — buy it ready made and serve it with the traditional neeps and tatties — and nips (of whisky)!

BEFOREHAND

Cock-a-leekie soup
Prepare the leeks the day before and keep in polythene bags in a cool place.

Spiced silverside
Soak overnight. Simmer in the morning and complete the oven-cooking in the evening.

Bashed neeps and chappit tatties
Peel the potatoes and swedes and keep covered in water.

Old English eggnog pie
Make the day before; decorate just before dinner.

DUBONNET ALMOND PUNCH

Metric
1 x 75 cl bottle red Dubonnet
150 ml Amaretto di Saronno
12 allspice berries
6 cloves
3 thin-skinned oranges
600 ml boiling water

Imperial
1 x 75 cl bottle red Dubonnet
¼ pint Amaretto di Saronno
12 allspice berries
6 cloves
3 thin-skinned oranges
1 pint boiling water

Heat the Dubonnet and Amaretto with the allspice, cloves and one of the oranges, thinly sliced. Heat almost to boiling point. Squeeze the juice from the remaining oranges and add to the punch with the boiling water. Serve hot.

Dubonnet almond punch.

COCK-A-LEEKIE SOUP

Metric
15 g butter
275-350 g chicken (2 small or
   1 large portion)
350 g leeks, trimmed
1.2 litres chicken stock
1 bouquet garni
1 x 2.5 ml spoon salt
Freshly ground black pepper
6 prunes

Imperial
½ oz butter
10-12 oz chicken (2 small or
   1 large portion)
12 oz leeks, trimmed
2 pints chicken stock
1 bouquet garni
½ teaspoon salt
Freshly ground black pepper
6 prunes

Scotland's national soup, this is one of her oldest and most popular traditional dishes.

Melt the butter in a large saucepan and fry the chicken quickly until golden on all sides. Meanwhile, cut the white part of the leeks into four lengthways and chop into 2.5 cm (1 inch) pieces. Finely shred the green parts of the leeks. Add the white parts to the pan and fry for 5 minutes. Add the stock, bouquet garni and seasoning. Bring to the boil and simmer for about 30 minutes or until the chicken is tender.

Add the prunes and the shredded green of the leeks and simmer for a further 30 minutes.

To serve, remove the chicken, cut the meat into large pieces, discard the skin and bones and place the meat in a warmed soup tureen. Adjust the seasoning of the soup and pour over the meat. Serve with oatcakes.

Below: Cock-a-leekie soup.

SPICED SILVERSIDE

Metric	Imperial
2 kg piece of salted silverside	4 lb piece of salted silverside
1 onion, peeled and sliced	1 onion, peeled and sliced
2 carrots, peeled and sliced	2 carrots, peeled and sliced
1 small turnip, peeled and sliced	1 small turnip, peeled and sliced
1-2 celery stalks, trimmed and chopped	1-2 celery stalks, trimmed and chopped
8 cloves	8 cloves
100 g soft brown sugar	4 oz soft brown sugar
1 x 2.5 ml spoon dry mustard	½ teaspoon dry mustard
1 x 5 ml spoon ground cinnamon	1 teaspoon ground cinnamon
Juice of 1 orange	Juice of 1 orange

Order the joint well ahead, to enable the butcher to salt it for you. Soak the meat for several hours or overnight, then drain and rinse. Put it in a large pan with the vegetables, cover with water and bring slowly to the boil. Remove any scum, cover with a lid and simmer until tender, allowing about 3 to 4 hours. Allow to cool in the liquid.

Drain the meat, put into a roasting tin and stick the cloves into the fat. Mix together the remaining ingredients and spread them over the meat. Bake in a preheated moderate oven (180°C/350°F, Gas Mark 4) for 45 minutes to 1 hour, basting from time to time.

BASHED NEEPS AND CHAPPIT TATTIES

Metric	Imperial
1 kg potatoes, peeled	2 lb potatoes, peeled
1 kg swedes, peeled and diced	2 lb swedes, peeled and diced
50 g butter	2 oz butter
Salt	Salt
Freshly ground black pepper	Freshly ground black pepper
150 ml hot milk	¼ pint hot milk
Chopped parsley to garnish	Chopped parsley to garnish

Cook the potatoes and swedes separately. Drain. Purée the swedes with half the butter. Cook over high heat to drive off the moisture. Season. Mash and cream the potatoes with the milk and remaining butter. Season. Pile the vegetables side by side in a warmed dish and garnish with chopped parsley.

Spiced silverside; Bashed neeps and chappit tatties.

OLD ENGLISH EGG NOG PIE

Metric	Imperial
125 g butter or margarine	4 oz butter or margarine
175 g plain flour, sifted	6 oz plain flour, sifted
3 x 15 ml spoons ground almonds	3 tablespoons ground almonds
6 x 15 ml spoons caster sugar	6 tablespoons caster sugar
3 egg yolks	3 egg yolks
1 x 15 ml spoon water	1 tablespoon water
300 ml milk	½ pint milk
1 x 1.25 ml spoon grated nutmeg	¼ teaspoon grated nutmeg
1 x 15 ml spoon powdered gelatine	1 tablespoon powdered gelatine
3 x 15 ml spoons rum	3 tablespoons rum
6 x 15 ml spoons double cream, lightly whipped	6 tablespoons double cream, lightly whipped
1 egg white	1 egg white
Chocolate curls to decorate	Chocolate curls to decorate

Rub the fat into the flour. Stir in the ground almonds with 3 x 15 ml spoons (3 tablespoons) of the sugar. Bind to a soft dough with 1 egg yolk and the water. Roll out the dough and use to line a deep 20 cm (8 inch) loose-bottomed flan tin. Bake blind in a preheated moderately hot oven (200°C/400°F, Gas Mark 6) for 20 minutes. Cool.

Bring the milk to just below boiling point. Beat the remaining egg yolks and sugar together and gradually stir in the hot milk and the nutmeg. Return to the pan and cook gently until the custard thickens, without boiling. Soak the gelatine in the rum and stir into the hot custard to dissolve. Allow to cool.

Fold the whipped cream into the half-set custard. Whisk the egg white until stiff and fold into the mixture. Turn into the flan case. Refrigerate until set. Remove the flan ring and leave for 30 minutes at room temperature. Decorate with chocolate curls.

Old English egg nog pie.

EASY WEEKENDS

Weekend entertaining doesn't have to involve two whole days of work in the kitchen. By cooking as much as possible in advance you can enjoy the weekend with everyone else. To help things to run smoothly, go through the menus in advance and make a detailed shopping list. Make a list of the menus, pin it up in the kitchen with reheating and roasting times alongside as a quick reminder. Don't forget to lay in a stock of drink including beer and soft drinks.

Start on Friday evening with an appetising meal that can be kept waiting if your guests are late. Make Saturday breakfast a particularly good one, then keep Saturday lunch simple. Serve a more formal menu for Saturday evening.

If your guests rise late on Sunday, our ideas for brunch will probably see them through to teatime; but if children are involved you'll want to provide a traditional Sunday lunch.

And whether you serve afternoon tea at four o'clock or high tea at six or a snack supper on Sunday, you'll find lots of ideas in this chapter.

FRIDAY DINNER FOR SIX

Cream of potato and watercress soup, Bread sticks/Beef pies, Green salad bowl with French dressing/Fresh fruit, Lemon shorties

BEFOREHAND

Cream of potato and watercress soup
Make the day before, but don't reheat after puréeing. Cool and refrigerate. Reheat, with cream, when needed.

Beef pies
Make the filling a day ahead and refrigerate. Top with crust at reheating time.

Green salad bowl
Prepare vegetables and refrigerate in polythene bags, ready for tossing with dressing when needed. Make enough dressing for this and other salads during the weekend and keep in a screwtop jar.

Lemon shorties
Make early in the day.

Beef pies.

CREAM OF POTATO AND WATERCRESS SOUP

Metric	Imperial
1 large bunch of watercress, trimmed	1 large bunch of watercress, trimmed
50 g margarine	2 oz margarine
1 x 15 ml spoon plain flour	1 tablespoon plain flour
600 ml milk	1 pint milk
600 ml water	1 pint water
75 g instant mashed potato granules	3 oz instant mashed potato granules
2 x 5 ml spoons salt	2 teaspoons salt
Freshly ground black pepper	Freshly ground black pepper
150 ml single cream	$\frac{1}{4}$ pint single cream
Butter and grated Parmesan cheese to garnish	Butter and grated Parmesan cheese to garnish

Set aside a few watercress sprigs for the garnish and roughly chop the remainder. Melt the margarine in a saucepan and cook the chopped watercress, covered, for about 15 minutes. Stir in the flour, milk and water and bring to the boil. Add the potato granules and seasoning and simmer gently for 20 minutes, stirring occasionally.

Purée the soup in a blender. Reheat gently with the cream, making sure the soup doesn't boil, or it may curdle. Garnish with the reserved sprigs of watercress, dots of butter and Parmesan. Serves 6 to 8

Cream of potato and watercress soup.

BEEF PIES

Metric	Imperial
2 x 15 ml spoons red wine vinegar	2 tablespoons red wine vinegar
300 ml pale ale	½ pint pale ale
1 garlic clove, crushed (optional)	1 garlic clove, crushed (optional)
1.5 kg stewing steak, cut into 2.5 cm cubes	3½ lb stewing steak, cut into 1 inch cubes
4 x 15 ml spoons plain flour	4 tablespoons plain flour
2-3 x 15 ml spoons oil	2-3 tablespoons oil
175 g onions, peeled and sliced	6 oz onions, peeled and sliced
1 x 142 g can tomato paste	1 x 5 oz can tomato paste
Salt	Salt
Freshly ground black pepper	Freshly ground black pepper
1 x 368 g packet frozen puff pastry, thawed	1 x 13 oz packet frozen puff pastry, thawed
Beaten egg	Beaten egg
Paprika	Paprika
Parsley sprigs to garnish	Parsley sprigs to garnish

Below: Lemon shorties.

Mix together the vinegar, ale and crushed garlic if used. Add the meat cubes and turn to coat. Leave to marinate overnight.

Drain the meat and reserve the marinade. Dredge the meat with the flour. Heat the oil in a frying pan and fry the onions until softened. Remove from the pan. Add the meat cubes, in batches, and brown on all sides. Return the onions to the pan with the tomato paste, seasoning and marinade and stir well. Bring to the boil and simmer for 2 to 3 minutes, then turn into a casserole. Cook in a preheated cool oven (150°C/300°F, Gas Mark 2) for 2 hours. Cool.

Roll out the dough to a rectangle, 35 by 45 cm (14 by 18 inches). Cut in half widthways. Brush with egg, sprinkle with paprika and roll up from the long sides. Cut at an angle into 6 mm (¼ inch) slices.

Divide the meat mixture between six 450 to 600 ml (¾ to 1 pint) ovenproof dishes. Spoon over 1 to 2 x 15 ml spoons (1 to 2 tablespoons) of the juices. Arrange the dough slices around the edge, overlapping. Brush with egg.

Bake just above the centre in a preheated moderately hot oven (200°C/400°F, Gas Mark 6) for about 30 minutes. Garnish with parsley. Reheat the meat juices to serve separately.

FRENCH DRESSING

Metric	Imperial
1 x 5 ml spoon salt	1 teaspoon salt
Pinch of freshly ground black pepper	Pinch of freshly ground black pepper
1 x 5 ml spoon dry mustard	1 teaspoon dry mustard
1 x 5 ml spoon sugar	1 teaspoon sugar
5 x 15 ml spoons vinegar	5 tablespoons vinegar
150 ml salad oil	¼ pint salad oil

Put the salt, pepper, mustard, sugar and vinegar in a bowl and whisk together. Add the oil and whisk until thick and creamy. Alternatively, put all the ingredients in a screwtop jar and shake well until thickened. Makes scant 300 ml (½ pint)

LEMON SHORTIES

Metric	Imperial
For the dough:	**For the dough:**
250 g plain flour	10 oz plain flour
100 g caster sugar	4 oz caster sugar
150 g butter, softened	6 oz butter, softened
2 egg yolks	2 egg yolks
For the filling:	**For the filling:**
25 g butter	1 oz butter
300 ml single cream	½ pint single cream
25 g plain flour	1 oz plain flour
50 g caster sugar	2 oz caster sugar
2 egg yolks	2 egg yolks
Grated rind of ½ lemon	Grated rind of ½ lemon
1 x 2.5 ml spoon vanilla essence	½ teaspoon vanilla essence
Icing sugar	Icing sugar

Sift the flour onto a working surface. Make a well in the centre and put in the sugar, butter and egg yolks. Using the fingertips of one hand, mix together and knead lightly. Chill for 30 minutes.

For the filling, heat the butter and half the cream in a small pan. Mix together the flour and sugar and stir in the remaining cream. Add gradually to the mixture in the pan, beating well until smooth. Remove from the heat and beat in the egg yolks, lemon rind and essence. Return to the heat and cook gently for 5 minutes. Cool.

Roll out the dough on a floured surface. Cut out about 14 rounds with a 7.5 cm (3 inch) plain cutter and 14 rounds with a 6.25 cm (2½ inch) fluted cutter. Line 14 deep patty pans with the plain rounds. Divide the filling between the pastry cases. Place the fluted lids in position and press down lightly.

Bake in a preheated moderately hot oven (200°C/400°F, Gas Mark 6) for 15 to 18 minutes until lightly browned. Allow to cool in the tins before turning out. Serve dusted with icing sugar. Makes about 14

SATURDAY BREAKFAST FOR SIX

Orange wake-me-up/Swiss apple muesli/Eggs and bacon, Bran muffins

BEFOREHAND

Swiss apple muesli
Remember to mix oats and fruit juice on Friday night.
Bran muffins
Make on Friday and heat through when needed.

ORANGE WAKE-ME-UP

Metric
Juice of 1 orange
1 x 15 ml spoon clear honey
1 egg

Imperial
Juice of 1 orange
1 tablespoon clear honey
1 egg

Put all the ingredients in an electric blender and switch on for 30 seconds. Or whisk with a rotary whisk. Serves 1

SWISS APPLE MUESLI

Metric
6 x 15 ml spoons rolled oats or medium oatmeal
About 200 ml fruit juice or water
3 dessert apples, cored and chopped
6 x 15 ml spoons cream or top of the milk
1.5 x 15 ml spoons honey
Brown sugar
75 g sultanas or seedless raisins, cleaned
Chopped nuts

Imperial
6 tablespoons rolled oats or medium oatmeal
About ⅓ pint fruit juice or water
3 dessert apples, cored and chopped
6 tablespoons cream or top of the milk
1½ tablespoons honey
Brown sugar
3 oz sultanas or seedless raisins, cleaned
Chopped nuts

Put the oats and fruit juice or water in a bowl and leave overnight. The next day, mix in the apples, cream or milk, honey, a little brown sugar and the fruit. Put into bowls and sprinkle with the nuts.

BRAN MUFFINS

Metric
200 g plain flour
1 x 5 ml spoon salt
2 x 15 ml spoons baking powder
100-125 g ready-to-eat bran
450 ml milk
50 g butter, softened
4 x 15 ml spoons caster sugar
2 eggs, beaten

Imperial
7 oz plain flour
1 teaspoon salt
2 tablespoons baking powder
4 oz ready-to-eat bran
1 pint less 6 tablespoons milk
2 oz butter, softened
4 tablespoons caster sugar
2 eggs, beaten

Grease twenty 6.5 cm (2½ inch) diameter deep muffin tins. Sift the flour, salt and baking powder together. Soak the bran in the milk for 5 minutes. Meanwhile, cream the butter and sugar together until light. Add the eggs and stir until smooth. Stir in the bran mixture, then add the flour mixture and stir until just mixed, no longer. Fill the muffin tins two-thirds full and bake in the centre of a preheated moderately hot oven (200°C/400°F, Gas Mark 6) for 25 minutes, or until well browned. Turn out onto a wire rack. To serve, split rather than cut open, and butter. Makes 20

Top: Bran Muffins. Left: Orange wake-me-up; Swiss apple muesli.

SATURDAY LUNCH FOR SIX

Chilled tomato juice/Cold glazed bacon, Chutney, Jacket potatoes, Chicory salad/Lemon delight/Cheese board, Fresh fruit

BEFOREHAND

Cold glazed bacon
Cook the joint the day before.
Potatoes
Scrub and keep in water.
Lemon delight
Make the day before, but do not decorate.

COLD GLAZED BACON

Metric
1 x 2 kg piece of collar or corner
    gammon bacon
1 x 15 ml spoon clear honey
2 x 15 ml spoons white vinegar
Demerara sugar

Imperial
1 x 4 lb piece of collar or corner
    gammon bacon
1 tablespoon clear honey
2 tablespoons white vinegar
Demerara sugar

Soak the bacon joint, which should be tied securely into shape with string, overnight in cold water. Drain. Place, skin side down, in a large pan and cover with fresh cold water. Bring slowly to the boil, removing any scum. When boiling, reduce the heat, cover and simmer for 1 hour 10 minutes. Always keep the joint under water.

Drain the joint, strip off the rind, and, using a sharp knife, score the fat in a lattice pattern. Place in a roasting tin. Heat the honey and vinegar until combined, then brush this mixture over the joint. Dredge with sugar and pat well in. Crisp in a preheated moderate oven (180°C/350°F, Gas Mark 4) for 30 minutes until golden. Baste with any excess honey glaze. Leave until cold, then wrap in foil and refrigerate. Serves 6 with leftovers

Below: Cold glazed bacon; Lemon delight; Chicory salad.

CHICORY SALAD

Metric
3 crisp eating apples, cored and
    diced
3 heads of chicory, thinly sliced
5-6 inner leaves of lettuce, torn
    into small pieces
3 firm tomatoes, skinned, seeded
    and chopped
3 x 15 ml spoons French dressing
    (see page 91)

Imperial
3 crisp eating apples, cored and
    diced
3 heads of chicory, thinly sliced
5-6 inner leaves of lettuce, torn
    into small pieces
3 firm tomatoes, skinned, seeded
    and chopped
3 tablespoons French dressing
    (see page 91)

Toss all the ingredients together in the French dressing and chill for 30 minutes before serving.

LEMON DELIGHT

Metric
1½ x 142 g lemon jelly tablet
200 ml water
Grated rind and juice of 1 lemon
200 ml medium white wine
3 eggs
3 egg yolks
75 g caster sugar

Imperial
1½ x 5 oz lemon jelly tablet
⅓ pint water
Grated rind and juice of 1 lemon
⅓ pint medium white wine
3 eggs
3 egg yolks
3 oz caster sugar

In a small pan, dissolve the jelly squares in the water over a very low heat, stirring. Pour into a measure. Add the lemon rind, juice and wine, then make up to 900 ml (1½ pints) with water. Cool until on the point of setting.

In a deep heatproof bowl placed over a pan of hot but not boiling water, whisk together the eggs, egg yolks and sugar until really thick. Allow to cool, whisking occasionally, then whisk in the jelly mixture. Turn into a serving dish and chill. Decorate if wished with lightly whipped cream or chocolate curls.

SATURDAY DINNER FOR SIX

Kipper pâté, Melba toast/Roast duckling with grapefruit sauce, Broccoli, Sweetcorn, Duchesse potatoes/Apple and blackberry compôte, or Fresh fruit

BEFOREHAND

Kipper pâté
Make one or two days beforehand and refrigerate, covered.
Roast duckling with grapefruit sauce
Make the grapefruit sauce the day before.
Duchesse potatoes
Peel and keep in water.
Apple and blackberry compôte
Make the day before.

KIPPER PÂTÉ

Metric	Imperial
350 g kipper fillets, skinned	12 oz kipper fillets, skinned
6 x 15 ml spoons dry white wine	6 tablespoons dry white wine
2 x 15 ml spoons lemon juice	2 tablespoons lemon juice
100 g butter, softened	4 oz butter, softened
Freshly ground black pepper	Freshly ground black pepper
6 tomato slices	6 tomato slices
Melba toast to serve	Melba toast to serve

Put the kipper fillets in a shallow dish and spoon the wine over. Cover and leave to marinate in a cool place for 4 hours.

Work the fillets and marinade to a paste with a wooden spoon, or purée them in an electric blender until smooth, adding the lemon juice to make a softer mixture. Beat in the softened butter and season with black pepper. Divide between six 120 ml (4 fl oz) ramekin dishes. Smooth over the tops and mark with a fork. Top each with a tomato twist. Serve with Melba toast.

ROAST DUCKLING WITH GRAPEFRUIT SAUCE

Metric	Imperial
2 x 1.75 kg duckling or 12 duckling pieces, thawed if frozen	2 x 3½ lb ducklings or 12 duckling pieces, thawed if frozen
Salt	Salt
Freshly ground black pepper	Freshly ground black pepper
2 x 15 ml spoons plain flour	2 tablespoons plain flour
1 x 178 ml can frozen concentrated unsweetened grapefruit juice, thawed	1 x 6¼ fl oz can frozen concentrated unsweetened grapefruit juice, thawed
1 x 15 ml spoon arrowroot	1 tablespoon arrowroot
2 grapefruit, peeled and segmented	2 grapefruit, peeled and segmented
Watercress to garnish	Watercress to garnish

The grapefruit juice gives the duck a rich fruity flavour. Orange juice can be used instead if preferred, in which case add a squeeze of lemon juice to the orange sauce to sharpen the flavour.

Joint each duckling into six or ask the butcher to do this for you. Trim off excess fat. Wipe the joints and prick well. Season. Place the duckling joints, skin side up, on a wire rack in a roasting tin containing the giblets. Cook near the top of a preheated moderate oven (180°C/350°F, Gas Mark 4) for about 1½ hours. Baste with the pan juices twice during cooking. Twenty minutes before the end of the cooking time, sprinkle with the flour and baste again.

Make the grapefruit juice up to 450 ml (¾ pint) with water. Mix a little with the arrowroot in a small pan, then gradually stir in the remaining juice and bring to the boil, stirring.

Transfer the cooked duckling joints to a warmed serving dish. Arrange the fruit segments on top. Return to the oven to keep hot. Drain the fat from the roasting tin, leaving the duckling juices, and add the grapefruit sauce. Scrape the bottom of the roasting tin to loosen any sediment. Bring to the boil, stirring well. Adjust seasoning. Strain. Glaze the duckling with some of the sauce and serve the rest separately. Garnish with watercress.

DUCHESSE POTATOES

Metric	Imperial
1 kg potatoes, peeled	2 lb potatoes, peeled
Salt	Salt
100 g butter	4 oz butter
2 eggs, beaten	2 eggs, beaten
Freshly ground black pepper	Freshly ground black pepper
Pinch of grated nutmeg	Pinch of grated nutmeg

Cook the potatoes in boiling salted water for 15 to 20 minutes. Drain them well, then sieve or mash them. Beat in the butter, eggs, seasoning and nutmeg. Cool the mixture, then spoon it into a piping bag fitted with a large rosette nozzle. Pipe onto a greased baking sheet. Cook in a preheated moderately hot oven (200°C/400°F, Gas Mark 6) for about 25 minutes, until set and golden brown.
Note: If serving the potatoes with the duckling, allow 35 minutes cooking time in a moderate oven (180°C/350°F, Gas Mark 4).

Left: Kipper pâté. Right: Roast duckling with grapefruit sauce; Duchesse potatoes; Broccoli; Apple and blackberry compôte.

APPLE AND BLACKBERRY COMPÔTE

Metric
1.25 kg eating apples, peeled, cored and thinly sliced
450 ml water
Pared rind of ½ lemon
75 g sugar
350 g blackberries
2 x 15 ml spoons Calvados or brandy

Imperial
2½ lb eating apples, peeled, cored and thinly sliced
¾ pint water
Pared rind of ½ lemon
3 oz sugar
12 oz blackberries
2 tablespoons Calvados or brandy

Poach the apple slices in the water with the lemon rind until transparent – about 7 minutes. Drain the apples and set aside to cool. Add the sugar to the cooking liquid. When dissolved, bring to the boil and continue boiling for 8 to 10 minutes or until reduced by half. Discard the lemon rind and pour this syrup over the apples.

Place half the apples in six individual dishes. Cover with half the blackberries. Add the Calvados or brandy to the remaining syrup and spoon it over the fruit. Fill up with layers of the remaining apples and blackberries. Chill well before serving with thick pouring cream.

SUNDAY BRUNCH FOR SIX

Melon/Kidney savouries, Floury baps

BEFOREHAND

Kidney savouries
The day before, prepare the bread rounds (but do not fry) and bacon rolls (but do not grill).
Floury baps
Make the day before and refresh when needed.

KIDNEY SAVOURIES

Metric
6 small thick slices of white bread
40 g butter
3 x 15 ml spoons corn oil
3 streaky bacon rashers, rinds removed
6 lambs' kidneys, skinned, halved and cored
12 pork chipolatas
3 tomatoes, halved
Parsley sprigs to garnish

Imperial
6 small thick slices of white bread
1½ oz butter
3 tablespoons corn oil
3 streaky bacon rashers, rinds removed
6 lambs' kidneys, skinned, halved and cored
12 pork chipolatas
3 tomatoes, halved
Parsley sprigs to garnish

Using an 8 cm (3¼ inch) plain pastry cutter, cut six rounds from the slices of bread. Heat 25 g (1 oz) of the butter and the oil in a frying pan and fry the bread rounds on both sides until crisp and golden. Drain on absorbent kitchen paper and keep warm. Stretch the bacon rashers with the back of a knife. Cut each in half. Roll up into six rolls and secure with half wooden cocktail sticks.

Melt the remaining butter in the pan and fry the kidneys for about 8 minutes. Meanwhile, grill the sausages and bacon rolls under a preheated moderate grill for 7 to 10 minutes, turning once. Grill the tomatoes for 4 minutes.

To assemble, place the fried bread rounds on a warmed platter. Place two sausages across each, then top with 2 kidney halves, a tomato half and finally a bacon roll and parsley sprig.

FLOURY BAPS

Metric
15 g fresh yeast
300 ml lukewarm milk and water mixed
450 g strong plain flour
1 x 5 ml spoon salt
50 g lard

Imperial
½ oz fresh yeast
½ pint lukewarm milk and water mixed
1 lb strong plain flour
1 teaspoon salt
2 oz lard

Mix the yeast with the liquid. Sift together the flour and salt and rub in the lard. Stir in the yeast liquid. Work the mixture to a firm dough, adding extra flour only if really needed, until the dough leaves the sides of the bowl clean. Knead on a floured surface for about 5 minutes. Place in a large bowl, cover with lightly oiled polythene and allow to rise until doubled in size.

Lightly knead the dough, then cut into eight or ten even-sized pieces. Shape each into a ball, place on a floured baking sheet and press down to flatten slightly. Cover with oiled polythene and allow to rise until doubled in size – 45 minutes at room temperature.

Dredge the tops lightly with flour and bake in a preheated moderately hot oven (200°C/400°F, Gas Mark 6) for 15 to 20 minutes. Cool on a wire rack. Makes 8 to 10

Kidney savouries; Floury baps.

SUNDAY LUNCH FOR SIX

Tomato bouillon / Rolled stuffed shoulder of lamb, Roast potatoes, Brussels sprouts / Rhubarb and apple snow

BEFOREHAND

Rolled stuffed shoulder of lamb
The day before, stuff the joint and keep, loosely wrapped, in the refrigerator. Weigh to calculate cooking time.
Rhubarb and apple snow
Make the purée on Friday. Fold the stiffly whisked egg whites through the purée about 1 hour before the meal.

TOMATO BOUILLON

Mix equal amounts of canned beef consommé and tomato juice. Garnish with thinly sliced lemon.

ROLLED STUFFED SHOULDER OF LAMB

Metric	Imperial
175 g streaky bacon rashers, rinds removed	6 oz streaky bacon rashers, rinds removed
25 g fresh white breadcrumbs	1 oz fresh white breadcrumbs
3 x 15 ml spoons chopped fresh mint	3 tablespoons chopped fresh mint
Salt	Salt
Freshly ground black pepper	Freshly ground black pepper
Beaten egg	Beaten egg
1 x 2-2.5 kg shoulder of lamb, boned	1 x 4-4½ lb shoulder of lamb, boned
1-2 x 15 ml spoons oil	1-2 tablespoons oil

Rhubarb and apple snow.

Finely scissor-snip the bacon and combine it with the breadcrumbs, mint and seasoning. Add sufficient beaten egg to bind the ingredients together. Spread out the lamb. Place the stuffing in the cavity where the bone was. Roll up the joint and secure with several bands of string. Weigh the joint.

Lightly grease a roasting tin with some of the oil. Place the joint in it and brush with the remaining oil. Cook in a preheated moderately hot oven (190°C/375°F, Gas Mark 5). Calculate the cooking time after stuffing by allowing 20 minutes per 450 g (1 lb) plus 30 minutes.

RHUBARB AND APPLE SNOW

Metric	Imperial
500 g pink rhubarb, trimmed and cut into 2.5 cm pieces	1 lb pink rhubarb, trimmed and cut into 1 inch pieces
500 g cooking apples, peeled, cored and sliced	1 lb cooking apples, peeled, cored and sliced
75 g granulated sugar	3 oz granulated sugar
1 x 5 ml spoon ground cinnamon	1 teaspoon ground cinnamon
4 x 15 ml spoons water	4 tablespoons water
2 egg whites	2 egg whites

Put the rhubarb and apples in a heavy-based pan with the sugar, cinnamon and water. Cover and stew gently until the fruits are quite soft. Cool.

Purée the fruits in a blender until smooth. Whisk the egg whites until stiff and fold through the fruit purée. Turn into six individual glass dishes. Cover and refrigerate for about 1 hour before serving, with sponge fingers.

Rolled stuffed shoulder of lamb; Tomato bouillon.

HIGH TEA FOR SIX

Cheese and chive hotties/Eggs with tomato-pepper sauce/Dark chocolate swirl cake, Biscuits, teabreads and spreads (see pages 134-53)

BEFOREHAND

Cheese and chive hotties
Can be partly prepared on Friday. Make the rolls, but don't bake them. Refrigerate, wrapped, and bake as directed when needed.

Eggs with tomato-pepper sauce
The sauce can be made on Friday and kept in the refrigerator. Reheat it in a saucepan while the eggs are being boiled.

Cookies, cakes and spreads
Can be made two or three days ahead and kept in airtight containers.

CHEESE AND CHIVE HOTTIES

Metric
1 medium fresh uncut white sandwich loaf
Soft butter or margarine
225 g red Leicester cheese, grated
Snipped fresh chives
Salt
Freshly ground black pepper
Melted butter
Paprika

Imperial
1 medium fresh uncut white sandwich loaf
Soft butter or margarine
8 oz red Leicester cheese, grated
Snipped fresh chives
Salt
Freshly ground black pepper
Melted butter
Paprika

Chill the fresh loaf in the freezing compartment of the refrigerator for 30 minutes to make slicing easier. Cut and butter as many thin slices as possible along the whole length of the loaf. Remove crusts.

Sprinkle each slice with cheese, chives and seasoning. Roll up each slice from the shorter edge and wrap each roll in dampened grease-proof paper. Chill for 30 minutes longer.

Unwrap the rolls. Arrange them on baking sheets. Brush with melted butter, dust with paprika and bake in a preheated very hot oven (230°C/450°F, Gas Mark 8) for 5 to 10 minutes. Serve oven-fresh, with dill pickles.

EGGS WITH TOMATO-PEPPER SAUCE

Metric
25 g butter
50 g onion, peeled and finely chopped
100 g green pepper, cored, seeded and finely chopped
500 g ripe tomatoes, skinned and chopped
1 garlic clove, crushed
Salt
Freshly ground black pepper
6-8 eggs

Imperial
1 oz butter
2 oz onion, peeled and finely chopped
4 oz green pepper, cored, seeded and finely chopped
1 lb ripe tomatoes, skinned and chopped
1 garlic clove, crushed
Salt
Freshly ground black pepper
6-8 eggs

Melt the butter in a saucepan and add the onion and green pepper. Cook gently until soft. Stir in the tomatoes and garlic, cover and simmer for 10 minutes. Adjust the seasoning.

Meanwhile, hard-boil the eggs. Cool slightly, then shell and halve lengthways. Arrange in a warmed shallow serving dish. Pour the hot sauce over the eggs and serve at once.

Cheese and chive hotties.

Eggs with tomato-pepper sauce.

Dark chocolate swirl cake.

DARK CHOCOLATE SWIRL CAKE

Metric	Imperial
175 g butter or block margarine	6 oz butter or block margarine
175 g caster sugar	6 oz caster sugar
2 eggs, beaten	2 eggs, beaten
5 x 15 ml spoons cocoa powder	5 tablespoons cocoa powder
175 ml milk	6 fl oz milk
1 x 5 ml spoon vanilla essence	1 teaspoon vanilla essence
225 g plain flour	8 oz plain flour
1.5 x 5 ml spoons bicarbonate of soda	1½ teaspoons bicarbonate of soda
Pinch of salt	Pinch of salt
1 square bakers' unsweetened chocolate, melted	1 square bakers' unsweetened chocolate, melted
125 g icing sugar	4 oz icing sugar
50 g plain chocolate-flavoured cake covering, melted	2 oz plain chocolate-flavoured cake covering, melted

Grease and bottom-line two straight-sided 19 cm (7½ inch) sandwich tins. Cream 125 g (4 oz) of the fat until soft. Gradually work in the caster sugar and continue creaming until light and fluffy. Beat in the eggs, little by little. Mix the cocoa and 6 x 15 ml spoons (6 tablespoons) of the milk to a smooth paste. Stir in the remaining milk with the essence.

Sift the flour with the bicarbonate of soda and salt and beat into the creamed ingredients, alternating with the cocoa liquid. Spoon into the prepared sandwich tins. Swirl the unsweetened chocolate around the top of one cake. Bake in a preheated moderate oven (180°C/350°F, Gas Mark 4) for about 30 minutes. Leave to cool in the tins before turning out.

Beat the remaining fat until soft. Sift in the icing sugar and continue to cream well. Work in the cake covering. Use to sandwich the cakes together. Makes a 19 cm (7½ inch) sandwich cake

SUNDAY NIGHT SNACK SUPPER FOR SIX

Cheese and tomato fries, Celery sticks, radishes and chicory/Fresh fruit or Melon and pear compôte

BEFOREHAND

Cheese and tomato fries
Can be made early in the day and fried when needed.
Celery sticks, radishes and chicory
Prepare and keep refrigerated in polythene bags or covered containers until needed.
Melon and pear compôte
Can be made on Friday or Saturday; keep refrigerated.

CHEESE AND TOMATO FRIES

Metric
12 slices of white bread
Butter or soft margarine
Dijon mustard
350 g Edam cheese, thinly sliced
225 g tomatoes, skinned and thinly sliced
Salt
Freshly ground black pepper
Oil and butter for frying
Watercress to garnish

Imperial
12 slices of white bread
Butter or soft margarine
Dijon mustard
12 oz Edam cheese, thinly sliced
8 oz tomatoes, skinned and thinly sliced
Salt
Freshly ground black pepper
Oil and butter for frying
Watercress to garnish

Spread the slices of bread with butter or margarine and mustard. Make six cheese and tomato sandwiches, placing the tomatoes in the centre with plenty of seasoning. Press well together. Cut off the crusts and cut each sandwich into triangles. Shallow fry quickly in mixed hot oil and butter until golden brown on both sides and the cheese starts to ooze. Serve as soon as possible, garnished with watercress.
Note: If preferred, the sandwiches can be grilled rather than fried. In this case, prepare by brushing or spreading the outside of the sandwich triangles with melted or softened fat.

MELON AND PEAR COMPÔTE

Metric
100 g sugar
300 ml water
4 x 15 ml spoons Kirsch
3 x 15 ml spoons lemon juice
4 large ripe pears, peeled, cored and sliced
1 medium ripe honeydew melon
Blanched finely shredded lemon rind to decorate

Imperial
4 oz sugar
½ pint water
4 tablespoons Kirsch
3 tablespoons lemon juice
4 large ripe pears, peeled, cored and sliced
1 medium ripe honeydew melon
Blanched finely shredded lemon rind to decorate

Dissolve the sugar in the water in a shallow pan. Bring to the boil and stir in the Kirsch and strained lemon juice. Add the pear slices, cover and poach gently until tender – about 20 minutes.

Meanwhile, divide the melon into eighths and discard the seeds. Remove the flesh from the skin in one piece and cut across into thin slices. Place in a large bowl. While still hot, pour the pears with their syrup over the melon and mix well together. Cool, cover and chill well before serving, decorated with lemon rind.

Above: Cheese and tomato fries. Right: Melon and pear compôte.

PARTIES
OUT OF DOORS

Whether for a picnic, a barbecue, or a buffet supper on the balcony, catering for any outdoor meal demands food to suit the occasion. For a picnic, take food which can be prepared in bake-and-take containers, such as quiches, flans and pâtés. Accompany them with salad greens, in polythene containers, with the dressing taken separately, and lots of fresh fruit.

Don't buy expensive and elaborate equipment unless you are regular outdoor-eaters. Polythene wraps and foil are usually adequate and disposable equipment is cheap enough for the odd occasion. If you take your picnicking seriously, you'll need a good suppy of rigid polythene containers of all sizes.

Take soups, ice cubes and fruit salads in wide necked vacuum flasks.

For barbecue parties at home, you'll need lots of foil, throwaway plates and extra-large absorbent paper napkins, tongs and a pair of thick gloves for whoever operates the barbecue. To drink, serve vin ordinaire, beer, a hot punch – or a chilled fruit cup on a warm summer's evening. Finish the meal with plenty of hot coffee.

SIMPLE PATIO PARTY FOR SIX TO EIGHT

Pan pizza, Blue cheese rarebits, Ratatouille aux champignons, Lemon-dressed avocado salad, Tossed green salad/Apricot cheesecake

BEFOREHAND

Pan pizza
Cook one in advance, as far as topping it with sardines and olives (see recipe note).

Blue cheese rarebits
Make the egg mixture early in the day; spread over the toast and grill when required.

Ratatouille aux champignons
Prepare the day before and refrigerate. Heat through, if required, in a preheated moderate oven (180°C/350°F, Gas Mark 4) for 45 minutes, or until hot.

Avocado salad
Prepare the cucumber and celery in the afternoon. Make the dressing. Prepare the avocados and complete the salad just before serving.

Tossed green salad
Prepare the vegetables and keep in polythene bags in the refrigerator.

Apricot cheesecake
Make the day before, but leave in mould in the refrigerator. Turn out and dredge with icing sugar when required.

PAN PIZZA

Metric	Imperial
325 g self-raising flour	12 oz self-raising flour
Pinch of salt	Pinch of salt
50 g butter or margarine	2 oz butter or margarine
About 175 ml water	About 6 fl oz water
4 x 15 ml spoons oil	4 tablespoons oil
4 x 15 ml spoons tomato paste	4 tablespoons tomato paste
1 x 397 g can tomatoes, drained and roughly chopped	1 x 14 oz can tomatoes, drained and roughly chopped
1 x 5 ml spoon dried oregano or marjoram	1 teaspoon dried oregano or marjoram
Freshly ground black pepper	Freshly ground black pepper
175 g Cheddar cheese, grated	6 oz Cheddar cheese, grated
1 x 250 g can sardines, drained	1 x 9 oz can sardines, drained
Black olives	Black olives

Sift together the flour and salt and rub in the fat. Add enough water to mix to a soft dough. Knead the dough gently. Divide in two and roll or press out half to fit a 25 cm (10 inch) diameter frying pan.

Heat half the oil in the frying pan and fry the dough until golden – about 5 minutes. Turn the dough over and spread half the tomato paste over the cooked side. Top with half of the tomatoes, herbs and pepper. Sprinkle half the cheese over. Top with half the sardines and olives. When the second side is brown – 5 to 7 minutes – place the pizza under a hot grill and cook until the cheese melts and bubbles. Serve in wedges from the pan. Make the second pizza the same way. Makes 2 pizzas, each to serve 3 to 4

Note: Cook one pizza in advance, as far as topping with sardines and olives. Remove carefully, sliding onto a heatproof plate, when the second side is brown. Keep warm and cook under the grill while the second pizza is cooking in the pan.

BLUE CHEESE RAREBITS

Metric	Imperial
225 g Danish blue cheese, grated	8 oz Danish blue cheese, grated
6 x 15 ml spoons dry white wine	6 tablespoons dry white wine
8 egg yolks	8 egg yolks
6 x 15 ml spoons milk	6 tablespoons milk
Freshly ground black pepper	Freshly ground black pepper
Salt	Salt
16 slices of rye bread, toasted	16 slices of rye bread, toasted

Blue cheese rarebits; Pan pizza; Ratatouille aux champignons; Lemon-dressed avocado salad.

Put the cheese and wine into a heavy-based saucepan and stir over a low heat until the cheese has melted. Beat the egg yolks with the milk and pepper. Off the heat, stir into the cheese mixture. Return to the heat, and cook gently, stirring constantly, until the mixture thickens. Adjust the seasoning, adding salt if necessary, and spoon onto the slices of toast. Pop them under a hot grill to glaze golden brown. Serve as soon as possible. Makes 16

RATATOUILLE AUX CHAMPIGNONS

Metric	Imperial
1 medium aubergine, thickly sliced	1 medium aubergine, thickly sliced
Salt	Salt
2 x 15 ml spoons oil	2 tablespoons oil
25 g butter	1 oz butter
500 g small button mushrooms	1 lb small button mushrooms
4 medium tomatoes, skinned, quartered and seeded	4 medium tomatoes, skinned, quartered and seeded
1 small green pepper, cored, seeded and sliced	1 small green pepper, cored, seeded and sliced
225 g courgettes, thickly sliced	8 oz courgettes, thickly sliced
1 garlic clove, crushed	1 garlic clove, crushed
2 x 15 ml spoons tomato paste	2 tablespoons tomato paste
Large pinch of ground coriander	Large pinch of ground coriander
Freshly ground black pepper	Freshly ground black pepper
Chopped parsley to garnish	Chopped parsley to garnish

Good hot or cold, coriander gives this dish a subtle flavour.

Sprinkle the aubergine slices with salt and leave for 40 minutes, then rinse under the cold tap to remove the excess salt. Drain well.

Heat the oil and butter in a large flameproof casserole. Reserve half the mushrooms and add the remainder with all the other vegetables, together with the garlic, tomato paste, coriander and seasoning. Stir well to mix thoroughly. Cover and cook in a preheated moderate oven (180°C/350°F, Gas Mark 4) for 50 to 60 minutes, stirring once or twice.

Ten minutes before the cooking is completed, stir in the reserved mushrooms. Adjust the seasoning and serve garnished with parsley.

LEMON-DRESSED AVOCADO SALAD

Metric	Imperial
½ small cucumber, peeled and diced	½ small cucumber, peeled and diced
Salt	Salt
150 ml vegetable oil	¼ pint vegetable oil
4 x 15 ml spoons lemon juice	4 tablespoons lemon juice
2 x 5 ml spoons thin honey	2 teaspoons thin honey
Freshly ground black pepper	Freshly ground black pepper
2 ripe avocados, peeled, stoned and sliced	2 ripe avocados, peeled, stoned and sliced
4 celery stalks, trimmed and thinly sliced	4 celery stalks, trimmed and thinly sliced
50 g salted peanuts	2 oz salted peanuts
Paprika or chopped parsley to garnish	Paprika or chopped parsley to garnish

Sprinkle the cucumber with salt and leave for 20 minutes to draw out the juices. Dry on absorbent kitchen paper.

Put the oil, lemon juice, honey, 1 x 2.5 ml spoon (½ teaspoon) salt and pepper to taste in a screwtop jar and shake well. Dice one avocado and toss both with the cucumber, celery, avocados and nuts. Pile into a serving dish. Serve immediately, dusted with paprika or parsley.

Apricot cheesecake.

APRICOT CHEESECAKE

Metric	Imperial
75 g granulated sugar	3 oz granulated sugar
200 ml water	⅓ pint water
500 g fresh apricots, halved and stoned	1 lb fresh apricots, halved and stoned
225 g semi-sweet biscuits, crushed	8 oz semi-sweet biscuits, crushed
175 g butter or block margarine, melted	6 oz butter or block margarine, melted
1 x 5 ml spoon mixed spice	1 teaspoon mixed spice
50 g caster sugar	2 oz caster sugar
4 x 5 ml spoons powdered gelatine	4 teaspoons powdered gelatine
Thinly pared rind and juice of 2 large thin-skinned lemons	Thinly pared rind and juice of 2 large thin-skinned lemons
225 g cream cheese	8 oz cream cheese
225 g cottage cheese	8 oz cottage cheese
1 large can condensed milk	1 large can condensed milk
Icing sugar	Icing sugar

Dissolve the granulated sugar in the water in a saucepan. Add the apricot halves and poach gently until tender. Then chop roughly.

Mix the biscuit crumbs with the melted butter or margarine, spice and caster sugar. Use three-quarters of the crumb mixture to line the bottom and sides of 21.5 cm (8½ inch) spring-release mould (bottom-lined with non-stick paper). Refrigerate until set.

Sprinkle the gelatine over the lemon juice in a heatproof cup to soften it. Place in a pan of hot water and stir to dissolve the gelatine. Put the lemon rind, cheeses, condensed milk and gelatine in a blender and blend until smooth. Fold in the chopped apricots. Pour the mixture into the crumb case. Scatter the remaining crumbs over and refrigerate until set.

Turn out, upside-down, dredge heavily with icing sugar and mark with a lattice design, using a knife.

PATIO PARTY FOR TWELVE TO SIXTEEN

Tunafish creams, Dressed leeks/Battalian beef bake, Red cabbage and sweetcorn salad, Tossed green salad/Peach and apple soufflé, Shortcake gâteau

BEFOREHAND

Tunafish creams
Make these the evening before; cover with cling film and refrigerate. Remove them from the refrigerator 2 hours before serving; garnish and cover again with film.

Dressed leeks
Prepare the leeks to the cooking stage the day before; store them in a polythene bag in a cool place. Make up the dressing. Finish preparing in the morning.

Battalian beef bake
Prepare up to the addition of the Parmesan; store, covered, in the refrigerator.

Red cabbage and sweetcorn salad
Prepare and finely shred the cabbage the day before; store in a polythene bag in a cool place.

Tossed green salad
Prepare the vegetables and keep in polythene bags in the refrigerator.

Peach and apple soufflé
Make the soufflé the day before and refrigerate; remove from the refrigerator 1 hour before serving. Discard the collar.

Shortcake gâteau
Make the walnut shortcake base the day before; wrap it in kitchen foil.

TUNAFISH CREAMS

Metric	Imperial
450 ml soured cream	¾ pint soured cream
4 x 15 ml spoons mayonnaise	4 tablespoons mayonnaise
Salt	Salt
Freshly ground black pepper	Freshly ground black pepper
Large dash of Worcestershire sauce	Large dash of Worcestershire sauce
2 x 15 ml spoons snipped fresh chives	2 tablespoons snipped fresh chives
4 x 5 ml spoons capers, chopped	4 teaspoons capers, chopped
1 x 15 ml spoon peeled and finely grated onion	1 tablespoon peeled and finely grated onion
1 x 12.5 g packet powdered gelatine	1 x ½ oz packet powdered gelatine
4 x 15 ml spoons water	4 tablespoons water
2 x 198 g cans tuna, drained and flaked	2 x 7 oz cans tuna, drained and flaked
4 eggs, hard-boiled and chopped	4 eggs, hard-boiled and chopped
To garnish:	**To garnish:**
3 firm tomatoes, sliced	3 firm tomatoes, sliced
Parsley sprigs	Parsley sprigs

Mix together the soured cream, mayonnaise, seasoning, Worcestershire sauce, chives, capers and onion. Dissolve the gelatine in the water in a small heatproof bowl over a pan of hot water. Cool slightly, then stir into the soured cream mixture, followed by the tuna and eggs. Mix thoroughly and spoon into individual soufflé or cocotte dishes. Chill until set. Garnish with tomato slices and parsley.

Below: Tunafish creams.

Battalian beef bake.

BATTALIAN BEEF BAKE

Metric
3 x 15 ml spoons corn oil
350 g onions, peeled and sliced
1 garlic clove, crushed
750 g prime collar or slipper of
  bacon joint, rind removed,
  cut into 1 cm cubes
1.25 kg lean minced beef
Thinly pared rind and juice of
  1 large orange
1 x 397 g can peeled tomatoes
2 bay leaves
Freshly ground black pepper
1 x 2.5 ml spoon Worcestershire
  sauce
Salt
2 kg potatoes, peeled
50 g butter or margarine
50 g plain flour
750 ml milk
1 x 5 ml spoon made mustard
100 g mature Cheddar cheese,
  grated
2 x 15 ml spoons freshly grated
  Parmesan cheese

Imperial
3 tablespoons corn oil
12 oz onions, peeled and sliced
1 garlic clove, crushed
1½ lb prime collar or slipper of
  bacon joint, rind removed,
  cut into ½ inch cubes
2½ lb lean minced beef
Thinly pared rind and juice of
  1 large orange
1 x 14 oz can peeled tomatoes
2 bay leaves
Freshly ground black pepper
½ teaspoon Worcestershire sauce
Salt
4 lb potatoes, peeled
2 oz butter or margarine
2 oz plain flour
1¼ pints milk
1 teaspoon made mustard
4 oz mature Cheddar cheese,
  grated
2 tablespoons freshly grated
  Parmesan cheese

Heat the oil in a large pan and fry the onions and garlic until soft but not coloured. Add the bacon and cook gently for 10 minutes, then stir in the mince. Cook for a further 10 minutes, stirring frequently.

Cut the orange rind into fine julienne strips and blanch in boiling water for 5 minutes. Drain. Add the orange strips, orange juice, tomatoes, with the can liquid, bay leaves, pepper and Worcestershire sauce to the meat mixture and bring to the boil. Cover the pan and simmer gently for 45 minutes. Check the seasoning and adjust if necessary.

Cook the potatoes in boiling salted water until almost tender. Drain, cool and slice. Turn the meat mixture into a shallow 3.4 litre (6 pint) casserole (or two 2.3 litre (4 pint) casseroles) and arrange the potato slices in an overlapping pattern over the meat.

Melt the butter or margarine in a saucepan. Stir in the flour and cook for 1 minute. Gradually stir in the milk and bring to the boil. Add seasoning and the mustard. Simmer for 3 minutes, then remove from the heat and stir in the Cheddar cheese until melted. Spoon the sauce over the potato slices and sprinkle with the Parmesan cheese.

Cook in a preheated hot oven (220°C/425°F, Gas Mark 7) for about 20 minutes.

Reduce the oven temperature to moderate (180°C/350°F, Gas Mark 4) and cook for a further 25 minutes or until really hot and the cheese is brown. Serve immediately.

DRESSED LEEKS

Metric
1.5 kg leeks
9 x 15 ml spoons oil
3 x 15 ml spoons cider vinegar
1 x 5 ml spoon French mustard
25 g peeled and finely chopped
  onion
2 x 5 ml spoons caster sugar
1 x 2.5 ml spoon salt
Freshly ground black pepper

Imperial
3 lb leeks
9 tablespoons oil
3 tablespoons cider vinegar
1 teaspoon French mustard
1 oz peeled and finely chopped
  onion
2 teaspoons caster sugar
½ teaspoon salt
Freshly ground black pepper

Trim about half the green part from the leeks. Cut the remainder of the leeks into 3mm (⅛ inch) slices and wash thoroughly. Drain, then blanch in boiling salted water for 3 to 4 minutes. Drain and cool quickly in cold water. Drain well.

In a screwtop jar, shake together the remaining ingredients. Pour over the leeks and toss together. Leave to marinate for at least 2 hours.

Dressed leeks.

Red Cabbage and Sweetcorn Salad

Metric	Imperial
1.5 kg red cabbage, cored and finely shredded	3 lb red cabbage, cored and finely shredded
150 ml French dressing (see page 91)	¼ pint French dressing (see page 91)
1 cucumber, diced	1 cucumber, diced
Salt	Salt
Freshly ground black pepper	Freshly ground black pepper
2 x 312 g cans sweetcorn kernels, drained	2 x 11 oz cans sweetcorn kernels, drained
1 x 2.5 ml spoon finely grated lemon rind	½ teaspoon finely grated lemon rind
1 x 5 ml spoon clear honey	1 teaspoon clear honey

Put the cabbage in a large bowl with the dressing. Toss and leave for 2 hours. Put the diced cucumber and seasoning in a bowl and leave for 2 hours.

Drain off any excess moisture from the cucumber and add with the corn, lemon rind and honey to the cabbage. Toss thoroughly.

Shortcake Gâteau

Metric	Imperial
250 g plain flour, sifted	10 oz plain flour, sifted
50 g ground rice	2 oz ground rice
200 g butter	8 oz butter
100 g caster sugar	4 oz caster sugar
Finely grated rind of 1 lemon	Finely grated rind of 1 lemon
50 g walnuts, finely chopped	2 oz walnuts, finely chopped
1 egg yolk	1 egg yolk
300 ml whipping cream	½ pint whipping cream
2 x 435 g cans loganberries or raspberries, or 225 g thawed frozen berries, well drained	2 x 15½ oz cans loganberries or raspberries, or 8 oz thawed frozen berries, well drained
Icing sugar	Icing sugar

Put the flour, ground rice, butter, sugar and lemon rind in a bowl and rub together until the mixture resembles breadcrumbs. Add the walnuts and egg yolk and knead together to give a soft dough. Chill, wrapped in a polythene bag, for 30 minutes.

Roll out two-thirds of the dough into a rectangle 30 by 15 cm (12 by 6 inches) and place carefully on a baking sheet. Roll out the remaining dough and cut into six 7.5 cm (3 inch) rounds with a fluted pastry cutter. Cut each in half to form semi-circles. Place on another baking sheet.

Bake in a preheated moderate oven (180°C/350°F, Gas Mark 4), allowing about 30 minutes for the rectangle and about 20 minutes for the semi-circles, or until light brown and firm to the touch. While on the baking sheet, cut the rectangle in half lengthways with a sharp knife. Cool on the baking sheet, then remove to a wire rack. Wrap in foil to store.

About 1 hour before required, whip the cream until stiff. With a forcing bag fitted with a large rose vegetable nozzle, pipe two-thirds in a thick line down the centre of one shortbread rectangle half. Spoon almost all the loganberries or raspberries over the piped cream. Place the second rectangle half over the berries and press down lightly. Pipe the remaining cream in whirls down the centre. Arrange the shortbread semi-circles along the cream and mount a whole berry between each. Dust with icing sugar.

Above: Red cabbage and sweetcorn salad. Right: Shortcake gâteau; Peach and apple soufflé.

Peach and Apple Soufflé

Metric	Imperial
500 g cooking apples, peeled, cored and sliced	1¼ lb cooking apples, peeled, cored and sliced
1 x 435 g can peach slices	1 x 15½ oz can peach slices
6 eggs, separated	6 eggs, separated
275 g caster sugar	10 oz caster sugar
2 x 15 ml spoons lemon juice	2 tablespoons lemon juice
5 x 5 ml spoons powdered gelatine	5 teaspoons powdered gelatine
3 x 15 ml spoons water	3 tablespoons water
2 x 15 ml spoons orange-flavoured liqueur	2 tablespoons orange-flavoured liqueur
150 ml single cream	¼ pint single cream
300 ml double cream	½ pint double cream
Few black grapes (some frosted) and candied angelica to decorate	Few black grapes (some frosted) and candied angelica to decorate

Stew the apples in 6 x 15 ml spoons (6 tablespoons) of the peach can syrup until soft. Cool. Sieve or liquidize with the drained peaches. Put the egg yolks, sugar and lemon juice in a heatproof bowl over a pan of hot water and whisk until very thick and creamy and the whisk leaves a trail when lifted. Remove from the heat and whisk until cool.

Dissolve the gelatine in the water in a heatproof bowl over a pan of hot water, then cool slightly. Whisk the fruit purée into the egg mixture, followed by the gelatine and liqueur. Whip the creams together until thick but not stiff and fold into the mixture. Finally, whisk the egg whites until stiff and fold in. Turn into a 1.5 litre (2½ pint) soufflé dish fitted with a paper collar and chill in the refrigerator until set.

Use a round-bladed knife to remove the collar from the soufflé, and decorate the top with grapes and angelica cut into diamonds. *Note:* To frost grapes, first dip them into egg white, then coat thoroughly in caster sugar. Leave to dry.

PICNIC FOR EIGHT ON BEACH OR BOAT, USING A CAMPING STOVE

Picnic stick/Sausage and apple burgers, Selection of cold meats, French bread, butter, Radishes/Ice cream, Butterscotch sauce

BEFOREHAND

Picnic stick
Prepare just before leaving and wrap in foil.
Sausage and apple burgers
These can be made at home the day before; if you make them at the picnic site, be sure you have enough containers (and water) for reconstituting, and mixing, the onion slices and apple flakes.
Butterscotch sauce
Make this at home and keep in an airtight screwtop jar.
Radishes
These can be topped and tailed before leaving home.

PICNIC STICK

Make two

Metric	Imperial
65 g butter	2½ oz butter
2 x 15 ml spoons milk	2 tablespoons milk
4 eggs, lightly beaten	4 eggs, lightly beaten
Salt	Salt
Freshly ground black pepper	Freshly ground black pepper
1 x 30 cm French loaf	1 x 12 inch French loaf
100 g salami, thinly sliced and skinned	4 oz salami, thinly sliced and skinned
2 firm tomatoes, sliced	2 firm tomatoes, sliced
Thinly sliced cucumber	Thinly sliced cucumber
Black olives	Black olives

Melt 15 g (½ oz) of the butter in a saucepan. Add the milk, then stir in the eggs and seasoning. Cook gently, stirring constantly, until the eggs thicken and become creamy. Don't let them become dry. Remove from the heat while still a little runny. Turn out of the pan and cool.

Split the French loaf lengthways, without cutting all the way through, and butter the cut surfaces using the remaining butter. Place a little of the scrambled egg in the centre of each salami slice. Fold or roll them up and wedge upright in the French loaf. Fill the gaps with any remaining scrambled egg and put slices of tomato and cucumber along the sides. Finish with black olives. Eat fresh.
Serves 4

SAUSAGE AND APPLE BURGERS

Metric	Imperial
1 x 40 g packet dried onion slices	1 x 1.4 oz packet dried onion slices
2 x 42 g packets quick-dried apple flakes	2 x 1½ oz packets quick-dried apple flakes
750 g pork sausage meat	1½ lb pork sausage meat
50 g fresh white breadcrumbs	2 oz fresh white breadcrumbs
2 x 5 ml spoons dried mixed herbs	2 teaspoons dried mixed herbs
Salt	Salt
Freshly ground black pepper	Freshly ground black pepper
1 egg, beaten	1 egg, beaten
25 g seasoned flour	1 oz seasoned flour
1 x 15 ml spoon oil	1 tablespoon oil

Reconstitute the onion slices and apple flakes separately as directed on the packets. Press out excess moisture and put them in a large bowl. With a wooden spoon, work in the sausage meat, breadcrumbs, mixed herbs and seasoning. Bind together with the beaten egg. Shape the sausage mixture into eight round cakes about 2 cm (¾ inch) thick. Turn in seasoned flour to coat.

Fry the burgers in the oil in a large pan for about 20 minutes, until well browned, turning once. Serve in soft buns with apple chutney, onion rings, tomato slices, etc.

A selection of cold meats to serve as an addition to this menu could include honey glazed ham, tongue, Danish salami, ham sausage, German garlic sausage and thinly sliced cold pork. Wrap each kind of meat separately in waxed or greaseproof paper and pack in a lidded plastic box. Take homemade chutney or French mustard to serve with the cold meats.

BUTTERSCOTCH SAUCE

Metric	Imperial
90 g dark soft brown sugar	3½ oz dark soft brown sugar
175 g golden syrup	6 oz golden syrup
50 g butter	2 oz butter
150 ml single cream	¼ pint single cream
2 x 15 ml spoons lemon juice	2 tablespoons lemon juice

Heat the sugar, syrup and butter in a pan for 5 minutes, stirring to dissolve the sugar. Off the heat, stir in the cream and lemon juice. (Keeps well in a screwtop jar for several days.)
Note: Remove the ice cream from the freezer at the last possible moment and take in an insulated container or wide-mouthed vacuum jar. (Or buy it near the picnic site!)

Above: Picnic stick. Right: Sausage and apple burgers; Selection of cold meats; Butterscotch sauce.

PICNIC IDEAS

HARVEST PASTIES

Metric
2 x 15 ml spoons oil
100 g peeled and diced carrot
100 g trimmed and diced celery
100 g diced leek
1 x 5 ml spoon yeast extract
1 x 5 ml spoon Worcestershire
    sauce
1 x 220 g can baked beans
Salt
Freshly ground black pepper
225 g shortcrust pastry, made
    with 225 g plain flour and
    100 g fat
1 egg, beaten

Imperial
2 tablespoons oil
4 oz peeled and diced carrot
4 oz trimmed and diced celery
4 oz diced leek
1 teaspoon yeast extract
1 teaspoon Worcestershire sauce
1 x 7¾ oz can baked beans
Salt
Freshly ground black pepper
8 oz shortcrust pastry, made with
    8 oz plain flour and 4 oz fat
1 egg, beaten

Heat the oil in a pan and fry the vegetables gently until soft – about 10 minutes. Stir in the yeast extract, Worcestershire sauce, baked beans and seasoning to taste. Cool.

Roll out the dough on a floured surface and cut out four rounds, each 16 cm (6½ inches) in diameter. Divide the vegetable mixture between the four rounds. Brush the edges with egg and bring the sides to the centre. Press together with the fingertips to seal. Place on a baking sheet. Using scissors, snip the pastry edge in diagonal cuts, about 1 cm (½ inch) inwards. Glaze with beaten egg and bake in a preheated moderately hot oven (190°C/375°F, Gas Mark 5) for 20 minutes. Glaze again with egg and return to the oven for a further 10 to 15 minutes baking. Wrap each pastry in foil for carrying to the picnic. Makes 4

MINI HEROES

Metric
1 x 454 g packet brown bread mix
Beaten egg
175 g butter or soft margarine
3 x 15 ml spoons horseradish
    relish
3 x 113 g packets sliced Danish
    salami
1 x 298 g can green cut asparagus
    spears, drained

Imperial
1 x 1 lb packet brown bread mix
Beaten egg
6 oz butter or soft margarine
3 tablespoons horseradish relish
3 x 4 oz packets sliced Danish
    salami
1 x 10½ oz can green cut asparagus
    spears, drained

Prepare and knead the dough according to the packet instructions. Wrap about one-sixth in greaseproof paper and keep in the refrigerator. Divide the remaining dough into 16 even pieces. Shape into finger rolls and place on lightly greased backing sheets. Loosely cover with oiled cling wrap and leave to rise in a warm place until double in size.

Shape the refrigerated dough into 16 plaits the same length as the rolls. Make an indentation along each proved roll and place a plait in each. Glaze with beaten egg. Bake in a preheated hot oven (220°C/425°F, Gas Mark 7) for 15 to 20 minutes. Cool.

Split the rolls (which should be eaten fresh) and spread each half with the butter or margarine and horseradish, creamed together. Fill with slices of salami rolled around asparagus pieces. Cover with cling wrap until required. (Wrap individually in cling wrap or foil for taking to the picnic.) Serves 8

Below: Harvest pasties; Mini heroes. Right: Picnic sandwich box; Tuna quiche.

PICNIC SANDWICH BOX

Metric
1 small uncut crusty bloomer
   loaf
75 g butter, melted
225 g pork sausage meat
100 g cooked ham, diced
100 g cooked tongue, diced
50 g onion, peeled and chopped
2 eggs
150 ml milk
Salt
Freshly ground black pepper
2 eggs, hard-boiled and halved

Imperial
1 small uncut crusty bloomer
   loaf
3 oz butter, melted
8 oz pork sausage meat
4 oz cooked ham, diced
4 oz cooked tongue, diced
2 oz onion, peeled and chopped
2 eggs
¼ pint milk
Salt
Freshly ground black pepper
2 eggs, hard-boiled and halved

Cut horizontally across the loaf, two-thirds of the way up, and remove this 'lid'. Gently ease away the bread from around the edge of the crust. Make 100 g (4 oz) breadcrumbs from the bread. Brush the cavity of the loaf and the lid with some of the melted butter.

Combine the sausage meat, chopped meats, breadcrumbs and onion. Beat the two eggs and milk together. Season well. Combine with the meat mixture. Place one third of the filling in the bread case and arrange the halved hard-boiled eggs lengthways on top. Pack around with the remaining filling, then top with the bread lid.

Secure the loaf in a parcel-like fashion with string. Use the remaining melted butter to brush all over the loaf. Place on a baking sheet. Bake in a preheated moderately hot oven (200°C/400°F, Gas Mark 6) for 15 minutes. Cover with foil and continue baking for 45 minutes. When cool, remove the string. Wrap in foil for carrying to the picnic. Cut in thick slices to serve. Serves 8

TUNA QUICHE

Metric
225 g dry shortcrust pastry mix
1 x 15 ml spoon oil
175 g plump spring onions,
   trimmed and cut into 6 mm
   slices
1 x 198 g can tuna, drained and
   flaked
2 eggs
300 ml milk
Salt
Freshly ground black pepper
Grated Parmesan cheese

Imperial
8 oz dry shortcrust pastry mix
1 tablespoon oil
6 oz plump spring onions,
   trimmed and cut into ¼ inch
   slices
1 x 7 oz can tuna, drained and
   flaked
2 eggs
½ pint milk
Salt
Freshly ground black pepper
Grated Parmesan cheese

Make up the pastry dough as instructed on the packet. Roll out and use to line a 23 cm (9 inch) flan dish. Bake blind in a preheated moderately hot oven (200°C/400°F, Gas Mark 6) for 15 minutes or until the pastry shows signs of browning.

Heat the oil in a frying pan and fry the spring onions for about 3 minutes. Drain well. Arrange the onions and tuna in the pastry case. Whisk together the eggs and milk and season well. Pour over the filling in the pastry case. Sprinkle the centre with Parmesan cheese. Bake in a preheated moderate oven (180°C/350°F, Gas Mark 4) for 30 to 35 minutes until the filling sets and lightly browns. Take to the picnic in the flan dish, foil wrapped. Serves 6

CURRIED BACON FLAN

Metric
175 g shortcrust pastry, made
  with 175 g plain flour 75 g fat
15 g margarine
100 g celery heart, sliced
100 g streaky bacon rashers,
  rinds removed, chopped
1 x 5 ml spoon mild curry powder
3 eggs, beaten
150 ml unsweetened natural
  yogurt
Salt
Freshly ground black pepper
225 g tomatoes, skinned and
  thinly sliced
Chopped parsley to garnish

Imperial
6 oz shortcrust pastry, made with
  6 oz plain flour and 3 oz fat
½ oz margarine
4 oz celery heart, sliced
4 oz streaky bacon rashers, rinds
  removed, chopped
1 teaspoon mild curry powder
3 eggs, beaten
¼ pint unsweetened natural
  yogurt
Salt
Freshly ground black pepper
8 oz tomatoes, skinned and
  thinly sliced
Chopped parsley to garnish

Roll out the dough and use to line a 21.5 cm (8½ inch) loose-bottomed French fluted flan tin. Bake blind in a moderately hot oven (200°C/400°F, Gas Mark 6) until the pastry is quite dry and just beginning to colour. Cool.

Melt the margarine in a small frying pan and fry the celery and bacon until the celery is golden brown. Stir in the curry powder and cook for 2 minutes to draw out the flavour.

Mix the eggs with the yogurt. Add the pan ingredients and seasoning, and turn into the flan case. Top with the tomato slices. Bake in a preheated moderately hot oven (190°C/375°F, Gas Mark 5) for about 25 minutes. Cool, then sprinkle with parsley. Carry in the tin. Serves 6

Left: Curried bacon flan. Above: Farmhouse cake.

FARMHOUSE CAKE

Metric
225 g wholemeal flour
225 g plain flour
1 x 5 ml spoon mixed spice
1 x 5 ml spoon bicarbonate of
  soda
175 g block margarine
225 g sugar
100 g sultanas, cleaned
100 g seedless raisins, cleaned
3 x 15 ml spoons chopped mixed
  peel
1 egg, beaten
300 ml milk

Imperial
8 oz wholemeal flour
8 oz plain flour
1 teaspoon mixed spice
1 teaspoon bicarbonate of soda
6 oz block margarine
8 oz sugar
4 oz sultanas, cleaned
4 oz seedless raisins, cleaned
3 tablespoons chopped mixed
  peel
1 egg, beaten
½ pint milk

Grease and flour a 20 cm (8 inch) cake tin. Sift the flours, spice and bicarbonate of soda into a bowl. Rub the fat into the dry ingredients until the mixture resembles fine breadcrumbs. Stir in the sugar, fruit and peel. Make a well in the centre and pour in the egg and some of the milk. Gradually work into the dry ingredients, adding more milk if necessary to give a dropping consistency. Put the mixture into the tin and level the top. Bake in a preheated moderate oven (160°C/325°F, Gas Mark 3) for about 2 hours, until firm to the touch. Turn out and cool on a wire rack. Wrap in foil and put in a firm container for carrying to the picnic.
Makes a 20 cm (8 inch) round cake

BARBECUES

Barbecue food needs to be spicy and satisfying. Choose your favourites from the following selection.

BARBECUE BASTING SAUCE

Combine a 225 g (8 oz) jar of tomato chutney, 1 x 5 ml spoon (1 teaspoon) each of dry mustard, soft brown sugar and salt, 1 x 15 ml spoon (1 tablespoon) Worcestershire sauce, 1 x 15 ml spoon (1 tablespoon) lemon juice, 120 ml (4 fl oz) each dry red wine and corn oil, a crushed garlic clove and a dash of Tabasco. This can be used for any meat or poultry.

With any barbecue grill, have a big salad bowl on hand, made with finely shredded cabbage, sliced radishes and sweet peppers, broken walnut pieces and snipped chives, moistened with French dressing or topped with mayonnaise.

Delicious extras for a barbecue are wedges of eating apple or halves of fresh juicy apricots, bacon-wrapped on skewers.

BARBECUE SAUCE

Metric	Imperial
50 g butter	2 oz butter
100 g onion, peeled and finely chopped	4 oz onion, peeled and finely chopped
1 x 226 g can tomatoes	1 x 8 oz can tomatoes
2 x 5 ml spoons tomato paste	2 teaspoons tomato paste
2 x 15 ml spoons vinegar	2 tablespoons vinegar
2 x 15 ml spoons demerara sugar	2 tablespoons demerara sugar
2 x 5 ml spoons dry mustard	2 teaspoons dry mustard
2 x 15 ml spoons Worcestershire sauce	2 tablespoons Worcestershire sauce

Melt the butter in a saucepan and fry the onion until soft but not browned. Stir in the remaining sauce ingredients and simmer, partially covered, for 25 minutes. Serve with barbecued chicken pieces, chops or sausages.

BARBECUE-STYLE MUSTARD CHICKEN

Several hours before, spread the mustard butter over the chicken pieces and keep them in the refrigerator until required for grilling.

Metric	Imperial
1 x 1.75 kg chicken	1 x 3½ lb chicken
50 g butter, softened	2 oz butter, softened
3 x 15 ml spoons coarse-grain mustard	3 tablespoons coarse-grain mustard
Grated rind of 1 lemon	Grated rind of 1 lemon
1 x 15 ml spoon lemon juice	1 tablespoon lemon juice
1 x 5 ml spoon chopped fresh tarragon or rosemary	1 teaspoon chopped fresh tarragon or rosemary
Salt	Salt
Freshly ground black pepper	Freshly ground black pepper

Joint the chicken into eight pieces and trim off any excess fat, leaving the skin on. In a bowl, cream the butter and work in the mustard a little at a time, using a wooden spoon. Add the lemon rind, then gradually beat in the lemon juice and the herbs. Season well. Spread the mustard butter over the chicken pieces, coating evenly.

Heat the grill and cook the chicken on the rack for 10 to 15 minutes on each side until the skin is crisp and golden and the chicken is tender. Some of the mustard mixture may slide off, in which case spoon it from the grill pan over the chicken when serving.

When cooking is done on a barbecue, keep back some of the mustard butter and spread it on the chicken pieces as they cook.
Serves 4 to 6

Barbecue-style mustard chicken, which can be cooked in batches.

HERRING PARCELS WITH MUSTARD BUTTER

The fish boats can be prepared several hours ahead and kept cool, covered, until needed for cooking.

Metric	Imperial
75 g butter, softened	3 oz butter, softened
2 x 15 ml spoons Dijon mustard	2 tablespoons Dijon mustard
2 x 15 ml spoons chopped parsley	2 tablespoons chopped parsley
Salt	Salt
Freshly ground black pepper	Freshly ground black pepper
2 herrings or mackerel, cleaned and heads removed	2 herrings or mackerel, cleaned and heads removed
½ lemon, cut into wedges	½ lemon, cut into wedges

Combine the softened butter with the mustard, parsley and seasoning. Shape two pieces of foil, each 23 by 23 cm (9 by 9 inches) into two boat-shapes suitable to hold the fish. Spread a little of the savoury butter on the bottom of the foil. Fill the cavity of each fish with more of the savoury butter, reserving 2 x 5 ml spoons (2 teaspoons). Make three slits at a slant on each side of each fish.

Place each fish in a foil 'boat' and top with the reserved butter. Cook over the barbecue for about 10 to 15 minutes, turning once during cooking. Serve in the boat to keep the juices and garnish with the lemon wedges. Serves 2

Note: For lemon tarragon butter, beat 125 g (4 oz) butter with 3 x 15 ml spoons (3 tablespoons) lemon juice, 1 x 15 ml spoon (1 tablespoon) chopped fresh tarragon and seasoning. Score the fish and spread with the butter. Place in foil boats and cook as above.

Below: Herring parcels with mustard butter. Right: Apricot cheese sponge cake; Strawberry mallows; Minced meat shashlik.

MINCED MEAT SHASHLIK

The meatballs can be made and threaded onto the skewers, with the onions and bay leaves, several hours ahead. Keep covered and cool. Brush with oil just before cooking.

Metric	Imperial
500 g lean minced beef (minced twice)	1 lb lean minced beef (minced twice)
1 x 5 ml spoon salt	1 teaspoon salt
1 x 1.25 ml spoon freshly ground black pepper	¼ teaspoon freshly ground black pepper
1 x 15 ml spoon peeled and grated onion	1 tablespoon peeled and grated onion
1 x 15 ml spoon Worcestershire sauce	1 tablespoon Worcestershire sauce
4 large onions	4 large onions
Bay leaves	Bay leaves
Oil	Oil
2 small tomatoes, halved	2 small tomatoes, halved
Fine strips of canned pimiento (optional)	Fine strips of canned pimiento (optional)

Combine the beef, salt, pepper, grated onion and Worcestershire sauce well together. Shape into small balls about the size of a large walnut. Put the onions in a bowl. Pour boiling water over and leave for 2 to 3 minutes. Drain and peel, then quarter. Thread onto four skewers with the meatballs and bay leaves. Brush with oil. Cook on the barbecue, turning until almost cooked.

Place the seasoned tomato halves on the skewers and cook for a further 5 minutes. Serves 4

Note: The shashlik can be cooked under a preheated grill for 10 minutes, turning once. The sliced pimiento can be added to the juices in the grill pan and spooned over the shashlik before serving.

APRICOT CHEESE SPONGE CAKE

Metric	Imperial
2 x 15 ml spoons apricot jam	2 tablespoons apricot jam
1 x 18 cm bought sponge flan case	1 x 7 inch bought sponge flan case
225 g cream cheese	8 oz cream cheese
1 sachet Dream topping	1 sachet Dream topping
150 ml milk	¼ pint milk
4 x 15 ml spoons lemon juice	4 tablespoons lemon juice
Grated rind of 1 lemon	Grated rind of 1 lemon
25 g sultanas, cleaned	1 oz sultanas, cleaned
Jam for topping	Jam for topping

Spread the apricot jam on the bottom of the flan case. Beat the cheese until soft. Make up the Dream topping with the milk and beat into the cheese. Beat in the lemon juice and rind and the sultanas. Pile into the flan case and drizzle on a little more jam. Serves 4 to 6

STRAWBERRY MALLOWS

Metric	Imperial
4 chocolate caramel bars	4 chocolate caramel bars
4 x 15 ml spoons single cream	4 tablespoons single cream
20 strawberries	20 strawberries
20 marshmallows	20 marshmallows

Round off the party in a spectacular — but simple — way. Melt the caramel bars gently (over a low heat or in a double saucepan), then stir in the cream. Keep warm.

Spear a berry and a marshmallow on a skewer and grill until the mallow starts to brown — but no longer. Dip into the chocolate caramel sauce and serve immediately. Serves 6

POSH PICNIC FOR SIX FOR TRANSPORTING IN THE BACK OF THE CAR

Cold avocado soup/Seafood quiches/Melton Mowbray pie, Chicory and black olive salad/Fresh lime mousse, Strawberries and cream

BEFOREHAND

Cold avocado soup
Make a day or two beforehand. When cool, refrigerate in a lidded polythene bowl or vacuum flask which can be put straight into the picnic basket on the day. Chop parsley or chives and keep in the refrigerator in a polythene bag. Stir soup before serving and sprinkle each cupful with the garnish.

Seafood quiches
Make the day before or on the morning of the picnic allowing time for the quiches to cool.

Melton Mowbray pie
Make a day or two beforehand and wrap lightly; keep refrigerated.

Chicory and black olive salad
Mix the dressing a day or two beforehand and keep in a screwtop jar (not in the refrigerator). Prepare chicory the day before; refrigerate in a polythene bag.

Fresh lime mousse
Make the day before and keep in refrigerator, lightly covered.

COLD AVOCADO SOUP

Metric	Imperial
25 g butter	1 oz butter
25 g plain flour	1 oz plain flour
150 ml milk	¼ pint milk
900 ml chicken stock	1½ pints chicken stock
1 x 1.25 ml spoon salt	¼ teaspoon salt
Freshly ground black pepper	Freshly ground black pepper
1 small green pepper, cored, seeded and chopped	1 small green pepper, cored, seeded and chopped
1 ripe avocado	1 ripe avocado
Chopped parsley or snipped fresh chives to garnish	Chopped parsley or snipped fresh chives to garnish

Melt the butter in a saucepan. Stir in the flour and cook gently over a low heat for about 3 minutes, without browning. Remove from the heat and gradually stir in the milk, then the stock. Add the salt, pepper and green pepper and bring to the boil. Simmer, covered, for 15 minutes.

Meanwhile, halve and stone the avocado. Scrape out the flesh and mash to a smooth cream. Mix some of the thickened stock with the avocado and stir it back into the pan. Cook the soup for a few minutes but do not boil it. Strain to remove the green pepper. Allow to cool. Serve garnished with parsley or chives. Take to the picnic in a vacuum flask.

SEAFOOD QUICHES

Metric	Imperial
200 g shortcrust pastry, made with 200 g plain flour and 115 g fat	7 oz shortcrust pastry, made with 7 oz plain flour and 3½ oz fat
100 g shelled prawns, chopped	4 oz shelled prawns, chopped
75 g smoked salmon, cut into strips	3 oz smoked salmon, cut into strips
300 ml single cream	½ pint single cream
4 egg yolks	4 egg yolks
Salt	Salt
Freshly ground black pepper	Freshly ground black pepper
2 x 15 ml spoons chopped parsley	2 tablespoons chopped parsley

Roll out the dough and use to line six 10 cm (4 inch) shallow patty pans or individual tartlet tins. Knock up the edges.

Divide the prawns and salmon equally between the uncooked pastry cases. Beat the cream and egg yolks together. Season to taste, remembering that the salmon tends to be salty. Add half the chopped parsley. Spoon into the pastry cases placed on a baking sheet. Bake in a preheated moderately hot oven (200°C/400°F, Gas Mark 6) for 10 minutes. Reduce the heat to moderate (180°C/350°F, Gas Mark 4) and cook for a further 20 to 25 minutes until the pastry is beginning to colour and the filling is lightly set.

Take in the patty pans, foil-wrapped and placed in a square container to hold firm, for transportation. Garnish with the remaining parsley just before serving. Makes 6

Cold avocado soup; Seafood quiches.

Melton Mowbray pie; Chicory and black olive salad.

MELTON MOWBRAY PIE

Metric	Imperial
For the pastry:	**For the pastry:**
225 g plain flour	8 oz plain flour
1 x 5 ml spoon salt	1 teaspoon salt
100 g lard	4 oz lard
5 x 15 ml spoons milk and water mixed	5 tablespoons milk and water mixed
Beaten egg to glaze	Beaten egg to glaze
For the filling:	**For the filling:**
500 g lean pork, finely diced	1 lb lean pork, finely diced
Salt	Salt
Freshly ground black pepper	Freshly ground black pepper
1 sage leaf, finely chopped, or 1 x 1.25 ml spoon dried sage	1 sage leaf, finely chopped, or ¼ teaspoon dried sage
2 x 15 ml spoons water	2 tablespoons water
Melted jellied stock	Melted jellied stock

Sift the flour and salt together and rub in 50 g (2 oz) of the lard. Melt the remaining lard in the milk and water and stir into the flour. Knead until smooth. Reserve one-quarter of the dough and keep covered. Roll out the remainder on a floured surface to a 25 cm (10 inch) circle. Use to line a 15 cm (6 inch) greased and bottom-lined round cake tin.

Mix the pork with seasoning, the sage and water. Fill the pastry case. Brush the top edge of the dough with beaten egg. Roll out the reserved dough into a circle and use to cover the pie. Crimp the edges to seal, cut a small hole in the centre and glaze with beaten egg. Bake in a preheated hot oven (220°C/425°F, Gas Mark 7) for 30 minutes, then reduce the heat to moderate (160°C/325°F, Gas Mark 3) and continue baking for 1½ hours.

Cool and remove from the tin. Top up the pie with melted jellied stock through the hole. Make sure the pie has cooled and the stock firmly jellied before wrapping it for the picnic.

CHICORY AND BLACK OLIVE SALAD

Metric	Imperial
2 x 15 ml spoons vinegar	2 tablespoons vinegar
2 x 5 ml spoons honey	2 teaspoons honey
2 onions, peeled and finely chopped	2 onions, peeled and finely chopped
4 x 15 ml spoons salad oil	4 tablespoons salad oil
2 x 15 ml spoons lemon juice	2 tablespoons lemon juice
Pinch of sugar	Pinch of sugar
Pinch of salt	Pinch of salt
4 heads of chicory, trimmed and thinly sliced	4 heads of chicory, trimmed and thinly sliced
12 black olives, stoned	12 black olives, stoned

Put the vinegar, honey, onions, oil, lemon juice, sugar and salt in a screwtop jar and shake well together. Put the chicory and olives in a large lidded plastic bowl and pour over the dressing. Toss. Place the lid firmly on top for transportation. Toss well again before serving.

FRESH LIME MOUSSE

Metric	Imperial
3 eggs, separated	3 eggs, separated
100 g caster sugar	4 oz caster sugar
Finely grated rind and juice of 2 limes	Finely grated rind and juice of 2 limes
1 x 15 ml spoon powdered gelatine	1 tablespoon powdered gelatine
150 ml double cream	¼ pint double cream
Sliced strawberries to decorate	Sliced strawberries to decorate

Put the egg yolks in a deep heatproof bowl over warm water with the sugar and lime rind and whisk until thick and mousse-like. (If using an electric mixer no heat is needed.) Meanwhile, soak the gelatine in the strained lime juice in a small heatproof bowl. Dissolve by standing the bowl in a pan of gently simmering water. Whip the cream to the floppy stage, then fold it through the mousse with the dissolved gelatine. Whisk the egg whites until stiff and fold in.

Turn into six individual unbreakable dishes or one large unbreakable plastic bowl. Refrigerate until firm. Decorate with sliced strawberries. Cover firmly with cling-wrap (or lids) before transportation. Keep as cool as possible.

Note: Instead of the rind and juice of the 2 fresh limes, 6 x 15 ml spoons (6 tablespoons) of "Lazy Lime Juice" can be used.

Fresh lime mousse.

BUFFET PARTIES

A help-yourself party is the best way of entertaining more than a handful of people, and careful planning can ensure that preparations go smoothly and that the party itself is a success. Choose a menu to suit your mood, your purse and your kitchen – and your culinary skill. Even if you haven't a freezer, you can do a lot of cooking beforehand, such as making meringues, gâteaux bases, pastry cases and fillings.
List the utensils and dishes you'll need for cooking as well as for serving, and borrow from friends if necessary. For the actual party, arrange the cold savouries, with cutlery, plates and napkins, on a table sited so that guests can move around freely and help themselves from all sides, and make sure there are enough serving spoons. Bring in hot dishes at the last possible minute. The desserts should be on another table or on a trolley in the kitchen, ready to be wheeled in; another table or sideboard will be needed for the drinks.

WINTER PARTY FOR TWELVE

Beef and wine potato pie, Courgette and orange salad, Platter salad (see page 128) /Caramel mousse

BEFOREHAND

Beef and wine potato pie
Prepare up to and including covering with mousseline potatoes. Cover and refrigerate.
Courgette and orange salad
Prepare the courgettes the day before, but don't combine with the dressing until the afternoon of the party.
Platter salad
Prepare, bag up and chill the salad items. If using chicory, wash it but leave slicing until assembly time. Fennel, if used, should be used sparingly; slice it thinly and brush at once with lemon juice or marinate in dressing. Prepare a large amount of mustardy French dressing (see page 91).
Caramel mousse
Make this the day before; keep it chilled, undecorated.

BEEF AND WINE POTATO PIE

Make two

Metric	Imperial
1.5 kg chuck steak	3 lb chuck steak
225 g lean streaky bacon, rinds removed	8 oz lean streaky bacon, rinds removed
50 g lard	2 oz lard
3 x 15 ml spoons plain flour	3 tablespoons plain flour
300 ml red wine	½ pint red wine
150 ml stock	¼ pint stock
1 x 2.5 ml spoon mixed herbs	½ teaspoon mixed herbs
1 bay leaf	1 bay leaf
1 garlic clove, crushed	1 garlic clove, crushed
225 g onions, peeled and sliced	8 oz onions, peeled and sliced
175 g small button mushrooms	6 oz small button mushrooms
For the mousseline potatoes:	**For the mousseline potatoes:**
1.5 kg old potatoes, peeled and boiled	3 lb old potatoes, peeled and boiled
150 ml hot milk	¼ pint hot milk
3 eggs, separated	3 eggs, separated
75 g Cheddar cheese, grated	3 oz Cheddar cheese, grated
50 g butter	2 oz butter
2 x 15 ml spoons chopped parsley	2 tablespoons chopped parsley
Salt	Salt
Freshly ground black pepper	Freshly ground black pepper

Mince the chuck steak and bacon, or ask your butcher to do it for you. Melt half the lard and quickly fry the mince until it starts to brown. Stir in the flour and cook for a few minutes. Add the wine and stock slowly, stirring all the time. Add the herbs, bay leaf and garlic. Turn the mixture into a large entrée-type ovenproof dish or a 30.5

cm (12 inch) diameter shallow casserole. Cover and bake in a preheated moderate oven (180°C/350°F, Gas Mark 4) for 30 minutes.
For the mousseline potatoes, sieve the potatoes. Beat the hot milk, egg yolks, grated cheese, butter and chopped parsley into the potatoes. Season to taste. Whisk the egg whites until stiff and fold in.
Melt the rest of the lard and fry the onions until golden. Add the mushrooms and cook for 5 minutes. Drain well and stir into the mince. Cover with the mousseline potatoes and return to a moderately hot oven (200°C/400°F, Gas Mark 6) to bake for about 30 minutes or until golden brown. Serves 6
Note: If preparing ahead of time, cover the mince with the mousseline potatoes, then allow to cool. Cover the dish or casserole and refrigerate. When needed, reheat in a moderately hot oven (200°C/400°F, Gas Mark 6) for 50 minutes, covering with foil after 30 minutes if the top is too brown.

COURGETTE AND ORANGE SALAD

Metric	Imperial
1.5 kg courgettes, cut into 1 cm slices	3 lb courgettes, cut into ½ inch slices
Salt	Salt
6 oranges	6 oranges
175 ml mayonnaise	6 fl oz mayonnaise
120 ml single cream	4 fl oz single cream
Chopped parsley to garnish	Chopped parsley to garnish

Blanch the courgettes in boiling salted water for 3 minutes. Drain and rinse in cold water. Pat dry on absorbent kitchen paper.
Grate the rind from the oranges and add to the mayonnaise with the cream. Peel the oranges and separate into segments. Put with any juice in a bowl with the courgettes. Toss in the mayonnaise mixture. Cover and chill for several hours.
Turn into a serving dish and garnish with parsley.

CARAMEL MOUSSE

Metric
4 eggs, separated
4 egg yolks
100 g caster sugar
1.2 litres lukewarm milk
500 g granulated sugar
400 ml warm water
9 x 5 ml spoons powdered
  gelatine
6 x 15 ml spoons lemon juice
600 ml whipping cream
Broken walnuts to decorate

Imperial
4 eggs, separated
4 egg yolks
4 oz caster sugar
2 pints lukewarm milk
1 lb 2 oz granulated sugar
14 fl oz warm water
9 teaspoons powdered gelatine
6 tablespoons lemon juice
1 pint whipping cream
Broken walnuts to decorate

Whisk all the egg yolks and caster sugar in a saucepan until thick. Add the milk and cook over a low heat without boiling, stirring all the time, until the custard thickens slightly. Cool.

Dissolve the granulated sugar in half the water. Boil to a rich dark caramel, then immediately pour in the remaining water. (Cover your hand while you do this as the caramel splutters.) Stir over a low heat to amalgamate, then pour into the custard.

Soak the gelatine in the lemon juice in a small heatproof bowl and dissolve by standing the bowl in a pan of simmering water. Add to the cool custard mixture. Chill until the mixture begins to set.

Lightly whip the cream. Whisk the egg whites until stiff. Fold half the cream and all the egg whites into the setting custard mixture. Turn into two 1.8 litre (3 pint) ring moulds or glass dishes and refrigerate until set. Decorate with whirls of the remaining whipped cream and walnuts. Makes 2 mousses, each to serve 6

Above: Caramel mousse. Below: Beef and wine potato pie; Courgette and orange salad.

Buffet Supper for Ten to Twelve Using Convenience Foods

Smoked mackerel salad, Tivoli salad, Walnut cheesies, Poppy seed knots/Lemon chiffon pie, or Apricot orange flan (see page 14)

BEFOREHAND

Smoked mackerel salad
Early in the day, prepare the potato, mackerel and celery up to the addition of the dressing. Keep in covered containers in the refrigerator.

Tivoli salad
Prepare the vegetables, meat and cheese on the morning of the party. Fold the mayonnaise through just before serving.

Walnut cheesies
Better made on the afternoon of the party, but can be made the day before; in this case, keep them whole and refresh when needed.

Poppy seed knots
Better if made fresh, but can be made before. Refresh when needed.

Lemon chiffon pie
Make the day before, apart from decoration.

Apricot orange flan
Make the flan cases a day or two before; keep in airtight containers, or foil-wrapped. Fill during the afternoon.

SMOKED MACKEREL SALAD

Metric	Imperial
1 kg small new potatoes (or use canned ones)	2 lb small new potatoes (or use canned ones)
750 g smoked mackerel fillets, skinned	1½ lb smoked mackerel fillets, skinned
300 ml soured cream	½ pint soured cream
120 ml mayonnaise	4 fl oz mayonnaise
6 x 15 ml spoons horseradish sauce	6 tablespoons horseradish sauce
Salt	Salt
Freshly ground black pepper	Freshly ground black pepper
500 g celery, trimmed and sliced	1 lb celery, trimmed and sliced
Paprika	Paprika
Lemon wedges	Lemon wedges

Boil the potatoes in their skins until tender, then peel, halve and cool. Divide the mackerel into fork-size pieces.

In a large bowl, mix the soured cream with the mayonnaise, horseradish and seasoning. Stir in the fish and vegetables. Cover and chill well. Serve the salad sprinkled with paprika and accompanied by lemon wedges.

TIVOLI SALAD

Metric	Imperial
3 x 340 g cans pork and ham, thickly sliced, or equivalent in thickly sliced cooked ham, cut into small cubes.	3 x 12 oz cans pork and ham, thickly sliced, or equivalent in thickly sliced cooked ham, cut into small cubes
350 g Samsoe cheese, cut into small cubes	12 oz Samsoe cheese, cut into small cubes
1 x 450 g (approx) can sweetcorn kernels, drained	1 x 16 oz (approx) can sweetcorn kernels, drained
1.5 x 15 ml spoons peeled and finely chopped onion	1½ tablespoons peeled and finely chopped onion
1 large crisp lettuce, separated into leaves	1 large crisp lettuce, separated into leaves
Snipped fresh chives to garnish	Snipped fresh chives to garnish
For the dressing:	**For the dressing:**
6 x 15 ml spoons mayonnaise	6 tablespoons mayonnaise
3 x 15 ml spoons cream	3 tablespoons cream
2-3 x 15 ml spoons lemon juice	2-3 tablespoons lemon juice
Freshly ground black pepper	Freshly ground black pepper

Mix together the meat, cheese, sweetcorn and onion. Combine the mayonnaise and cream with lemon juice to sharpen. Season with pepper. Fold the mayonnaise dressing through the meat and cheese.

Arrange a bed of lettuce on a dish and pile the meat and cheese mixture on top. Garnish with chives. Serves 10

Left: Smoked mackerel salad.

Walnut cheesies; Poppy seed knots; Tivoli salad.

WALNUT CHEESIES

Metric
1 x 283 g packet brown bread mix
100 g cream cheese
1-2 x 15 ml spoons single cream
25 g walnuts, finely chopped
Salt
Freshly ground black pepper

Imperial
1 x 10 oz packet brown bread mix
4 oz cream cheese
1-2 tablespoons single cream
1 oz walnuts, finely chopped
Salt
Freshly ground black pepper

Make up and knead the dough according to the packet instructions. Roll out on a floured surface to a 30 cm (12 inch) square. Beat the cheese with the cream, walnuts and seasoning and spread over the dough. Roll up like a Swiss roll and cut into nine even-sized slices. Place, cut sides down, in a greased and bottom-lined 16 cm (6½ inch) square cake tin. Cover loosely with oiled cling wrap and leave to rise until double in size, about 40 minutes.

Bake in a preheated very hot oven (230°C/450°F, Gas Mark 8) for about 20 minutes. Cool on a wire rack. Serve slightly warm, pulled apart like Chelsea buns. Makes 9

POPPY SEED KNOTS

Metric
1 x 283 g packet white bread mix
200 ml lukewarm milk
Beaten egg to glaze
Salt
Poppy seeds

Imperial
1 x 10 oz packet white bread mix
7 fl oz lukewarm milk
Beaten egg to glaze
Salt
Poppy seeds

Make up the dough according to the packet instructions, using the milk instead of water. Divide the kneaded dough into eight and roll each piece into a long sausage shape. Tie into a single knot. Place well apart on a greased baking sheet, cover loosely with oiled cling wrap and leave to rise in a warm place for about 40 minutes, or until double in size.

Brush evenly with beaten egg to which a pinch of salt has been added. Sprinkle with poppy seeds and bake in a preheated very hot oven (230°C/450°F, Gas Mark 8) for about 12 minutes. Cool. Break open and spread with butter to serve. These are at their best on the day they are made. Makes 8
Note: To vary, use celery seeds instead of poppy seeds, and grate 50 g (2 oz) mature cheese into the dry bread mix before making up.

Lemon chiffon pie; Apricot orange flan (see recipe page 14).

LEMON CHIFFON PIE

Make two

Metric	**Imperial**
125 g digestive biscuits, crushed	4 oz digestive biscuits, crushed
50 g butter, melted	2 oz butter, melted
1 x 2.5 ml spoon ground ginger	½ teaspoon ground ginger
2 medium lemons	2 medium lemons
1 small can condensed milk, or ½ large can	1 small can condensed milk, or ½ large can
1 x 5 ml spoon powdered gelatine	1 teaspoon powdered gelatine
1 egg white	1 egg white
150 ml whipping cream, lightly whipped	½ pint whipping cream, lightly whipped

Mix the biscuits with the melted butter and ground ginger. Press into an 18 cm (7 inch) loose-bottomed flan tin, lining the bottom and sides. Place in the refrigerator to firm up.

Pare a few strips of lemon rind free of all white pith. Cut into fine shreds and blanch in boiling water for a few seconds. Drain well. Grate the remaining lemon rind and squeeze the juice from the lemons. Whisk the condensed milk with 5 x 15 ml spoons (5 tablespoons) strained lemon juice and the grated lemon rind until the mixture thickens. Soak the gelatine in a further 1 x 15 ml spoon (1 tablespoon) lemon juice in a small heatproof bowl, then dissolve by standing the bowl in a pan of simmering water. Add to the condensed milk mixture.

Whisk the egg white until stiff and fold into the lemon mixture, then pour into the flan case. Refrigerate until set. Decorate with whirls of lightly whipped cream and the shreds of lemon rind.
Serves 3 to 4

Summer Buffet for Twenty

Curried cucumber soup (cold) /Liver pâté, Blue cheese quiche, Pink mushrooms, French bread, Garlic bread, Cold glazed bacon (see page 93), Rice salad, Greek-style, Platter salad with Celery seed dressing /Grape and banana vacherin, Compôte of peaches, Lemon sugar cookies

Beforehand

Curried cucumber soup
Make the day before and keep refrigerated, covered. Remove from the refrigerator about 30 minutes before serving, and garnish when serving.

Liver pâté
Make several days ahead; keep, covered, in the refrigerator.

Blue cheese quiche
Prepare and cook the pastry the day before. Complete the quiches during the afternoon of the party.

Pink mushrooms
Make the day before and keep, covered, in the refrigerator.

Garlic bread
Prepare in the morning of the party and wrap ready for heating through later.

Cold glazed bacon
Prepare two or three days ahead; keep, covered, in the refrigerator.

Rice salad
Make the day before and keep in a cool place or the refrigerator. Unmould about 2 hours before serving; leave in a cool place (not the refrigerator).

Platter salad
Prepare during the afternoon of the party. Prepare the dressing the day before.

Grape and banana vacherin
Make the meringue rounds several days ahead; foil-wrap. Assemble with cream and fruit just before the party.

Compôte of peaches
Prepare the day before, but don't add the almonds until just before serving.

Lemon sugar cookies
Make several days ahead. Keep in airtight container.

Liver pâté; Curried cucumber soup.

Curried Cucumber Soup

Metric	Imperial
150 g butter	5 oz butter
750 g onions, peeled and very finely chopped	1½ lb onions, peeled and very finely chopped
5 cucumbers	5 cucumbers
1 x 15 ml spoon mild curry powder	1 tablespoon mild curry powder
5 x 15 ml spoons plain flour	5 tablespoons plain flour
10 chicken stock cubes	10 chicken stock cubes
4 litres boiling water	7 pints boiling water
2 litres milk	3½ pints milk
Salt	Salt
Freshly ground black pepper	Freshly ground black pepper
Cucumber slices to garnish	Cucumber slices to garnish

Melt the butter in a large pan and fry the onions, without colouring, for 10 minutes. Add the cucumbers, grating them coarsely straight into the pan. Fry for a further 5 minutes. Stir in the curry powder and flour and cook for a few minutes.

Dissolve the stock cubes in the water and add to the pan, stirring. Bring to the boil. Cover, reduce the heat and simmer for 30 minutes.

Add the milk and reheat without boiling. Adjust the seasoning. Chill and serve cold with a garnish of wafer-thin slices of cucumber.

Liver Pâté

Metric	Imperial
225 g pigs' liver	8 oz pigs' liver
225 g calves' liver	8 oz calves' liver
500 g fat pork	1 lb fat pork
75 g onion, peeled and chopped	3 oz onion, peeled and chopped
1 garlic clove, crushed	1 garlic clove, crushed
Salt	Salt
Freshly ground black pepper	Freshly ground black pepper
150 ml dry white wine	¼ pint dry white wine
5 x 15 ml spoons brandy	5 tablespoons brandy
5 x 15 ml spoons olive oil	5 tablespoons olive oil
1 x 2.5 ml spoon dried thyme	½ teaspoon dried thyme
225 g streaky bacon rashers, rinds removed	8 oz streaky bacon rashers, rinds removed
2 eggs, beaten	2 eggs, beaten
100-125 g chicken livers, quartered	4 oz chicken livers, quartered
Juniper berries	Juniper berries
3 bay leaves	3 bay leaves
150 ml liquid aspic jelly	¼ pint liquid aspic jelly

Divide the liver and pork into small strips, discarding any skin and ducts. Place these in a bowl with the onion, garlic, seasoning, wine, brandy, oil and thyme. Cover and marinate overnight.

Stretch the rashers of bacon, using a blunt-edged knife, and use to line a 1.5 litre (2½ pint) capacity terrine dish, leaving the rashers hanging over the edge of the terrine. Drain the marinade from the other ingredients and reserve the liquid. Mince the liver mixture and return to the marinade with the eggs and chicken livers. Mix well. Turn into the lined dish. Draw the rashers over the top, cover and bake in a water bath in a preheated moderate oven (160°C/325°F, Gas Mark 3) for 1 hour. Lower the heat to cool (150°C/300°F, Gas Mark 2) and cook for a further 1¼ to 1½ hours or until firm.

Place a weight on the pâté and leave to cool overnight. Decorate with juniper berries, bay leaves and aspic for serving.

BLUE CHEESE QUICHE

Make two

Metric	Imperial
For the pastry:	**For the pastry:**
225 g plain flour	8 oz plain flour
150 g butter or margarine	5 oz butter or margarine
1 egg yolk	1 egg yolk
2 x 15 ml spoons water	2 tablespoons water
For the filling:	**For the filling:**
175 g onions, peeled and chopped	6 oz onions, peeled and chopped
175 g streaky bacon rashers, rinds removed, chopped	6 oz streaky bacon rashers, rinds removed, chopped
225 g Stilton cheese, crumbled	8 oz Stilton cheese, crumbled
2 eggs	2 eggs
1 egg yolk	1 egg yolk
150 ml double cream	$\frac{1}{4}$ pint double cream
150 ml milk	$\frac{1}{4}$ pint milk
Salt	Salt
Freshly ground black pepper	Freshly ground black pepper

Sift the flour into a bowl. Rub in the butter or margarine until the mixture resembles breadcrumbs, then bind with the egg yolk and water. Roll out and use to line a 24 cm (9½ inch) flan dish. Bake blind in a preheated moderately hot oven (200°C/400°F, Gas Mark 6) for about 25 minutes, or until the pastry is beginning to colour and the bottom is quite dry. Cool.

Meanwhile, fry the onions and bacon together until the fat runs and the onion is tender. Cool, then scatter into the pastry case. Sprinkle the cheese on top of the onion and bacon. Whisk the eggs and egg yolk with the cream, milk and seasoning. Pour into the flan case.

Bake in a preheated moderately hot oven (190°C/375°F, Gas Mark 5) for about 45 minutes or until golden brown and set, covering if necessary with foil or greaseproof paper to prevent over-browning.

PINK MUSHROOMS

Metric	Imperial
1 kg button mushrooms	2 lb button mushrooms
300 ml dry red wine	$\frac{1}{2}$ pint dry red wine
300 ml vegetable oil	$\frac{1}{2}$ pint vegetable oil
4 x 15 ml spoons red wine vinegar	4 tablespoons red wine vinegar
2 x 5 ml spoons sugar	2 teaspoons sugar
1 x 5 ml spoon dry mustard	1 teaspoon dry mustard
Few grains of cayenne	Few grains of cayenne
12 cocktail onions, finely chopped	12 cocktail onions, finely chopped
8 small pickled gherkins, finely chopped	8 small pickled gherkins, finely chopped
3 x 15 ml spoons chopped parsley	3 tablespoons chopped parsley
Salt	Salt
Freshly ground black pepper	Freshly ground black pepper
Chopped parsley to garnish	Chopped parsley to garnish

Trim the mushroom stems level with the caps. Simmer the whole mushrooms in the wine in a saucepan for about 15 minutes or until the wine evaporates and the mushrooms turn pink. Tip into a bowl. Shake together the remaining ingredients in a screwtop jar. Spoon over the warm mushrooms. Leave them to cool and chill well before serving, garnished with parsley.

Right: Blue cheese quiche; Garlic bread.

RICE SALAD, GREEK-STYLE

Metric	Imperial
900 g brown rice	2 lb brown rice
150 ml French dressing (see page 91)	$\frac{1}{4}$ pint French dressing (see page 91)
225 g onions, peeled and finely chopped	8 oz onions, peeled and finely chopped
1 green pepper, cored, seeded and chopped	1 green pepper, cored, seeded and chopped
1 red pepper, cored, seeded and chopped	1 red pepper, cored, seeded and chopped
4 celery stalks, trimmed and chopped	4 celery stalks, trimmed and chopped
1 x 397 g can pimientos, drained	1 x 14 oz can pimientos, drained
Black olives, stoned	Black olives, stoned

Cook the rice as directed on the packet. Drain the rice and, while still hot, pour over the dressing. Mix well. Add the onions, green and red peppers and celery. Chop all but two of the pimientos and stir into the rice mixture.

Brush two 1.5 litre (2½ pint) plain ring moulds with oil. Make a pattern on the bottom using the remainder of the pimientos, sliced and the black olives. Carefully spoon the rice mixture into the ring moulds. Cool to set, then turn out onto flat plates.

Makes 2 salads, each to serve 10

PLATTER SALAD

Prepare a salad of diced red and green eating apples, chopped walnuts and celery and dress with lemon juice. Arrange in the centre of a round dish. Surround with diced cucumber, sliced radishes and thinly sliced chicory. Serve with a dressing made with 150 ml (¼ pint) French dressing (see page 91) to which 1 x 5 ml spoon (1 teaspoon) each of celery seeds and creamed horseradish have been added.

Rice salad Greek-style; Pink mushrooms; Platter salad.

GRAPE AND BANANA VACHERIN

Make two

Metric	Imperial
6 egg whites	6 egg whites
350 g caster sugar	12 oz caster sugar
300 ml whipping cream, whipped	½ pint whipping cream, whipped
3 large bananas, sliced	3 large bananas, sliced
225 g black grapes, halved and pipped	8 oz black grapes, halved and pipped
Lemon juice	Lemon juice
Chocolate curls to decorate	Chocolate curls to decorate

Whisk four of the egg whites until stiff, then beat in 4 x 5 ml spoons (4 teaspoons) of the sugar and continue whisking until the mixture will stand up in stiff peaks. Fold in a further 200 g (7 oz) sugar. Pipe the mixture in two 25 cm (10 inch) rounds on non-stick paper-lined baking sheets, using a 1 cm (½ inch) plain nozzle. Dry in a preheated very cool oven (120°C/250°F, Gas Mark ½) for 1 hour.

Make up the remaining egg whites and sugar into a meringue mixture as above. Pipe a border of small meringues round the edge of one of the baked meringue rounds. Return this to the oven and dry both rounds for a further hour. Remove the paper and cool.

Sandwich the meringue rounds together with the whipped cream, bananas and grapes. Lightly brush any exposed pieces of banana with lemon juice to prevent discoloration. Serve as soon as possible, decorated with chocolate curls.

COMPÔTE OF PEACHES

Metric	Imperial
550 g sugar	1¼ lb sugar
1.5 litres water	2½ pints water
Piece of vanilla pod	Piece of vanilla pod
20 yellow flesh peaches, peeled, stoned and sliced	20 yellow flesh peaches, peeled, stoned and sliced
5 x 15 ml spoons lemon juice	5 tablespoons lemon juice
Flaked almonds	Flaked almonds

Dissolve the sugar in the water with the vanilla pod. Bring to the boil and boil for 3 minutes. Discard the vanilla pod and add the peach slices. Cook gently for 5 minutes. Remove the pan from the heat. Add the lemon juice and leave the fruit until cold.

Brown a few flaked almonds under the grill and sprinkle over the peaches in a serving dish. Serve with thin crisp biscuits or soft sponge fingers. (See Lemon sugar cookies, below.)

Note: To peel the peaches, place them in boiling water, count to 10, then plunge them into cold water. Carefully remove the skins.

LEMON SUGAR COOKIES

Metric	Imperial
225 g plain flour	8 oz plain flour
1 x 5 ml spoon baking powder	1 teaspoon baking powder
Pinch of salt	Pinch of salt
Pinch of grated nutmeg	Pinch of grated nutmeg
100 ml vegetable oil	4 fl oz vegetable oil
100 g caster sugar	4 oz caster sugar
1 egg	1 egg
Grated rind of 1 small lemon	Grated rind of 1 small lemon
Granulated sugar	Granulated sugar

Sift together the flour, baking powder, salt and nutmeg. Combine the oil and caster sugar in a bowl, then beat in the egg and lemon rind. Add the dry ingredients to the oil mixture. Mix well. Shape into balls about 2 cm (¾ inch) in diameter. Dip the tops of the balls into granulated sugar and place, sugar side up, on greased baking sheets, about 5 cm (2 inches) apart. Press the tops of the biscuits with the prongs of a fork to make a criss-cross pattern. Bake in a preheated moderately hot oven (190°C/375°F, Gas Mark 5) for 10 to 12 minutes. Cool on a wire rack. Makes 30

Lemon sugar cookies; Compôte of peaches; Grape and banana vacherin.

Slimmers' Special for Eight

Apple tuna salad/Swiss veal, Tossed green salad/Grape delight

BEFOREHAND

Apple tuna salad

Make up the salad about 1½ hours before serving time. The apple shouldn't discolour if you use sufficient lemon juice.

Swiss veal

This can be partly prepared, up to but not including the addition of the egg yolks and yogurt, the day before. To reheat when required, put the mixture in a casserole and cook in a preheated moderate oven (180°C/350°F, Gas Mark 4) for about 1 hour. Then add the egg yolks and yogurt and complete the preparation according to the recipe.

Tossed green salad

Prepare the vegetables and store in polythene bags in the refrigerator.

Grape delight

Halve and pip the grapes the day before; store in the refrigerator. Make up the sweet 1 hour before serving time.

APPLE TUNA SALAD

Metric	Imperial
2 x 198 g cans tuna, drained and flaked	2 x 7 oz cans tuna, drained and flaked
2 small green peppers, cored, seeded and chopped	2 small green peppers, cored, seeded and chopped
8 medium red-skinned apples	8 medium red-skinned apples
For the cheese dressing:	**For the cheese dressing:**
225 g cottage cheese	8 oz cottage cheese
Juice of 1 lemon	Juice of 1 lemon
Salt	Salt
Freshly ground black pepper	Freshly ground black pepper

Mix the tuna with the green peppers. Core the apples and scoop out the inside of each, leaving a 6 mm (¼ inch) wall. Chop the scooped-out apple and add to the tuna mixture.

Combine the cottage cheese, lemon juice and seasoning and sieve or blend until smooth and creamy. Add 1 to 2 x 15 ml spoons (1 to 2 tablespoons) to the tuna mixture and mix thoroughly. Pile into the apple shells and chill. Serve the rest of the dressing separately.

SWISS VEAL

Metric	Imperial
2 kg pie veal, cubed	4 lb pie veal, cubed
Seasoned flour	Seasoned flour
2 x 15 ml spoons cooking oil	2 tablespoons cooking oil
225 g carrots, peeled and diced	8 oz carrots, peeled and diced
225 g shallots, peeled and chopped	8 oz shallots, peeled and chopped
1 x 15 ml spoon lemon juice	1 tablespoon lemon juice
300 ml stock	½ pint stock
150 ml dry white wine	¼ pint dry white wine
1 bouquet garni	1 bouquet garni
4 egg yolks, beaten	4 egg yolks, beaten
300 ml unsweetened natural yogurt	½ pint unsweetened natural yogurt
Salt	Salt
Freshly ground black pepper	Freshly ground black pepper
Chopped parsley to garnish	Chopped parsley to garnish

Dust the veal lightly with the seasoned flour. Heat the oil and fry the veal until pale golden. Add the carrots, shallots, lemon juice, stock, wine and bouquet garni and simmer gently until the meat is tender – about 1½ hours. Alternatively, turn the mixture into a casserole and cook in a preheated moderate oven (180°C/350°F, Gas Mark 4) for about 1½ hours.

Mix the egg yolks with the yogurt. Add a little of the hot stock, then stir into the meat mixture and adjust the seasoning. Reheat gently without boiling and serve sprinkled with chopped parsley.

GRAPE DELIGHT

Metric	Imperial
3 egg whites	3 egg whites
450 ml apricot yogurt	¾ pint apricot yogurt
225 g black grapes, halved and seeded	8 oz black grapes, halved and seeded
225 g white grapes, halved and seeded	8 oz white grapes, halved and seeded

Whisk the egg whites until stiff and fold in the yogurt. Layer the yogurt and grapes into eight glasses. Top with grapes.

Above: Grape delight. Right: Apple tuna salad; Swiss veal.

COFFEE PARTIES

There are lots of good reasons for giving a coffee party; to welcome a new neighbour, or to say goodbye to an old one; to raise money for a favourite cause; or simply to be sociable and entertain friends. If it's to be a money-raising venture, it's a good idea to start planning ahead.

Biscuits, buns and cakes can all be made in advance and stored in airtight containers until they're needed. The home-made preserves and pickles in this chapter keep well – chutneys actually mature with keeping. Lemon curd, fudge and truffles all keep for 2 or 3 weeks. Label jars clearly – and put sweets and biscuits in transparent bags or in small boxes. Wrap them with cling film and stick a descriptive label on top.

The cakes, teabreads and other goodies in this chapter can be made for eating at the coffee morning – or for selling. If larger quantities than those indicated in the basic recipe are needed, make two or three batches, instead of doubling or trebling the ingredients.

COFFEE PARTY FOR TWELVE

Parkerhouse rolls with unsalted butter, honey, apricot jam, Salted twisters and Cheese crescents (see page 66; double the quantity), Malt bread with unsalted butter/Date streusel, Coffee battenberg, Cherry Madeira ring, Spiced carrot cake

COFFEE

The coffee should be piping hot when you serve it, accompanied by hot – but not boiled – milk. It must be fresh; if you can't get it freshly roasted and freshly ground, buy the coffee in flavour-sealed containers (cans or bags). Make it in the way you find most successful, whether it's in a jug, percolator, or cafetière, or whether you use the espresso or filter method.

For every 24 to 26 servings (allow 200 ml (⅓ pint) per serving) you'll need 275 to 350 g (10 to 12 oz) of fresh or instant coffee, 3.5 litres (6 pints) of water, and 1.75 litres (3 pints) of milk. Allow 500 g (1 lb) of sugar for these quantities. If you are using instant coffee and want to make it in bulk, allow 100 g (4 oz) to 3.5 litres (6 pints) of water.

If you make the coffee in advance – and this will almost certainly be necessary if you are to be prepared for most of your guests to arrive simultaneously – strain it after infusion and then reheat it, without boiling, when required. If you have, or can borrow, some large vacuum flasks or jugs, it's a good idea to fill them with freshly made coffee beforehand and to keep them topped up as the party progresses. Milk can be kept hot in this way, or in a double saucepan.

Malt bread; Parkerhouse rolls.

PARKERHOUSE ROLLS

Make two batches

Metric	Imperial
1 x 283 g packet white bread mix	1 x 10 oz packet white bread mix
2 x 15 ml spoons finely chopped fresh thyme	2 tablespoons finely chopped fresh thyme
200 ml water, hand hot	⅓ pint water, hand hot
Melted butter to glaze	Melted butter to glaze

Mix together the dry bread mix and chopped thyme and stir in the water. Mix the dough together in the bowl, then turn onto a lightly floured surface and knead for about 5 minutes. Roll out the dough to 1 cm (½ inch) thick. Cut out eight rounds with a 6.5 cm (2½ inch) plain cutter, re-rolling the dough as necessary. With the dull edge of the knife, make a crease just off-centre of each round. Brush with melted butter and fold over so that the larger part overlaps, pressing well together. Place on baking sheets, cover with oiled cling film and leave to rise in a warm place until doubled in size.

Brush again with melted butter and bake in a preheated very hot oven (230°C/450°F, Gas Mark 8) for 10 to 12 minutes. Transfer from baking sheets to a wire rack to cool. Eat fresh. (Any leftovers are delicious split and toasted.) Makes 8

MALT BREAD

Metric	Imperial
25 g fresh yeast	1 oz fresh yeast
About 350 ml tepid water	About 13 fl oz tepid water
450 g plain flour	1 lb plain flour
1 x 5 ml spoon salt	1 teaspoon salt
3 x 15 ml spoons malt extract	3 tablespoons malt extract
2 x 15 ml spoons black treacle	2 tablespoons black treacle
25 g butter or margarine	1 oz butter or margarine
225 g sultanas, cleaned	8 oz sultanas, cleaned
For the glaze (optional):	**For the glaze (optional):**
1 x 15 ml spoon sugar	1 tablespoon sugar
1 x 15 ml spoon water	1 tablespoon water

Cream the yeast and water together. Sift the flour and salt into a mixing bowl. Warm the malt extract, treacle and butter or margarine until just melted, then stir into the flour with the yeast liquid. Combine well. Add the sultanas and beat for 5 minutes.

Divide the mixture between two greased 20.5 x 10 cm (8 x 4 inch) top measurement loaf tins. Cover and leave to rise in a warm place for 45 minutes, or until the dough almost fills the tins.

Bake in a preheated moderately hot oven (200°C/400°F, Gas Mark 6) for 40 to 45 minutes. When cooked the loaves may be brushed with the sugar and water glaze. Makes 2 loaves

Date Streusel

Make two

Metric	Imperial
125 g shortcrust pastry, made with 125 g plain flour and 60 g fat	4 oz shortcrust pastry, made with 4 oz plain flour and 2 oz fat
350 g stoned dates, chopped	12 oz stoned dates, chopped
3 x 15 ml spoons lemon juice	3 tablespoons lemon juice
4 x 15 ml spoons soft dark brown sugar	4 tablespoons soft dark brown sugar
1 x 2.5 ml spoon bicarbonate of soda	½ teaspoon bicarbonate of soda
6 x 15 ml spoons water	6 tablespoons water
75 g plain flour	3 oz plain flour
1 x 2.5 ml spoon mixed spice	½ teaspoon mixed spice
40 g butter or block margarine	1½ oz butter or block margarine
25 g granulated sugar	1 oz granulated sugar
Grated rind of 1 lemon	Grated rind of 1 lemon

Bottom-line a 21.5 cm (8½ inch) straight-sided sandwich tin with greaseproof paper. Roll out the dough and use to line the tin. Prick with a fork and bake blind in a preheated moderately hot oven (200°C/400°F, Gas Mark 6) for 15 minutes.

Place the dates in a small saucepan with the lemon juice, brown sugar, bicarbonate of soda and water. Heat gently to dissolve the sugar and soften the dates. Cool.

Sift the flour with the spice. Rub in the fat, then stir in the granulated sugar and lemon rind. Spread the date mixture in the pastry case and sprinkle the crumble mixture on top. Bake in a preheated moderately hot oven (190°C/375°F, Gas Mark 5) for about 25 minutes, or until golden brown. Cool in the tin.

Coffee battenberg; Date streusel.

Coffee Battenberg

Metric	Imperial
175 g butter or margarine	6 oz butter or margarine
175 g caster sugar	6 oz caster sugar
3 eggs, beaten	3 eggs, beaten
175 g self-raising flour, sifted	6 oz self-raising flour, sifted
4 x 5 ml spoons coffee essence (Camp)	4 teaspoons coffee essence (Camp)
1 x 15 ml spoon milk	1 tablespoon milk
10 x 15 ml spoons ginger marmalade or apricot jam	10 tablespoons ginger marmalade or apricot jam
2 x 226 g packets marzipan	2 x 8 oz packets marzipan
Crystallised ginger, chopped, to decorate (optional)	Crystallised ginger, chopped, to decorate (optional)

Grease a 20 cm (8 inch) square cake tin or two 24 by 11 cm (9½ by 4½ inch) loaf tins – top measurement. Divide the square tin in half by bottom-lining with foil, making a pleat down the centre. Support by cardboard inside the pleat.

Cream the fat and sugar well together and gradually beat in the eggs, keeping the mixture fairly stiff. Lightly beat in the flour. Divide the mixture in half. Fold the coffee essence into one portion and the milk into the other.

Spoon one flavour into each side of the tin (or separate loaf tins). Bake in a preheated moderately hot oven (190°C/375°F, Gas Mark 5) for about 30 minutes. Turn out onto a wire rack and cool.

Trim each piece of cake and divide in half lengthways. Sandwich alternately together with half of the marmalade or jam. Measure the Battenberg lengthways, and also add up the total of the four sides. Cut out a sheet of non-stick paper to these measurements and cut out the marzipan on top to fit it exactly. Spread the remaining marmalade or jam over the marzipan and wrap closely around the cake. Pinch the top edges and press in the crystallised ginger.

CHERRY MADEIRA RING

Make two

Metric	Imperial
125 g butter	4 oz butter
125 g caster sugar	4 oz caster sugar
Grated rind and juice of 1 large juicy lemon	Grated rind and juice of 1 large juicy lemon
2 large eggs, beaten	2 large eggs, beaten
175 g glacé cherries, halved	6 oz glacé cherries, halved
175 g plain flour	6 oz plain flour
1 x 5 ml spoon baking powder	1 teaspoon baking powder
125 g icing sugar	4 oz icing sugar

Cream the butter, caster sugar and lemon rind together until really light. Beat in the eggs, little by little, keeping the mixture stiff. Mix 125 g (4 oz) of the cherries with the flour and baking powder sifted together. Fold the flour and cherries lightly into the cream ingredients with 2 x 15 ml spoons (2 tablespoons) lemon juice. Turn into a greased 1.5 litre (2½ pint) plain ring mould. Bake in a preheated moderate oven (160°C/325°F, Gas Mark 3) for about 45 minutes, or until firm to the touch. Turn out onto a wire rack to cool.

Dissolve the sifted icing sugar in 1 to 2 x 15 ml spoons (1 to 2 tablespoons) lemon juice to give a coating consistency. Drizzle over the cake. Decorate with the remaining cherries before the icing sets.

Spiced carrot cake.

SPICED CARROT CAKE

Metric	Imperial
450 g wholemeal flour	1 lb wholemeal flour
Large pinch of salt	Large pinch of salt
1 x 2.5 ml spoon bicarbonate of soda	½ teaspoon bicarbonate of soda
1 x 15 ml spoon ground cinnamon	1 tablespoon ground cinnamon
1 x 2.5 ml spoon grated nutmeg	½ teaspoon grated nutmeg
1 x 1.25 ml spoon ground cloves	¼ teaspoon ground cloves
125 g butter	4 oz butter
500 g juicy carrots, peeled and grated	1 lb juicy carrots, peeled and grated
125 g dark brown sugar	4 oz dark brown sugar
75 g clear honey	3 oz clear honey
75 g treacle	3 oz treacle
About 2 x 15 ml spoons milk	About 2 tablespoons milk
2 x 15 ml spoons demerara sugar	2 tablespoons demerara sugar

Grease and bottom-line a 20 cm (8 inch) cake tin. Mix together the flour, salt, bicarbonate of soda and spices in a large bowl. Rub in the butter, then stir in the carrots. Warm the sugar, honey and treacle together over a low heat. Pour into a well in the centre of the dry ingredients. Mix to a stiff dropping consistency with the milk and turn into the prepared cake tin. Sprinkle with the demerara sugar and bake in a preheated moderately hot oven (190 °C/375°F, Gas Mark 5) for 1 to 1¼ hours until a skewer inserted in the centre comes out clean and dry. Turn out and cool on a wire rack.
Makes a 20 cm (8 inch) cake

Cherry Madeira ring, which may also be baked in a 1 kg (2 lb) loaf tin.

COFFEE PARTY FOR TWENTY

*Date and apple teabread, Marmalade teabread, Chocolate butter crunch, Boston brownies, Cornish fairings,
Ginger fridgies, Honey whirls*

DATE AND APPLE TEABREAD

Make two

Metric	Imperial
225 g cooking apples, peeled, cored and sliced	8 oz cooking apples, peeled, cored and sliced
Grated rind of 1 lemon	Grated rind of 1 lemon
3 x 15 ml spoons lemon juice	3 tablespoons lemon juice
125 g stoned dates, chopped	4 oz stoned dates, chopped
125 g butter or block margarine	4 oz butter or block margarine
125 g soft dark brown sugar	4 oz soft dark brown sugar
2 eggs	2 eggs
225 g self-raising flour, sifted	8 oz self-raising flour, sifted

Put the apples into a heavy-based pan. Add the lemon rind and juice, cover tightly and stew until the apples are soft. Beat the apple purée until smooth (or use a potato masher) and, while still warm, stir in the dates. Cool.

Cream the butter or margarine and sugar together thoroughly. Beat in the eggs, flour and apple mixture until evenly mixed. Turn into a greased and bottom-lined 1.2 litre (2 pint) loaf tin. Bake in a preheated moderate oven (180°C/350°F, Gas Mark 4) for about 1 hour or until firm to the touch.

Turn out of the tin and cool on a wire rack. Wrap and keep for at least a day before serving, sliced and buttered.

Note: The teabread should have a cracked, rounded top.

MARMALADE TEABREAD

Make two

Metric	Imperial
225 g plain flour	8 oz plain flour
1.5 x 5 ml spoons baking powder	1½ teaspoons baking powder
1 x 2.5 ml spoon bicarbonate of soda	½ teaspoon bicarbonate of soda
	1 teaspoon salt
1 x 5 ml spoon salt	2 oz block margarine
50 g block margarine	4 oz demerara sugar

100 g demerara sugar	¼ pint milk
150 ml milk	1 egg, beaten
1 egg, beaten	4 tablespoons marmalade
4 x 15 ml spoons marmalade	5 oz seedless raisins, cleaned
150 g seedless raisins, cleaned	2 oz walnuts, chopped
50 g walnuts, chopped	

Grease and line a 23 by 11.5 cm (9 by 4½ inch) loaf tin (top measurements). Sift together the flour, baking powder, bicarbonate of soda and salt. Rub in the margarine and add the sugar. Combine the milk, beaten egg and marmalade and stir lightly into the batter, followed by the raisins and walnuts. Turn the batter into the prepared tin. Level the top and bake in a preheated moderate oven (180°C/350°F, Gas Mark 4) for about 1¼ hours. Cool for 10 minutes in the tin, then turn out and cool on a wire rack. Serve thickly sliced and buttered.

CHOCOLATE BUTTER CRUNCH

Metric	Imperial
125 g butter	4 oz butter
50 g caster sugar	2 oz caster sugar
125 g plain flour, sifted	4 oz plain flour, sifted
50 g ground rice	2 oz ground rice
Finely grated rind of 1 orange	Finely grated rind of 1 orange
50 g plain chocolate-flavoured cake covering, finely grated	2 oz plain chocolate-flavoured cake covering, finely grated

Grated chocolate and orange on a rich butter base make deliciously different shortbread. Cream the butter until soft, then gradually beat in the sugar until the mixture is light and creamy. Mix together the flour, ground rice and orange rind, then work into the creamed mixture with the chocolate. Knead lightly until the mixture forms a stiff dough. Pat into a 29 by 19 cm (11½ by 7½ inch) Swiss roll tin. Bake in a preheated moderate oven (160°C/325°F, Gas Mark 3) for 35 to 40 minutes until crisp and lightly browned. Cut into 16 fingers and leave in the tin to cool. Makes 16

Date and apple teabread; Marmalade teabread.

Chocolate butter crunch.

BOSTON BROWNIES

Metric	Imperial
4 x 15 ml spoons pure corn oil	4 tablespoons pure corn oil
50 g plain chocolate	2 oz plain chocolate
175 g caster sugar	6 oz caster sugar
75 g self-raising flour	2½ oz self-raising flour
1 x 1.25 ml spoon salt	¼ teaspoon salt
2 eggs, beaten	2 eggs, beaten
1 x 2.5 ml spoon vanilla essence	½ teaspoon vanilla essence
50 g walnuts, roughly chopped	2 oz walnuts, roughly chopped

Lightly oil and flour a 20 cm (8 inch) square tin. In a heatproof bowl over hot water, heat the oil and chocolate until melted. Sift together the dry ingredients and, off the heat, add to the chocolate mixture with the remaining ingredients. Beat well, then turn into the prepared tin. Bake in a preheated moderate oven (180°C/350°F, Gas Mark 4) for about 35 minutes. Leave in the tin to cool, then cut into squares or finger-shaped pieces. Makes about 24

CORNISH FAIRINGS

Make two batches

Metric	Imperial
100 g plain flour	4 oz plain flour
Pinch of salt	Pinch of salt
1 x 5 ml spoon baking powder	1 teaspoon baking powder
1 x 5 ml spoon bicarbonate of soda	1 teaspoon bicarbonate of soda
1 x 5 ml spoon ground ginger	1 teaspoon ground ginger
1 x 2.5 ml spoon mixed spice	½ teaspoon mixed spice
50 g block margarine	2 oz block margarine
50 g caster sugar	2 oz caster sugar
3 x 15 ml spoons golden syrup	3 tablespoons golden syrup

Sift the flour, salt, baking powder, bicarbonate of soda and the spices into a bowl. Rub in the margarine, then add the sugar. Warm the syrup and work into the flour to give a fairly stiff mixture. Roll into small balls and arrange, well spaced, on greased baking sheets. Bake fairly near the top of a preheated moderately hot oven (200°C/400°F, Gas Mark 6) for 5 to 8 minutes. Cool on a wire rack. Makes about 24

GINGER FRIDGIES

Make two batches

Metric	Imperial
225 g plain flour	8 oz plain flour
1 x 2.5 ml spoon bicarbonate of soda	½ teaspoon bicarbonate of soda
1 x 2.5 ml spoon salt	½ teaspoon salt
1 x 5 ml spoon ground ginger	1 teaspoon ground ginger
100 ml pure corn oil	4 fl oz pure corn oil
100 g soft brown sugar	4 oz soft brown sugar
100 g caster sugar	4 oz caster sugar
1 egg	1 egg
1 x 2.5 ml spoon vanilla essence	½ teaspoon vanilla essence
50 g flaked almonds	2 oz flaked almonds

Sift together the dry ingredients. Beat the oil, sugars, egg and essence together, then add to the dry ingredients with the nuts. Work together to give a manageable dough. Shape into a roll and wrap in greaseproof paper. Chill in the refrigerator for several hours, or overnight. Next day, or when required, cut the roll into 6 mm (¼ inch) slices and place them, widely spaced, on greased baking sheets. Bake in a preheated moderately hot oven (200°C/400°F, Gas Mark 6) for 10 to 12 minutes. Cool on a wire rack. Makes about 36

HONEY WHIRLS

Make two batches

Metric	Imperial
1 x 212 g packet frozen puff pastry, thawed	1 x 7½ oz packet frozen puff pastry, thawed
50 g margarine	2 oz margarine
4 x 15 ml spoons thick honey	4 tablespoons thick honey
Pinch of salt	Pinch of salt
50 g salted peanuts or walnut pieces, finely chopped	2 oz salted peanuts or walnut pieces, finely chopped

Roll out the dough thinly to an oblong 25 by 30 cm (10 by 12 inches). Mix together the remaining ingredients and spread evenly all over the surface. Roll up the dough from both the long edges so that the two rolls meet in the middle. Cut the roll into 14 even-sized pieces. Place, cut sides down, in an 18 cm (7½ inch) sandwich tin which has been greased and bottom-lined with non-stick paper. Bake in a preheated very hot oven (220°C/450°F, Gas Mark 8) for 20 minutes, or until brown and crisp. (The centre will be soft, but will harden on cooling.) Turn out immediately onto a plate, and pull apart into sections when cooler. Makes about 14

Left: Cornish fairings; Ginger fridgies; Boston brownies.
Below: Honey whirls.

BRING AND BUY IDEAS

CHERRY FUDGE

Metric	Imperial
900 g caster sugar	2 lb caster sugar
600 ml milk	1 pint milk
2 x 5 ml spoons powdered glucose	2 teaspoons powdered glucose
100 g butter	4 oz butter
100 g glacé cherries, chopped	4 oz glacé cherries, chopped
Vanilla essence	Vanilla essence

Butter a 23 cm (9 inch) square toffee tin. Dissolve the sugar in the milk in a large heavy-based saucepan. When completely dissolved, stir in the glucose and butter. Bring to the boil and boil gently until the temperature reaches 125°C/240°F. Add the cherries and a few drops of vanilla essence.

Stand the saucepan in cold water and beat the mixture until it turns thick and creamy. Pour at once into the buttered tin. Mark into squares when half set and leave until set. Makes 1 kg (2¼ lb)

Note: Make this a week ahead and leave wrapped. Cut into squares and put into polythene bags a day before the sale.

CHOCOLATE TRUFFLES

Metric	Imperial
225 g plain chocolate, grated	8 oz plain chocolate, grated
1 small can evaporated milk	1 small can evaporated milk
1 x 175 g packet trifle sponges, crumbled	1 x 6 oz packet trifle sponges, crumbled
65 g ground almonds	2½ oz ground almonds
350 g icing sugar, sifted	12 oz icing sugar, sifted
1-2 x 15 ml spoons rum	1-2 tablespoons rum
Chocolate vermicelli or desiccated coconut to decorate	Chocolate vermicelli or desiccated coconut to decorate

Put the chocolate and milk in a small saucepan and heat gently to melt the chocolate. Off the heat, stir in the remaining ingredients except the vermicelli or coconut. Allow the mixture to cool. Shape the mixture into bite-size balls and roll in vermicelli or coconut, or press into rigid foil sweet cases. Makes about 60

Note: Make up to a week ahead and store, covered, in the refrigerator.

MERINGUE SHELLS

Metric	Imperial
3 egg whites	3 egg whites
150 g caster sugar	6 oz caster sugar

Make these from the whites left over when you've used the yolks in biscuits and other goodies. Pack them by the half-dozen or dozen in polythene bags.

Line a baking sheet with non-stick paper. Whisk the egg whites until stiff, then whisk in half the sugar until the mixture becomes stiff again. Fold in the remaining sugar. Spoon into small heaps – or use a large star vegetable nozzle – keeping them well apart, on the baking sheet. Bake in a preheated very cool oven (130°C/250°F, Gas Mark ½) for 1½ to 2 hours or until dry. Leave to cool on a rack.
Makes 18 to 24 (depending on size)

Right: Meringues. Far right: Lemon honey curd; Cherry fudge; Chocolate truffles; Lemon and apple chutney.

Note: Preserve fruits and vegetables in season for selling later. Always use scrupulously clean pots. Wash them in very hot water and dry them in a warm oven. Pots should be warm when filled.

LEMON AND APPLE CHUTNEY

Metric	Imperial
2 lemons	2 lemons
300 ml cider vinegar	½ pint cider vinegar
6 x 15 ml spoons thin honey	6 tablespoons thin honey
225 g granulated sugar	8 oz granulated sugar
1 x 2.5 ml spoon ground ginger	½ teaspoon ground ginger
225 g cooking apples, peeled, cored and sliced	8 oz cooking apples, peeled, cored and sliced
100 g onion, peeled and thinly sliced	4 oz onion, peeled and thinly sliced
25 g sultanas, cleaned	1 oz sultanas, cleaned

Halve the lemons lengthways, slice them thinly and discard the pips. Put the lemon slices in a pan, add water to cover and simmer, covered, for 45 minutes or until tender. Remove the slices from the liquid and reserve. Add the vinegar, honey, sugar and ginger to the liquid and heat gently until the sugar is dissolved.

Add the apples, onion, sultanas and cooked lemon slices and bring to the boil. Simmer uncovered for 20 to 25 minutes until the onion is soft and the liquid well reduced.

Pot and cover in the usual way with vinegar-proof covers. To allow the chutney to mature, store in a cool, dry place for 2 to 3 months before eating. Makes about 1 kg (2 lb)

LEMON HONEY CURD

Metric	Imperial
Finely grated rind and juice of 4 lemons	Finely grated rind and juice of 4 lemons
5 eggs, beaten	5 eggs, beaten
100 g butter	4 oz butter
225 g thick honey	8 oz thick honey
50 g caster sugar	2 oz caster sugar

Put all the ingredients into the top of a double boiler or into a deep heatproof bowl which fits over a saucepan. Place over a pan of simmering water and stir until the sugar has dissolved and the curd is thick enough to coat the back of a wooden spoon; this will take from 10 to 20 minutes. Do not allow the curd to boil or it will curdle. Stir continuously. Pour the curd into small pots and cover as for jam. Store in a cool place, preferably the refrigerator. Keeps about 1 month. Makes about 1 kg (2 lb)

Note: There should be 175 ml (6 fl oz) lemon juice, so squeeze another lemon, if necessary.

Lemon and
Apple

Lemon + apple
Chutney

PINEAPPLE RELISH

Metric	Imperial
3 x 825 g cans pineapple	3 x 1 lb 13 oz cans pineapple
6 dried chillies, crushed	6 dried chillies, crushed
3 large garlic cloves, crushed	3 large garlic cloves, crushed
40 g mustard seeds	1½ oz mustard seeds
6 pieces of root ginger	6 pieces of root ginger
1.5 x 5 ml spoons ground mace	1½ teaspoons ground mace
1 x 5 ml spoon turmeric	1 teaspoon turmeric
450 ml white wine vinegar	¾ pint white wine vinegar
1 x 15 ml spoon salt	1 tablespoon salt

A slightly hot relish, this is good with ham, cold bacon or roast chicken.

Drain the pineapple, reserving 450 ml (¾ pint) of the syrup. Purée the fruit, with the measured syrup, in small amounts, to a medium-coarse texture. Put the chillies, garlic, mustard seeds and ginger in a muslin bag.

Put the puréed pineapple, muslin bag of spices, mace, turmeric, vinegar and salt in a pan and boil gently, stirring occasionally, until there is no free liquid. Discard the muslin bag. Pot into warm jars and seal with vinegar-proof covers. Makes six 225 g (8 oz) jars

BREAD AND BUTTER PICKLE

Metric	Imperial
6 large cucumbers, cut into chunks	6 large cucumbers, cut into chunks
750 g onions, peeled and thinly sliced	1½ lb onions, peeled and thinly sliced
6 x 15 ml spoons salt	6 tablespoons salt
1.2 litres distilled white vinegar	2 pints distilled white vinegar
350 g sugar	12 oz sugar
2 x 5 ml spoons celery seeds	2 teaspoons celery seeds
2 x 5 ml spoons mustard seeds	2 teaspoons mustard seeds

This pickle is especially good with English farmhouse Cheddar or Cheshire or cream cheese, wholemeal bread and country butter.

Put the cucumbers, onions and salt in a bowl. Toss and leave to stand for 1 hour. Pour off the brine, rinse well and drain.

Heat the vinegar, sugar and seeds and boil for 3 minutes. Pack the vegetables in jars. Add the hot vinegar mixture to cover and seal at once with vinegar-proof covers. Makes six 450 g (1 lb) jars

Bread and butter pickle.

Pineapple relish; Apple-mint jelly.

APPLE-MINT JELLY

Metric	Imperial
3 kg cooking apples, cut into pieces	6 lb cooking apples, cut into pieces
1.2 litres water	2 pints water
225 g fresh mint with stalks	8 oz fresh mint with stalks
750 g sugar	1½ lb sugar
175 ml lemon juice	6 fl oz lemon juice
900 ml distilled white vinegar	1½ pints distilled white vinegar
Green food colouring	Green food colouring

Traditional with lamb, this is a good way of using large windfall apples. Put the apples and water in a large pan and cook them to a pulp. Strain through a jelly bag. Boil the strained liquid for 15 minutes with half the mint, then remove the mint. Add the sugar, lemon juice and vinegar to the liquid and stir to dissolve the sugar. Bring to a fast rolling boil and boil for about 20 minutes or until setting point (110°C/222°F) is reached.

To test without a thermometer, spoon a little jelly onto a saucer, cool, then push it gently with your finger. It should wrinkle. If it does not, return to the heat and continue boiling and testing.

Stir in the rest of the mint leaves, chopped, and the green colouring. Cool the jelly until the mint is suspended. Pot and cover as for jam. Makes nine 225 g (8 oz) jars

SPICED PEPPER CHUTNEY

Metric	Imperial
500 g green peppers, cored, seeded and chopped	1 lb green peppers, cored, seeded and chopped
500 g onions, peeled and chopped	1 lb onions, peeled and chopped
1 kg tomatoes, quartered	2 lb tomatoes, quartered
1 kg cooking apples, peeled, cored and chopped	2 lb cooking apples, peeled, cored and chopped
225 g demerara sugar	8 oz demerara sugar
1 x 5 ml spoon ground allspice	1 teaspoon ground allspice
450 ml malt vinegar	¾ pint malt vinegar
1 x 5 ml spoon peppercorns	1 teaspoon peppercorns
1 x 2.5 ml spoon mustard seeds	½ teaspoon mustard seeds

Put the green peppers, onions, tomatoes, apples, sugar, allspice and vinegar in a large pan and stir well. Tie the peppercorns and mustard seeds in muslin and put in the pan. Bring to the boil and simmer, uncovered, for about 1½ hours or until well reduced. Discard the muslin bag. Pot and seal. Makes 2.3 kg (5 lb)

CORN RELISH

Metric	Imperial
6 ripe corn cobs, trimmed	6 ripe corn cobs, trimmed
550 g white cabbage, cored	1¼ lb white cabbage, cored
2 medium onions, peeled	2 medium onions, peeled
2 red peppers, cored and seeded	2 red peppers, cored and seeded
2 x 5 ml spoons salt	2 teaspoons salt
2 x 5 ml spoons plain flour	2 teaspoons plain flour
1 x 2.5 ml spoon turmeric	½ teaspoon turmeric
175 g granulated sugar	6 oz granulated sugar
2 x 5 ml spoons dry mustard	2 teaspoons dry mustard
600 ml distilled white vinegar	1 pint distilled white vinegar

Blanch the corn in boiling water for 3 minutes. Drain and cut the corn kernels away from the cobs. Coarsely mince the cabbage, onions and peppers. Mix the salt, flour, turmeric, sugar and mustard in a saucepan and gradually stir in the vinegar. Bring to the boil and add the minced vegetables and corn kernels. Simmer, stirring occasionally, for 30 minutes. Pour at once into hot jars. Cover with vinegar-proof paper. Makes seven 450 g (1 lb) jars

RASPBERRY CONSERVE

Metric	Imperial
2 kg raspberries	4 lb raspberries
2 kg sugar	4 lb sugar
A little butter	A little butter

Simmer the raspberries gently in a large pan in their own juice for about 15 minutes. Add the sugar, stir until dissolved, then bring to a fast rolling boil. Add a small knob of butter and boil until setting point (110°C/220°F) is reached – in about 10 minutes. To test for setting point, see Apple mint jelly above. Don't overboil. Pot as for jam. Makes about 3.2 kg (7 lb)

Below: Corn relish; Spiced pepper chutney; Raspberry conserve.

TEA PARTIES

Tea parties may be family affairs, get-togethers for friends or neighbours, a pleasant way of holding an informal committee meeting, or an enjoyable setting for a money-raising event.

If you are serving sandwiches, keep them small and dainty – we give you ideas for fillings later in the chapter. But more substantial savouries, some hot, based on bread rolls or scone mixes, will be welcome too. Provide Indian and China tea with lemon slices as well as milk and sugar.

If you are catering for a fairly large number of people, hand round the sandwiches and other goodies on trays lined with doilies or paper napkins; more varieties can be attractively presented that way. Label sandwiches with sandwich flags.

It's a good idea, if you are combining your tea party with a bring-and-buy sale, to make an extra supply of the cakes, biscuits and teabreads which you are serving, for your guests to buy and take home. Our choice of recipes will give you tempting ideas for tea parties of all kinds.

SANDWICHES AND SANDWICH FILLINGS

If you buy uncut sandwich loaves, you can control the thickness of the slices (and slicing is considerably simplified) if you use an electric carving knife! A large loaf, about 800 g (28 oz), gives 20 to 24 slices. A small loaf, about 400 g (14 oz), gives 10 to 12 slices. A long sandwich loaf, about 1.5 kg (3½ lb) gives 50 slices. About 100 g (4 oz) butter or margarine will be needed for spreading 10 to 12 sandwiches, and 225 g (8 oz) for bread rolls.

Ring the changes on different types of white bread – brown, white, wholemeal, granary, rye and so on, varying them with rolls on occasions.

Fillings should be well flavoured, so that they are not overwhelmed by the double layer of bread and butter. They must also be easy to spread or arrange. Don't use anything very moist, unless the sandwiches are to be eaten at once, or the filling will soak into the bread, making it soggy.

If you are using bread other than a sandwich loaf, pair the slices accurately to give a neat appearance. Stack up the made sandwiches and cut them in halves or quarters (after first removing the crusts). Use a really sharp knife. Wrap the sandwiches in polythene, aluminium foil or greaseproof paper, or put them in a plastic box. Store in a cool place until they are needed.

Below: A variety of sandwich fillings and different types of bread.
Right: Cheese flakies; Cheese toast racks.

FILLINGS

Shelled cooked shrimp, chopped celery, shredded pineapple and mayonnaise. Cream cheese, chopped walnuts and seedless raisins. Minced cooked chicken, minced cooked ham and finely chopped pineapple. Chopped cooked ham, sliced hard-boiled egg and chopped pickled gherkin. Cream cheese, chopped celery and chopped green pepper. Chopped cooked tongue, mayonnaise, pinch of curry powder and chopped hard-boiled egg. Flaked canned crabmeat, chopped avocado and mayonnaise. Canned pâté and thinly sliced cucumber.

Cut the sandwiches into quarters or fancy shapes after removing the crusts – triangles, rounds and fingers. For an attractive effect, use brown and white bread together.

CHEESE TOAST RACKS

Metric	Imperial
1 x 283 g packet white bread mix	1 x 10 oz packet white bread mix
50 g mature Cheddar cheese, finely grated	2 oz mature Cheddar cheese, finely grated
2 x 15 ml spoons Parmesan cheese	2 tablespoons Parmesan cheese
200 ml warm water	$\frac{1}{3}$ pint warm water
40 g butter	$1\frac{1}{2}$ oz butter
1 x 2.5 ml spoon made mustard	$\frac{1}{2}$ teaspoon made mustard

Tip the bread mix into a bowl. Add the cheeses and mix with the warm water, according to the packet instructions. Knead for 5 minutes. Cut the dough in half, knead lightly and roll out each half to a 23 cm (9 inch) square.

Melt the butter with the mustard and brush half over the squares. Cut each square into 5 strips and stack these on top of each other. With a sharp knife, cut both stacks into four. Hold each quarter, cut side uppermost, and pinch the bases together. Press down well into greased deep bun tins. Prove, covered, in a warm place for about 45 minutes or until doubled in size.

Brush with the remaining butter mixture and bake in a preheated hot oven (220°C/425°F, Gas Mark 7) for about 25 minutes or until they sound hollow when tapped. Makes 8

CHEESE FLAKIES

Metric	Imperial
15 g fresh yeast	$\frac{1}{2}$ oz fresh yeast
5 x 15 ml spoons warm water	5 tablespoons warm water
25 g lard	1 oz lard
225 g plain flour, sifted	8 oz plain flour, sifted
1 x 2.5 ml spoon salt	$\frac{1}{2}$ teaspoon salt
1 egg, beaten	1 egg, beaten
125 g butter, softened	5 oz butter, softened
75 g Gruyère cheese	3 oz Gruyère cheese
Beaten egg to glaze	Beaten egg to glaze
Poppy seeds	Poppy seeds
1 x 112 g can sardines, drained	1 x $4\frac{3}{8}$ oz can sardines, drained
Grated Parmesan cheese	Grated Parmesan cheese
2 firm tomatoes, sliced	2 firm tomatoes, sliced

Mix the yeast with the water. Rub the lard into the flour and salt, then stir in the yeast mixture and egg. Mix and knead to a soft dough. Place in an oiled polythene bag and leave for 10 minutes in a cool place. Shape the butter into an oblong 23 by 7.5 cm (9 by 3 inches).

Roll out the dough to a 25 cm (10 inch) square. Place the butter in the centre. Fold the dough sides over and seal the top and bottom. Roll out to a 38 x 12.5 cm (15 x 5 inch) oblong. Fold the top third down and the bottom third up. Rest the dough for 10 minutes.

Repeat the process twice, then rest the dough for 30 minutes.

Divide the dough in half. Roll out one half to a 25 cm (10 inch) square. Cut into four squares, then halve each diagonally. Divide 50 g (2 oz) of the Gruyère cheese into eight cubes. Place a cube at the base of each dough triangle. Roll up into crescents. Egg-glaze and sprinkle with poppy seeds.

Roll out the remaining dough to a 30 x 20 cm (12 by 8 inch) oblong. Cut into six 10 cm (4 inch) squares. Place 3 sardines diagonally across each of three squares. Fold the corners over. Glaze and sprinkle with Parmesan. Use the tomatoes in the remaining three squares. Glaze and sprinkle with the remaining Gruyère cheese, grated. Leave, lightly covered, on baking sheets in a warm place for 20 minutes.

Bake in a preheated hot oven (220°C/425°F, Gas Mark 7) for 10 to 15 minutes. Cool on a rack. Makes 14

FROSTED HAZELNUT LAYER CAKE

Metric	Imperial
175 g plain flour	6 oz plain flour
2 x 5 ml spoons baking powder	2 teaspoons baking powder
225 g caster sugar	8 oz caster sugar
50 g demerara sugar	2 oz demerara sugar
50 g browned hazelnuts, chopped	2 oz browned hazelnuts, chopped
Finely grated rind of 1 lemon	Finely grated rind of 1 lemon
2 eggs, separated	2 eggs, separated
3 x 15 ml spoons vegetable oil	3 tablespoons vegetable oil
120 ml water	4 fl oz water
1 egg white	1 egg white
2 x 15 ml spoons lemon juice	2 tablespoons lemon juice
Pinch of cream of tartar	Pinch of cream of tartar
40 g butter, softened	1½ oz butter, softened

Grease and bottom-line two straight-sided 18 cm (7 inch) sandwich tins. Sift the flour and baking powder into a large mixing bowl. Stir in 50 g (2 oz) of the caster sugar, the demerara sugar, 40 g (1½ oz) of the nuts and the lemon rind. Whisk the egg yolks with the oil and water and stir into the dry ingredients. Beat well. Whisk the two egg whites until stiff and fold into the cake mixture. Turn into the prepared tins and bake in a preheated moderately hot oven (200°C/400°F, Gas Mark 6) for about 25 minutes. Turn out and cool on wire racks.

Split each cake into two layers. Whisk the remaining caster sugar, the egg white, lemon juice and cream of tartar in a deep heatproof bowl over a pan of simmering water until the mixture stands in stiff peaks. Whisk off the heat until cool, then beat into the softened butter. Sandwich the cake layers with the lemon icing, swirling the final layer of icing over the top. Decorate with the remaining nuts. Makes an 18 cm (7 inch) sandwich cake

COCONUT AND APRICOT SWISS ROLL

Metric	Imperial
2 large eggs	2 large eggs
65 g caster sugar	2½ oz caster sugar
50 g plain flour	2 oz plain flour
4 x 15 ml spoons desiccated coconut	4 tablespoons desiccated coconut
6 x 15 ml spoons apricot jam, warmed	6 tablespoons apricot jam, warmed

Grease a 28.5 by 18.5 by 2 cm (11¼ by 7¼ by ¾ inch) Swiss roll tin. Bottom-line with greaseproof paper, then grease again and dust with caster sugar and flour. Whisk the eggs and sugar in a deep heatproof bowl placed over a pan of hot water until thick. Remove from the heat and continue whisking until cold. Fold in the sifted flour with 3 x 15 ml spoons (3 tablespoons) of the coconut. Spread into the Swiss roll tin.

Bake in a preheated hot oven (220°C/425°F, Gas Mark 7) for about 8 minutes, or until the crust is golden brown and springs back when pressed lightly with a finger. Turn out at once onto a sheet of greaseproof paper dusted with the remaining coconut and a little caster sugar. Trim the edges. Spread straight away with the warm jam and roll up from the narrow edge using the paper to help roll it. Keep wrapped in the paper on a wire rack until cool. Serve on day of baking.

PEPPERKAKER

Metric	Imperial
100 g butter or block margarine	4 oz butter or block margarine
100 g demerara sugar	3½ oz demerara sugar
200 g molasses or golden syrup	7 oz molasses or golden syrup
1 x 5 ml spoon ground ginger	1 teaspoon ground ginger
1 x 5 ml spoon ground cinnamon	1 teaspoon ground cinnamon
1 x 2.5 ml spoon ground cloves	½ teaspoon ground cloves
2 x 5 ml spoons bicarbonate of soda	2 teaspoons bicarbonate of soda
1 egg	1 egg
500 g plain flour	1 lb 2 oz plain flour

Roughly cut up the butter or margarine and place in a large bowl. In a saucepan, bring the sugar, molasses or syrup and the spices to boiling point. Add the bicarbonate of soda and pour over the butter. Stir until the butter has melted. Beat in the egg and slowly mix in the sifted flour. Knead in the bowl to a smooth, manageable dough. Roll out and cut into a variety of shapes.

Place the biscuits on baking sheets and bake in a preheated moderate oven (160°C/325°F, Gas Mark 3) for 10 to 15 minutes. Cool on a wire rack. Makes about 48

MOCHA CUP CAKES

Metric	Imperial
2 x 15 ml spoons coffee essence (Camp)	2 tablespoons coffee essence (Camp)
200 ml water	⅓ pint water
75 g butter	3 oz butter
75 g caster sugar	3 oz caster sugar
1 x 15 ml spoon golden syrup	1 tablespoon golden syrup
225 g plain flour	8 oz plain flour
2 x 15 ml spoons cocoa powder	2 tablespoons cocoa powder
1 x 5 ml spoon bicarbonate of soda	1 teaspoon bicarbonate of soda
3 x 15 ml spoons milk	3 tablespoons milk
1 x 2.5 ml spoon vanilla essence	½ teaspoon vanilla essence
For the icing:	**For the icing:**
75 g plain eating chocolate	3 oz plain eating chocolate
40 g butter	1½ oz butter
4 x 15 ml spoons water	4 tablespoons water
300 g icing sugar	11 oz icing sugar

A rich fudgy frosting and syrup in the cake mixture keep these cakes deliciously moist. Bake each paper-caseful in a bun tin to keep its shape. In a large pan, gently heat together the coffee essence, water, butter, caster sugar and syrup, stirring until the sugar dissolves. Bring to the boil and simmer for 5 minutes. Cool. Sift the flour and cocoa together into the cool mixture. Dissolve the bicarbonate of soda in the milk and add to the pan with the vanilla essence. Beat until smooth.

Spoon the chocolate mixture into 20 paper cases (bottom measurement 5 cm/2 inches) and bake in a preheated moderate oven (180°C/350°F, Gas Mark 4) for 15 to 20 minutes. Cool on a wire rack.

To make the icing, melt the chocolate and butter in the water in a heatproof bowl over hot water. Sift in the icing sugar and beat until smooth. Keep the icing liquid over the hot water, adding a little extra water if necessary and beating it if it begins to set. Put a large spoonful of icing on each cake, tipping it to reach the edges. Makes about 20

Coconut and apricot Swiss roll; Frosted hazelnut layer cake; Pepperkaker; Mocha cup cakes.

WALNUT COFFEE ROCK CAKES

Metric
100 g butter or block margarine
225 g self-raising flour, sifted
50 g walnuts, chopped
75 g demerara sugar
1 egg
2 x 15 ml spoons coffee essence
About 3 x 15 ml spoons milk
75 g icing sugar

Imperial
4 oz butter or block margarine
8 oz self-raising flour, sifted
2 oz walnuts, chopped
3 oz demerara sugar
1 egg
2 tablespoons coffee essence
About 3 tablespoons milk
3 oz icing sugar

Rub half the fat into the flour. Mix in the chopped walnuts and demerara sugar. Beat the egg with 1 x 15 ml spoon (1 tablespoon) of the coffee essence and the milk. Add to the dry ingredients and mix to a firm dough, adding more milk only if really necessary. Spoon the mixture into 12 heaps on lightly greased baking sheets, allowing them room to spread. Bake in a preheated moderately hot oven (200°C/400°F, Gas Mark 6) for 15 to 20 minutes. Cool on wire racks.

Soften the remaining fat and beat in the sifted icing sugar and remaining coffee essence. Cut a small cap off each bun and sandwich back with the coffee buttercream. Dust with icing sugar for serving.
Makes about 12

Right: Walnut coffee rock cakes.
Below: Cheese scones (see recipe page 61); Toasted devilled fingers.

TOASTED DEVILLED FINGERS

Metric	Imperial
1 small crusty loaf	1 small crusty loaf
100 g butter or soft margarine	4 oz butter or soft margarine
Mild mustard chutney	Mild mustard chutney

Cut the loaf into average slices and butter liberally. Spread with a thick layer of chutney and sandwich in pairs. Just before they are required, toast the sandwiches on both sides under a hot grill. Cut into chunky fingers to serve. Serves 6 to 8

ST. CATHERINE'S CAKES

Metric	Imperial
125 g butter	4 oz butter
125 g caster sugar	4 oz caster sugar
1 large egg, beaten	1 large egg, beaten
225 g self-raising flour	8 oz self-raising flour
1 x 5 ml spoon mixed spice	1 teaspoon mixed spice
4 x 15 ml spoons ground almonds	4 tablespoons ground almonds
50 g currants, cleaned	2 oz currants, cleaned

St. Catherine is the patron saint of lace-making and in Honiton, East Devon, a place noted for its lace, these wheel-shaped biscuits are still eaten on her feast day, November 24. Traditionally they are eaten hot, with mulled ale and cider. Cream the butter and sugar together until light and fluffy. Gradually beat in the egg. Sift in the flour and spice and stir in the almonds and currants. Mix, handling lightly, until the dough begins to bind together, then knead again lightly. Roll out the dough on a floured surface to 6 mm (¼ inch) thick and 20 cm (8 inches) wide. (This is easier if only half the dough is handled at once.) Cut in 1 cm (½ inch) strips and wind round to form a Catherine wheel.

Arrange on greased baking sheets and bake in a preheated moderately hot oven (190°C/375°F, Gas Mark 5) for 10 to 15 minutes or until pale golden. Cool on a wire rack. Makes about 30

DANISH ALMOND FINGERS

Metric	Imperial
225 g plain flour	8 oz plain flour
Pinch of salt	Pinch of salt
25 g lard	1 oz lard
15 g fresh yeast	½ oz fresh yeast
5 x 15 ml spoons warm water	5 tablespoons warm water
1 egg, beaten	1 egg, beaten
1 x 15 ml spoon caster sugar	1 tablespoon caster sugar
150 g butter or margarine	5 oz butter or margarine
350 g almond paste (see page 77), cut into fingers	12 oz almond paste (see page 77), cut into fingers
Beaten egg to glaze	Beaten egg to glaze
Glacé icing (see page 57) to decorate	Glacé icing (see page 57) to decorate

Sift the flour and salt into a bowl and rub in the lard. Mix the yeast with the water. Make a well in the centre of the flour mixture and add the yeast mixture, egg and caster sugar. Mix to a soft dough. Knead until smooth. Cover and leave in a cool place for 10 minutes. Work the fat to a block 23 by 7.5 cm (9 by 3 inches).

Roll out the dough to a 25 cm (10 inch) square and place the butter in the centre. Fold the dough sides up over it. Roll out the dough to a 38 by 12.5 cm (15 by 5 inch) oblong. Fold the top third down and the bottom third up. Put it in a polythene bag and leave to rest for 10 minutes in a cool place. Repeat the process twice, resting finally for 30 minutes.

Roll out the dough to a 30 by 20 cm (12 by 8 inch) oblong. Cut into 12 strips 2.5 cm (1 inch) wide. Wrap loosely around the almond paste fingers. Place on a greased baking sheet. Cover and leave in a warm place for about 20 minutes, until spongy.

Brush with beaten egg and bake in a preheated hot oven (220°C/425°F, Gas Mark 7) for about 15 minutes. Brush with thin glacé icing while still warm. Makes 12

Danish almond fingers; St. Catherine's cakes.

SUSSEX PLUM HEAVIES

Metric	Imperial
225 g self-raising flour	8 oz self-raising flour
Pinch of salt	Pinch of salt
Pinch of ground cinnamon	Pinch of ground cinnamon
75 g lard	3 oz lard
75 g margarine	3 oz margarine
100 g currants, cleaned	4 oz currants, cleaned
50 g soft brown sugar	2 oz soft brown sugar
About 120 ml milk	About 4 fl oz milk
Beaten egg to glaze	Beaten egg to glaze

These are said to have been eaten in the open by shepherds and woodmen. Originally they were made with plain flour, which meant that they were indeed "heavy". By using self-raising flour, the result is a cross between a scone and flaky pastry. They are best eaten the day that they are made.

Sift the flour, salt and cinnamon into a bowl. Mix the fats together and rub one quarter into the flour. Add the currants and sugar and mix to a soft manageable consistency with the milk. Knead the dough lightly on a floured board and roll out to an oblong about 30 by 10 cm (12 by 4 inches).

Mark the dough into three and flake one-third of the remaining fat over the top two-thirds of the dough. Fold the bottom third up and the top third down and roll out to the original size. Repeat twice more until all the fat has been used. Leave to rest in the refrigerator for 1 hour.

Roll out the dough to 6 mm (¼ inch) thick and stamp out 5 cm (2 inch) rounds. Remove a 1 cm (½ inch) hole from the centre of each round. Place on lightly greased baking sheets and brush with beaten egg. Bake in a preheated very hot oven (230°C/450°F, Gas Mark 8) for about 7 minutes, then reduce the heat to moderately hot (190°C/375°F, Gas Mark 5) and bake for a further 5 minutes.
Makes 24

Porter cake.

PORTER CAKE

Metric	Imperial
225 g butter	8 oz butter
Finely grated rind of 1 lemon	Finely grated rind of 1 lemon
225 g soft dark brown sugar	8 oz soft dark brown sugar
3 large eggs, beaten	3 large eggs, beaten
225 g seedless raisins, cleaned	8 oz seedless raisins, cleaned
225 g sultanas, cleaned	8 oz sultanas, cleaned
50 g chopped mixed peel	2 oz chopped mixed peel
50 g glacé cherries, quartered	2 oz glacé cherries, quartered
50 g almonds, chopped	2 oz almonds, chopped
275 g plain flour	10 oz plain flour
2 x 5 ml spoons mixed spice	2 teaspoons mixed spice
150 ml Guinness	¼ pint Guinness

In this traditional recipe, Guinness replaces the porter, a weak form of stout no longer produced. This moist, rich cake improves if aged for at least 24 hours, but preferably for a week. Wrap in foil and put in a tin. Cream the butter with the lemon rind and sugar until soft. Gradually add the eggs, beating well between each addition. Place the fruit and nuts in a large mixing bowl. Sift the flour and spice together and mix half into the fruit. Fold the remaining flour into the creamed ingredients, then the fruit, adding about 6 x 15 ml spoons (6 tablespoons) of the Guinness to give a dropping consistency.

Put the mixture in an 18 cm (7 inch) greased and lined round cake tin. Bake in a preheated moderate oven (160°C/325°F, Gas Mark 3) for 1 hour, then reduce the heat to cool (150°C/300°F, Gas Mark 2) and bake for a further 2 hours. Cool slightly in the tin, then while still warm, remove the cake from the tin. Prick the base well and spoon over the remaining Guinness. Makes an 18 cm (7 inch) cake

MIXED FRUIT SLAB CAKE

Metric	Imperial
450 g plain flour	1 lb plain flour
1 x 5 ml spoon baking powder	1 teaspoon baking powder
225 g clarified dripping	8 oz clarified dripping
250 g light soft brown sugar	9 oz light soft brown sugar
350 g mixed dried fruit, cleaned	12 oz mixed dried fruit, cleaned
125 g glacé cherries, halved	4 oz glacé cherries, halved
4 eggs, beaten	4 eggs, beaten
About 6 x 15 ml spoons milk	About 6 tablespoons milk

Make ahead – this improves with keeping. Sift together the flour and baking powder. Lightly rub in the dripping. Stir in the sugar, dried fruit and glacé cherries. Make a well in the centre and add the beaten eggs and milk. Mix to a stiff dropping consistency. Turn the mixture into a 20.5 cm (8 inch) square cake tin. Level the surface.

Bake in a preheated moderate oven (180°C/350°F, Gas Mark 4) for 30 minutes, then turn the heat down to cool (140°C/275°F, Gas Mark 1) and bake for 1½ to 2 hours longer or until golden and firm to the touch. Cool on a wire rack. Wrap in foil and keep in a tin.

Mixed fruit slab cake; Sussex plum heavies.

SIMNEL CAKE

Metric	Imperial
450 g (ready made weight) almond paste (bought or see page 77)	1 lb (ready made weight) almond paste (bought or see page 77)
225 g plain flour	8 oz plain flour
Pinch of salt	Pinch of salt
1 x 2.5 ml spoon grated nutmeg	$\frac{1}{2}$ teaspoon grated nutmeg
1 x 2.5 ml spoon ground cinnamon	$\frac{1}{2}$ teaspoon ground cinnamon
225 g currants, cleaned	8 oz currants, cleaned
100 g sultanas, cleaned	4 oz sultanas, cleaned
75 g chopped mixed peel	3 oz chopped mixed peel
100 g glacé cherries, quartered	4 oz glacé cherries, quartered
175 g butter	6 oz butter
175 g caster sugar	6 oz caster sugar
3 eggs	3 eggs
Milk to mix (if required)	Milk to mix (if required)
Egg white or apricot glaze	Egg white or apricot glaze

Grease and line an 18 cm (7 inch) round cake tin. Shape one-third of the almond paste into a round slightly smaller than the cake tin. Sift together the flour, salt and spices. Mix the currants, sultanas, peel and cherries.

Cream the butter and sugar together until pale and fluffy, then beat in the eggs, one at a time. Fold in the flour mixture, adding a little milk, if required, to give a dropping consistency. Fold in the fruit.

Put half the mixture into the prepared tin and place the round of almond paste on top. Cover with the rest of the mixture, spreading it evenly. Bake in a preheated cool oven (150°C/300°F, Gas Mark 2) for 2½ to 3 hours, until the cake is a rich brown and firm to the touch. Leave to cool on a wire rack.

From half the remaining almond paste, shape eleven small balls. Shape the rest into a round to fit the top of the cake. Brush the top surface of the cake with egg white or apricot glaze and place the almond paste round in position. Smooth it slightly with a rolling pin and pinch the edges into scallops with finger and thumb. Score the surface with a knife. Arrange the almond paste balls around the edge and, if liked for extra glaze, brush the whole with egg white. Grill until light golden brown, and finish with a ribbon and a bow when cold. Makes an 18 cm (7 inch) cake

CARAMEL SHORTBREAD

Metric	Imperial
175 g plain flour	6 oz plain flour
50 g caster sugar	2 oz caster sugar
175 g butter	6 oz butter
50 g soft brown sugar	2 oz soft brown sugar
1 large can condensed milk	1 large can condensed milk
100 g plain chocolate	4 oz plain chocolate

Sift the flour into a bowl. Add the caster sugar and rub in 125 g (4 oz) of the butter lightly with the fingertips until the mixture resembles fine crumbs. Press the mixture evenly into a Swiss roll tin measuring 29 by 19 cm (11½ by 7½ inches). Bake in a preheated moderate oven (170°C/325°F, Gas Mark 3) for about 30 minutes until just coloured. Allow to cool in the tin.

Heat the remaining butter and the soft brown sugar together in a saucepan. Stir in the condensed milk and heat gently until the sugar dissolves. Bring to the boil and cook, stirring continuously, until the caramel mixture is a creamy fudge colour. Pour over the shortbread and spread evenly. Leave to cool.

Melt the chocolate in a heatproof bowl over hot but not boiling water and pour over the caramel. Tap the tin on a hard surface to level the chocolate. Leave to set, then cut into fingers.
Makes about 32

MELTING MOMENTS

Metric	Imperial
100 g butter or block margarine	4 oz butter or block margarine
75 g sugar	3 oz sugar
1 egg yolk	1 egg yolk
Few drops of vanilla essence	Few drops of vanilla essence
150 g self-raising flour, sifted	5 oz self-raising flour, sifted
Crushed cornflakes	Crushed cornflakes

Cream the fat and sugar together and beat in the egg yolk. Flavour with vanilla essence, then stir in the flour to give a really stiff dough. Divide the dough into 20 to 24 portions. Form each into a ball and roll in crushed cornflakes.

Place the balls on greased baking sheets, well apart, and bake in a preheated moderately hot oven (190°C/375°F, Gas Mark 5) for 15 to 20 minutes. Cool on the baking sheets for a few moments before lifting onto a wire rack. Makes 20 to 24

Above: Simnel cake.

Caramel shortbread; Melting moments.

FOR A GRAND OCCASION

A wedding reception at home need not be a headache for the bride's mother providing she caters only for the numbers she can confidently manage. The celebration menu here would be just as suitable for an anniversary party as it is for a wedding reception. It is planned for 25 people, which in some cases means making double the quantity of the recipe. Unless you have very big pans and bowls, which in any case are heavy and awkward to cope with, it is more practical to make up recipes in two or more batches (we tell you when to do this). If you feel you can cater for more people, the quantities can be increased again but by making the recipes in three or more batches. The same basic advance preparation rules apply as for buffet parties.

Lay the buffet table so that people can help themselves from each end. Serve drinks from a separate table and brief some of the family to help.

BUFFET FOR TWENTY TO TWENTY-FIVE FOR A GRAND OCCASION

Crème vichyssoise or Cream of lemon soup, Walnut sablés/Cheese and asparagus quiche, Quiche lorraine/Rolled ham with chicken and almond mayonnaise, Jubilee eggs, Tossed green salad, Orange and chicory salad, Jellied beetroot and apple salad/Chocolate and rum cheesecake pie or Lemon cheesecake pie, Fruit salad or Strawberries or raspberries and cream/Cheese and biscuits/Coffee

BEFOREHAND

Several days ahead
Make the walnut sablés and keep in airtight tins. (When needed, refresh them in a preheated cool oven (150°C/300°F, Gas Mark 2) for a few minutes, then cool on a wire rack.)

The day before
Make the soup; refrigerate, covered. Make dry mix for the quiche pastry. Cook the chicken early in the day. Prepare the ham rolls, but don't glaze them; cover closely with cling film and keep in a cool place. Prepare the green salad ingredients; store in polythene bags in the refrigerator. Make up French dressing. Make the beetroot and apple salads. Make the cheesecakes without decorating them.

The morning of the party
Make up the fruit salad, without the bananas; keep cool. Make the quiches. Glaze the ham rolls.

The afternoon of the party
Decorate the cheesecakes. Make the orange and chicory salad.

At the last possible moment
Toss the salad. Add sliced bananas to the fruit salad. Reheat the quiches, if wished, in a preheated moderate oven (180°C/350°F, Gas Mark 4) for 30 minutes. Garnish dishes with parsley, etc. Make coffee when needed – the fresher the better.

CRÈME VICHYSSOISE

Make two batches

Metric	Imperial
6 leeks	6 leeks
50 g butter	2 oz butter
2 small onions, peeled and sliced	2 small onions, peeled and sliced
1 kg potatoes, peeled and diced	2 lb potatoes, peeled and diced
1.8 litres white stock	3 pints white stock
2 egg yolks	2 egg yolks
300 ml single cream	½ pint single cream
Salt	Salt
White pepper	White pepper
Snipped fresh chives to garnish	Snipped fresh chives to garnish

Trim the leeks, discarding most of the green tops, and slice thinly. Melt the butter in a 4.5 litre (8 pint) saucepan. Add the leeks and onions, and soften them without browning. Add the potatoes and stock and simmer for about 30 minutes. Sieve or purée in an electric blender. Return the purée to the saucepan. Add the egg yolks mixed with the cream and stir well. Reheat without boiling and adjust the seasoning. Chill and serve garnished with chives. Serves 12

CREAM OF LEMON SOUP

Make two batches

Metric	Imperial
75 g butter or margarine	3 oz butter or margarine
350 g onions, peeled and sliced	12 oz onions, peeled and sliced
350 g carrots, peeled and sliced	12 oz carrots, peeled and sliced
4 litres turkey or chicken stock	7 pints turkey or chicken stock
Thinly pared rind and juice of 3 large lemons	Thinly pared rind and juice of 3 large lemons
1 bouquet garni	1 bouquet garni
3 x 15 ml spoons arrowroot	3 tablespoons arrowroot
Salt	Salt
Freshly ground black pepper	Freshly ground black pepper
450 ml single cream	¾ pint single cream
Thin lemon slices to garnish	Thin lemon slices to garnish

Melt the butter or margarine in a large saucepan. Add the onions and carrots and cook gently until tender, stirring frequently. Stir in the stock and bring to the boil. Reduce the heat and cook for 5 minutes.

Meanwhile, pour boiling water over the lemon rind and leave for 1 minute. Drain. Add the rind, lemon juice and bouquet garni to the pan. Cover and cook for 1 hour or until the vegetables are really soft. Remove the bouquet garni.

Purée the soup, a little at a time, in an electric blender. In a clean pan, dissolve the arrowroot in a little of the soup, then add the remainder, stirring. Bring to the boil, stirring. Adjust the seasoning before adding the cream. Reheat but do not boil. Garnish with lemon slices. Serves 12

WALNUT SABLÉS

Metric	Imperial
100 g plain flour	4 oz plain flour
100 g butter	4 oz butter
100 g mature Cheddar cheese, grated	4 oz mature Cheddar cheese, grated
Pinch of salt	Pinch of salt
Pinch of dry mustard	Pinch of dry mustard
Beaten egg	Beaten egg
Few chopped walnuts	Few chopped walnuts

Sift the flour into a bowl. Rub the butter into the flour with the fingertips until the mixture resembles fine crumbs. Add the cheese, salt and mustard and work together to form a dough.

Roll out the dough to about 6 mm ($\frac{1}{4}$ inch) thick on a lightly floured board. Neaten the edges and cut into 5 cm (2 inch) squares. Cut each in half diagonally. Brush the sablés with beaten egg. Sprinkle with nuts and press them lightly into the dough. Place on a baking sheet and bake in a preheated moderately hot oven (200°C/400°F, Gas Mark 6) for about 10 minutes. Cool on a wire rack. Makes 30

Above: Walnut sablés. Below: Crème vichyssoise; Cream of lemon soup.

CHEESE AND ASPARAGUS QUICHE

Make two

Metric	**Imperial**
200 g shortcrust pastry, made with 200 g plain flour and 100 g fat	7 oz shortcrust pastry, made with 7 oz plain flour and 3½ oz fat
25 g butter or margarine	1 oz butter or margarine
3 x 15 ml spoons plain flour	3 tablespoons plain flour
300 ml milk	½ pint milk
100 g cheese, grated	4 oz cheese, grated
Salt	Salt
Freshly ground black pepper	Freshly ground black pepper
1 x 340 g can green asparagus spears, drained	1 x 12 oz can green asparagus spears, drained

Roll out the dough and use to line a 20 cm (8 inch) flan ring or deep pie plate. Bake blind in a preheated hot oven (220°C/425°F, Gas Mark 7) for 15 to 20 minutes or until the pastry is cooked but not browned.

Melt the fat in a saucepan. Stir in the flour and cook for 2 to 3 minutes. Remove the pan from the heat and gradually stir in the milk. Bring to the boil and continue to cook, stirring, until the sauce has thickened. Remove from the heat and stir in 75 g (3 oz) of the cheese and seasoning.

Place the asparagus in the pastry case, retaining a little for decoration. Pour the sauce over and decorate with the remaining asparagus. Sprinkle with the remaining cheese and brown under a preheated hot grill or in a preheated moderate oven (180°C/350°F, Gas Mark 4) for 30 minutes, before serving. Serves 8 to 10

Quiche lorraine.

Cheese and asparagus quiche.

QUICHE LORRAINE

Make two

Metric	**Imperial**
100 g shortcrust pastry, made with 100 g plain flour and 50 g fat	4 oz shortcrust pastry, made with 4 oz plain flour and 2 oz fat
2 eggs, beaten	2 eggs, beaten
1 x 5 ml spoon chopped fresh herbs (if available)	1 teaspoon chopped fresh herbs (if available)
150 ml double cream	¼ pint double cream
150 ml single cream	¼ pint single cream
Grated nutmeg	Grated nutmeg
Salt	Salt
Freshly ground black pepper	Freshly ground black pepper
100 g lean streaky bacon rashers, rinds removed	4 oz lean streaky bacon rashers, rinds removed
100-175 g Gruyère cheese, thinly sliced or diced	4-6 oz Gruyère cheese, thinly sliced or diced

Roll out the dough very thinly and use to line a 20 cm (8 inch) flan ring placed on a baking sheet. Bake blind in a preheated hot oven (200°C/425°F, Gas Mark 7) for 15 to 20 minutes.

Meanwhile, mix together the eggs, herbs, creams, nutmeg and seasoning. Fry the bacon rashers gently until just cooked. Drain on absorbent kitchen paper.

Arrange the cheese on the bottom of the pastry case. Place the bacon rashers on top and pour on the egg mixture. Continue to bake in a moderate oven (180°C/350°F, Gas Mark 4) for about 35 to 40 minutes or until just set. Serve warm, cut in wedges. Serves 6 to 7

ROLLED HAM WITH CHICKEN AND ALMOND MAYONNAISE

Metric	Imperial
1 x 1.6 kg oven-ready chicken	1 x 3½ lb oven-ready chicken
600 ml water	1 pint water
1 small onion, peeled and sliced	1 small onion, peeled and sliced
1 carrot, peeled and sliced	1 carrot, peeled and sliced
Slivers of lemon rind	Slivers of lemon rind
1 bay leaf	1 bay leaf
4 peppercorns	4 peppercorns
Salt	Salt
25 g butter	1 oz butter
25 g plain flour	1 oz plain flour
2-3 x 15 ml spoons mayonnaise	2-3 tablespoons mayonnaise
50 g flaked almonds, toasted	2 oz flaked almonds, toasted
20 slices of canned ham (about 750 g)	20 slices of canned ham (about 1¾ lb)
Aspic glaze (optional)	Aspic glaze (optional)
Stuffed olives to garnish	Stuffed olives to garnish

Put the chicken in a saucepan with the water, onion, carrot, lemon rind, bay leaf, peppercorns and salt. Bring to the boil, reduce the heat, cover and simmer until the chicken is tender – about 40 minutes. Drain the chicken, reserving the liquor and leave to cool.

Melt the butter in another saucepan. Add the flour and cook for 1 to 2 minutes. Gradually stir in the strained chicken cooking liquor.

Bring to the boil and simmer for 3 to 4 minutes. Leave to cool, covered with buttered paper to prevent a skin forming.

Skin the chicken and remove the meat from the bones. Dice the meat and add to the sauce with mayonnaise to taste and the flaked almonds. Divide the chicken filling between the ham slices, placing it towards one end. Roll up. If liked, brush the rolls with aspic glaze. When set, press half a stuffed olive into the end of each roll, cut side outwards. Keep in a cool place until required. Makes 20

JUBILEE EGGS

Metric	Imperial
25 eggs, hard-boiled	25 eggs, hard-boiled
225 g liver pâté	8 oz liver pâté
120 ml thick mayonnaise	4 fl oz thick mayonnaise
Salt	Salt
Freshly ground black pepper	Freshly ground black pepper
Stoned green olives	Stoned green olives
Paprika	Paprika

Cut the eggs in half lengthways and carefully remove the yolks. Pass the yolks through a nylon sieve. Divide in half and add the pâté to one half. Beat very thoroughly until smooth. To the rest of the yolk add the mayonnaise and seasoning. Beat well.

Pipe the pâté mixture into half the egg whites, using a 1.25 cm (½ inch) plain nozzle. Pipe the mayonnaise mixture into the remaining egg whites with a star nozzle. Garnish the pâté eggs with sliced olives and the mayonnaise eggs with paprika. Makes 50

Rolled ham with chicken and almond mayonnaise; Jubilee eggs.

ORANGE AND CHICORY SALAD

Metric	Imperial
3 x 15 ml spoons lemon juice	3 tablespoons lemon juice
1 x 5 ml spoon salt	1 teaspoon salt
Freshly ground black pepper	Freshly ground black pepper
1 x 5 ml spoon French mustard	1 teaspoon French mustard
1 x 15 ml spoon clear honey	1 tablespoon clear honey
9 x 15 ml spoons vegetable oil	9 tablespoons vegetable oil
9 oranges	9 oranges
12 heads of chicory, trimmed	12 heads of chicory, trimmed

Put the lemon juice, salt, pepper, mustard, honey and oil in a screwtop jar. Shake well until the dressing is smooth and creamy. Grate the rind from six of the oranges and add to the dressing. Remove the skin and pith from the all the oranges. Divide them into segments and place in a salad bowl together with any juice.

Reserving a few chicory leaves for garnish, thinly slice the remainder and add to the bowl. Pour over the dressing and toss gently. Leave for 1 to 2 hours. Garnish with the reserved chicory leaves.

Jellied beetroot and apple salad.

Orange and chicory salad.

JELLIED BEETROOT AND APPLE SALAD

Make three

Metric	Imperial
1 x 142 g red jelly tablet	1 x 5 oz red jelly tablet
300 ml boiling water	½ pint boiling water
150 ml vinegar	¼ pint vinegar
2 x 15 ml spoons lemon juice	2 tablespoons lemon juice
50 g walnut halves	2 oz walnut halves
500 g cooked beetroot, skinned and sliced or diced	1 lb cooked beetroot, skinned and sliced or diced
2 eating apples, peeled, cored and sliced	2 eating apples, peeled, cored and sliced
Chicory to garnish	Chicory to garnish

Break up the jelly tablet. Put it in a bowl and dissolve it in the boiling water. Mix together the vinegar and lemon juice and make up to 300 ml (½ pint) with cold water. Add to the hot jelly liquid.

Put the walnut halves in the bottom of a 1.2 litre (2 pint) ring mould and add the beetroot and apples in layers. Pour on the liquid jelly and leave to set in the refrigerator. When required, unmould onto a flat plate and garnish with chicory. Serves 6

Note: Use shallow dishes if you don't have enough ring moulds to make three salads.

160

CHOCOLATE AND RUM CHEESECAKE PIE

Make three

Metric

For the biscuit base:
150 g digestive biscuits, crushed
75 g caster sugar
75 g butter, melted

For the filling:
100 g cottage cheese, sieved
100 g cream cheese
100 g caster sugar
100 g plain chocolate
15 g powdered gelatine
2 x 15 ml spoons water
2 x 15 ml spoons rum
150 ml double cream, whipped

Imperial

For the biscuit base:
6 oz digestive biscuits, crushed
3 oz caster sugar
3 oz butter, melted

For the filling:
4 oz cottage cheese, sieved
4 oz cream cheese
4 oz caster sugar
4 oz plain chocolate
½ oz powdered gelatine
2 tablespoons water
2 tablespoons rum
¼ pint double cream, whipped

For the decoration:
150 ml double cream
1 x 15 ml spoon milk
Curls of chocolate
Icing sugar

For the decoration:
¼ pint double cream
1 tablespoon milk
Curls of chocolate
Icing sugar

Mix the biscuits with the caster sugar and butter. Use to line the bottom and sides of a 20 cm (8 inch) fluted flan dish. Press into place with the back of a spoon. Chill until firm.

Cream the cheeses together and add the caster sugar. Melt the chocolate in a heatproof bowl over hot water. Add the chocolate to the cheese mixture and beat well. Dissolve the gelatine in the water in a heatproof bowl placed in a pan of hot water. Stir into the cheese mixture and chill until almost set.

Add the rum, then fold in the cream. Pour the filling into the crumb crust. Chill until firm.

To decorate, whip the cream with the milk and swirl this over the chocolate filling. Top with curls of chocolate dusted with icing sugar. Serves 6 to 8

Chocolate and rum cheesecake pie.

LEMON CHEESECAKE PIE

Make three

Metric	**Imperial**
For the biscuit base:	**For the biscuit base:**
150 g digestive biscuits, crushed	6 oz digestive biscuits, crushed
75 g caster sugar	3 oz caster sugar
75 g butter, melted	3 oz butter, melted
For the filling:	**For the filling:**
1½ x 142 g lemon jelly tablets	1½ x 5 oz lemon jelly tablets
3 x 15 ml spoons water	3 tablespoons water
2 eggs, separated	2 eggs, separated
150 ml milk	¼ pint milk
Grated rind of 2 lemons	Grated rind of 2 lemons
4 x 15 ml spoons lemon juice	4 tablespoons lemon juice
350 g cottage cheese, sieved	12 oz cottage cheese, sieved
2 x 15 ml spoons caster sugar	2 tablespoons caster sugar
150 ml double cream, whipped	¼ pint double cream, whipped
To decorate:	**To decorate:**
150 ml double or whipping cream, whipped	¼ pint double or whipping cream, whipped
Angelica	Angelica

Mix the digestive biscuits with the caster sugar and butter. Use to line the bottom and sides of a 23 cm (9 inch) or 1.2 litre (2 pint) shallow open pie plate. Press in with the back of a spoon. Chill until firm.

Dissolve the jelly in the water in a pan over low heat. Do not boil. Beat together the egg yolks and milk and stir into the jelly. Heat for a few minutes without boiling. Remove from the heat and add the lemon rind and juice. Cool until beginning to set.

Stir in the sieved cottage cheese (or blend the jelly mixture and unsieved cheese in an electric blender). Whisk the egg whites until stiff. Add the caster sugar and whisk again until stiff. Fold quickly into the cheese mixture followed by the whipped cream. Spoon into the crumb crust, piling it up slightly. Chill until set, then decorate with the additional whipped cream and angelica, if liked.
Serves 6 to 8

FRUIT SALAD

Metric	**Imperial**
1 x 818 g can sliced peaches	1 x 1 lb 13 oz can sliced peaches
1 x 425 g can pineapple rings	1 x 15 oz can pineapple rings
2 dessert apples, cored and thinly sliced	2 dessert apples, cored and thinly sliced
4 oranges, peeled and segmented	4 oranges, peeled and segmented
225 g strawberries, hulled and sliced	8 oz strawberries, hulled and sliced
225 g white grapes, peeled and seeded	8 oz white grapes, peeled and seeded
4 x 15 ml spoons orange-flavoured liqueur	4 tablespoons orange-flavoured liqueur
Lemon juice	Lemon juice
4 bananas	4 bananas

Turn the contents from the cans into a large bowl. Cut the pineapple rings in half. Add the apples, oranges, strawberries, grapes, liqueur and lemon juice to taste. Stir well. Leave for at least 1 hour for the flavours to mix.

Just before serving, slice the bananas and add to the salad.
Serves 15

COFFEE FOR TWENTY

Allow 200 ml (⅓ pint) of coffee per person. You will need 275 g (10 oz) of ground coffee, 3.4 litres (6 pints) of water and 1.2 litres (2 pints) of milk, or 600 ml (1 pint) of single cream, for 20 people. Allow 500 g (1 lb) of sugar – demerara, white, or coffee crystals.

Below: Coffee for a crowd. Left: Lemon cheesecake pie; Fruit salad.

DROP IN FOR DRINKS

A drinks party calls for more than the crisps and other bits and pieces. Make a few of the goodies shown here – three or four cold ones, and at least one hot one, such as Talmouse, and a savoury dip – and your party will be a sure success. Serve dips in a bowl on a tray and surround the bowl with colourful bite-size pieces of raw carrot, cauliflower and celery or small crisp biscuits or potato crisps. Keep hot and cold savouries separate and serve some crisps and other bits and pieces – cocktail sausages, olives, gherkins, nuts.

If you're using any pastry cases or bases, they can be made a day or two in advance and kept in airtight tins. Refresh them shortly before filling by putting them into a warm oven for 10 to 15 minutes. Allow them to cool before adding the filling or topping. Do this as near as possible to serving time. The same applies to canapés based on savoury biscuits, whether homemade or bought.

TALMOUSE

Metric	Imperial
1 x 212 g packet smoked haddock fillets	1 x 7½ oz packet smoked haddock fillets
15 g butter	½ oz butter
15 g plain flour	½ oz plain flour
150 ml milk	¼ pint milk
Salt	Salt
Freshly ground black pepper	Freshly ground black pepper
1 x 368 g packet frozen puff pastry, thawed	1 x 13 oz packet frozen puff pastry, thawed
Beaten egg	Beaten egg

Cook the haddock fillets according to the directions on the packet. Allow to cool, then discard the skin and any bones and flake the flesh. Melt the butter in a saucepan. Add the flour and cook, stirring, for 1 minute. Remove from the heat and gradually stir in the milk. Return to the heat and bring to the boil, stirring constantly. Simmer until thickened. Remove the sauce from the heat. Season to taste with salt and pepper and fold in the flaked fish.

Roll out the pastry dough thinly and, with a 7.5 cm (3 inch) plain cutter, stamp out as many rounds as possible. Re-roll the dough as necessary. Brush the rim of each dough round with beaten egg. Put a little of the fish mixture in the centre of each round and shape up the round into a tricorn. Brush with more beaten egg and place on a baking sheet.

Bake in a preheated moderately hot oven (200°C/400°F, Gas Mark 6) for 20 minutes or until golden. Serve hot. Makes 24

DEVILS ON HORSEBACK

Metric	Imperial
1 x 450 g can prunes, drained	1 x 15½ oz can prunes, drained
34 whole browned almonds	34 whole browned almonds
350 g lean streaky bacon rashers, rinds removed	12 oz lean streaky bacon rashers, rinds removed

There should be 34 prunes in the can. Cut each almost in half and discard the stones. Replace with an almond.

Stretch the bacon rashers on a flat surface with the back of a knife, then cut each in half. Wrap a half rasher around each prune. Grill slowly until the bacon is brown and crisp. Serve on cocktail sticks. Makes 34

CHEESE OLIVES

Metric	Imperial
225 g full fat cream cheese	8 oz full fat cream cheese
15 stuffed olives	15 stuffed olives
Chopped walnuts	Chopped walnuts

Cream the cheese until it is soft. Take a heaped 5 ml spoonful (teaspoonful) and roll it around a stuffed olive to enclose it completely. Lightly coat in chopped walnuts. Cover the remaining olives in the same way. Chill the olives for about 1 hour. Before serving, cut each in half with a sharp knife. Makes 30

SARDINE PYRAMIDS

Metric	Imperial
20 to 24 cocktail grielle (rusk biscuits)	20 to 24 cocktail grielle (rusk biscuits)
Butter	Butter
2 x 106 g cans sardines, drained	2 x 4 oz cans sardines, drained
Lemon juice	Lemon juice
Salt	Salt
Freshly ground black pepper	Freshly ground black pepper
Paprika	Paprika
Chopped fresh parsley	Chopped fresh parsley

Lightly spread the cocktail grielle with butter. Mash the sardines with a seasoning to taste of lemon juice, salt and pepper. Mound some of the sardine mixture on each grielle and shape into a pyramid. Using a damp skewer, mark in a cross with paprika and chopped parsley. Makes 20 to 24

Left: Talmouse. Right: Sardine pyramids; Devils on horseback; Cheese olives.

PÂTÉ FLEURONS

Metric	Imperial
1 x 212 g packet frozen puff pastry, thawed	1 x 7 oz packet frozen puff pastry, thawed
Beaten egg	Beaten egg
1 x 107 g tube liver pâté	1 x 4¼ oz tube liver pâté
50 g butter	2 oz butter

Roll out the pastry dough thinly. Using a 3.7 cm (1½ inch) fluted round cutter, stamp out as many rounds as possible. Re-roll as necessary. Brush the rounds with beaten egg and fold over into semi-circles. Place on a baking sheet and leave in a cool place for at least 30 minutes.

Brush the semi-circles with beaten egg and bake in a preheated moderately hot oven (200°C/400°F, Gas Mark 6) for about 15 minutes. With a sharp knife, cut almost through the pastry to allow the steam to escape. Leave to cool on a wire rack.

Beat together the liver pâté and butter. Put into a piping bag fitted with a cake icing no. 8 nozzle. Pipe in a shell shape down the centre of each pastry fleuron. Makes about 52

PRAWN TITBITS

Metric	Imperial
100 g cheese pastry, made with 100 g plain flour (see page 56)	4 oz cheese pastry, made with 4 oz plain flour (see page 56)
Beaten egg	Beaten egg
1 x 100 g can prawns, drained	1 x 4 oz can prawns, drained
100 g butter, softened	4 oz butter, softened
1 x 2.5 ml spoon tomato paste	½ teaspoon tomato paste
Parsley sprigs to garnish	Parsley sprigs to garnish

Roll out the pastry dough to a rectangle 20 by 30 cm (8 by 12 inches). Trim the edges and cut into 2.5 cm (1 inch) wide strips, 5 cm (2 inches) long. Place on baking sheets and brush with beaten egg. Bake in a preheated moderately hot oven (200°C/400°F, Gas Mark 6) for about 15 minutes or until golden. Cool.

Sieve half the contents of the can of prawns. Beat in the butter and tomato paste. Put the shrimp butter into a piping bag fitted with a star vegetable nozzle and pipe lines on the cheese pastry bases. Garnish with the remaining whole canned prawns and parsley sprigs. Makes 48

CELERY SLICES

Metric	Imperial
100 g Danish blue cheese	4 oz Danish blue cheese
75 g full fat cream cheese	3 oz full fat cream cheese
8 celery stalks, trimmed	8 celery stalks, trimmed

Cream together the blue and cream cheeses. Put the cheese mixture into a piping bag fitted with a plain nozzle and pipe into the hollow of each celery stalk. Fit the celery stalks together in pairs, slightly interlocking them. Secure each end of each pair with an elastic band and leave in a cool place – not the refrigerator – for the stalks to firm up. Using a sharp knife, cut into approximately 1 cm (½ inch) slices. Makes about 30

SAVOURY BITES

Metric	Imperial
For egg and horseradish bites:	**For egg and horseradish bites:**
50 g butter	2 oz butter
2 x 5 ml spoons creamed horseradish	2 teaspoons creamed horseradish
24 salted crackers	24 salted crackers
3 eggs, hard-boiled and sliced	3 eggs, hard-boiled and sliced
24 pickled gherkin fans	24 pickled gherkin fans
For tomato bites:	**For tomato bites:**
225 g full fat cream cheese	8 oz full fat cream cheese
20 salted crackers	20 salted crackers
Tomato butterflies	Tomato butterflies
Black olives, stoned	Black olives, stoned

For the egg and horseradish bites, cream the butter and horseradish together well and spread onto the crackers. Top each with a slice of egg and a gherkin fan.

For the tomato bites, beat the cream cheese until soft. Put it into a piping bag fitted with a star vegetable nozzle and pipe a whirl of cheese onto each cracker. Garnish with tomato butterflies and a piece of black olive.

Prepare both these canapés as near as possible to serving time, as the crackers may soften. Makes 44

SALAMI CUSHIONS

Metric	Imperial
1 x 212 g packet frozen puff pastry, thawed	1 x 7 oz packet frozen puff pastry, thawed
100 g salami, finely chopped	4 oz salami, finely chopped
Beaten egg to glaze	Beaten egg to glaze

Roll out the dough to an oblong about 38 by 30 cm (15 by 12 inches). Cut in half. Dot the salami at 4 cm (1½ inch) intervals on one sheet. Brush the remaining sheet with water and lay it, wet side down, on the first sheet. Press the pastry well to form 'parcels' and cut into squares with a sharp knife or pastry wheel. Glaze with beaten egg and bake in a preheated hot oven (220°C/425°F, Gas Mark 7) for 8 to 10 minutes. Cool on a wire rack. Makes about 40
Note: These can be prepared the day before the party, but bake them just before they are needed. Wrap the uncooked 'cushions' in polythene and keep in the refrigerator overnight.

Left (clockwise from top): Celery slices; Prawn titbits; Egg and horseradish bites; Pâté fleurons; Tomato bites. Right: Salami cushions.

SPANISH DIP WITH MUSHROOMS

Metric	Imperial
25 g butter or margarine	1 oz butter or margarine
225 g tomatoes, skinned and chopped	8 oz tomatoes, skinned and chopped
1 large garlic clove, crushed	1 large garlic clove, crushed
1 x 2.5 ml spoon dried basil	½ teaspoon dried basil
2 x 15 ml spoons tomato paste	2 tablespoons tomato paste
Salt	Salt
Freshly ground black pepper	Freshly ground black pepper
150 ml thick mayonnaise	¼ pint thick mayonnaise
500 g small button mushrooms	1 lb small button mushrooms

Mushrooms make ideal dunkers, their special crispness contrasting deliciously with this rich velvety sauce.

Melt the butter or margarine in a small frying pan. Add the tomatoes, garlic, basil, tomato paste and seasoning and simmer gently for about 10 minutes, or until the tomato is well pulped. Cool slightly, then purée in a blender or sieve and leave to go cold.

Mix in the mayonnaise and adjust the seasoning. Serve as a dip with the mushrooms skewered on cocktail sticks. Serves 12 to 16

CHEESE AND WALNUT DIP

Metric	Imperial
500 g Wensleydale or mild soft cheese	1 lb Wensleydale or mild soft cheese
200 ml top of the milk	⅓ pint top of the milk
25 g onion, peeled and grated	1 oz onion, peeled and grated
Tomato paste	Tomato paste
Salt	Salt
Freshly ground black pepper	Freshly ground black pepper
40 g walnuts, finely chopped	1½ oz walnuts, finely chopped

With a fork, work the cheese until creamy, adding the milk a little at a time. Beat in the grated onion, tomato paste to taste and seasoning. Finally fold in the chopped walnuts. Serve with crisps, crackers and pretzels. Makes 600 ml (1 pint)

Spanish dip with mushrooms; Cheese and walnut dip.

PIQUANT COCKTAIL CROQUETTES

Metric	Imperial
25 g butter or margarine	1 oz butter or margarine
25 g plain flour	1 oz plain flour
150 ml milk	¼ pint milk
50 g pickled gherkins, very finely chopped	2 oz pickled gherkins, very finely chopped
1 x 15 ml spoon capers, very finely chopped	1 tablespoon capers, very finely chopped
25 g green olives, stoned and very finely chopped	1 oz green olives, stoned and very finely chopped
2 x 15 ml spoons chopped parsley	2 tablespoons chopped parsley
Salt	Salt
Freshly ground black pepper	Freshly ground black pepper
Beaten egg	Beaten egg
Fresh white breadcrumbs	Fresh white breadcrumbs
Oil for deep frying	Oil for deep frying

Melt the fat in a saucepan. Stir in the flour and cook for 1 minute. Gradually stir in the milk and bring to the boil. Simmer, stirring, for 1 minute. Add the gherkins, capers, olives, parsley and seasoning. Mix well, then turn the mixture onto a plate. Refrigerate until cold.

Shape the mixture into small barrels and coat with egg and breadcrumbs. Deep fry in oil heated to 190°C/375°F until crisp and golden. Drain on absorbent kitchen paper. Serve hot.
Makes about 20
Note: These can be made the day before and refreshed in a preheated moderately hot oven (200°C/400°F, Gas Mark 6) for 5 to 8 minutes. (Store them overnight in a polythene bag in the refrigerator.)

SCOTCH CHEESIES

Metric	Imperial
100-125 g Gorgonzola, Dolcelatte or Danish blue cheese, rind removed	4 oz Gorgonzola, Dolcelatte or Danish blue cheese, rind removed
500 g sausagemeat	1 lb sausagemeat
1 x 15 ml spoon French mustard	1 tablespoon French mustard
Salt	Salt
Freshly ground black pepper	Freshly ground black pepper
Plain flour	Plain flour
1 egg, beaten	1 egg, beaten
25 g dry white breadcrumbs	1 oz dry white breadcrumbs
Oil for deep frying	Oil for deep frying

Divide the cheese into 12 even-sized pieces. Pound the sausagemeat with the mustard and seasoning until well mixed. Divide into 12 portions. Roll each piece of cheese in sausagemeat, making sure the cheese is completely encased. Coat the balls lightly in flour, beaten egg and breadcrumbs, in that order, pressing the crumbs on well. Chill for 30 minutes to set the crumbs.

Deep-fry in oil heated to 190°C/375°F until golden brown. Drain well on absorbent kitchen paper. Leave to cool before serving. Makes 12

Left: Piquant cocktail croquettes; Scotch cheesies. Below: Herb chicken goujons with cucumber dip.

HERB CHICKEN GOUJONS WITH CUCUMBER DIP

Metric	Imperial
4 x 100 g chicken breasts, skinned and boned	4 x 4 oz chicken breasts, skinned and boned
Plain flour	Plain flour
Salt	Salt
Freshly ground black pepper	Freshly ground black pepper
1 egg, beaten	1 egg, beaten
1 x 85 g packet herby stuffing mix	1 x 3 oz packet herby stuffing mix
3 x 15 ml spoons oil	3 tablespoons oil
25 g butter	1 oz butter
For the dip:	**For the dip:**
75 g piece of cucumber, peeled and grated	3 oz piece of cucumber, peeled and grated
150 ml thick mayonnaise	¼ pint thick mayonnaise
Dash of Tabasco sauce	Dash of Tabasco sauce

With a sharp knife, slice each chicken breast into six long strips. Coat the strips evenly in lightly seasoned flour, then in egg and finally in dry stuffing mix. Heat the oil in a frying pan. Add the butter and when frothing, but not brown, fry the chicken goujons, half at a time, for 2 to 3 minutes on each side until golden brown. Drain well on absorbent kitchen paper. Leave to go cold.

To make the dip, mix the cucumber with the mayonnaise. Add a few drops of Tabasco and seasoning. Serve the goujons on cocktail sticks with the sauce separately. Serves 12

Party Drinks

A drinks party can provide a very convivial way of entertaining without the need for a great deal of cooking but do provide some home-made savouries (see pages 166-71).
If you're not adept at making cocktails, stick to sherry (fino and amontillado), vermouth (sweet and extra dry) and white wine (dry and medium dry) or a non-vintage champagne or sparkling wine. Serve the vermouth straight, with ice and a sliver of lemon. For winter parties a hot mulled wine is popular and in summer a wine cup is very refreshing. Have a good supply of tonic water, ginger ale, tomato juice, orange juice and beer on hand. Order the drinks early, on a sale or return basis, paying only for bottles which are opened. Make lots of ice in advance if you have a freezer; or buy it in large bags from your off-licence.
Site the bar on a large table, covered with a cloth or sheet, at one end of the room. Remove most of the chairs and place ashtrays and coasters strategically to protect carpets and furniture.

COCKTAILS

HOW MANY DRINKS TO THE BOTTLE?

Sherry, port and vermouth, straight: 12 to 16 glasses.
Vermouths and spirits, in single nips for mixes: 30 drinks.
Spirits, served with tonic, soda or other minerals: 16 to 20 drinks.
A split bottle of tonic or soda: 2 to 3 drinks.
Table wines: 5 to 6 glasses.
A 600 ml (1 pint) can of tomato juice: 4 to 6 drinks.
A bottle of fruit cordial, diluted with 4 litres (7 pints) of water: 20 to 26 drinks.

SUGAR SYRUP FOR DRINKS

Metric	Imperial
450 g sugar	1 lb sugar
300 ml water	½ pint water

When making cups and punches, it is often more convenient to add the sugar in the form of a syrup, which dissolves more readily. Put the sugar in a saucepan with the water and dissolve it slowly. Bring it to the boil and boil to 105°C/220°F. Cool and bottle. Use as required. Makes about 600 ml (1 pint)

Dry martini; Sweet martini.

CHAMPAGNE COCKTAIL

Metric	Imperial
4 dashes of Angostura bitters	4 dashes of Angostura bitters
1 small sugar lump	1 small sugar lump
Juice of ¼ lemon	Juice of ¼ lemon
1 x 15 ml spoon brandy (optional)	1 tablespoon brandy (optional)
Champagne, chilled in the bottle	Champagne, chilled in the bottle
Lemon slice to decorate	Lemon slice to decorate

Pour the bitters over the sugar lump in a champagne glass. Add the strained lemon juice and brandy, if used, and fill up with Champagne. Float a wafer-thin slice of lemon on top. Serves 1

BUCK'S FIZZ

Metric	Imperial
1 part fresh orange juice	1 part fresh orange juice
2 parts non-vintage Champagne	2 parts non-vintage Champagne

Chill the ingredients and stir together well just before serving. Serves 1

Buck's fizz; Bronx; Champagne cocktail.

Kir; Screwdriver.

BRONX

Metric	Imperial
Equal parts dry gin, Italian vermouth and French vermouth	Equal parts dry gin, Italian vermouth and French vermouth
Juice of ¼ orange	Juice of ¼ orange
Crushed ice	Crushed ice

Shake together the ingredients, then strain into a cocktail glass. Serves 1

DRY MARTINI COCKTAIL

Metric	Imperial
2 parts French vermouth	2 parts French vermouth
1 part dry gin	1 part dry gin
Cracked ice	Cracked ice
Stuffed olives or lemon rind curls	Stuffed olives or lemon rind curls

Shake the vermouth and gin together with some cracked ice in a shaker. Strain into a glass and add a stuffed olive or a curl of lemon rind. (The proportions of a martini are a matter of personal taste. Some people prefer two parts of gin to one of vermouth; others like equal parts of gin and vermouth.) Serves 1

SWEET MARTINI COCKTAIL

Metric	Imperial
2 parts Italian vermouth	2 parts Italian vermouth
1 part dry gin	1 part dry gin
Few drops of orange bitters (optional)	Few drops of orange bitters (optional)
Cracked ice	Cracked ice
1 Maraschino cherry	1 Maraschino cherry

Shake the vermouth, gin, bitters, if used, and ice together in a shaker. Strain into a glass. Serve with a cherry. Serves 1

SCREWDRIVER

Metric	Imperial
1 measure of vodka	1 measure of vodka
Orange juice	Orange juice

Put some ice cubes into a glass and pour in the vodka. Add orange juice to taste and stir lightly. Serves 1

KIR

Metric	Imperial
4 parts dry white wine (Chablis or similar)	4 parts dry white wine (Chablis or similar)
1 part crème de cassis	1 part crème de cassis

Chill the wine thoroughly before combining it with the cassis. Serve in a claret glass. Serves 1

JOHN COLLINS

Metric	Imperial
Juice of ½ lemon	Juice of ½ lemon
Dash of Angostura bitters	Dash of Angostura bitters
2 x 5 ml spoons caster sugar	2 teaspoons caster sugar
2 measures of gin	2 measures of gin
Ice	Ice
Soda water	Soda water
Lemon slice	Lemon slice

Shake the lemon juice, bitters, sugar and gin together and strain into a tall glass over ice. Fill with soda water and add a slice of lemon.

For a quick John Collins, mix two measures of gin and a dash of Angostura bitters, add ice and fill up the glass with fizzy lemonade. Serves 1

FRESH TOMATO COCKTAIL (NON-ALCOHOLIC)

Metric	Imperial
150 ml unsweetened natural yogurt	¼ pint unsweetened natural yogurt
4 ripe tomatoes, skinned and puréed and strained	4 ripe tomatoes, skinned and puréed and strained
2 drops of Worcestershire sauce	2 drops of Worcestershire sauce
1-2 drops of lemon juice	1-2 drops of lemon juice
Paprika	Paprika
Fresh mint sprigs	Fresh mint sprigs

Whisk together the yogurt, tomatoes, Worcestershire sauce and lemon juice with a dusting of paprika. Serve in tall glasses with a float of fresh mint. Serves 2 to 3

John Collins; Fresh tomato cocktail.

COLD CUPS AND PUNCHES

WHITE WINE CUP

Metric
Crushed ice
3 bottles of medium white wine
¾ bottle of dry sherry
4 x 15 ml spoons
   orange-flavoured liqueur
4 "splits" tonic water
3 cucumber slices, 1 slice of apple
   and 1 fresh borage sprig per jug

Imperial
Crushed ice
3 bottles of medium white wine
¾ bottle of dry sherry
4 tablespoons orange-flavoured
   liqueur
4 "splits" tonic water
3 cucumber slices, 1 slice of apple
   and 1 fresh borage sprig per jug

Mix all the ingredients in one or more jugs and chill before serving.
Serves 19 to 20

RED WINE CUP

Metric
2 bottles of red wine (preferably
   Rioja), well chilled
1 bottle (same capacity as the
   wine bottles) of soda water,
   well chilled
Sugar to taste, dissolved in
   water, or sugar syrup
   (see page 174)
Large pinch of ground
   cinnamon
Lemon and orange slices

Imperial
2 bottles of red wine (preferably
   Rioja), well chilled
1 bottle (same capacity as the
   wine bottles) of soda water,
   well chilled
Sugar to taste, dissolved in
   water, or sugar syrup
   (see page 174)
Large pinch of ground
   cinnamon
Lemon and orange slices

This is a simple version of Spanish sangria. Mix together the wine,
soda water, dissolved sugar or sugar syrup and cinnamon. Pour into a
punch bowl and stir in the fruit slices. (Ice cubes and a glass or two of
sherry or brandy could be added.) Serves about 12

Red wine cup; White wine cup.

Midsummer Night's Dream.

MIDSUMMER NIGHT'S DREAM

Metric
1 bottle of Riesling
1 bottle of Beaujolais
3 x 15 ml spoons
   orange-flavoured liqueur
1 dessert apple, cored and sliced
Pieces of melon
Orange slices, quartered
Few strawberries
Crushed ice
750 ml fizzy lemonade
Sugar syrup (see page 174) to
   taste

Imperial
1 bottle of Riesling
1 bottle of Beaujolais
3 tablespoons orange-flavoured
   liqueur
1 dessert apple, cored and sliced
Pieces of melon
Orange slices, quartered
Few strawberries
Crushed ice
1¼ pints fizzy lemonade
Sugar syrup (see page 174) to
   taste

Red wine and orange punch; Barbados rum punch.

Pour the wines and liqueur over the fruit and ice in a bowl. Chill, then add the lemonade and sugar syrup to taste. Serve ice-cold. Serves about 10

BARBADOS RUM PUNCH

Metric	**Imperial**
Rum	Rum
Orange juice	Orange juice
Grated nutmeg	Grated nutmeg

Mix rum with orange juice in the proportions you like and top up with ice-cold water. Serve in tumblers with just a sprinkling of nutmeg.

RED WINE AND ORANGE PUNCH

Metric	**Imperial**
1 orange	1 orange
12 cloves	12 cloves
2 bottles of red Burgundy	2 bottles of red Burgundy
1 x 540 ml can unsweetened orange juice	1 x 19 fl oz can unsweetened orange juice
24 sugar lumps	24 sugar lumps
6 x 15 ml spoons orange-flavoured liqueur	6 tablespoons orange-flavoured liqueur

Stud the orange with the cloves. Slice it and place it in a punch bowl. Pour the Burgundy and orange juice into a saucepan, add the sugar lumps and bring nearly to the boil. Add the liqueur and heat but don't boil. Pour over the orange slices. Serves 12

HOT PUNCHES AND CUPS

HUCKLE-MY-BUFF

Metric
1.2 litres draught beer
6 eggs, beaten
50 g sugar
Grated nutmeg
Brandy to taste

Imperial
2 pints draught beer
6 eggs, beaten
2 oz sugar
Grated nutmeg
Brandy to taste

A perfect drink to serve round the bonfire on Guy Fawkes night or after a Boxing Day walk in the country. Heat 600 ml (1 pint) of the beer with the eggs and sugar, but do not boil. Remove from the heat and add the remaining beer, a generous amount of nutmeg and brandy to taste. Serve in heatproof glasses.

You will need a large saucepan or flameproof casserole to make this punch. Serve it with a ladle. Serves 6

Huckle-my-buff.

HOT HONEY TODDY

Metric	Imperial
1 bottle of medium dry white wine	1 bottle of medium dry white wine
Thinly pared rind and juice of 1 lemon	Thinly pared rind and juice of 1 lemon
2 x 15 ml spoons thin honey	2 tablespoons thin honey
Few pieces of mace blade	Few pieces of mace blade
1 x 5 cm cinnamon stick	1 x 2 inch cinnamon stick
4 x 15 ml spoons brandy	4 tablespoons brandy

Heat the wine, lemon rind and juice, honey and flavourings to just below boiling point. Remove from the heat, cover and leave to infuse for 1 hour.

Reheat the punch, but do not boil it. Strain it into a warmed jug. Add the brandy and serve immediately. (Run the punch into the glasses over the back of a spoon to prevent their cracking.)
Serves 6 to 8

GLÜHWEIN

Metric	Imperial
600 ml red wine	1 pint red wine
75 g brown sugar	3 oz brown sugar
2 x 5 cm cinnamon sticks	2 x 2 inch cinnamon sticks
1 lemon stuck with cloves	1 lemon stuck with cloves
150 ml brandy	¼ pint brandy

Put all the ingredients except the brandy in a pan, bring to simmering point and simmer gently, covered, for 2 to 4 minutes. Remove from the heat, add the brandy, strain and serve at once.
Serves about 4

JULGLÖGG (CHRISTMAS WINE)

Metric	Imperial
1 bottle of aquavit or gin	1 bottle of aquavit or gin
2 bottles of Burgundy	2 bottles of Burgundy
75 g seedless raisins, cleaned	3 oz seedless raisins, cleaned
100 g sugar	4 oz sugar
1 x 15 ml spoon cardamom seeds (optional)	1 tablespoon cardamom seeds (optional)
6 cloves	6 cloves
1 x 5 cm cinnamon stick	1 x 2 inch cinnamon stick
Small piece of lemon rind	Small piece of lemon rind

Pour half the aquavit or gin into a saucepan with the wine. Add the raisins and sugar. Tie the spices and lemon rind in muslin and add to the pan. Cover and bring very slowly to the boil. Simmer for 30 minutes.

Add the remaining aquavit or gin and remove from the heat. Take out the muslin bag of spices and, just before serving, ignite the punch with a match. Serve in tumblers or punch glasses.
Serves 12 to 13

Glühwein; Julglögg; Hot honey toddy.

Non-Alcoholic Cups and Punches

Verandah Punch

Metric
Juice of 2 large juicy oranges
Juice of 3 thin-skinned lemons
150 ml sugar syrup (see page 174)
300 ml freshly made tea
3 x 175 ml bottles of ginger ale, well chilled
3 x 175 ml bottles of soda water, well chilled
Ice cubes
Orange slices to decorate

Imperial
Juice of 2 large juicy oranges
Juice of 3 thin-skinned lemons
¼ pint sugar syrup (see page 174)
½ pint freshly made tea
3 x 6 fl oz bottles of ginger ale, well chilled
3 x 6 fl oz bottles of soda water, well chilled
Ice cubes
Orange slices to decorate

Mix the fruit juices with the sugar syrup and tea. Cool, then strain into a bowl and chill. Just before serving, mix in the ginger ale and soda water. Add ice cubes and orange slices. Serves 9

Spicy Fruit Punch

Metric
600 ml fresh or canned orange juice
300 ml canned pineapple juice
Pared rind and juice of 1 lemon
1 x 2.5 ml spoon grated nutmeg
6 cloves
1 x 2.5 ml spoon mixed spice
600 ml water
100-175 g sugar
6 'splits' of American ginger ale, chilled
Crushed ice
Pared orange or lemon rind to garnish

Imperial
1 pint fresh or canned orange juice
½ pint canned pineapple juice
Pared rind and juice of 1 lemon
½ teaspoon grated nutmeg
6 cloves
½ teaspoon mixed spice
1 pint water
4-6 oz sugar
6 'splits' of American ginger ale, chilled
Crushed ice
Pared orange or lemon rind to garnish

Mix the fruit juices, lemon rind and spices in a large jug. Put the water and sugar into a saucepan and heat gently to dissolve the sugar. Cool, then add the other ingredients from the jug. Chill. Strain the liquid and add the ginger ale and crushed ice just before serving. Garnish with pared orange or lemon rind. Serves 20

Grapefruit or Lime Soda

Metric
1 ice cube, crushed
½ glass of soda water
2 x 15 ml spoons grapefruit juice or 1 x 15 ml spoon lime juice
1 x 15 ml spoon ice cream

Imperial
1 ice cube, crushed
½ glass of soda water
2 tablespoons grapefruit juice or 1 tablespoon lime juice
1 tablespoon ice cream

Whisk all the ingredients together with a rotary whisk until frothy, or blend at maximum speed for 1 minute in an electric blender. Pour into a large glass. Serves 1

Ginger Soda

Metric
¾ glass of ginger beer
¼ glass of lemonade
1 x 15 ml spoon ice cream

Imperial
¾ glass of ginger beer
¼ glass of lemonade
1 tablespoon ice cream

Make as for grapefruit or lime soda. Serves 1

Pineapple Crush

Metric
1 x 539 ml can pineapple juice
Juice of 1 orange
Juice of 1 lemon
Sugar
1.2 litres ginger ale (chilled in the bottle)

Imperial
1 x 19 fl oz can pineapple juice
Juice of 1 orange
Juice of 1 lemon
Sugar
2 pints ginger ale (chilled in the bottle)

Combine the fruit juices, sweeten to taste and chill. Just before serving, add the ginger ale. Serves about 9

Hot Spiced Pineapple Cup

Metric
2 x 400 ml cans pineapple juice
4 x 15 ml spoons sugar
2 x 15 ml spoons lemon juice
1 x 10 cm cinnamon stick

Imperial
2 x 15 fl oz cans pineapple juice
4 tablespoons sugar
2 tablespoons lemon juice
1 x 4 inch cinnamon stick

Simmer all the ingredients together for 10 minutes. Remove the cinnamon and pour the liquid into glasses. Serves 5

Hot spiced pineapple cup; Spicy fruit punch; Pineapple crush; Verandah punch.

LEMON CIDER CUP

Metric	Imperial
3 lemons	3 lemons
100 g caster sugar	4 oz caster sugar
1 cinnamon stick	1 cinnamon stick
600 ml boiling water	1 pint boiling water
1.2 litres cider, chilled	2 pints cider, chilled
1 'split' of soda water, chilled	1 'split' of soda water, chilled
Lemon slices	Lemon slices

Pare the rind from two of the lemons, free of any pith. Squeeze the juice from all the lemons. Put the rind, juice, sugar and cinnamon stick in a large jug. Pour on the boiling water and stir until the sugar has dissolved. Leave to cool, then strain into a bowl. Just before serving, add the cider, soda water and a lemon slice to float in each glass. Serves 12

APRICOT CIDER CUP

Metric	Imperial
1 x 820 g can apricots, drained	1 x 1 lb 13 oz can apricots, drained
1 x 5 cm cinnamon stick	1 x 2 inch cinnamon stick
15 g sweet almonds, blanched	½ oz sweet almonds, blanched
1.2 litres cider	2 pints cider
4 'splits' of tonic water	4 'splits' of tonic water

Rub the apricots through a sieve and put the purée into a large jug. Put the cinnamon, almonds and 300 ml (½ pint) of the cider in a pan. Bring to the boil, then remove from the heat and leave to stand for about 10 minutes. Cool, then add to the apricot purée. Just before serving, add remaining cider and tonic water and stir well. Serves 6

Below: Lemon cider cup; Ginger soda; Grapefruit or lime soda; Apricot cider cup.

QUANTITY GUIDE
APPROXIMATE QUANTITIES FOR BUFFET PARTIES

	1 portion	24-26 portions	Notes
Soups: cream or clear	200 ml (⅓ pint)	4.75 litres (1 gallon)	Serve garnished in mugs or cups.
Fish cocktail: shrimp, prawn, tuna or crab	25 g (1 oz)	750 g (1½ lb) fish 2-3 lettuces 900 ml (1½ pints) sauce	In stemmed glasses, garnished with a shrimp or prawn.
Meat with bone	150 g (5 oz)	3.25-3.50 kg (7-8 lb)	Cold roasts or barbecued chops.
boneless	75-100 g (3-4 oz)	2.25-3 kg (5-6½ lb)	Casseroles, meat balls, sausages, barbecued steaks.
Poultry: turkey	75-100 g (3-4 oz) boneless	7 kg (16 lb) (dressed)	
chicken	1 joint 150-225 g (5-8 oz)	6 x 1-1.5 kg (2½-3 lb) birds (dressed)	Serve hot or cold.
Delicatessen: ham or tongue	75-100 g (3-4 oz)	2.25-3 kg (5-6½ lb)	Halve the amounts if making stuffed cornets.
pâté for wine-and-pâté party	75-100 g (3-4 oz)	2.25-3 kg (5-6½ lb)	Halve the amount if pâté is starter course.
Salad vegetables lettuce	⅙	3-4	Dress at last minute.
cucumber	2.5 cm (1 inch)	2	
tomatoes	1-2	1.5 kg (3 lb)	
white cabbage	25 g (1 oz)	750 g (1½ lb)	For winter salads.
boiled potatoes	50 g (2 oz)	1.5 kg (3 lb)	For potato salads.
Rice or pasta	40 g (1½ oz) uncooked	1 kg (2 lb)	Can be cooked a day ahead; reheated for 5 min. in boiling water.
Cheese (for wine-and-cheese party)	75 g (3 oz)	1.75-2.25 kg (4½-5 lb) of at least 4 types	You'll need more if you serve a cheese dip, too.
Cheese (for biscuits)	25-40 g (1-1½ oz)	750 g-1 kg (1½-2 lb) cheese plus 500 g (1 lb) butter, 1 kg (2 lb) biscuits	Allow the larger amounts for an assorted cheese board.

APPROXIMATE TEA AND COFFEE QUANTITIES

	1 Serving	24-26 Servings		Notes
Coffee ground, hot	200 ml (⅓ pint)	225-250 g (8-9 oz) coffee 3.5 litres (6 pints) water	1.75 litres (3 pints) milk 500 g (1 lb) sugar	If you make the coffee in advance strain it after infusion. Reheat without boiling. Serve sugar separately.
ground, iced	200 ml (⅓ pint)	350 g (12 oz) coffee 3.5 litres (6 pints) water	1.75 litres (3 pints) milk sugar to taste	Make coffee (half sweetened, half not), strain and chill. Mix with chilled milk. Serve in glasses.
instant, hot	200 ml (⅓ pint)	50-75 g (2-3 oz) coffee 3.5 litres (6 pints) water	1.25 litres (2 pints) milk 500 g (1 lb) sugar	Make coffee in jugs as required. Serve sugar separately.

	1 Serving	24-26 Servings		Notes
instant, iced	200 ml ($\frac{1}{3}$ pint)	75 g (3 oz) coffee 1.25 litres (2 pints) water	3.5 litres (6 pints) milk sugar to taste	Make black coffee (half sweetened, half not) and chill. Mix with chilled creamy milk. Serve in glasses.
Tea Indian, hot	200 ml ($\frac{1}{3}$ pint)	50 g (2 oz) tea 4.75 litres (8 pints) water	900 ml (1$\frac{1}{2}$ pints) milk 500 g (1 lb) sugar	It is better to make tea in several pots rather than in one outsize one.
Indian, iced	200 ml ($\frac{1}{3}$ pint)	75 g (3 oz) tea 4.25 litres (7 pints) water	1.25 litres (2 pints) milk sugar to taste	Strain tea immediately it has infused. Sweeten half of it. Chill. Serve in glasses with chilled milk.
China	200 ml ($\frac{1}{3}$ pint)	50 g (2 oz) tea 5.5 litres (9 pints) water	2-3 lemons 500 g (1 lb) sugar	Infuse China tea for 2-3 minutes only. Put a thin lemon slice in each cup before pouring. Serve sugar separately.

SAVOURIES AND SWEETS

	Ingredients	Portions	Notes
Sausage rolls	675 g (1$\frac{1}{2}$ lb) shortcrust or flaky pastry or 2 x 312 g (2 x 12 oz) pkts frozen shortcrust or flaky pastry; 1 kg (2 lb) sausagemeat	25-30 medium or 50 small rolls	Pastry based on 675 g (1$\frac{1}{2}$ lb) flour, 350-450 g ($\frac{3}{4}$-1 lb) fat.
Boucheés	450 g (1 lb) puff pastry or 2 x 227 g (2 x 8 oz) pkts frozen puff pastry; 600 ml (1 pint) thick white sauce; 275 g (10 oz) prepared filling	50 boucheés	Pastry based on 450 g (1 lb) flour, 350 g (12 oz) butter. Fillings: chopped cooked ham, chicken, egg, mushrooms, shrimps.
Cheese straws	225 g (8 oz) cheese pastry	100 cheese straws	225 g (8 oz) flour, 125 g (4 oz) fat, 125 g (4 oz) cheese.
Meringues	6 egg whites; 350 g (12 oz) caster sugar; 450 ml ($\frac{3}{4}$ pint) whipped cream	50 (small) meringue halves	2 halves per head with cream; 1 half with fruit and cream, or ice cream.
Jelly	3 litres (2$\frac{1}{2}$ quarts)	25	
Trifle	2.5 litres (4 pints) custard; 25 sponge fingers; 1 large can fruit	25	Decorate with cream, glacé cherries, nuts, angelica.
Fruit salad	3 kg (6$\frac{1}{2}$ lb) fruit; 1.75-2.5 litres (3-4 pints) sugar syrup; 1 litre (1$\frac{1}{2}$ pints) cream	25	Can be prepared a day ahead and left submerged in syrup, but bananas should be added just before serving.

SALAD DRESSINGS

Mayonnaise	600 ml (1 pint) for 12 salad portions	900 ml-1 litre (1$\frac{1}{2}$-1$\frac{3}{4}$ pints) for 24-26 salad portions	For 600 ml (1 pint), use 3 egg yolks, 400 ml ($\frac{3}{4}$ pint) oil, 3 x 15 ml spoons (3 tablespoons) vinegar, 1.5 x 5 ml spoons (1$\frac{1}{2}$ teaspoons) each of dry mustard, salt and sugar, and 1 x 5 ml spoon (1 teaspoon) pepper.
French dressing	300 ml ($\frac{1}{2}$ pint) for 12 salad portions	450-600 ml ($\frac{3}{4}$-1 pint) for 24-26 salad portions	Make in a lidded container and shake together just before serving.

HOW A FREEZER CAN HELP

Food and Storage time*	Preparation and Freezing	Thawing and Serving*
Meat and poultry, cooked dishes, casseroles, stews, curries, etc: 3 months If highly seasoned: 2 months	Prepare as desired; do not overcook. Have enough liquid to cover meat completely. Freeze when quite cold in rigid containers, foil dishes or foil-lined cookware.	Reheat in casserole from frozen. Allow at least 1 hour in oven at 200°C/400°F, Gas Mark 6. Reduce heat to 180°C/350°F, Gas Mark 4 and cook for 40 minutes, or until really hot.
Meat loaves, pâtés: 1 month	Follow recipe. When cold freeze in tin or dish, and when frozen remove from dish, wrap tightly in foil and overwrap in polythene.	Thaw overnight in refrigerator. For quicker thawing slice before freezing, place waxed paper between slices and wrap (see left).
Fish, cooked pies, fish cakes: 1-2 months	Follow recipe but omit any hard-boiled eggs from mixture. Freeze when cold in foil-lined containers. Remove when hard, then pack in sealed bags.	Thaw overnight in refrigerator or put straight in oven in ovenproof dish at 180°C/350°F, Gas Mark 4 until heated through.
Sauces, soups, stocks: 3 months If highly seasoned: 2 weeks	Prepare as usual. When cold, pour into rigid containers, seal well and freeze.	Thaw, covered, at room temperature, or heat in pan until boiling point is reached.
Pizza (yeast mixture) baked: up to 2 months	Bake as usual. When cold pack in foil or polythene, and freeze flat. When frozen pack in twos or threes in polythene bags.	Remove packaging and place frozen in oven at 200°C/400°F, Gas Mark 6, for about 20 mins. If thawed, reheat as above for 10-15 mins.
Pastry, cooked Pastry cases: 6 months Meat pies: 3-4 months Fruit pies: 6 months	Prepare and cook as usual. Brush pastry cases with egg white before filling. Cool. Wrap carefully (very fragile) in foil.	Thaw at room temperature for 2-4 hours. Then reheat if required hot. Allow flans to thaw for about 1 hour. Refresh in a warm oven.
Pancakes, unfilled: 3 months	Add 1 x 15 ml spoon (1 tablespoon) corn oil to basic 100 g (4 oz) flour recipe. Make pancakes; cool on a wire rack. Interleave with polythene film. Seal in polythene bags or foil. Freeze.	Thaw in packaging overnight in refrigerator or 2-3 hours at room temperature. To reheat place stack of pancakes, wrapped in foil, in oven at 190°C/375°F, Gas Mark 5 for 20-30 mins. Or separate pancakes and reheat in a lightly greased pan, 30 seconds on each side.
Desserts Mousses, creams, soufflés, etc: 2-3 months	Make as usual. Freeze unwrapped in foil-lined container until firm, then remove container and place dessert in polythene bag. Soufflés can be left in soufflé dish placed in polythene bag when firm.	Unwrap and thaw in refrigerator overnight (at least 6 hours).
Cream, fresh: 3 months	Use only pasteurised double or whipping cream. Half whip with a little sugar, 1 x 5 ml spoon (1 teaspoon) to 150 ml (¼ pint). Pack in waxed carton, leaving space for expansion.	Thaw in refrigerator for 24 hours or 12 hours at room temperature.
Cakes Sponges and layer cakes: 3 months (Frosted cakes lose quality after 2 months)	Bake in usual way. Leave until cold. Wrap in polythene film or foil. Freeze frosted cakes unwrapped. When firm, wrap, seal and pack in boxes for protection.	Unwrap frosted and cream cakes before thawing. Leave plain cakes in package. Allow 1-2 hours for small cakes, 4 hours for frosted and larger cakes at room temperature.
Scones and teabreads: 3 months	Bake in usual way. Freeze in polythene bag or foil.	Thaw in wrapping at room temperature for 2-3 hours.

Food and Storage time*	Preparation and Freezing	Thawing and Serving*
Frozen chicken: 12 months Turkey, duck: 9 months	Keep in the freezer in original wrapping.	Thaw in wrapping, preferably in refrigerator. Allow: 12 hours for birds up to 1.8 kg/4 lb; 24 hours for birds up to 5.5 kg/ 12 lb; 48-72 hours for birds over 5.5 kg/ 12 lb; joints 6 hours.

***Note:** The storage times given are the recommended maximum times food will keep in peak condition in a freezer. It will start to lose flavour and texture after that time. Although the change may be difficult to discern, the food remains safe to eat provided it is properly handled and cooked.

*Thawing times cannot be accurate as they depend on the temperature of the room, or the quantity of food already in the refrigerator and also the size of pack, but the times given in this table are a useful guideline.

PASTRY AND FILLING GUIDE

Tin sizes can only be approximate as manufacturers' ranges vary. Pastry amounts are generous to allow a certain flexibility for depths and metric proportions. Leftover trimmings can be used to make a pasty, turnover or a few tartlet cases.

Size of Tin	Pastry Required to Line
15 cm (6 inch)	100 g (4 oz) flour, etc.
18 cm (7 inch)	150 g (5 oz) flour, etc.
20.5 cm (8 inch)	200 g (7 oz) flour, etc.
23 cm (9 inch)	250 g (9 oz) flour, etc.
25.5 cm (10 inch)	300 g (11 oz) flour, etc.
28 cm (11 inch)	350 g (12 oz) flour, etc.

NB As a fluted flan *ring* is deeper than its equivalent size fluted flan tin, you'll need to use a size larger tin for a recipe that specifies a ring.

Fillings
15 cm (6 inch) flan needs half the amount of 20.5 cm (8 inch)
18 cm (7 inch) flan takes half the quantity of a 23 cm (9 inch)
25.5 cm (10 inch) flan needs twice the amount of a 20.5 cm (8 inch).

To bake blind:
Line the flan tin with rolled out pastry. Cover the pastry with greaseproof paper, or foil and dried beans, and bake at the usual temperature. Remove the beans and paper 5 to 10 minutes before the end of the cooking time. Small tartlet tins lined with pastry need only be pricked before baking.
To refresh savoury biscuits and pastries, flans or quiches, heat them in a warm oven (160°C/325°F, Gas Mark 3) for 5 to 10 minutes according to size and quantity.

INDEX

ACKNOWLEDGMENTS

The publishers would like to thank the following companies for their kindness in providing materials and equipment used in the photography for this book:
Liberty, Elizabeth David, Craftsmen Potters Association of Great Britain, David Mellor, Spode.
We should also like to thank the following who were concerned in the preparation of the book:
Carol Macartney, Consultant Editor; Margaret Coombes, Food Editor; Norma MacMillan, Editor; Brenda Holroyd, Associate Editor; Jill Eggleton, Caroline Young, Diana Wilkins and Alex Dufort, Home Economists.

Photography by: Barry Bullough: 2-8, 30, 31, 90-92, 106, 107, 110-119, 157 (bottom), 158-163; Paul Kemp: 12-23, 26, 27, 34-43, 54-59, 61, 126-129, 131, 146-148, 150-152, 153 (bottom right), 164-181; Philip Dowell: 10, 11, 24, 25, 32, 33, 44, 45, 52, 53, 60, 62, 63, 68, 69, 72, 73, 88, 89, 102, 103, 120, 121, 123-125, 130, 132, 133, 140-145, 153 (bottom left), 154, 155, 157 (top); Melvin Grey: 28, 29, 46-51, 64-67, 70, 71, 75-87, 93-101, 104, 105, 108, 109, 134-139; Robert Golden: jacket photograph p 185.

TWICE BITTEN

TWICE BITTEN

Gerald Hammond

CHIVERS LARGE PRINT
BATH

British Library Cataloguing in Publication Data available

This Large Print edition published by Chivers Press, Bath, 1999.

Published by arrangement with Macmillan.

U.K. Hardcover ISBN 0 7540 3691 X
U.K. Softcover ISBN 0 7540 3692 8

Printed and bound in Great Britain by
Redwood Books, Trowbridge, Wiltshire

I am grateful to Alan Wood of the United Kingdom Blade Association, Mr Wilson of Wilson and Sons (Dundee) Ltd., dog-food manufacturers, and to Keith Erlandson, the gun dog guru, for patiently answering a lot of daft questions.

PREFACE

It was cold on the hill, and all the colder for what we had just found. The body itself was warmer than we were by far, but it had been roasted as if for some cannibal meal. I had smelled burnt bodies before, in the Falklands and elsewhere, and it was always shocking, not by virtue of what it was and certainly not because the smell itself was bad, but because it smelled like any other roasting meat.

But this was all the worse because I thought that I knew who it was.

The crime had grown from seeds planted years earlier, although I could not have known it at the time. I say 'the crime', but in my opinion there were two crimes and the one recognized by the law was the lesser.

Our involvement had begun more than a year before . . .

1

CHAPTER ONE

I remember the night early that spring when Mim was born. The occasion stands out from all the other births which have now rather merged together in my memory, only the latest whelping ever being distinct in my mind. We have had rather a lot of springer spaniel and other litters at Three Oaks Kennels over the years.

Either Daffy or Hannah (our two kennel-maids) would normally attend a whelping. Bitches can usually manage very well on their own and when one of them beats the calendar and fools us she can be counted on to show us a perfect litter with pride next morning. (Puppies, like babies, are nearly always born in the small hours.) So we have never made a rule about it, but the girls are conscientious and involved and they share the duty of attending the *accouchement* according to a roster of their own devising. If there is any reason to expect a problem, Isobel, a partner and a qualified vet, will keep the sitter-up company or be available 'on call'. But this was not Hebe's first litter and no trouble was foreseen.

On this occasion Rex, Daffy's husband, was away on the oil rig so when Hebe was seen to be moving restlessly and making a nest for

3

herself, Daffy dozed in the armchair in the heated whelping shed. All went well. Daffy even managed a few hours of sleep and had been home for a shower and change. Isobel, who had expressed every confidence in the outcome, was as anxious as anybody and arrived in a rush long before her usual time, just as Beth and I descended the stairs in the old farmhouse and deposited Sam on top of the two cushions on his chair in the big kitchen. Beth and Daffy set about making breakfast. Beth whipped up something special for Sam and, to his indignation, Isobel started spooning it into him. There are no lines of demarcation at Three Oaks Kennels.

'How did it go?' Beth asked Daffy.

'Seven,' Daffy said. 'All thriving.'

Isobel picked up immediately on the reserve in Daffy's voice and flashed her pink-framed spectacles at the younger woman. 'You don't sound very sure,' she said.

'One of them looks slightly odd.'

That was enough for Isobel. The occasional stillborn pup could be accepted, but oddities might indicate a genetic freak affecting the whole of our carefully sculptured breeding line. She left Sam to feed himself, which he was quite capable of doing with only occasional lapses, and was out of the house like a whippet. She was well into her fifties but if anything was wrong with one of the dogs she could show a remarkable turn of speed. A quick flash of sunshine, a slam of the door and she was gone.

'Look who's talking,' Beth said.

Daffy looked up from the frying pan and put out her tongue. This, bearing in mind that Beth is the third partner, was a piece of impertinence. Daffy also shook her head. I was mildly disappointed to see that although she was still as always an eccentric dresser she had given up wearing a violently coloured stripe in her hair. I had rather enjoyed the daily changing splash of colour. 'There's nothing much wrong with her,' she said plaintively. 'Or nothing very much. I only said that she looks slightly odd.'

'She,' Beth said. 'Damn!' Bitch pups, as well as commanding a higher price, were essential to our breeding programme. 'What else have we got?'

'Three dogs, three bitches.'

'What do you mean, "odd"?' I asked Daffy.

'Nothing awful. Her ears are black, but the rest of her looks grey rather than black and white. And her face doesn't look quite right. The bitch couldn't have been served twice?'

'No,' I said. 'She couldn't.'

Hannah came in from feeding the other youngsters. Adhering rigidly to the job in hand, she had, with more restraint than the rest of us would have shown, passed by the whelping kennel without looking in on the new litter. Before we had finished explaining,

5

Isobel returned, relief showing clearly on her homely face. 'Not to panic,' she said, brooding over Sam again. 'What we've got is a—'

The last word was lost to me in a splutter from the frying pan.

'A loony?' Daffy said doubtfully.

'A Clunie,' Isobel corrected. 'That's what they're commonly known as.' She looked round our faces. The two girls were frankly puzzled. Beth put a plate of bacon and eggs in front of me and waited for elucidation. I got on with my breakfast and tried to look as though I knew what Isobel was talking about. Sam made it clear that he could not have cared less and concentrated on the more important subject of breakfast. Isobel, who studies gun dog bloodlines so intensely that she knows them better than the lines on her own face, resumed in tones which might have been used by one explaining the mysteries of the universe to a class of four-year-olds. 'A throwback to Champion Clunie of Netherbrae. It's a very strong set of genes and when they come back together, which they do now and again, the result takes after her in both appearance and temperament. I warned you when you chose the sire, you may remember. He has Clunie for a great-great-grandam and Hebe has the same only one generation further back.'

Now that she mentioned it I remembered that Isobel had uttered a few cautionary words, but she had made the risk sound remote and she is inclined to prophesy doom whenever gun dog genetics is under discussion. 'Surely,' I said, 'if Clunie was a champion . . .'

'She was a very talented bitch,' Isobel said. 'Quite brilliant on her day, but temperamental. She was sort of brindled with small spots instead of the larger patches of the usual spaniel, so that she looked grey from a distance. And she had a slightly undershot jaw, just like this pup. Not the kind of appearance to attract an owner. And her temperament was both nervous and headstrong.'

'And those of her descendants who inherit her looks have her temperament as well?' I asked, hoping that Isobel might have changed her opinion within the last few minutes.

'In my experience, invariably.'

'Oh dear!' I said mildly. We tried to be very careful of our language now that Sam was not only articulate but approaching school age. He had developed an uncanny knack of singling out the rude word and then picking on the very occasion when we would least like to hear it repeated. But as the principal trainer in the firm I knew that a headstrong dog which was also of a nervous and sensitive disposition was a trainer's nightmare. Whatever one did would be wrong for one side or the other of its nature. 'I'll take a look as soon as I've finished my breakfast,' I said. 'In your opinion, what do we do?'

'You certainly don't invest time and money training her to work,' Isobel said. 'And you can't sell her as a pup for an owner to train without damaging our reputation for only breeding the best. I don't see anyone buying her for a pet. We'd better put her down— unless HM Government wants her for a sniffer dog. Clunie had one of the finest noses in the business.'

There was a moment of uncomfortable silence. None of us had the least compunction about putting down the old and sick; each of us, indeed, would have supported the legalization of euthanasia. But we hated to put down any creature only because it was unwanted.

'Put me down,' Sam said suddenly. He meant that he wanted to be helped down from the cushion which raised him to a convenient height for feeding.

'Don't think we haven't thought of it,' Beth said affectionately. She heaved up her first-born and set him on his feet.

'Please,' Daffy said, 'don't decide just yet. Let's see what she looks like when her eyes open. If you want a good home for her . . . I might take her. I've been wanting one to train on my own account.'

'My dear girl,' said Isobel, 'you don't know what you'd be taking on.'

'If she's going to have the same temperament as Clunie,' Daffy said

8

stubbornly, 'and Clunie was made up to Champion—'

'By the great Harry Stimson,' Isobel said. 'One of the greatest trainers ever and while he was at the height of his career. You'd be walking a tightrope between being too harsh and too soft.'

'I could learn to walk a tightrope,' Daffy said. 'Couldn't I?' she added in my direction.

Sam was dashing round and round the table, tooting in imitation of an Intercity train. It made rational thinking difficult but I tried very hard. Strictly, the duties of the two kennel-maids were concerned with feeding, cleaning, grooming and exercising our stock and the occupants of the boarding and quarantine kennels. But training followed by success in competition brought in both revenue and reputation. The girls, and Daffy in particular, had been expected to play with and 'humanize' the young pups. Daffy had also undertaken much of the elementary training. She had helped me by throwing dummies and firing blank cartridges during more advanced lessons. I had found that she had learned by watching, so that I could tell her to 'Go and give so-and-so a lesson with the dummy launcher,' and know that it would be done with skill and sensitivity.

I had never dared to say so aloud, but I had rather hoped that when Isobel, who was the oldest of us three partners, retired from doing most of the handling in field trials, Daffy might be ready to take over. Since the illness which had ended my army career, I had remained subject to occasional fainting attacks that the doctors put down to vagal inhibition, in addition to which I had neither the stamina nor the steadfastness needed for consistent success in competition, both of which qualities Isobel had in plenty and Daffy seemed to be developing. A dog of her own might be the spur to further progress, and the more difficult the dog the further might be the progress. I could see a definite advantage in Daffy learning such lessons from mistakes made on her own dog rather than on one of the firm's.

'You've been coming on,' I said cautiously. 'But you still have a lot to learn.'

'You can teach me,' Daffy said. She caught Sam on his next circuit, sat him on her knee and popped a piece of toast into his mouth.

I was about to object to this bland assumption that I would spend my valuable time and energy on training a possible future rival in the field, when Beth chipped in. 'Let her try,' she said. 'We owe Daffy a lot.'

'I've no objection,' Isobel said, 'provided, first, that she doesn't carry our kennel-name and second, that she's never bred from.'

Probably they were both influenced by the blissful but temporary silence. Daffy, however, seized the moment. 'That's agreed, then,' she

10

said, transferring Sam to Isobel's knee. 'Work to be done. Come on, Hannah.' She headed out of the room before anybody could think of any counter-arguments.

*   *   *

The pup was named Mimulus—Mim for short, although there had already been a Mimosa. At eight weeks, she was removed and ownership transferred to Daffy. But we soon began to see a lot of her. Rex, Daffy's husband, was often to be seen leading the fast-growing pup around on a plaited leather leash, but when Rex was offshore (two weeks out of four) Mim came to Three Oaks with Daffy and mingled with our dogs.

For half a year, all went well. Love and patience seemed to be achieving what conventional wisdom could not. Mim learned to sit, stay, come, lie down and walk reliably at heel. She made progress at retrieving dummies. I was adamant that she must not be introduced to retrieving real game too early— that way lies the mortal sin of running-in—but she learned to retrieve dummies decorated with pheasant wings or rabbit skins by marking, memory, hand signals or scenting.

Sam also was learning. The first and most essential lesson for a child around a kennels was not to provoke a dog into biting him. One sharp nip taught him sense without, I was

11

pleased to see, giving him any real fear. The second was to wash thoroughly after mingling with the dogs and before touching food or his face. Once those two lessons had been ingrained he was free to visit the dogs, admire the young pups or help the girls with the chores. Young children can sometimes develop a better rapport with dogs than their elders. A dog has little reasoning power but a child, even one who would be going to school in a year or so, not being particularly well furnished in that direction, does not expect it. Sam took a particular fancy to Mim. Daffy insisted that without his company as playmate and assistant trainer, Mim would never have made the progress that she did.

One of Mim's admirers was Quentin Cove. Quentin owned a large farm over to the west of Cupar. He lived alone but he was a sociable man, a back-slapper with a loud laugh and a huge appetite for food and drink and, it was said, despite his bachelor status, women. I got on well enough with him although Beth usually managed to avoid him. Like many Scotsmen of rural upbringing but good education, he was well spoken but inclined to lapse into the Scots tongue when excited.

When the economic climate and the Government between them turned against farming, Quentin had decided to diversify. He was the third generation of Coves to own Ardrossie, so capital was not in short supply.

Some lightweight, modern buildings had been erected on a corner of his land and he had set up as a manufacturer and supplier of dog-food. He was adamant that the move arose from no more than sound economics, but I suspected that he had had in mind the interests of his farm-workers who were being displaced by advancing technology. The day-to-day management of the farm was left to his farm manager, Dougal Webb, a graduate from agricultural college but not too proud to drive a tractor or handle a shovel.

We made Quentin's acquaintance soon after our arrival at Three Oaks. He was newly started in the dog-food business at the time and was acting as his own sales manager. He called to see me, offering an unusual deal which had already been turned down by several of our more established rivals. Although, as a shooting man himself, he kept several dogs, he needed greater feedback than he could manage from his own resources. If we would keep daily records of how our dogs thrived on his products and also allow the use of our competition successes in his advertising, he would supply us with his dog-food at half price, without limit of time.

The offer seemed almost too good to be true. After a trial period, which proved to my and even Isobel's satisfaction that Quentin's product was as good as any and better than most, I jumped at it. At the factory the various

13

mixtures were compressed into small and easily crumbled cakes of exact bulk, so that it was easy to count out the proper diet for a dog of any size and energy need. At first, Quentin was also his own delivery driver. Later, as his business grew, he employed others to drive his vans although most often our supplies were brought by Dougal Webb. The dog-food business was, strictly speaking, nothing to do with Dougal, but he was courting Hannah at the time and glad of the excuse to call.

During the summer Quentin, on one of his visits, met Daffy with Mim in the drive. He was very much taken with the spaniel, which was not surprising. Mim was becoming a very charming little dog. She had developed a habit, when Daffy held out her hand at hip level, of rearing up on her hind legs and thrusting her head against the hand, thus obtaining a pat without putting her mistress to any trouble. He enquired as to her pedigree and seemed very knowledgeable about Clunie of Netherbrae, which was not particularly surprising; Quentin's dogs were cousins to our stock. He told Daffy that if she ever wanted to part with Mim she could expect a good offer. Daffy said that Mim was a champion of the future and advised him not to hold his breath.

Mim's progress was too good to last.

One morning, at Daffy's home beyond the village and only a few days after Quentin's

14

visit, a metal basin which Daffy was taking down from a high shelf slipped from her fingers. The noise, she said later, was just as she imagined a bomb would sound and, by mischance, the basin landed beside the sleeping Mim and caught the spaniel a crack over the nose as it bounced.

The effect on a nervous young dog may be imagined. Poor Mim developed a fear of loud noises which was resistant to normal treatments. In vain we fed her titbits while hands were gently clapped at varying distances. It took only the sound of a carelessly closed door to send her into the shelter of the nearest pair of friendly legs.

Worse was to follow. One week later, Rex was walking with Mim in farmland on the other side of the village. The spaniel seemed to be in better spirits and was quartering the grass, picking up scents and, no doubt, wondering what they might foretell. They reached a crest crowned by gorse bushes. Drawn by the scent of rabbits, Mim pushed into the cover.

Nobody can be quite sure what happened next, but it seems that the farmer was also looking for rabbits, but on the far side of the bushes. He saw a rabbit. There are rabbit holes just there and bunny probably went to ground. But the farmer saw a grey shape flitting through the bushes, which was almost certainly Mim. Whatever the explanation, Mim heard the sound of a shot and collected about a dozen pellets of Number Six shot.

The farmer was as horrified as Mim and Rex. He Land Rovered them straight to us at Three Oaks. While Isobel Kitts struggled to remove any pellets which were in danger of aggravating the physical damage, Rex sat with his head in his hands and told the story.

'What put the bloody lid on it for me,' he finished, 'was that when we reached the road and were lifting her into the Land Rover, Sanctimonious Pratt drove by. And he wagged a finger at us. He must have thought that one of us had run the dog over.'

I was duly sympathetic. Timothy Pratt, a freelance photographer and cameraman, was well known locally. He was often nicknamed 'Sanctimonious' because of his habit of sermonizing over anyone who he had at a moral disadvantage. He had political ambitions and by strange chance often figured heroically on television in his own film clips. At the moment he was admired without being liked. Millions of viewers had seen him attempting to rescue an injured motorcyclist and being himself burned in the attempt. Whatever characteristics Sanctimonious Pratt might lack, courage was not one of them; but it must have been gall and wormwood to Rex to be admonished by him at such a time and from a safe distance.

Isobel managed to tidy Mim up without

16

serious harm, but the damage to Mim's morale could never be repaired and I was forced to agree that she was now totally and incurably gun-shy.

Daffy, as far as I know, never reproached Rex, but Rex never forgave himself. Daffy was heartbroken. She loved Mim but she had set her heart on bringing a pup of her own to field trial standard. A chronically gun-shy dog would be a total loss for trials and might very well pass on her nervousness to any kennel-mate. Very reluctantly, Daffy and Rex agreed that Mim would have to go.

Daffy approached Quentin Cove and, although she was perfectly honest about the gun-shyness, received an acceptable offer. Mim was handed over. Daffy was subdued and occasionally tearful for several days but eventually another puppy which Rex, nobly abandoning for the moment his intention of building a sports car from a kit, insisted was properly bought and paid for this time, took her mind off Mim although she never forgot some of the lessons she had learned. They named the new puppy Sarda—the acronym of the Search and Rescue Dogs Association although, as Isobel pointed out more than once, the name would have more properly suited a Labrador.

For the moment, all seemed well.

*   *   *

The critical stage in the training of any dog which is to compete in field trials or be sold as a working gun dog is the introduction to live quarry. For this purpose, rabbits are useful and sometimes essential. The dog may have been schooled in all the basic skills, will have learned to quarter the ground, to obey whistles and hand signals, to ignore rabbits in the rabbit pen and to retrieve cold game. It may even have learned the futility of chasing after an airborne pheasant. But a running rabbit is an open invitation to chase. Perhaps the biggest hurdle in training is for the dog to learn to hunt the rabbit out of cover and then to stop dead, just when temptation is at its strongest, until sent for the retrieve. Happily for the dog trainer, most farmers regard the rabbit much as a fond mother regards the common nit. A shooter with a dog, both of whom can be trusted to respect crops and livestock, is usually welcomed.

That year, myxomatosis broke out again in our neighbourhood. It was not as total as in previous years—the infection is carried by the rabbit flea, which is mostly transferred in tightly occupied burrows, but rabbits now live more above-ground than they used to. And rabbits have developed a resistance to the virus. It was becoming quite common to gather a healthy rabbit with old mixy scars around the eyes. But those bunnies that caught the infection were seriously ill while it lasted. The disease was not communicable to dogs, but rabbits which hopped slowly or sat still were going to teach the dogs nothing that I wanted them to know and much that I hoped they would never find out.

Late that summer, Dougal Webb made the regular run with a supply of dog-food. He was a thickset young man with black, curly hair, a round and ruddy face and a square jaw. Beth and I both felt, for reasons that we could not put into words, that he was not a man for a young girl, or anybody else, to trust. He was just a little too sure of his welcome, too pleased with himself and certain that his allure would have the desired effect. For Hannah, it did just that. As far as she was concerned, the sun shone out of his every orifice. She could hardly utter a coherent word while he was around. Beth said that this was because he brought with him his own cloud of pheromones and testosterone and God alone knew what else. I couldn't see it myself. Dougal Webb also had a taste for life's more luxurious capital goods. I put forward the theory that free spending on a man's part might be a more powerful aphrodisiac than a whole cloud of personal chemicals. Beth, who was out of patience with me at the time, said that she wouldn't know about that, never having experienced either of them.

Dougal Webb was certainly a free spender though more, as far as I could judge, on his own comforts and status than on his lady friends. He dressed well and ran around in a Lotus quite unsuited to life on a farm. He wore a Rolex watch which I frankly envied. At first glance I had supposed it to be a fake, but the movement of the second hand confirmed that it was the genuine article. I had only once seen a similar model, and that had been on the wrist of one of the local landowners.

Although Dougal was devoted to expensive possessions, he was remarkably thrifty about little things. The abhorrence of waste which had probably endeared him to Quentin as a farm manager extended even to finishing every last crumb on his plate, so although Dougal once explained his lifestyle with a passing reference to a legacy, I guessed that he had known hard times. His visit was timed, as usual, to suit an invitation to the snack which passes with us for lunch, but whether this was due to thrift or lust was uncertain.

For once, nobody was away competing or engaged in some task too urgent to be left. We all managed to sit down together, so that the table in the big kitchen was crowded around and almost covered with crockery. In addition to Dougal, Sam and the five members of the firm, Henry, Isobel's husband, had walked over to join us, as was his frequent habit.

The myxomatosis that was still rife around

Three Oaks had struck earlier further south and passed on, leaving a slightly reduced but still thriving population behind. Sam, who was passing through a garrulous phase—or so we hoped—had been almost monopolizing the conversation but I seized on a moment when his mouth was full. 'I need to do some training on rabbits within the next day or two,' I told Dougal. 'Will it be all right if I come and work two or three dogs through your set-aside land?'

Dougal swallowed quickly. 'I'm afraid not,' he said. 'Mr Cove tells me that he's let the rough shooting over the farm, so he doesn't feel that he can let anybody else on. It wasn't any of my doing,' he added in what seemed to be genuine apology.

'I understand,' I said.

The loss of access to one farm was not a serious blow. I had been cultivating farmers for a long time, always asking each for an introduction and recommendation to his neighbours. Although it meant a big outlay on thank you bottles at Christmas, at least I was never without land to train on. But Henry may have thought that either Dougal or I would appreciate a quick change of subject, because he suddenly asked Dougal, 'How's Quentin getting on with Mim?'

This subject was more sensitive than the other. Hannah was looking at Dougal as though he had been handing down tablets of

21

stone, but I saw Daffy and Sam exchange a look of sadness. Spaniels are very loving little dogs. Once in a while one meets up with one of their number which is exceptionally both loving and giving. Sarda, Mim's replacement, was one of these; but Mim had had a special place in Daffy's heart and Sam's.

Dougal shrugged. 'That's the spotted one? I don't have much to do with the dogs. I believe he's very pleased with her.'

'Is he managing to do anything about the gun-shyness?' Henry persisted.

'He hasn't said anything, but I saw him working her with the dummy launcher the other day. I don't think he can be having too much trouble.'

I saw Daffy bite her lip. I knew that she was thinking that I was a false prophet. Perhaps, if she had persevered . . .

After lunch, I caught Daffy on her own. 'Don't blame yourself,' I said, 'or me. If he's had any success with the gun-shyness it may have been at the expense of something else. And even if Mim becomes a Dual Champion, it doesn't follow that you could have achieved the same. Just be happy for her.'

'You're probably right,' Daffy said. But I could see that she did not believe it.

CHAPTER TWO

Soon after that, autumn came round again, the shooting season opened and we were too busy to think about Quentin Cove. My own shooting engagements were infrequent, but I was picking-up several times in most weeks. The job of the pickers-up is to observe from behind the standing Guns and to use their dogs to collect any fallen birds other than those gathered by the Guns themselves. The opportunity is not to be missed, offering the trainer the ideal chance to give his dogs a final polish while at the same time having to himself the most enjoyable part of the day's sport and even being paid for it—albeit a comparative pittance. Trustworthy handlers and dogs are in demand by shoot organizers, to put birds in the bag and to give a merciful end to any not killed outright by the shot.

Along with shooting season, the season of field trials came rushing at us. Keeping our name before the shooting public and a series of field trial champions in our dogs' pedigrees was the only way to convince the shooting man that one of our stock would be a more dependable purchase than the untried progeny of the bitch next door. Isobel, who had a remarkable talent and temperament for handling dogs under competition conditions, was competing almost every weekend. This, unfortunately, tied up at least one other member of the firm, because Isobel, who had a very poor head for those inevitable celebratory drinks, had succumbed once too often to temptation and had lost her driving licence— to the general relief because, even sober, she had been the sort of driver who causes other motorists to wake up in the small hours, gibbering.

It was my responsibility to bring the dogs through the successive stages of training and to send them off with Isobel as prepared as they could be to acquit themselves well in competition. At the same time, it was necessary for the other dogs which I was training to sell as workers, the guests in boarding and the virtual prisoners in the quarantine kennels to be fed and watered, cleaned and groomed and, with the exception of those in quarantine who had to make do with an illicit period of chasing a ball in the quarantine courtyard, walked. And during all this activity it was inevitable that any brood bitch who had failed to conceive in the spring and was now in an interesting condition would pick the most frantically inconvenient moment to produce her litter.

During the occasional brief intervals in this frenetic activity, we were much too tired to give more than a passing thought to absent friends. It was not until late October that Mim was brought to our notice again. By then, the first rush of activity on the grouse moors was over and estates were giving that year's pheasants a little more time to mature, so that there was a comparative lull. My picking-up engagements were at a standstill, but I had three dogs to prepare for imminent competitions. The local rabbit population was still very low and unlikely to increase until spring. One of my favourite farms had been heavily poached by ferreters and another had received its annual visit from a team who shot at night by lamp from the back of a Land Rover. I was driven to try some of the farms where active game-shooting took place but, as I feared, I would not be welcome at that time of year. As a next-to-last resort I phoned Alec Hatton.

Alec's farm, Lincraigs, lay between Ardrossie, Quentin Cove's farm, and Marksmuir, the wide-spread estate of Sir Ian Bewlay. Without compromising on the efficiency of his farming, Alec ran a small shoot with a syndicate of middle-income executives mostly from Glenrothes. He managed the shoot very well and at a modest subscription, by making use of volunteer labour from among his members, tucking small patches of game crops into every otherwise unusable corner of his land, releasing a modest number of pheasant poults and depending on an inward migration of birds from the much larger numbers reared and released for the commercial shooting on Marksmuir.

Alec hesitated. He was usually a generous man although he always managed to sound grudging. It was only a mannerism. 'The morn's morn?' he said. 'Aye. That'll be fine, if you'll go round and dog the boundaries. Turn my birds back, like. Speak to me after.'

Dog training with a gun is best not done solo. The act of shooting distracts from the dog handling and rabbits in particular are adept at breaking out of cover on the far side from the lone hunter. Beth always resisted my going off alone in case one of my blackouts overtook me while I was out of reach of ready help. Isobel, who would normally have come along to work the dogs while I used the gun, had seized on what would probably be the last quiet spell before February to take Henry away on a visit to a relative in Oban.

'Who's coming with me?' I asked the world in general.

Beth was usually willing to come along and to shoot, quite competently, while I got on with the training, but Sam had developed a cough. 'You go,' she told Daffy. 'Hannah and I can manage the chores.'

Daffy nodded happily.

In the morning, there was a thin covering of fresh snow, the first since the early spring, but the roads were passable. I had hardly slowed the car outside the cottage where she lived with Rex before Daffy was out of the door and running down the path. Sarda was too young to progress beyond obedience training and the retrieval of dummies but, with the prospect of her own dog to bring on for competitions, Daffy was as keen as any young pup to learn. In wellingtons and a full set of Barbours, she looked almost normal or perhaps even a member of the Establishment.

Twenty minutes later we passed Ardrossie Farm and the clutch of new buildings, dominated by silos and a square aluminium tower, out of keeping with the ancient countryside, where the dog-food was made. As we bounced up the potholed farm-road to Lincraigs Alec Hatton, a distant figure on a tractor, waved to us.

Lincraigs Farm covered a large acreage and to dog the whole boundary would have taken more time than we could spare. But I could guess that it was the boundary with Marksmuir that concerned Alec. A farm track took us that way and I parked beside an enormous black-wrapped sausage of straw a hundred yards long. Evidently Alec was taking the fullest advantage of the new technology.

It was a marvellous day. Unexpected sunshine struck a sparkle from the snow without being warm enough to trigger a thaw. Beyond the boundary, Marksmuir was heavily wooded with beech and birch and rowan. On Lincraigs, tree strips and small copses had been preserved. A mild autumn had seen the leaves turn but they had not yet fallen. That first, light powdering of snow outlined the branches against a blue sky, and among the tracery the leaves glowed in the sunshine, gold and brown and orange and scarlet. It was a day to remember. Daffy had brought a camera for the sake of the dogs. An enlarged print of one of her shots hangs over my desk as I write. In the foreground, a rowan blazes with berries while beneath its branches a spaniel, with one paw raised and eyes alight, awaits the command, 'Get on!' The picture may be pretty rather than beautiful. It may belong on the lid of a chocolate-box. But it can still bring a glow to my heart.

But we were not there to enjoy the scenery. Daffy put away the camera and took my gun from me. She was becoming a more than competent shot.

The snow made scenting difficult but it held a record of every creature that had set foot on it. In particular, it saved us wasting time hunting for rabbits where there were none. It also showed the arrowhead footprints of many pheasants. Most of them had been drawn over the boundary from Marksmuir into a long and narrow strip of kale along the boundary of Lincraigs and towards grain-filled feed-hoppers strategically placed among scattered gorse-bushes. The deliberate tempting of a neighbour's birds across the boundary was perfectly legal. It would have been generally denounced as un-neighbourly, but while Daffy knocked over the occasional rabbit, I worked the dogs, one at a time, with a clear conscience and sent pheasants onwards towards the two small woods at the heart of the Lincraigs shoot. Sir Ian Bewlay had never been among my favourite people and I was tickled by the thought of how the wandering would have infuriated his thrifty spirit.

In the cold air, sound travelled. On Gifford Hill, which humped up to the south of us, foresters were felling the conifer plantation, clearing the roots and waste branches by building the foundation for a huge future bonfire. In the process, a house was emerging where previously I had only seen a roof and chimneys. The sound of the foresters' voices came clearly between the bursts of chainsaw.

The spaniels seemed to be enjoying the beauty of the day. They worked with zest but stayed under control, making only occasional tries to test their handler's firmness as spaniels always will.

Between Lincraigs and Gifford Hill ran another back-road and where the boundary met the road stood a small but stoutly built cottage with a slated roof and walls of stone. The small garden was tidy but the flowers were over and the vegetables almost finished. I had seen the place before but never its occupant. That morning, as we reached the road a figure was entering the garden gate, a woman of around sixty. She was very small and even in her youth could never have been a beauty, having a flat nose, a disproportionately large mouth and a noticeable squint. The spaniel at work just then, Pru, being even more sociable than the rest, pushed through the hedge and went to make her acquaintance and she squeaked with delight and went down on her knees to pet the dog. (This was a breach of discipline on the part of Pru but it was too late to do anything much about it; the dog had already been rewarded with praise.)

She stood up, without becoming much taller, and came close to the hedge. 'Yon's gey bonny dogs you hae there,' she said. Although her speech was broad her voice was pure and she had a ready grin. Despite her goblinlike appearance, I found myself inclined to like her. Pru evidently agreed, because she reappeared at the woman's side bearing one of the rabbits that we had collected and delivered the limp body into her hands. The old woman accepted it without any sign of squeamishness. When she held it out to me I said, 'Keep it, if you'd like it.'

She smiled with the warmth that redeemed her face. 'I'd like it fine,' she said. 'Rabbit flesh is hailsome meat. I'm Elsie Dundee,' she added.

'John Cunningham.'

'I ken that,' she said. 'You're the dog man.'

I bade her a slightly cool farewell. I dislike being addressed as Captain but I once threatened to sue a journalist who referred to me as a dog man.

All went well until we were almost back at the car and ready to leave, when the youngest dog put up a cock pheasant which rocketed, gaudy in the sunshine, only to hit an overhead wire in a puff of bronze feathers and come spiralling down with a broken wing, just over the boundary. Burn, the oldest dog, brought it to me for the *coup de grâce*.

Even so early in the season, the game dealers were giving only the price of a pint of beer for a pheasant and this would soon be reduced to less than half. All the same, I was in no doubt that I must deliver the bird to Alec with an apology. One can feel totally alone in the countryside; but break a single rule and an observer will pop out of every bush. I turned the car and picked my way between the potholes back towards Lincraigs Farmhouse.

*   *   *

In the farmyard the tractor was muttering to itself like a bad-tempered old man, but at the farmhouse door Alec Hatton was talking to a visitor. As I stopped the car at the mouth of the yard they both looked round and I saw that the visitor was Dougal Webb, dressed for once not in his elegant casuals but in dusty jeans and a sweater. A few more quick words were exchanged before Dougal turned away. He gave us a cheerful nod as he went by. He vanished into a dip leading down through a field of set-aside land towards Ardrossie.

Alec Hatton followed more slowly. He was around forty, lightly built though I knew that he was very strong. I got out of the car to meet him, holding out the pheasant. 'You'd better take this,' I said.

He smiled to Daffy who was still in the car, then looked at me in surprise for several seconds. His weather-beaten face was as thin as his body and seemed have melted slightly so that his lower lip, his nose and even his eyelids seemed to droop despondently. He took the pheasant out of my hands and felt for the wing-tag. 'You mistook it for a flying rabbit?' he suggested.

'He flew into the overhead wires,' I explained.

He shook his head. 'I bet one of your dogs pegged it.'

This was almost fighting talk. For a trained dog to pick up an unpricked bird which was sitting tight would be an eliminating fault in a field trial and very close to being a cardinal sin. But I kept my temper. I had only lived in the area for seven or eight years, and it was quite customary for the native Fifer to needle one who would still be counted a stranger, just to

32

test his reaction. 'You'd better pluck it for yourself,' I said patiently. 'You'll find a broken wing. And I wrung his neck. That's all. No shot. Do you want a dozen rabbits?'

My reply passed the test. He smiled suddenly, dissipating the apparent gloom of his features, and thrust the pheasant back at me. 'You keep it,' he said. 'Anyway, it's a Marksmuir bird, one of last year's from the tag. Yon mannie Cove might buy your rabbits.'

We both looked towards Ardrossie. The Lincraigs buildings were set on the edge of a rise overlooking the other farm. Below us, Dougal Webb had reached the boundary fence. I saw him put one hand on a fence post and vault nimbly over the barbed wire before unhesitatingly hopping the overhung ditch between two hawthorn trees. He seemed to be familiar with his way across. We could see over the corrugated roofs of the new buildings in their anodized, pastel colours to the sturdy old farm buildings. As we watched, Quentin Cove came out of the factory buildings and looked towards us, shading his eyes.

'I'll keep them,' I said. 'There's no point selling them cheap to him and then buying them back in his dogfood at three times the price. And I'll bet he's got plenty of rabbits on Ardrossie.'

Alec nodded. 'That's for sure,' he said. 'He'd likely be glad of a hand with them.'

'You'd think so,' I said. 'But he told young

33

Dougal to tell me that he'd taken money for the rough shooting, so he couldn't in fairness give away permissions. Who would the shooting tenant be?'

Alec pushed back his cap and scratched a balding scalp. 'Dashed if I know. I've never seen a soul with a gun. Nor heard a shot since the last time you were over the ground a month or two back, except for Mr Cove hisself training his dogs. Are you and the lassie coming in for a fly cup?'

'We'll do that,' I said. Mrs Hatton's baking was the best for miles around, rivalled only by that of her two daughters. Also, you never know when some oddment of farming gossip may come in useful, if only as a topic of conversation.

The farmhouse kitchen was filled with delicious smells. There were fresh scones on the table and raspberry jam, and big mugs of tea. It was a comfortable haven after the crispness and activity of the morning.

Mrs Hatton was unashamedly stout. The two daughters were strapping girls who would probably go the same way as their mother in time. Alec Hatton had no employees but ran the farm with their help and making use of outside contractors. The girls were much in demand socially. Dorothy, the elder girl, we learned was engaged to be married to the son of a big farmer near Leslie. Her younger sister, Emily, was frankly envious. I hoped for

34

Hannah's sake that Dougal Webb's visits to Lincraigs were business rather than pleasure. And yet, perhaps a jilting would not be the worst that could come to her. She was young enough to recover. We, on the other hand, might never find another such kennel-maid.

The topic of Dorothy's leaving the nest and its repercussions on the farm lasted until we were almost ready to leave. Then Daffy, who, with her own husband safely in the bag, had been listening with only half an ear, asked Alec, 'Do you see Mr Cove often, training his spaniels?'

'Most days, for an hour or so in the morn and again after his dinner. You can't help but see him,' Alec explained. 'If he's in a hurry, he just takes them onto the bittie rough ground at the end of the big barn. It's right under our noses, as you might say.'

'You said that you heard shots when he was training them.'

'That's right. He uses the gun, but I've seen him more often with the dummy thrower.'

'Have you seen him working with Mim? That's the brindled young bitch he got from us. But she'd look grey at a distance,' Daffy explained carefully.

Alec looked blank. His interest in dogs only extended as far as working collies and the dogs of his syndicate members. His daughters were the spaniel fanciers. Dorothy had a spaniel of Three Oaks breeding.

35

'I've seen her,' Dorothy said.

'Is she all right?' Daffy asked. 'Did she look happy and fit?'

'For all you can tell at a quarter-mile,' said Dorothy. 'She seemed to have plenty of energy.'

'Has he been complaining about gun-shyness?'

Alec laughed while eating cake and almost choked. 'We never discuss dogs with him these days. Not after the matter he made of it when Dorothy's dog covered one of his bitches.'

We got up to leave, but we were not to drive off straight away. Somebody had removed all four valves from the tyres of my car. Alec was very apologetic although the whole family had been in the kitchen with us when the deed was done. He set off immediately in his own car to obtain a set of valves from the nearest service station and then fetched a compressor from his tractor shed to reinflate the tyres. We agreed that it must have been the work of small boys, with whom the area was over-provided.

*   *   *

Soon after that, life began to gather pace again.

Ash was entered in a novice stake for the Saturday. I was determined, as usual, to send him out with all his lessons fresh in his little

36

mind. Familiarity with the 'real thing' is essential to a working dog's upbringing, but Ash was not short of experience picking-up. Conversely, to take him out on a solo expedition into the field would have been to risk a blank and wasted day. With a little ingenuity, all the basic lessons could be reinforced in the comfortably familiar atmosphere of home.

The snow had thawed, to be replaced by dull and sometimes drizzly weather. I had long before covered several dummies with pheasant skins. On the Friday morning, I fetched them out of the bag of fresh pheasant feathers in which, so that the scent would remain familiar, they were stored. In another field of set-aside land behind the house I set up several spring-operated devices of my own making which could toss a dummy, after the manner of a Roman ballista, in a reasonable mimicry of a rocketing pheasant. I fetched my gun, a blank adapter, some blank cartridges, Isobel and Henry, on the way out passing Dougal Webb who was making eyes at Hannah.

We spent a useful hour in the set-aside land. Isobel worked Ash to and fro, keeping him always under control. From time to time I would send up a dummy from one or another of my devices, Henry would fire a blank cartridge and the dummy would fall in the cover. When we were sure that Ash was steady and as closely in tune with his job as he ever would be, we knocked off before boredom could set in and undo the good work.

The trial was to be in Ayrshire. Isobel, chauffeured by Daffy, would have to set off that afternoon and make an overnight stay so, instead of going back to his kennel, Ash went into a travelling box in the back of my car.

The kitchen, containing both the range and the central-heating boiler, tends to overheat, so the back door often stands ajar. We found Dougal still leaning against the jamb in an attitude of calculated negligence, aiming flirtatious remarks at Hannah who, to do her justice, was concentrating on the preparation of a meal for the latest litter of pups. Dougal could seem almost dapper in his carefully chosen 'smart' gear, but today he was still in his dusty working clothes and looked almost ungainly.

Dougal, it seemed, was not so fixated on concupiscence as to forget other manly pursuits. He glanced round and stiffened like a pointer. 'Nice gun,' he said. 'May I look?' I was carrying one of my dummy traps in one hand. He took my Dickson Round Action from under my other arm without waiting for my permission, dropped the barrels and looked through at the daylight outside. The gesture proved nothing except that he knew how to operate the top-lever. With the blank cartridge adapters in place he could have seen very little. But he inspected the sparse engraving and tried the gun to his shoulder several times.

Hannah, noticeably piqued, was making little noises to attract his attention but was ignored in the face of more macho attractions. 'Very nice indeed,' Dougal said, closing and handing back the gun. 'I bet that cost you a bob or two.'

I was too disgusted by what I considered to be his bad manners to feel like recounting the story of how I had come by the gun. It was, in fact, very valuable and I was still slightly ashamed of the bargain which had been almost forced on me. I jumped at the excuse provided by Henry's arrival with two more of my dummy traps and turned away to unlock the door which led to my workshop.

Dougal returned his attention to Hannah.

* * *

Daffy and Isobel got away after lunch. We received the usual phone call to confirm their safe arrival and that Ash had travelled well and taken his dinner.

And after that, nothing. On the next day, Daffy would invariably have phoned to report on success or failure and the probable time of their return, but we waited through Saturday afternoon and into the evening.

Henry, who had been left behind to attend to one or two of his own business affairs, had spent some of the day helping us with the

39

chores. He was becoming openly anxious, the deep lines of ageing in his face filled with darker shadows. 'Somebody would have let us know if there'd been an accident, surely,' he said.

'Of course they would,' I said stoutly. But it was only too easy to visualize the car wrecked, the dog dead or loose on the motorway and Isobel and Daffy injured and not wanting to worry us until we could be given definitive news. Pessimism feeds on ignorance. The effort of trying to think of something else only emphasized our worrying.

Henry ate with us and we spent a miserable evening together. Even Sam was fretful and rebellious but went to bed at last. Just before midnight, two hours or more after we would have expected them back, we heard the sound of a car in the drive.

Hannah was first outside into the cold night but I was close on her heels, flicking on the outside lights as I passed the switch. The car was ours. It looked travel-stained but undamaged. As far as I could see, there was nothing wrong with Ash. Daffy got out of the car, stiff from the long drive and looking fed up but all in one piece. Isobel followed. She looked sorry for herself but there were no bandages.

Beth spoke first. 'What's wrong? Why didn't you phone?'

'Didn't want to worry you.' I wondered how

much worry is caused by the wish not to cause worry. 'And too difficult to explain on the phone. We'll tell you inside,' Daffy said, shivering. She was wearing a quilted anorak, so I put her coldness down to nerves.

We moved towards the house. Hannah fetched Ash out of the car. 'Have you eaten?' Beth asked, putting first things first.

'We had a snack at a Little Chef,' Isobel said. 'Nothing filling. I could handle a bowl of soup.'

'And Ash?' Hannah asked quickly.

'Of course he's had his dinner,' Daffy said indignantly. 'We wouldn't forget that.'

Instead of taking Ash back to his kennel as the house rules dictated, Hannah brought him into the kitchen with us. She put on the kettle. 'But what *happened*?' she demanded, adding, 'Soup coming up. Who'd like a bacon sandwich?'

Between relief and the cold, it seemed that hunger was as powerful as curiosity. We all wanted bacon sandwiches. While Beth and Hannah bustled about and the rest of us took seats at the big table, Henry demanded again to be told what disasters had befallen.

There was something more important on my mind. 'Did we win?' I asked.

'It's all part and parcel,' Isobel said thickly.

I looked at Daffy.

'Did we hell!' Daffy said. 'Mrs Kitts was great and Ash worked his little backside off.

41

Late on, he put up a hen pheasant that the other dog had gone past and then retrieved it from water. I could see that the judges were pleased. At that point I was sure it was in the bag but—would you believe?—we were pushed into second place by Mr Cove with Mim.'

There were gasps round the table. 'Never!' I said.

'It's true,' Isobel said, nodding. 'And well deserved.'

'I'm afraid it was,' Daffy confirmed. 'She was perfection. And not a trace of being gun-shy. I couldn't take my eyes off her.' She looked at me reproachfully. There could be no doubt that I had fallen from my pedestal. 'And then, to cap it all, I got breathalysed.'

'Did you pass? But you must have been all right or they wouldn't have let you drive home,' Beth said.

'I was slightly over on the breathalyser,' Daffy said, 'so I insisted on a blood test. That's where the time went. But my blood was all right. It's been quite a day.'

'You were lucky,' Beth said severely. 'I thought you knew better than to drink when you're driving Isobel around.'

Daffy managed to look indignant, puzzled and innocent, all at the same time. 'But I didn't,' she protested. 'That's what's so maddening. I thought I'd only had two soft drinks. Somebody must have spiked them.'

'Well, I just don't understand it,' I said. 'I don't mean the drinks. You probably picked up one that was meant for somebody else. But Mim's only about nine months old. And even if Quentin Cove has a cure for gun-shyness—which I don't believe—he couldn't possibly have done it in the time.'

'You're quite right,' Daffy said, 'except that she was there and handling beautifully, hunting like a dream, and one of the guns took a rabbit with a shot just over her head—a damned sight closer than was safe, if you ask me—and she never even blinked. If only I'd known . . .' She heaved a sigh that nearly blew the plates off the table.

'It doesn't follow that you'd have been able to work the same miracle,' Henry said gently. 'Quentin Cove has years more experience than you do and now that the business is running itself he has the time to apply that experience patiently. I take it that she was responding normally to the whistle?'

'Perfectly,' Daffy said. 'He hadn't plugged up her ears with wax, if that's what you're thinking. After the awards were given out I went over to say hello to both of them, but Mr Cove popped Mim into that Shogun of his before I got there. He said that he didn't want her to remember other times. He thought that we might remind her of her fear of guns. I didn't want to stand around in a bitter wind and argue about it so I just congratulated him

43

and came away.

'Then, when we got away, we called at the first hotel we came to.'

'My fault,' Isobel said. 'I felt the need of a little comfort.'

We all nodded. Isobel always needed a drink in the let-down after a competition. She was still breathing a faint aroma of brandy into the smell of frying bacon.

'I was thirsty too,' Daffy said. 'Anyway, Mr Cove came in, almost on our heels. He was very nice and quite apologetic. He said that he felt he'd been rude when we spoke earlier and he insisted on buying us both drinks. I left mine on the bar while I went to the Ladies, so you could be right,' she told me. 'The place was crowded. Perhaps someone mistook it for somebody else's and spiked it, or else I swapped glasses by mistake. I was feeling all right, but Mrs Kitts had got over her disappointment—'

'Second place wasn't bad for Ash's first time out,' Isobel explained.

'It was very good,' Hannah said stoutly, distributing mugs of soup, 'but it doesn't count for anything.'

'—and she was being very jolly,' Daffy resumed, 'so I only thought that that was why I was having a fit of the giggles. I certainly didn't think there was anything wrong with me. And I honestly don't think there was anything wrong with my driving either, but a few miles up the

44

road we were pulled over and they made me blow into a little machine. You know the rest.'

I still felt the need to justify myself. 'If I had to advise you again,' I said, 'I'd still say that Mim was incurable. It's all very well being wise in hindsight—'

'It's all right,' Daffy said kindly. 'I'm not blaming you. I'm sure you thought you were right at the time.'

Beth spluttered with laughter. I was less amused. But the bacon sandwiches were served out just then and the company lost interest in my honour as a prophet, instead demanding every least detail of each flush and retrieve, which dog had run in, which had been put out for pegging game and who had wiped whose eye. I comforted myself with the thought that the first time Mim trod on a thorn just as a shot went off she would undoubtedly revert to her earlier state.

CHAPTER THREE

Most of my picking-up engagements were for Saturdays, the prime shooting day of the week but the one day when we were most likely to be short-handed because of field trial commitments. For midweek shoots, enough keepers were usually free to pick up for each other and they usually preferred to keep the

45

modest extra income within their own ranks. The keeper at Lincraigs, however, was not popular and always had difficulty raising a full squad of beaters, let alone skilled dog-handlers; but I was prepared to put up with abuse and mind-changing in order to get in the maximum of retrieving practice for as many dogs as possible.

On the Wednesday following Daffy's brush with the law, I set off to Marksmuir with six dogs in the car—two aspiring champions, three that I was bringing on to sell as workers and one that I was training for another owner. The weather was fine and it was a perfect occasion for training the dogs, but beyond that point it was an event that I would cheerfully have missed. The Marksmuir shoots were sometimes for invited guests—distinguished company who could foster Sir Ian's ambitions. This one, however, was primarily a commercial shoot intended to subsidize the other kind, although I was surprised to note the presence of 'Sanctimonious' Pratt in the group and guessed that he was an invitee to make up numbers. Timothy Pratt, who had managed so much to aggravate Rex without uttering a word, in common with his friend Sir Ian Bewlay was a parsimonious man, not given to spend money on frivolous pleasures unless status or useful friendships would follow on. Dougal Webb, I thought, was out of the same mould.

I have a dislike of commercial shoots, for which the visiting Guns pay so much per bird and have no interest in the land beyond its scenic value. Even so, most keepers take a pride in presenting the birds high and fast and then adjusting their difficulty so that the bag ends at or very close to the planned total at the end of a full day. But McNair, Sir Ian Bewlay's keeper, placed the Guns and drove his birds so that if the Guns had been even moderately good shots they would have reached their target before lunch and then been forced to choose between an early finish or an extra cost. The presence of Timothy Pratt, who was a competent shot, could be explained. He was there to ensure that the guests shot, and so paid for, their intended bag.

There were only two other pickers-up—one of Sir Ian's estate workers with a clumsy but efficient golden retriever and Joe Little, a fellow breeder and trainer who was similarly glad of the opportunity to train his dogs under real conditions. I was pleased at this paucity, because there would be more work for my dogs, but not impressed. The modest fee paid to a picker-up is amply recovered from the cost to the Guns of a single bird in the bag which might otherwise have been missed.

Joe was a distinguished trainer and a regular field trial judge. He bred Labradors, not spaniels, so we were not rivals and could

47

afford to be good friends. At the break for lunch, usually taken by the Guns in what seemed once to have been the servants' hall of the big house and by the keeper, beaters and pickers-up in a former wash-house, I made sure that the dogs were warm and dry and then headed to overtake Joe.

The house was a rambling structure of local stone, its pleasing lines half hidden by ivy and Virginia creeper. Its condition was slightly rundown and the garden was definitely overgrown, further evidence of Sir Ian's genius for the false economy. The place deserved a better owner.

As I crossed the cobbled yard, Sir Ian, who seemed to have been lying in wait, popped out of the back door. He was usually around on shooting days, keeping watch to see that everything was paid and accounted for.

'Cunningham,' he said.

I slowed to a halt, reluctantly. From a rough count of beaters' heads I had already worked out that my chances of claiming one of the more comfortable chairs had gone and I was now more concerned whether there would be as much as a sausage roll left for me. The exercise and fresh air had sharpened my fallible appetite.

As already mentioned, Sir Ian was not one of my favourite people. He was large—not that I counted his height against him but his girth was unattractive. He was also red-faced, pop-eyed and with an exaggerated idea of his own importance. But he was a valuable source of dog-work, so I returned his greeting politely.

'You were shooting on Lincraigs the other day.' He paused. 'Well?'

'I was,' I said.

'You shot a pheasant on my land. Do you know how much each bird costs?' Sir Ian was a self-made man who had been knighted for some unspecified services to industry. His accent was intended to convey an impression of old money and an ancient baronetcy but it did not quite manage it. He had picked up the Marksmuir estate at a bargain price many years earlier and if a visitor jumped to the conclusion that Sir Ian, and possibly his ancestors, had been born and raised there, the misapprehension was never corrected.

My aggravation at being spoken to as if I was an errant schoolboy was increased by the arrival a moment earlier of another man, Timothy Pratt. (Pratt and Sir Ian were often to be found together. Each had political ambitions, but whereas Pratt was only aiming, for the moment, at a seat on a nearby Regional Council Sir Ian had his sights set on Parliament. Each could help the other with his ambitions. Sir Ian could give Sanctimonious Pratt many useful introductions while Pratt could ensure that Sir Ian's least good deed, be it a minuscule donation to charity or a kiss reluctantly bestowed on an even more

49

reluctant baby, was faithfully recorded and found its way to the media. Pratt was a small man, younger than Sir Ian and about my own age, burdened with a thin face and very close-set eyes. He was very much inclined to sermonize any captive audience, and especially the readers of his column in a local paper, on any subject which he could claim as dear to his heart, though by a strange coincidence each could be expected to appeal to a wide public and alienate only a minority. Among these was the eternally thorny subject of Animal Rights. Timothy Pratt was, of course, thoroughly in favour of them without ever specifying just what rights an animal should have. But he was conspicuously against live exports, fox hunting and battery poultry-farming. He was a pillar of every animal protection society in Scotland. Yet there was one right of animals which seemed to disturb him deeply. He was eternally advocating legislation to penalize anyone daring to allow a dog to foul any public place. He had once taken to court a critic who suggested that, if Timothy Pratt could have his way, any owner of a dog so offending would be made to eat the offence. His endless preaching on these and kindred subjects had earned him the sobriquet of 'Sanctimonious' Pratt. He saw no contradiction between his fondness for shooting and his support of Animal Rights, and on that one subject I agreed with him.)

50

In point of fact, I probably had a better idea of the cost of rearing birds than Sir Ian did. It was generally believed that his keeper was ripping him off. But I kept a firm grip on my temper. 'I did not shoot a pheasant on your land,' I told Sir Ian firmly and patiently, 'and I do have a good idea what every bird costs. One of my dogs put up a pheasant on Lincraigs. It hit the overhead wires—still on the Lincraigs side of the march, as you know—and broke a wing.' While I spoke, I was thinking that only one house stood high enough for the occurrence to have been seen from it. 'I dare say that it would have looked like a shot bird at the distance, to someone at Gifford House. If he was behind double glazing he wouldn't have heard the sound of a shot anyway. The bird landed on your side of the fence. I did not cross the boundary, with or without a gun. I picked up the dog and lifted him over the fence.'

'Ha! You admit it!'

'I heard him,' said Pratt excitedly. 'I can bear witness.' I noticed that his wrists still bore the scars of his old burns and reminded myself to make allowances. At least he had courage.

'Why shouldn't I admit it?' I asked reasonably. 'What I did was quite legal and normal practice. Would you rather that I'd left the bird to feed the foxes?'

Sir Ian drew himself up to his considerable height, thereby thrusting his belly at me.

'There are no foxes on my land!'

That was a black lie. The prints had been clear in the snow, of foxes coming out of Marksmuir land and stalking rabbits on Lincraigs. What is more, he knew that it was a lie. So there was nothing to be gained by arguing about it. Sir Ian had made no comment on my reference to Gifford House, any more than I had mentioned that the bird's wing-tag had shown it to have been released on Marksmuir.

'I think you'll find that I was behaving properly,' I said. 'I have a witness to exactly what happened. But if you really want the bird, it's hanging in my garage. I'll make you a present of it. I should warn you that it's a cock with spurs an inch long. I wouldn't expect it to be good for more than game soup or pâté. Shall I bring it to you or will you collect it?'

It seemed to dawn on him for the first time that if he insisted on taking possession of the pheasant the story would do the rounds, growing all the while. Sir Ian was known to be a wealthy man. He might have parliamentary ambitions but his growing reputation for petty meanness was making him locally into a laughing-stock. He glanced at his watch to suggest a more important appointment elsewhere. The watch, I noticed, was a Rolex and not the one that I had seen on his wrist the previous year. 'Keep the damn bird,' he said, turning away.

'You should have taken the bird,' I heard Pratt say. 'You're too soft with these people and it only encourages them to take greater liberties next time.' Thankfully I was out of earshot before I heard enough to make me really blow my top.

I was in time to capture a sandwich and one sausage roll. I took them back to the car where I could sit comfortably in the tail, talk to the dogs as I ate and enjoy the winter sun while I waited for my temper to cool. Joe joined me after a few minutes, which was a help. We relaxed in the partial shelter, surrounded by contented dogs. I remarked that Sir Ian was an odd sort of character. 'Penny wise and pound foolish,' I amplified. 'He worries himself sick over a tough old bird shot beyond his boundary, but he's wearing a new Rolex.' Then I remembered that Marksmuir had been burgled the year before and I added, 'But, to be fair, perhaps it was an insurance replacement.'

'I doubt it,' Joe said. 'He was away at the time of the burglary and his Rolex is never off his wrist. He put it about that he fancied treating himself to a new watch and so he sold the old one.'

'I'd place a small bet that somebody got robbed.'

The beaters were crowding into their trailer. A few minutes later the first Guns appeared, among them 'Sanctimonious' Pratt

53

accompanied by a cowed Labrador. 'I was surprised to see him here,' I said. 'He's another skinflint. I don't believe for a moment that he coughed up the price of a driven day.'

'Not in a million years,' Joe agreed. 'He and Sir Ian formed a mutual back-scratching association years ago. Pratt bought that dog from me. He haggled over the price and then, when he wanted me to train it, jibbed at the cost and decided to train it himself. He ballsed it up, of course—'

'Of course,' I said.

'—and he came back to me, wanting me to cure the dog of running-in. But once again we fell out over the cost.'

'He came to me after that,' I told Joe. 'He said that you were a bare-faced robber with delusions of grandeur. When I quoted my rates he said that I was worse than you were.'

'That figures,' Joe said. 'He was probably right. The upshot was that he was saddled with a chronic runner-in. You weren't here when it came to a head—I think you were abroad. I saw the whole thing and so did some of the beaters. A rabbit came past the guns. Pratt fired at it and missed and his dog took off after it.'

'Oh dear!' I said. I could see what was coming.

'Yes indeed. I've known men try to cure running-in with a cartridge loaded with rock salt. It stings like hell but does no permanent damage. I've also known idiots who let the dog get about seventy yards out, to where the pellets have lost much of their energy, and then let the dog have a dose of Number Six. But either Pratt has a poor judgement of distance or else he was in a rage. He shot the dog up the arse from thirty yards. He was sorry afterwards—or so he said, and it was probably true because it cost him money. The dog was in even worse agony, of course.'

'It's a wonder he didn't kill it.'

'I believe it was touch and go. As it was, the dog had to be castrated. And it's still a chronic runner-in,' Joe added.

The rest of the Guns emerged and we prepared to follow them to the next drive.

*   *   *

I was home, and with the dogs fed and kennelled, in time for the drinks in the sitting room with which we usually mark the end of the working day. Henry and Isobel were away so that it was a more intimate gathering than usual. It was a time for relaxing in front of a flickering fire, toasting the toes and sipping a drink, but it was also the time for discussion. When I had reported on the performance of each of the dogs I went on to recount my exchange with Sir Ian Bewlay.

Daffy confirmed that my version of the event was the true one. Beth was justly indignant. 'That man is getting himself despised,' she said, 'and not least by me. With the game dealer paying about one-fifty a brace—for *good* birds, not ones that have been strutting around since the Gulf War—he was off his rocker to make a song and dance about it. Why alienate yet another voter?'

'He wasn't exactly thumping his chest,' I said mildly, 'and if I had gone onto his ground to shoot he'd have been within his rights to create hell. A bird costs enough to rear, never mind how little the dealer pays for it after it's shot. What really annoyed me was that "Sanctimonious" Pratt was egging him on. I noticed that Bewlay didn't deny that somebody at Gifford House had been telling tales.'

'That could only be Mrs Macevoy,' Daffy said. 'I met her at a party given by some newcomers who didn't know about her. She has an awful reputation. A plump and middle-aged, dyed redhead whose hair looks as if it's been set in fibreglass. She hardly ever goes out locally—nobody can stand her. I suppose that she and Sir Ian might be drawn together because they've both more or less run out of other friends. She goes on a cruise for about a month each winter and I suppose she gets all her socializing over in one burst, in the company of people who can't escape without jumping overboard.'

'You said that she had an awful reputation.

56

What does she have such an awful reputation *for*?' Hannah asked.

'The usual things plus plus,' Daffy said. By some process beyond my comprehension, Daffy seems to know the history and personal foibles of anyone you care to mention. 'There was a big scandal at one time, but it was before you came here. I wasn't really old enough to be told about it but I sneaked looks at the newspapers when my parents weren't looking and I had friends who seemed to know everything.

'Her husband got himself into real trouble. They were both promiscuous, but he was worse than she was. Even so, it seems to have been a real shock when he was accused of rape. It happened a long way from here, but from the word that went round it wasn't very much of a rape—the lady's reputation wasn't any better than his and people were saying that she'd only brought the case because his cheque bounced or he refused to take his weight on his elbows or something.' Now that she was a married woman, Daffy felt free to make that sort of remark but I could see Hannah blushing.

'Then,' Daffy continued, 'there was another scandal. It came out that somebody had been embezzling from the firm he worked for—he was financial manager in a solicitor's office—but they never found any trace of the money and that prosecution was dropped for lack of evidence.

'The next thing was that when the rape case came on, Mrs Macevoy gave evidence against her husband. I thought,' she said, 'that a wife couldn't do that.'

'A wife can't be compelled to give evidence against her husband,' I explained, 'but there's nothing to stop her doing so if she wants to.'

'Can I really?' Beth said delightedly. 'You'd better behave, or you'll be amazed to hear what you've done.'

'Now I understand,' said Daffy. 'Somebody told me that he'd have got off but for her evidence. Anyway, she really dropped him in it—swore that she heard the other woman weeping and begging for mercy and so on and so forth. She made it sound like a Victorian melodrama. He got sent down for about ten years.

'At first, everybody seemed sorry for her and impressed by her devotion to the truth. But then it came out that she'd sold her story to at least one of the tabloids. "My Life With A Sex Fiend", that sort of thing. It was only discussed in hushed tones, but when I was considered old enough to hear about such things my mother explained that the Macevoys seemed to have been running out of money—scraping the bottom of the barrel, was how she put it— and that there was no doubt that her evidence had been heavily weighted against her husband so that she could get her hands on the money

58

she got for telling, or inventing, the story.'

'If they were going broke,' Beth said, 'it doesn't sound as though he was embezzling.'

'One of them could have been gambling,' I pointed out. 'Or he may have been hiding his ill-gotten gains from her so as to be able to get out of her clutches.'

'I wouldn't have blamed him for that,' Daffy said. 'Anyway, allowing for good behaviour he should be out soon and then the fur will fly. They say that she stands looking out of the front window in case he's coming. Ready to bolt out of the back door, I suppose. That would explain how she came to see us on Lincraigs. And talking of coming, I must be going. Rex is due home any minute. It's all right, Ducky,' she said to Hannah. 'I won't see you stuck. I'll come and relieve you so that you can go out to play with your Dougal.'

'Saturday?' Hannah said quickly.

'I don't know about Saturday,' Daffy said, shrugging into her coat. 'I think we're going away. But now and again. Cheerio!'

*   *   *

That weekend, for the first time that season, Isobel was due to compete in an open stake— that is to say, a trial for dogs which have qualified by winning a novice stake.

By long-standing custom Daffy, who pulled more than her weight at other times, was

59

allowed to work part-time while Rex, her husband, was ashore. The pair were to meet friends for a weekend in Paris.

We were quite used to our logistics being thrown into disarray by the unexpected. After some discussion, it was arranged that Hannah would drive Isobel on the understanding that she would accept no drinks from anybody but Isobel herself and keep her hand over the glass containing any that either of them bought for her. Henry by then felt the weight of years too heavy for undertaking long drives. I think that he would have liked to go along with Hannah and his wife as a passenger, spectator and relief driver, but he nobly stayed behind and spent much of the Saturday in helping with the still necessary chores. By early that evening the work was done and we had even managed to give every trainee a few minutes' workout. Henry, who was to stay and eat with us, fell into an exhausted sleep in the sitting room. Sam, who had been carrying feeding dishes and holding leashes with the rest, had flaked out in the other chair, the two of them snoring in occasional synchronization.

I could see that Beth was tired but when I tried to help her with the meal she shook her head. 'You look pooped,' she said. 'Go and have a zizz with the other two.'

'I don't feel like it,' I said. 'I slept last night. If I sleep now, I'll lie awake tonight. And have you heard the noise they're making?'

60

'Then go down to the pub.' This was Beth's panacea whenever I seemed to be in low spirits. It was her contention that draught Guinness and a change of company helped to restore me in body and spirit. After consideration I decided that for once I felt like following her advice.

'I think I will.'

'Wrap up warmly.'

I blew a raspberry. There is nothing more annoying than being told to do something that one was going to do anyway except, perhaps, being warned not to do something which one would not have done on a bet.

The pub in our village was a former coaching inn, long since bypassed, which had been extended several times and then, happily, left alone. The stone-flagged bar wandered round unexpected corners where several open fires competed for the available draught. I penetrated to the furthest corner where I knew that the fire threw out the greatest warmth and knocked on a serving-hatch. It was early and there were only two or three customers making pit stops. During the week it would have been busy with customers on the way home—perhaps, I thought, gathering strength to face the pandemonium of family life after the peace and quiet of the office.

I sat down, made a small inroad into my pint of Guinness and let my mind drift. Business, I decided, was going as well as could be expected in an economic recession and a highly competitive, leisure-oriented market. (It was a renewable source of surprise and relief to me to find that that, however much Mr Average had to tighten his belt, there were always plenty of customers with money to spend on luxury goods.) My family life was better than most. I should have been quietly contented. But there was a ripple in the pattern. Something not quite right was cruising at the back of my mind.

My reverie was interrupted before that thought could surface. Dougal Webb's thickset form penetrated my nook. 'Mr Cunningham!' he said. 'Are you ready for another of those?'

'This will last me, thanks,' I said, wondering whether the offer would have been made if I had not been nursing a nearly full pint glass. He knocked on the hatch and bought a half-pint of lager.

'Do you mind if I join you?'

I could hardly refuse without creating a hostility which might have rubbed off on Hannah. He took the chair opposite and leaned back comfortably. He was very smart in fawn slacks, a soft tweed jacket very slightly too large for him and a white shirt with cravat. I was getting the measure of Dougal Webb. He worked hard but he expected his money to do the same, a pound doing the work of a fiver. The jacket, I suspected, had come from the

Nearly New shop.

'Hannah's not back yet,' I said.

'Mrs Cunningham told me. She said I'd find you here.'

I suspected that Beth had betrayed my whereabouts in order to get rid of him. We chatted for a few minutes about the weather, the harvest, the shooting season and our progress with the dogs but my mind was elsewhere and so, I thought, was his. Eventually he came to the point. 'That's a good gun you have,' he said.

I acknowledged that the Dickson was a very good gun, hiding my surprise that he recognized the quality of a design which to the uninformed eye looks no more than efficient and unobtrusive.

'How much do you want for it?' he asked me bluntly.

'It's not for sale,' I told him.

'I'll give you a hundred,' he said grandly.

His nerve almost took my breath away. I had had several offers for the gun, not one of them for less than two thousand. 'I suppose you'd want a "lucky penny" back as well,' I said. 'Nothing doing.'

His square jaw seemed to get squarer and his eyes narrowed. 'I suppose my money isn't good enough for you?'

'It's good enough,' I said. 'There just wouldn't be enough of it even if my gun was for sale, which it isn't.'

'I'll give you a receipt for whatever figure suits you. You can use it as a tax loss.'

'Watch my lips,' I told him. 'My gun is not for sale.'

'Everything is for sale,' he said with conviction. 'It just needs the right inducement. Let's keep it friendly. You'd best accept my offer.'

Either he was out of his mind or I was being blackmailed. 'Or what?' I asked curiously.

'Or you'll be very sorry. I know what's been going on.'

'Then you'd better tell me, because I can't think of anything.'

He looked at me, hard faced, through slitted eyes, and then glanced round to make sure that we were not overheard. 'No, I can't swallow that. You know damn well what I'm talking about. And you wouldn't like it if I told the Kennel Club. That would cost you a damn sight more than the price of a gun, you and my boss both.' He got to his feet. 'You think it over and I'll ask you again. You'll be glad to take me up on my offer. You'll thank me one of these days.' He turned away.

'I'll see you in hell first,' I said to his receding back.

My peaceful interlude of contemplation was over. I finished my pint and walked out into the patchy lighting of the car park. There was no sign of Dougal Webb nor of his highly unsuitable car. I walked to the end of the pavement and took to the grass verge by the light of my torch, pondering as I walked.

At home, Henry and Sam were awake. 'Hannah phoned,' Beth said. 'They'll be a little late—you know what a slow driver she is—so we'll eat and I'll keep theirs in the oven.'

'How did they get on?'

'Certificate of Merit.'

I grunted. A Certificate of Merit might be valuable if we wanted to sell the dog but it was no help towards the Field Trial Champion status that alone would enhance every subsequent pedigree.

Sam was a terror for remembering odd snatches of conversation and repeating them just when and where they would be least appreciated so I asked Henry, who was ready to walk home, to wait until the boy was asleep and I persuaded Beth to put Sam to bed in good time. That gave me a few minutes before Hannah, with Isobel in tow, arrived home and I told them, in as much detail as I could remember, of my conversation with Dougal Webb.

'It's off-putting,' I finished, 'to be blackmailed and not know what it's about. We haven't done anything we wouldn't want the Kennel Club to know about, have we?'

'You've cursed them up hill and down dale for a bunch of short-sighted idiots, ruining good breeds with unrealistic breed standards and a closed gene-pool policy,' Beth pointed

65

out.

'That's different,' I said. 'I don't mind them knowing about that. I want them to know what asses they are. I hate to think that they're going around with delusions of competence.'

'Well, just don't expect them to thank you. I can't think of anything else,' Beth said.

'What are you going to do about it?' Henry asked. 'If anything.'

'I can't complain to the police if I don't even know what the threat would have been,' I said. 'And he didn't want to say it aloud. Anyway, I've no witness. He's certainly not getting my Dickson. That's the one thing I'm sure of. I'm not so sure what to do about Hannah.'

'Yes,' Beth said thoughtfully. 'She wouldn't believe you anyway.'

'And,' Henry said, 'what attitude do you adopt if he visits here socially? If you exclude him from the house you'll have to give Hannah a reason.'

'And lose a good kennel-maid,' Beth said. 'Say nothing for the moment.'

'A policy of masterly inactivity is often the best,' Henry agreed. 'But if they seem to be plotting matrimony, or something equally drastic—'

'Then we'll have to tell her,' Beth said. 'And only then.'

'*Is* there anything equally drastic?' I asked.

Beth threw a cushion at me.

CHAPTER FOUR

When Hannah and Isobel returned, Hannah paused only to regale us with tales of game passed over, runners missed, eye-wipes, triumphs and tragedies, how Polly—Throaks Polygonum, to give her her full name—had failed at the last hurdle and been pushed out of the places by a half-witted tyke that had fluked the final retrieve. She then ate a meal appropriate for one of her youth and appetite before heading towards the phone to call the farm cottage where her Dougal pursued his bachelor lifestyle. The pair, we soon gathered, had then made another date for the following evening.

'I hope you apologized for standing him up,' Beth said severely. The two kennel-maids had started with us while they were in their teens and Beth, though very few years older, still felt the need to hand out motherly guidance on behaviour. On the whole they usually took it very well, with only the occasional sigh and casting up of eyes.

'I don't know why he came here at all,' Hannah said. 'I told him I couldn't be back in time. He must have forgotten. He tried to tell me that I never said any such thing, but I remember my very words and what he answered.'

Hannah spent the Sunday emulating a quick-change artist. She began the morning in jeans and a thick sweater. When the first round of chores was done, she put on a demure suit and, being in the midst of a mildly religious phase, went off to the kirk. But Daffy was in Paris and dogs, more particularly puppies, take no cognizance of the Lord's Day, so Hannah spent the afternoon back in her jeans and wellingtons, walking a succession of dogs in small groups in the cold and drizzle around the nearby fields while I undertook a little elementary training in the old barn. We carried out the evening feed and clean-up together. Hannah ate with us and then, much too early, went for a bath and reappeared in a much less demure frock and some jewellery borrowed from Beth. Even Sam seemed impressed.

When Sam was asleep, Beth and I retired to watch the television in the sitting room. Hannah came with us, but spent her time looking through the curtains at countryside prettily lit by the rising moon, holding her breath whenever the lights of a car approached from the direction of the village and releasing it explosively as the car went past. When Dougal's arrival was definitely overdue, she tried to phone the cottage and then Quentin Cove's farmhouse, but neither number answered.

At last she came and asked for the keys of

my car. 'Something must be wrong,' she said.

'If you go chasing after him,' Beth said, 'you'll seem too eager. Men don't like that.'

'He'll lap it up,' I promised. 'Drive carefully. If he turns up after you've left, we'll send him back by the main road.' With a flea in his ear, I added to myself.

'You shouldn't encourage her,' Beth said as the sound of our car faded in the distance. 'Knowing what he is.'

'If I hadn't said what I did, she might have invited him in,' I pointed out.

'You have a point.'

Later, when we were watching a film on video and beginning to yawn, the telephone sounded. I had the cordless with me so I answered it. It was Hannah. 'He hasn't been here,' I told her.

'Mr Cove arrived back,' Hannah said. 'I'm phoning from his house. He doesn't know where Dougal's got to. There's no sign of him or his car and I'm worried.'

'There'll turn out to be some quite simple explanation.'

'Like some other lady-friend? That's not exactly a weight off my mind, Mr Cunningham.' For a moment Hannah sounded almost light-hearted but when she spoke again her spirits had dropped. 'I'm going to bide here for a while.'

'All right,' I said. 'Don't get cold.'

'Mr Cove says I can sit in front of his fire.

Don't wait up for me. Dougal won't come looking for me this late. You go to bed. I'll see you in the morning.'

We disconnected and I relayed Hannah's words to Beth. Beth was immediately anxious but not about Dougal. 'Should she be alone in Ardrossie farmhouse with Quentin?' she asked me. 'From what I hear, he's a danger to women.'

'But not to girls,' I said. 'Hannah can look after herself.'

'She shouldn't have to.'

'She went there of her own accord,' I pointed out. 'But if you think she needs a chaperon, phone for a taxi and go and join her. Or would you rather that I went and sat with her?'

It was a cold night and I was tired. The fire was comforting. Into my voice I deliberately put more enthusiasm than I was feeling. That was enough for Beth. 'As you said, Hannah's quite capable of looking after herself,' she said.

There were times when both Hannah and Daffy spoke to us as though we were elderly parents verging on senility, but her last words had been sensible advice and we took it. I for one was sure that, if Dougal had not found himself other company, he was playing tit for tat with Hannah for standing him up the day before. But then I remembered that Hannah had not been at fault. The date had been

Dougal's error. The remainder of the video got less than my full attention.

We woke in the morning to the sound of brisk footsteps outside and the jingle of the trolley that we used to transport feed around the kennels. Beth squinted one-eyed at the clock. 'Five thirty!' she said. 'The dogs won't know what day it is!'

'They don't care what day it is,' I said. 'As long as there's food on the go, every day is Christmas.' I closed my eyes for a few seconds during which a sombre daylight arrived and Beth disappeared. There was a warm cup of tea beside the bed. I was usually the first to rise in the morning but, in deference to my sometimes uncertain health, Beth always left me to sleep in if she was the first to wake.

When I came downstairs, Beth was presiding over a pan on the stove. 'I heard you in the bathroom,' she said in explanation, as she always did. I had come to dislike the implications of the wording. Hannah, her back to us, was in jeans again. She was washing puppy dishes at the porcelain sink which was never used for non-canine washing-up. I glanced at the newer stainless steel sink but there were no dirty dishes there. Either Hannah had done the washing-up from one breakfast, which was not part of our routine, or she had not felt like eating. I raised my eyebrows at Beth and she screwed up her face.

Hannah turned round suddenly. There were

71

dark stains under her eyes. 'Dougal hadn't come back by the time I gave up, around four. I've phoned the police and his car hasn't been in an accident.'

'But, Hannah,' Beth said, 'haven't you been to bed at all?'

'I couldn't have slept.'

'You haven't eaten either.'

'Honestly, I'm not hungry.'

Beth shared out the scrambled eggs and toast between three. 'There's no point making yourself ill,' she said firmly. 'Sit down and eat this and then go to bed.'

Obediently, Hannah sat. 'I'll phone again soon. Mr Cove is probably up by now. Daffy should be back soon. I'll go and rest when she comes in.' She looked at her plate suspiciously and then fell to with the hunger of youth, wiping her eyes, secretly as she thought, with a paper napkin.

'Mrs Kitts will be here any minute,' Beth said, 'and probably Henry too. You've already done most of the work. We can manage for the moment. But I don't know what we'll do in the longer term if you fret yourself into a breakdown.'

Hannah looked mollified. When she had eaten and made her fruitless phone calls, she went obediently to her bed.

*　　　*　　　*

72

All through the Monday and Tuesday we endured Hannah's misery. To be fair, she did her work and tried not to inflict her worry on the rest of us, but she was so obviously unhappy and frightened, and made so many wasted phone calls in the hope of getting some news, that her anxiety seemed to colour everything that we did. We tried to be careful of what we said, but so many topics had suddenly become taboo that inevitably we put our several feet right in it from time to time. Only Sam found the right words. With a child's uncanny ability to put a finger right on the hub of a problem, he marched up to Hannah while she was sitting still beside the phone after another useless call, a dispirited figure like Patience on the toilet, and climbed onto her knee. 'I'm still here,' he said. Hannah choked, clutched him tightly, broke down and howled. Sam hugged her. He knew the therapeutic value of a good cry.

'She'll be better now,' Beth said. Privately, I doubted it; but we were both right. Hannah had not yet come to terms with worry but had partially suppressed it. She was subdued but if she shed any more tears she did so in privacy.

The weather had turned suitably miserable to match Hannah's mood. Each day came grey and dank. A recurrent drizzle kept the ground sodden so that even if the weather went into remission for an hour or two a spaniel was soon made soaking wet. As I had once said—

and the girls repeated it back to me whenever that particular work was getting on top of them—God made spaniels and sponges on the same day. A platoon of wet and muddy dogs to be cleaned, dried and brushed was more than the ladies of the business cared to cope with, so only those dogs for whom outdoor training was essential were allowed out for more than token exercise. The others underwent training in the barn.

On Wednesday, Detective Inspector Ewell arrived.

Ewell had been our local sergeant some years previously. His removal to headquarters in Kirkcaldy, transfer to CID and eventual promotion just when it seemed that he was destined to coast towards retirement as a perpetual sergeant, had all been due, he had told me in an expansive moment, largely to a case with which we had given him a little help and all the credit. He was a thin man, his hair now fully grey; and he was in plain clothes, looking just as neat as he invariably had in uniform. He had a friendly face which always looked as though a smile was imminent though it never actually appeared.

I had never presumed on our acquaintance. Gratitude can too easily turn to resentment. For the moment, however, it seemed that we were still on good terms although there was a touch of embarrassment in his manner. I sat the three young dogs and took a seat on one of the straw bales furnishing the corner of the barn. The Inspector considered the effect of straw on his smart cavalry twills and decided to remain standing.

'Would you rather we went into the house?' I asked him.

'This is fine. I wanted a word in private with you. Can you think what about?' He had an unusually soft voice for a policeman although he could bark when a bark was called for.

'You're not bringing bad news?' (He shook his head.) 'Then I can only suppose that somebody has reported Dougal Webb as a missing person. Have they?'

This time he nodded sadly. 'His employer once and Miss Hannah Hopewell four times. The young lady sounded very upset.'

'She's usually a sensible girl, but she was becoming very much attached to young Webb. She's naturally concerned.'

'That I can understand,' Ewell said. 'I'll be as gentle as I can. I thought that I might have a word with you first and then perhaps you'd be present—'

We were interrupted by the arrival of Hannah herself in the barn doorway. Her face was white and her eyes looked enormous.

'No news,' I said quickly. 'Hannah, would you kennel these three for me, please? Give us a few minutes and then come back. The leads are hanging on the door.'

When she was out of earshot I said, 'I can't

tell you much more than that Hannah was away with Mrs Kitts on Saturday and missed a date with Webb, or so he seemed to think. She phoned him and then told us that they'd made a fresh date for Sunday evening. She got all dolled up for the date but he never showed. Around nine thirty she borrowed my car and went to see if he was asleep or collapsed or drunk or injured or a combination of two, three or all four. Elevenish, she phoned from Mr Cove's farmhouse, to say that there was no sign of him and she was going to wait a little longer.' I hesitated, uncertain if and how to introduce the subject of blackmail. 'That's about all that I can tell you from my own knowledge.'

He looked up from the book in which he was making a few terse notes and regarded me shrewdly. 'Is that really so?' he enquired. 'Perhaps you'd care to tell me about the quarrel you had with him on the Saturday evening?'

I tried not to let my irritation show. Gossip travels like a heather fire in the neighbourhood. Webb and I had been well away from the bar but the hatch had been nearby and Mrs Hebden was a notorious chatterbox. Instead of volunteering my information I would apparently now be making an admission under questioning.

'There's not a lot to tell,' I said. 'Young Webb had admired my shotgun—'

'The Dickson?' His tone was respectful. As a sergeant, Ewell had been responsible for implementing shotgun and firearms legislation in the area and he knew about guns.

'Yes,' I said. 'He joined me in the bar. He said that when he called for Hannah and found her missing Beth had told him that I'd be there. Hannah is sure she'd made it quite clear that she couldn't get back in reasonable time, but that may be by the way.'

'She's a reliable sort of girl? Not given to fantasizing?'

'Yes, very reliable,' I said, 'and no, no more than any other young lady of an age for romantic dreams. Webb brought up the subject of my gun. He offered me a hundred for it.'

The Inspector clicked his tongue. 'The young man was looking for a thief's bargain?'

'Very much so. When I told him that he didn't have a hope in hell, he began to utter vague threats. He seemed to be suggesting that I'd been doing something that the Kennel Club wouldn't approve.'

'And had you?'

'Nothing that they don't know about. I've criticized their policies up hill and down dale. Young Webb seemed to be suggesting that his boss was concerned with me in something nefarious, though apart from buying dog-food off him I've had no dealings with Cove in years. I suppose we raised our voices. That was as far as it went. If it hadn't been that we weren't even talking the same language, I suppose that it could have been called a blackmail attempt. But we'd come up against a barrier of total mutual incomprehension.'

'It didn't occur to you to tell the police?'

'Tell them what?' I demanded irritably. 'There was no witness. At least, not that I knew of at the time,' I amended. 'And the words themselves could almost have been innocuous. After all, it's no crime to make somebody an unacceptable offer for some possession and I could hardly point to any threats when I didn't know what if anything was being threatened. But one thing occurred to me since. If he's in the habit of using threats to gain what you called a "thief's bargain", it might be worth finding out how much he paid for his watch or for the fancy car he drives around in. And any other expensive acquisitions.'

Detective Inspector Ewell thought it over while contemplating me mildly. I remembered him as an officer who was never brusque but instead was given to comfortable chats over a cup of tea or a beer, which probably gained him far more information than any amount of interrogation would have done. 'You realize what you're suggesting?' he asked finally.

'I'm not suggesting anything,' I retorted, perhaps untruthfully. 'I'm giving you the facts. If you want to suggest—' I was about to put words into the Inspector's mouth as he nearly had into mine. The thought hanging in the air between us was that blackmailers have been known to disappear, sometimes for ever, when a victim has been pushed too far. I was interrupted by the return of Hannah. She paused in the doorway looking, I thought, rather like a trapped moth awaiting the arrival of the spider.

'Come in, come in,' Ewell said at his most fatherly. Perhaps the thought about the spider had not been wholly inappropriate. 'Do sit down.' (Hannah perched one neat buttock on another straw bale and looked at me pleadingly.) Ewell introduced himself. 'I've asked Mr Cunningham to bide with us while we talk. Is that all right? I thought you might prefer it.'

Hannah nodded more confidently.

'Aye well,' the Inspector said. He pretended to flip back through his notes but he was watching Hannah out of the corner of his eye. 'How long have you been going out with Mr Webb?'

'About a year,' Hannah said very softly. It was little more than a whisper.

'When did you last see him?'

'About ten days ago. On the Saturday. There was a dance at the Royal Hotel.'

'And you made a date for a week later, Saturday last?'

'But I phoned him during the week,'

Hannah insisted. 'I was driving Mrs Kitts to a field trial and I knew that I couldn't possibly get back at a reasonable time. The trials usually go on until almost dusk, then there's the results and presentations. And Mrs Kitts likes to stop on the way home. So I told him that I'd phone and make another date.'

'Then why did he come here asking for you?'

'Perhaps he forgot that I'd phoned him,' Hannah said after a pause. 'Perhaps habit took over. Saturday nights were—are—usually our time together.'

'Would you say that he was absent-minded?'

'No. But anybody can forget things if they have something else on their mind.'

'What did Mr Webb have on his mind?'

The day was still overcast and daylight was failing early. Under the harsh fluorescent lights in the barn, Hannah was looking older than her years. 'Nothing that I know of,' she said carefully. 'But I hadn't seen him for a week. You'd better ask Mr Cove.'

Ewell nodded. 'But when you phoned again—on the Saturday evening, was it?— what was his reaction? Did he sound like a man who had forgotten your call and was angry at having been stood up? Or was he apologetic for having made a silly mistake? Angry with himself, perhaps?'

'None of those.' Hannah was becoming

80

more confident. 'He sounded quite normal. I said that it was me and I was back now but it was too late to go out, just as I'd expected. And he said yes it was and that he thought he'd have an early night for a change and how about tomorrow evening? I said that that would be fine and I asked him why he'd come looking for me. He said that he'd come over on spec and he asked how we'd got on and I told him and he said he'd spent most of the day dismantling a tractor and he'd rather have gone along with us. He said that he'd pick me up at about eight the next evening. And that was it, really.'

'That was absolutely all? You're sure of that?'

Hannah turned pink and became tongue-tied.

'Have a heart, Inspector,' I said. 'I'm sure you wouldn't expect a young couple to hang up straight away. You wouldn't have done so yourself when you were courting. Equally, you can't expect one participant to quote the fond exchanges out of context. Words which were memorable gems between the two would sound quite insane when quoted in public.'

Hannah looked at me gratefully.

'I suppose that's so,' Ewell said. 'Well then, Miss Hopewell, I'll put it another way. Was the rest of your conversation limited to an exchange of . . . endearments?'

The pink of Hannah's cheeks became tinged

with scarlet but she nodded.

'And during that exchange, was his manner as usual?'

Hannah got up, walked to the doorway and turned. I thought that she was holding back the tears with an effort and wanted to be able to duck out of sight if the effort failed. 'Absolutely as usual,' she said defiantly. 'I told him that I loved him and he said that he loved me.'

'But on the Sunday evening, he never arrived?'

'No. I tried to phone but I got no answer. So I borrowed Mr Cunningham's car and drove there. Dougal's cottage was dark and there was no sign of his car. I sat there for hours, until about eleven, playing the radio and sometimes running the engine to keep warm. Then Mr Cove drove home. He let me come in and use his phone to call back here and say that I'd be late. He sat with me for a while and had a drink of whisky, because he said that he'd been needing a good dram all evening but he couldn't take more than a drop because he'd be driving. He went off to bed after that but he said that I could wait in his house if I promised to drop the lock behind me as I left. So I did that. In the end, between three and four, I decided that it was too late. If he came home at that time, I wouldn't want to face him. So I gave up and came back here.'

'Was it unusual, for him to stand you up like

that?'

'He's always very dependable,' Hannah said. 'He wouldn't do it on purpose, I'm sure of that.'

'The two of you are close?'

'Yes, we are.' Hannah's cheeks, which had lost their colour, flushed again and her mouth hardened. 'But to save you asking, Inspector, we haven't slept together. In fact, I'm a virgin. I don't think that he is, but I certainly am.'

It was the Detective Inspector's turn to redden. 'I was not, in fact, going to ask you such a question. Does he see other girls?'

'I don't know, Inspector. If he does, he never told me and I wouldn't expect him to.' And with that Parthian shot and a quick sob, Hannah turned and stalked off towards the house, injured dignity in every step.

'A young woman of spirit,' Ewell remarked. 'But I seem to remember that, not so long ago, she was a real hellion.'

'Teenage rebellion,' I said. 'As soon as she started working with animals she cooled right down. It's the best therapy in the world.'

'I must try it some time.' The Detective Inspector paused for thought. 'Might she have heated up again if she was the woman scorned? If, say, while she was waiting in your car he had arrived home with another woman's lipstick on his face and her perfume hanging around him? What do you think?'

I tried to imagine Hannah as the woman

scorned and found that it was easy. She was more a natural victim than an aggressor. 'She would be hurt more than angry,' I said. 'There might have been words. There would certainly have been tears. No more than that. You've checked that he isn't lying in hospital somewhere, unidentified?'

'Not unless he had changed his sex and aged about thirty years.'

'Oh,' I said. It seemed to be the only possible comment. But I was not ready to give up yet. 'Tell me, have you found his car?'

'Aye, we have. I see no reason not to tell you. It was in the station yard at Cupar, undamaged.'

'There you are, then. He's got fed up and run off. People do.'

'They do that,' the Inspector acknowledged. 'And I ken it better than you do. But when somebody vanishes, we must aye consider the possibility that . . . he didn't just run off. If he did run off, was he threatened? Bribed? Was he running away from guilt of some crime? We have to consider these things.'

'I suppose you must,' I admitted. 'But you needn't consider that possibility in respect of Hannah Hopewell or me. I didn't have a car, remember. And even if he did make Hannah angry enough to dot him one, what would she have done with the body? I can't see her managing to handle the agricultural machinery well enough to bury him about the farm and

84

leave no trace.'

'No more can I,' Ewell said. 'But mind this, Mr Cunningham, she was sitting almost on the doorstep of a deserted pet-food factory.'

*   *   *

The next few days were spent in a sort of limbo. We were the rabbit waiting for the eagle's strike, the condemned waiting under the guillotine. Something was going to happen. We had no way of guessing what it would be, but it would not be pleasant for Hannah. Dougal Webb might come back with an explanation, credible or otherwise, to account for his disappearance. He might be found wandering with amnesia. Or he might turn up dead or injured, in which eventuality Hannah and I might have more questions to answer. Detective Inspector Ewell had hinted—and my mind shied away from the hypothesis—that a pet-food factory might be the ideal place for the disposal of an unfaithful lover or an aspiring blackmailer.

Hannah, to do her justice, tried to cope with her job but for once her heart was elsewhere. She sank into a state of unhappy apprehension, comforted only by a lopsided faith in a God of her own imagining. The big dining table in the kitchen was often the scene for lively discussions or arguments on any subject that took our fancy and we had been made aware of Hannah's views. She made no secret of them. She admitted that, logically, she could not give credence to the idea of a personal God. She was an avid reader in such spare time as we left her and she was aware of a growing view that, if the evidence of the Dead Sea Scrolls was to be accepted, the traditional view of Christ was the imagining of Saul of Tarsus after he had suffered a stroke on the road to Damascus and that Jesus, rather than the son of the deity, had more probably been a political agitator. These things she knew and part of her mind accepted. But, she would argue, the churches were the only force striving for all the old moralities and might be forgiven for clouding the issues with myths. And yet that very mythology gave rise to the philosophy and ritual of the Christian religion which had such appeal and comfort for her that she made a conscious leap clean over disbelief and into a faith that was not blind but deliberately unseeing.

Daffy, while her husband was at home, should have been working part-time, but with Hannah distracted by worry and liable to vanish without warning in the direction of the church, she gave up much of her leisure to help out rather than have me put pressure on Hannah to pull her weight. In particular, she and Rex agreed to escort Isobel to an open stake to be held near Perth at the weekend.

Our order of various grades of dog-food was delivered that week by Quentin Cove—to Hannah's distress, because it was yet another reminder of her Dougal's absence, although she helped with the fetching and carrying. When the last bag was stowed in the store Quentin, at Beth's invitation, took a seat in the kitchen. I joined them for coffee while the girls went back to work.

'Taking it badly, is she?' Quentin said. 'I'm sore vexed for the lassie.' I noticed the slip back towards the language of his childhood on the farm and took it for a sign that his concern was genuine.

'She'll get over it,' I said. 'The not knowing is the worst. Are you getting by without him?'

Quentin helped himself to more sugar and cream. 'Aye,' he said. 'We're managing. It's a quiet time of year. But, truth to tell, I'm glad to get back to running the farm. It only takes four men to keep the factory working and I've moved them around to cover for me. If it works out we'll maybe leave it that way. That's if young Dougal doesn't come back,' he added quickly.

'Do you think he will?' Beth asked him.

'I've no way to tell. I saw him go off in yon wee car on Sunday morning. I thought he was maybe heading to see Hannah or some other lass—you know what these lads are—but he was wearing jeans and his working boots. He came back later to change his clothes.'

87

Quentin Cove paused and looked thoughtful. 'Leastwise I heard his car—there was no mistaking the sound of it. I never needed to watch his comings and goings—he's a worker, I'll say that for him, so that I could always trust him to take time off to go beating or do his courting or whatever and I'd know that he'd make it up when it suited him. Did you ken that his cottage was broken into?'

'The things people do!' Beth said. 'Do you suppose it was somebody who'd heard that Dougal was missing?'

'That I don't know. I doubt it. On Monday, when he didn't show up for work, I took the spare key that I'd kept and went across to see had he maybe slept in or fallen ill. From outdoors it looked all right and tight, but the inside was all ... all tapsalteerie and when I looked around I could see that a window had been forced. There was no sign of Dougal. That's when I decided to report him missing. I'll tell you this, between these four walls.' Quentin lowered his voice. 'I'm not wishing any ill on him, but I can do without his kind around the place. There!' Looking rather pleased with himself, Quentin bit into one of Daffy's rock cakes.

'We know what you mean. If she wasn't so heart-sore I'd say that'—Beth paused and chose her words—'the best thing for Hannah would be not to see him again.'

Quentin nodded and changed the subject.

88

'It didn't put you out, not being able to train on my land?' he asked me. 'I've seen you on Lincraigs.'

I said that we were getting by. But Ardrossie had been a valuable standby when rabbits were in short supply around home and I wondered whether another arrangement would be possible. 'Who did you let the rough shooting to?' I asked.

To my surprise, Quentin showed a trace of embarrassment. 'You'd not know him,' he said. 'A lad from Anstruther. Maybe I can make it up to you. They're nearly finished felling on Gifford Hill. That's where most of the rabbits have been coming from. One of my factory staff has ferrets, but many of the rabbits are lying out and some of the buries have more holes than you'd believe. I want them cleared out and the factory could make use of the meat. How do you fancy shooting over ferrets on Saturday?'

'Very much,' I told him. Several of the dogs could still do with steadying to rabbits, while those dogs being trained as workers rather than field triallers would be the better for experience of working around ferrets. It was sometimes an extra selling point.

'I'll have him phone you.'

'I didn't know that Gifford Hill was yours,' I said.

'It belongs to Marksmuir. It's been let to Ardrossie since my granddad's time, but it's

89

not good land and on a north slope so I leased it for the forestry. If I'd known that I was leasing it as a nursery for the bloody rabbits,' Quentin said, 'begging your pardon, Mrs Cunningham, I'd have let them keep their money and gone on growing neips for cattle on it. Which is what my father aye did.'

Later that day, when I was helping with the preparation of the main meal, I took up a handful of the small cubes. Then it came to me that what I was holding in my hand might contain a trace of Dougal Webb's mortal remains and I dropped them hastily. But dogs must be fed and I had had no great fondness for young Dougal. I let the evening feed go ahead. No such thought had occurred to Hannah but I noticed that Daffy only took up the cubes with the scoop provided for the purpose.

CHAPTER FIVE

Henry elected to come with me to Gifford Hill. On the Saturday, he lent a hand with an early session of feeding and walking. As soon as we were sure that Beth (helped by Sam), with Hannah and Isobel, could easily cope, we loaded four dogs and both guns into my car and set off, right on time. It had rained in the night but had turned into the sort of day that makes comfortable dressing problematic—warm in the sunlight but with a cold breeze when the wandering clouds hid the sun, and with a threat of showers. It would be cold up on the hill but warm work climbing it.

Forestry work on Gifford Hill was finished. The ground was now bare except for the few outcrops of rock which had previously only been visible as gaps in the conifers. Even the stumps had been pulled and heaped on the huge bonfire that was now reduced to dross and ashes and charred lumps of root, but smoke or steam still drifted into the cold air. Gifford House, home to Mrs Macevoy of dubious reputation, stood boldly out of the landscape, its walled garden an oasis in the desert.

Jack Gilchrist, Quentin Cove's employee and ferreter, was waiting beside a motorbike and sidecar in the road below. He had only been a voice on the phone to me, but the moment I saw him I remembered encountering him more than once when he had been acting as a beater on various shoots, usually in the company of Dougal Webb. He was a cheerful, tubby little man. With his big ears and prominent teeth he looked rather like a rabbit himself, so that I half expected his ferrets to take him by the neck; but they were well-kept little animals, very affectionate but very much under his thumb. He had already worked the small, isolated burrows and a dozen paunched rabbits were cooling behind one of the few surviving sections of hedge to prove it.

A common error would have been to hunt the spaniels first, pushing any lying-out rabbits underground ready to be bolted again by the ferrets. But Jack had found, as I had over the years, that unless you can spare the time to wait for anything up to a couple of hours before putting in the ferrets, the rabbits may prefer to face the ferrets underground rather than the danger above. Even the sound of shots would be less of a deterrent. If a ferret killed underground we might have been faced with a lengthy lie-up. We decided to walk quietly up to the largest outcrop, which was also the highest, and work our way down. That way, the bag would only be carried downhill. We would then finish with a hunt in the open.

The hillside had originally been planted ridge-and-furrow and then had been further disturbed by the rooting out of the trees, so that the ground had been left in a wildly uneven state. Rather than make frequent trips to the bottom and back up over the difficult going, I put leads on all four dogs and took them along. Each caught the scent of many rabbits and became eager to start the hunt, but they were there to learn restraint.

The rocky outcrops had been fragmented by age and weather. The rabbits had entries or exits through long fissures as well as between and below fallen boulders. Jack's purse-nets could never have attempted coverage. At each outcrop, I found a secure place for the screw-in anchorage and attached the dogs. The ferrets went in and I had time to glance at the spectacular view over the sparse chessboard of winter countryside. When the rabbits began to spurt out, Henry and I attended to their slaughter. For all his advancing years, Henry was still an excellent shot. Then I would free one dog and do the picking-up and out would come our knives for paunching.

The operation began well. The dogs soon realized that this was not an occasion for riotous behaviour and performed rather better than adequately. The ferrets came back to hand with very few lie-ups. Although at that time of year the rabbit population would have been at its lowest, our game-bags were getting heavy.

It was too good to last. We were just finishing at the third of the rocky outcrops, which happened to be nearest to the house, when a stout female figure emerged through a side-gate in the garden wall and hobbled towards us in unsuitable shoes, picking her way as best she could over the bumps and hollows. From Daffy's description of her hair, which was red and so lacquered as to look synthetic, I could guess her identity.

Mrs Macevoy was in a state of high indignation. We were disturbing the tranquillity for the sake of which she lived so far from civilization. What was worse, we were doing it at the weekend and close to her house. We were upsetting her cats. She was going to call the police. When I had managed to convince her that our activities were perfectly legal, she switched ground. We were being cruel.

That was too much for Henry. 'Madam,' he said, 'the rabbits would not live for ever and they do not die in their beds. Which of the methods open to them do you think they would prefer? Myxomatosis? Starvation? Freezing to death? Or being taken by a fox or one of your cats?' Mrs Macevoy emitted a squawk of protest but Henry rolled on. 'Do you realize, madam, that more wildlife is killed by domestic cats than by the entire field sports fraternity, and more painfully? So who, then, is being cruel?'

For some reason that defies analysis, when Henry speaks people listen. Mrs Macevoy listened with her mouth open. Whether she was convinced, whether she even took in Henry's argument, I had no way of knowing, but I thought that she was going to turn on her unsuitable heel and totter back to her house.

Jenny (short for Gentian) had been helping with the pick-up, but while I was distracted she had started to hunt. She was always a fast mover. (Beth called her Twinkletoes.) She was also a friendly little dog. When in ebullient mood and if she felt that she was getting less than her fair share of attention, she would pluck at one's trouser-leg as she went by, as if to say, *Look at me—aren't I beautiful*?

Jenny chose that moment to appear from nowhere and to give a tug at Mrs Macevoy's skirt as she passed by. It was no more than a friendly gesture, but the woman chose to let out a screech. 'Your dog attacked me!' she announced. 'Look!' She exhibited a very small hole near the hem. It looked to me like an old cigarette-burn—Mrs Macevoy's fingers were stained yellow—and I was sure that Jenny, who had never left behind a visible tooth-mark, had only touched the other side of the garment.

'Rubbish!' I said.

She rounded on Henry and Jack. 'You saw?'

They shook their heads. Jack was grinning.

Her face flamed. 'Get out of here, you *bloody* men. I'm going to call the police.'

I am not proud of what came next. I can only say that Mrs Macevoy had exhibited all the traits that I most despise, in particular uttering the word *men* as though it was a dire insult. I can only put up with stupidity allied to bad manners for just so long. 'How much attention do you think the police will pay to a woman who shopped her own husband in order to sell the story to the gutter press?' I

95

asked politely. Evilly inspired, I added, 'Isn't he due out soon?'

She turned white and then back to red. Without another word, she turned and made off back towards the house, stamping her way so that she almost fell.

'Not a nice woman,' Henry said without lowering his voice. He shot a sly glance at me. 'But perhaps she feels that she is politically correct.'

Henry knew that the words *politically correct* are to me as a red rag to a bull. In any other context a reference to politics implies a whole field of deviousness and expediency. There would have been no need to devise such a phrase as political correctness except as a more acceptable way of saying *I know it's rubbish but I want it to be true so you must believe it anyway*. Outdated attitudes were changing without the extra leverage, and the label of *political correctness* was now too often being used to damn attitudes which had been adopted because the experience of a thousand generations had shown that they were what the majority wanted, rightly or wrongly, to believe. But this was not the time for a dialectic argument. Some day soon, I would take my verbal revenge. 'Shall we get on?' I suggested coldly.

'In due course,' Henry said, grinning. 'We seem to have another visitor.'

I followed his eyes. The tiny but indomitable

figure of Mrs Dundee was struggling up the uneven slope. I greeted her arrival warmly and introduced her to Henry—partly to give her time to recover her breath, but I had genuinely liked the old thing.

'Would you like another rabbit?' I asked her. She looked relieved and I guessed that that had been the object of her climb. 'Take a brace,' I said. 'In fact, two brace.'

'You hae plenty?'

'Far more than we need,' Jack said.

I noticed that her cheery smile had vanished, leaving only the goblin looks. Had she been so haggard when we met not long before? I thought not. She was holding a plastic carrier-bag which gaped open, exposing several handfuls of kale and a turnip which had been partially nibbled by sheep. She saw my glance at it and bit her lip. 'I lost my morning job,' she whispered. 'My afternoon work doesna pay. And I'm no old enough for the pension just yet. My Jimmy will see to't when he gets hame soon frae the sea. Meantime, I maun just get by.'

'You don't have to explain,' I said. 'But have you been to the Benefit Office? Nobody's left to starve, these days.'

'I'll no tak charity.' The occasional rabbit between friends, it seemed, was neither here nor there. 'My Jimmy left me some money when he was last ashore, but he didna hae muckle and it's a gone.'

97

'Please take this to tide you over.' I found that I only had a fiver on me so I handed that to her. Henry matched it. She thanked us gravely and turned away, back down the hill.

'I didn't know,' Jack said simply. 'But I'll see she's never short of a few rabbits till her boy gets back.'

I brought Jenny back under command and we finished gathering the slain. When these were paunched and the guts disposed of down a rabbit hole, Henry's game-bag and mine would have been more than filled. We were about halfway back to the car but none of us fancied repeating the stiff climb if it could be avoided.

'Hang on a moment,' Jack said. 'We need a pole.'

Henry and I gladly took seats on the stones and rested our wearying legs. Getting about on that sort of surface was as tiring as twenty times the distance on level ground. Jack was quite right. A heavy load of rabbits is most easily carried slung on a pole between two men. The foresters had done their work well and there was very little in the way of loppings left lying, but Jack was heading for the area where the bonfire had been. I watched him idly and saw him single out a long branch from the partly burnt fringe, produce a large knife and begin to trim off the twigs. Then he stopped and stared. He turned, sheathed his knife and hurried back towards us.

He arrived breathless and shaking. 'There's a dead man,' he said, gasping. 'Leastwise, I think there is. It's that brunt you can hardly tell.'

Although the unexplained disappearance of Dougal Webb had kept the possibility of a dead body in our minds for several days, now that the possibility had become a probability our first reaction was disbelief. Henry and I wanted to see for ourselves.

We left the guns and our heavy game-bags with the ferret-box and I sat the dogs to guard them. 'Probably some farmer's way of disposing of a dead sheep,' Henry said as we hopped and staggered across the uneven ground.

'I hope so,' said Jack shakily, 'but I don't think it.'

The bonfire had been built on a relatively flat area, from all the otherwise wasted limbs and roots and loppings. The heat met us twenty yards off. From among the smells of warm earth and conifer logs I scented others and I judged that it had been fired by the most usual method—paraffin and a few old tyres. There was also another smell, familiar but so out of place that it was like a blow to the face. The centre of the fire was now a hump of white ash and charred roots and around the edges was a ring of unburned twigs and branches. Part-way in from one edge was the body.

It was certainly dead. I could understand Jack's uncertainty. The body was curled and partly consumed, almost indistinguishable from the scorched and shapeless roots, but it had once been human. I had seen burnt bodies during the Falklands War and I was in no doubt of it.

Henry was in agreement. 'No point standing here gawking,' he said. 'We'd better call the police.'

Jack looked unhappily in the direction of Gifford House. 'I'll not go knocking on that woman's door and asking to use her phone,' he said firmly, 'and that's definite.'

'No need.' Henry patted his pockets until he found what he wanted. 'Thought so,' he said. 'I have my mobile with me. There should be a passable signal up here. Nine-nine-nine, you think?'

'It's hardly an emergency,' I said. 'He's not going anywhere. But it's the only number I can remember offhand. Should we be getting back to the dogs?'

Henry had already keyed in the number. He made a brief report to the police before answering me. 'We're warmer here,' he said.

Jack was more practical. 'They rabbits should be hung up or laid out to cool,' he suggested. He looked at Henry. 'You can bide in the warmth if you like.'

But Henry came with us. He admitted to me later that his eyes had been constantly drawn

100

to the gruesome sight among the ashes and he had no wish to be left alone with it. We decided that the police would prefer us to disturb the whole scene as little as possible, so instead of carrying the rabbits down to the car we laid them out to cool and then found ourselves the best seats we could among the bumps and hollows.

'You reckon that's him?' Jack asked suddenly. 'Young Dougal?'

'It looked too small for him,' Henry said.

'They always do,' I said. 'Fat burns. They lose a lot of bulk in a fire and they curl up.' Jack looked ready to be sick, so I hurried to find at least a partial change of subject. 'It would be a bit of a coincidence, a man going missing and a different body turning up in strange circumstances. But coincidences do happen.'

'I think you understated the case,' Henry remarked. 'What we have here is a man going missing and a murdered body turning up. And that is a little too much coincidence for anyone to swallow. Unless, of course, you can find a more innocent explanation for how it came to be where it is. You're not going to suggest that a tramp crawled in there for shelter and was still asleep when they lit the bonfire?'

'He could have passed out with hypothermia,' I suggested doubtfully. 'Or drink.'

'Suicide,' Jack said firmly. 'That'll be it. He

101

could ha crawled in and takken poison, thinking to be wholly brunt.' Like many others, when disturbed he was becoming broader in his speech. 'They go to all kinds of lengths, whiles, to leave no trachle ahint. Or maybe it was for the insurance.'

I guessed that Jack was suggesting that there might have been an insurance policy with a suicide clause. But if the deceased had intended to do a favour for his nearest and dearest by concealing the fact of suicide he, or possibly she, would certainly have got it wrong if the body had indeed been wholly consumed. Insurance companies do not readily pay out on mysterious disappearances unless or until a court gives the family leave to presume death. Without mentioning blackmail I said as much and suggested, as being marginally more possible, such scenarios as somebody having had a heart attack in the wrong bed or else a hit-and-run accident, conceivably to Dougal Webb himself. In either case it might have seemed more convenient for the corpse to disappear for ever. This triggered a meandering argument which touched on various other explanations, of escalating improbability, and lasted until the first police car arrived on the road below us, disgorging no less than five officers.

That was the moment for all hell to break loose. Handling a number of leashes while carrying a gun and a game-bag comes close to my idea of hell. As each dog had done its working stint, blowing off steam and becoming more biddable, I had left it off the lead. While we sat and talked I had been vaguely conscious of a huddle of dogs around me without bothering to count them. I had not noticed Joshua, who had been brought to me for retraining, sneak away to begin an exploration of all the alluring scents around. At that critical moment he nosed a rabbit which had been sitting tight in the concealment of a drift of twigs, cones and coniferous needles. The rabbit did the sensible thing and bolted for the nearest holes, a course which took it close past our feet.

The result was inevitable. I had taken those dogs out just because they needed steadying to fur; but even a fully steadied spaniel may sometimes succumb to the temptation of a rabbit being hotly pursued by a rival. Joshua swept up the other three into a yelping pack which in turn bolted several more rabbits.

Any reader who thinks of the springer spaniel as a slow and lumbering dog has only seen an overweight, show-bred fireside pet. Instead, he should witness a fit young springer of working stock going flat out. It may not be a match for a greyhound but it can give a rabbit a good run for its money.

They knew that they had broken discipline. Guilt was written all over them. As each dog raced with ears flying, above its head there might well have been a little 'thinks' balloon, reading, *I'm wicked but it's worth it.*

I was not altogether unsympathetic. To have four legs and hunt a rabbit must rank among the world's most exhilarating sports. But to me as a trainer, this was disaster. Weeks of work were being undone in seconds. In theory I should have run after each dog in turn, catching it in full cry and administering a good shaking. The trouble was that, even if I had not been as stiff as a very old man from sitting uncomfortably in the cold wind, they could still have run much faster than I could. On the other hand, punishing a dog after it has returned to you conveys precisely the wrong message.

It was a time for compromise and for leaving the mess to be sorted out later. I tried to run and blow the stop whistle at the same time, never an easy combination. The first dog to pass close by expressed its sentiments in every frantic movement—*Can't stop now, busy, busy, busy!* At the third try Jenny heeded the whistle and I managed to grab her and blow the whistle in her ear as a powerful reminder. Jack, who realized the seriousness of the situation, took her back to Henry on a lead while I went after the next. To the police it must have looked like a textbook example of what should never happen. To the sound of whistles, shrill yelps and much shouting, their death scene was being swept and trampled by dogs, rabbits and human feet. To make matters worse, Henry had collapsed into helpless laughter. 'View hulloa!' he shouted and 'Tally-ho!' The last, stemming as it does from the French *Il est hault* (he is lame), probably applied more to me than to either the dogs or the rabbits.

The arrival of Detective Inspector Ewell in a shining but otherwise undistinguished Range Rover probably saved us from arrest or worse. Ewell knew at least something about gun dogs—indeed, during his time as our local sergeant he had occasionally whiled away part of a boring shift by helping me on the Moss, tirelessly throwing dummies or discharging the dummy launcher, and he recognized the disastrous nature, from my point of view, of the riot. As he hurried up the hill, a rabbit went to ground a few yards ahead of him. One of the dogs buried its head and shoulder in the hole so that its excited yelps came from all the neighbouring holes. Ewell pulled the culprit out and held her up by the scruff of the neck until Jack could collect her. At the same moment, my grab for another neck latched onto a tail. The last miscreant, realizing that the fun was over and that all odium was now focused on him, came to heel, trying to look hurt and surprised that I should think that he had been among the rioters. *Who? Me? I was trying to catch those others for you . . .*

We came together, puffing, and Henry, now

serious again, took charge of the four leads.

'Now that that's sorted,' Ewell said, 'you can tell me what's adae. Somebody reported a dead body, partly burned, so I came to see for mysel.' He looked from one to the other of us, awaiting explanations.

'I found it,' Jack Gilchrist told him proudly.

'And I phoned you,' Henry added.

'And it's over there,' I said, pointing. 'We haven't touched it and I don't think we've seen anything helpful or caused any more disturbance than we could help, but we'll stick around anyway.'

'Aye. That you will,' said Ewell.

'I take it,' said Henry, 'that sport is over for the day. Is it all right if we load up our rabbits and wait in the car?'

'No, it is definitely not.' The Detective Inspector looked around him and decided not to make three usually responsible citizens stand around in the cold, for which I was thankful. During the chase, I had sweated under my waxed cotton coat and the chill breeze was beginning to bite. 'You can wait in my Range Rover,' Ewell said. 'Take your guns and the dogs but leave the rabbits where they are.' He nodded to a uniformed sergeant who had followed him up the hill.

'Well, all right,' Jack said. He glanced sideways at Ewell. 'But, mind, the rabbits are counted.'

The sergeant preceded us down the hill. I

hung back a few yards. 'Sometimes I feel a bit Bolshy too,' I told Jack softly. 'Inspector Ewell isn't a bad sort but he can be firm if he's crossed. Better not to annoy him or we may never get home.'

'That's a very well,' he grumbled, 'but what for will he no let us clear up and go home?'

'You don't want to know,' I said. Jack was obviously puzzled but Henry looked at me and nodded. I could see for myself what Inspector Ewell would be thinking, because I would have thought the same in his shoes. Dougal Webb was missing. Now there was word of a dead body. If the body had not died on the spot, it would have had to be conveyed there. He knew that each of us had some connection with Dougal Webb. To cap it all, the finders of a body are usually suspect. Ewell would undoubtedly want our vehicles to be examined before he allowed us near them again.

We put the dogs into the rear of the Range Rover alongside a nest of traffic cones and then sat three abreast in the back seat. Jack nursed the ferret-box on his knees. Henry and I held our bagged guns. Jenny stood up against the back of the seat and panted in my ear.

The Sergeant was far from the conventional image of a police sergeant. She was a young woman, very smart and tidy in uniform. It was unusual, in my limited experience, for a sergeant who was driving and dogsbodying for

107

a plain-clothes inspector to wear uniform. I decided that this departure must be to lend her the authority that her apparent youth would otherwise have denied her. Like Beth and other slim, long-legged ladies she looked very young—too young to be in the police at all, let alone have earned her sergeant's stripes. On closer scrutiny of her hands and eyes and throat I decided that she was more mature than first impressions suggested but no less attractive. Even in uniform, her figure was temptation incarnate, her legs creations of beauty. Her dark eyes and full lips raised an otherwise modestly pretty face from the ordinary. Her skin was very good. In short, she was a walking mantrap and I suspected that she knew it, but her manner was perfectly neutral.

She took the front passenger seat, turning round towards us and, I supposed, tucking her legs under her in that loose-hipped way that women have. She rested a notebook on the back of the driver's seat and began a series of questions. It was soon clear that she was well educated and no novice. Her questions were precise and to the point and she took down our answers in a neat shorthand.

When she was satisfied she had the bones of the story and that we were not withholding any startling revelations, she came back to the visit of Mrs Macevoy.

'What did you think was behind her

approach to you?' The Sergeant looked at each of us in turn.

'Behind it?' Jack said.

'Was she really disturbed by the sound of shots. Did she really have a fellow-feeling for the rabbits?'

Jack shrugged. The Sergeant switched her gaze to Henry. Henry sucked his stomach in. If he had had a moustache, he would have given it a twirl. 'I was surprised by that attitude,' he said. 'The woman—I won't call her a lady—has been living there for some years. From what I've seen, her garden is not in the class that gets opened to the public, but from a distance it looks cared for and there's been some attempt to grow flowers and vegetables. It's walled, but the gates are by no means rabbit-proof. There would be food there for rabbits and none in the forestry plantation. Overnight, they probably gorge themselves at her expense. I think that by now she must be totally fed up at the damage that rabbits do. In similar circumstances, most householders are begging for somebody, anybody, to come and reduce the numbers.'

The Sergeant turned her big brown eyes from Henry to me. I tried not to smirk. 'Did she just want to make you go away?' she asked.

'It could have been that,' I said. 'At the time, I put her down as one of those people who have no importance of their own and who try to give themselves a little brief and synthetic importance by handing out a lot of aggravation. You know what I mean?'

'I know *exactly* what you mean,' the Sergeant said, nodding in spite of herself. 'But, from what you remember of her manner at the time, what do you think now?' When none of us hurried to answer she spoke again, slowly and clearly as if to children. 'Could she have been trying to head you away from finding the body?'

I had disliked Mrs Macevoy intensely, but that was all the more reason to try to be fair to her. 'Now,' I said, 'I'm not sure. She could. I can't say that she gave that impression.'

'But she used the words, "Get out of here you bloody men"?'

'Yes,' we said together. 'Accent on bloody,' Henry added.

'And said that she was going to call the police?'

'Yes.'

'But she didn't.' The Sergeant was making a statement. She made a long note. 'What about Mrs Dundee?'

'All she was after was rabbits,' Jack said. 'I think,' he added.

The Sergeant's shorthand might be neat but it was not very speedy. This had all taken time, during which I had watched the comings and goings. It was soon evident that Ewell, as was to be expected, was treating the death as

110

suspicious. I had recognized the police surgeon. A photographer arrived and then another car with men who I assumed to be Scene of Crime Officers.

The Sergeant looked at me again. 'Your car key?'

I handed it over. Detective Inspector Ewell had descended to meet the newcomers. The Sergeant got out to join the throng. I saw her read from her notes. Ewell nodded. At a word from him, two of the newcomers went and fussed around my car.

I rapped on the window. The Sergeant came back and resumed her seat. 'Yes?'

'To save them a lot a wasted excitement,' I said, 'you may as well explain to them that I'm in the habit of carrying shot rabbits and game in the car. Any bloodstains, in the rear end or behind the driver's seat, will be from that.'

She frowned. 'You don't stick to the one place?'

I suppressed a sigh. The most maddening aspect of a police inquiry, I had discovered in the past, was the need to verbalize explanations of the obvious. 'Some dogs travel well in travelling boxes, where they can lie down and not be rolled around. That lets me put game in beside them. But if a dog is car sick, it travels better standing up and looking out. If there's a dog loose in the back of the car I daren't leave anything edible in with it, so shot game goes on the floor behind the driver.

111

But that doesn't mean that you won't find bloodstains anywhere else.'

The Sergeant wrinkled her pretty nose. She made a final note and closed her book. 'I'm glad that I don't share a car with you,' she said austerely.

'I, on the other hand, am sorry,' I replied without taking time to think. The Sergeant dithered for a moment, uncertain how to react. 'It was a compliment,' I added. 'Just ignore it. But you might point out to Inspector Ewell that we're getting hungry.'

Without comment, the Sergeant got out again. She slammed the door of the Range Rover more vigorously than before. We were left to stare through the windscreen. Mrs Dundee was at her gate, watching.

'Even when I had my youth and vigour,' Henry said, 'I never made sexual advances to a policewoman on an empty stomach.'

'Did they not have women constables in the Bow Street Runners?' I asked him.

Soon after that, we were allowed to collect our rabbits and go. Jack offered us a share of the bag but we both declined. I never wanted to see those particular rabbits again. We told him to give our share to Mrs Dundee.

CHAPTER SIX

When we got back to Three Oaks, Beth was pacing up and down outside the house. Her temper was conspicuously high, which for her was unusual. She was speaking, loudly so as to be heard through the glass, before the car had quite stopped. 'Where have you *been*? I have been waiting and waiting for the car and there was no sign of you except for about three words from Henry on his mobile to say that you were held up and I've got to get to the shops before they close because Sam knocked over a whole jug of milk and we're almost out. Have you had anything to eat?' she asked on a second breath as I opened the door.

'Nothing. I want a word with you.'

'Later. There's lunch for both of you in the oven, mostly, if it hasn't burnt. Hannah and Sam are walking the last batch of dogs in the field. I've got to go.'

'I have to talk with you now,' I said, getting out of the car.

'No time,' Beth said, getting in and groping for the key which I had been careful to take with me. 'What happened to the floor-mats?'

'The shops won't close for more than an hour and I'll go and get milk before then. The police have the mats for examination. They'll be looking for bloodstains.'

113

That stopped her. 'What happened?'

'That's what he's trying to tell you about,' Henry explained.

As usual, Beth listened to Henry. 'What is it, then?'

'And I need Hannah,' I said. 'Help me with the dogs. They need their dinners too.'

Not even the usually overriding topic of the dogs' dinners distracted Beth this time. She was looking dazed. 'Why do you want Hannah?'

'I'll explain if I ever get a chance to talk to you calmly, with her and with Henry, indoors, fed and seated. I am not embarking on a lengthy subject standing out here, cold and hungry. And neither is Henry.'

Beth gave up fumbling for the key and got out of the car. Between us we fed, brushed and kennelled the four dogs. Henry cleaned both our guns and we managed to snatch a late and hasty lunch before the dog-walkers returned. Sam, luckily, was yawning after the dose of concentrated fresh air and was put down to rest. Beth had lit the fire in the sitting room and we others settled in front of the hearth. Hannah knew that something was coming and she was perched on the edge of her chair, her hands clasped together so tightly that I thought she would draw blood.

Without more delay I said, 'Hannah, you'd better brace yourself for a shock. We don't know anything for sure, but we found a body this morning. It had been inside a big bonfire of forestry waste so it may be some time before it's identified, but there's obviously a possibility, if not a probability, that it is or was Dougal Webb. As far as we know, he's the only person to have gone missing.'

I had been looking into the fire as I spoke. Now I glanced back at Hannah and away again. She had turned very white and closed her eyes but her chin was still high. 'Please tell me it all,' she said in little more than a whisper.

'You're sure?'

'Yes.'

So I told the story of our day, with Henry interpolating when I missed out any details.

At the end, Hannah asked, 'How can they ever make sure who it is? I mean, if it's so badly burnt . . .'

'You'd have to ask the police about that,' Henry said, 'but the necessary information usually comes from dental records.'

'They won't help very much,' said Hannah. 'Dougal always boasted—boasts—that he's got perfect teeth and never went to a dentist in his life.'

'Then if they find that the body has fillings in its teeth . . .' Beth began gently.

'That might not help. You see, Dougal isn't always very truthful about that sort of thing. He doesn't mean to tell lies.' Hannah looked earnestly at each of us in turn. 'It's just that he likes to brag a little. I can quite imagine him saying that he had perfect teeth because perfect teeth are better than teeth full of fillings and so from his point of view it was the right thing to say at the time, just to score points off the other person. Scoring points is important to him.'

That, I thought, said quite a lot about Dougal's humble origins.

'Don't worry about it,' Henry told her. 'They can do a great deal with the length of bones, the shape of a skull and any old operations or fractures. They can even rebuild the features, just from the skull. They'll find out for sure. Meantime, you can only wait and hope.'

'I expect so.' Hannah sighed shakily. She was turning palely green at Henry's ramblings.

I did not share Henry's faith in forensic science. Skulls can burst in intense heat. But, for Hannah, a detailed description of the head of the corpse in the bonfire might be the last straw. 'It's a little early in the day,' I said, 'but I think we could call it knocking-off time. Hannah, you'd like a drink? A stiff one for a change?' I had it in mind to give Hannah a good stiff mixture of port and brandy. Nothing can beat it as a settler for a queasy stomach.

Hannah shook her head and got to her feet. 'I'm going out,' she said hoarsely. 'Dogs to walk.' She hurried out of the room.

I looked at Beth, who shook her head. 'The

dogs have all been walked,' she said. 'But never mind. Hannah won't want anybody to see her face for now. The light's going. Walking dogs in the fresh air and twilight may be the best therapy for her. It won't do the dogs any harm, either. What was that about a stiff drink?'

'That was for Hannah's benefit,' I told her. 'I'll have to be going if I'm to fetch milk.'

'Never mind about the milk,' Beth said—or words to that effect. 'Hannah can walk some more dogs up to the farm later. Did you mean to imply that the police think that Mrs Macevoy was trying to head you away from finding the body?'

'That would be putting it a bit strong,' Henry said. He was already at the side table and pouring our customary drinks. 'All we can tell you is that the woman sergeant who took our preliminary statements seemed to think that it was one question that Mr Ewell would ask later, so she'd better have the answer.'

Beth considered. 'It could be,' she said. 'If Mrs Macevoy had carried the body from the house and hid it in the bonfire and then found today that it wasn't completely burned—heavy rain woke me during the night, it could have damped down the remains of the bonfire—she could have been planning to go out after dark to bury it or move it, as soon as it was cool, or even to rekindle the bonfire.'

'You haven't seen the place,' Henry said. 'It

117

had originally been planted ridge-and-furrow and then, so that the roots would be out and ready to burn, they'd taken down the trees by pulling them out with a tractor. That would be at the landowner's insistence,' he added, resuming his chair with a substantial whisky to hand. 'The ground was like the aftermath of a major battle in World War One, all trenches and shell-holes. The woman could hardly get herself over it—in fact, I found it hard going myself.'

'I certainly couldn't carry a body over it,' I said. 'Especially in the dark.'

'Would a barrow have made it easier?'

'The reverse.'

Beth was reluctant to abandon a nicely compact theory. 'With a male accomplice . . . Oh well, we can think about it when we know a little more.'

'I don't want to think about it at all,' I said.

Beth seemed to accept what I said at face value. 'You don't have to think about it if you don't want to. So what happens now? When will the rest of us know something?'

'The media will know even less than we do, for the moment,' I said. 'The police will be asking questions. The more they find out the more questions they'll ask. You know that, you've seen them in action.'

'And they'll be handing out information like a tiger giving up its kill,' said Henry.

'You can make a lot of informed guesses

118

from the questions they ask,' Beth said. 'And sometimes even more from what they don't ask. If it's Sergeant Ewell—'

'Detective Inspector Ewell,' Henry and I corrected her in unison.

'If it's Mr Ewell,' Beth began again, 'I'll pick his brains, just you see if I don't.'

*   *   *

Once again we were in a state of limbo. From the media, I gathered that Jack Gilchrist, as the actual discoverer of the body, was giving interviews galore and would continue to do so for as long as the body was news and his stories continued to grow in dramatic appeal—or until an arrest was made and the whole subject became sub judice. Of hard news, there was none.

I told Hannah that she could take time off, go home, do anything that would help her to get through the period of uncertainty, but she said that she would go mad if she had nothing to occupy her mind. That was all very well and quite understandable. I would have felt the same. But there is no helper more counter-productive than one who promises to do something and then forgets. As long as Hannah was liable to fall into a trance or suddenly hurry out of sight to hide a burst of weeping, she was more of a nuisance than a help. Beth and Daffy tried to comfort her, which usually made bad worse and also hindered their own labours. As a result, we endured two days during which the work of the kennels went forward, if at all, in fits and starts. The dogs soon knew that our minds were not on them and they began playing us up.

When Detective Inspector Ewell arrived unheralded at mid-morning on the Tuesday, accompanied by his Sergeant—still glamorous though still in uniform—it was, more than anything, a relief.

Ewell wanted to speak first to Hannah and Hannah asked me to be present. When Ewell made no objection, Beth, after a speculative glance at the Sergeant, managed to suggest that perhaps another woman, and not of the police, should attend in case comfort was called for. That also was accepted after a judicious pause, but when Daffy (accompanied by Sam) and Isobel tried to add themselves to the party, he drew the line. They were excluded, firmly but politely. Henry, who would probably have managed to include himself in the conclave by dint of the mere authority of his presence, was away.

We settled in the sitting room. The hearth had not been cleared, which was a measure of our disturbed state, but two firelighters soon kindled a fire of logs above the old ashes. The flames performed their usual magic, transforming the sometimes cheerless room into a welcoming haven. I saw the Sergeant glance up at the painting above the fireplace, of a skein of geese over an estuary.

Hannah was looking towards the Inspector as a rabbit might look at a stoat.

'Mr Cunningham told you about the find on Saturday?' Ewell asked her. The question seemed superfluous. I suspected that he had put off this particular interview until he could be quite sure that I had done the job for him. As a sergeant, I remembered, the breaking of bad news had been the only part of his work which he faced with less than enthusiasm.

Hannah nodded.

Ewell, who had seemed as apprehensive as Hannah herself, looked happier. 'I still have no definite information for you,' he admitted. 'So far, that body has not been positively identified. You'll understand that we have to consider the possibility—'

'That the body is all that's left of Dougal Webb,' Hannah said bravely. 'I understand. Mr Cunningham explained. He also told me how badly burned it was.'

The Detective Inspector looked still more relieved. 'And that's one reason I've come to you. We are in some difficulty. Mr Webb seems almost to have appeared out of nowhere. His employer knows very little about him. The job was advertised, Mr Webb applied. Mr Cove checked on his college diploma and left it at that. The addresses at which Webb was living

121

when he took his course and when he made his application were both lodgings in Falkirk. Can you, for instance, tell us who Mr Webb's dentist is?'

Hannah repeated what she had told us, that Dougal Webb had boasted of his perfect teeth, and paused.

'Hannah had her reservations as to whether that was necessarily true,' I said.

'From what we've been able to find out so far,' Ewell said, 'he seems to have been a model of truthfulness—at least in that one respect.'

'And the body had good teeth?' Beth put in.

'Well, yes. We know which medical practice Mr Webb signed on with, but he never seems to have needed more attention than a bandaged cut or a prescription for cough mixture. They don't even have a record of his height and weight. We can make an estimate of those from the clothes left in his cottage, but that's a poor basis for an identification. The body, as you say, was badly burned and—'

I saw Beth wince. 'If that's all you want from Hannah, can she go now?' Beth asked. 'Surely she needn't hear the gory details?'

'It's all right,' Hannah said quickly, 'Somebody's died. That's all I care about— that, and whether or not it was Dougal.'

'I would never give what you call "gory details" to a member of the public,' Ewell said with dignity. 'I was only going to say that we recovered some of Mr Webb's hairs from his hairbrush and there was a bloodied sticking-plaster in his bathroom. There should be no difficulty isolating his DNA—what they call "genetic fingerprinting". That may take about ten days. But the body's DNA may present more of a problem.'

Despite the Inspector's fine words, I was sure that he had been on the point of explaining that they had hopes of an identification by genetic fingerprint *if the body was not cooked beyond the point at which DNA could still be isolated*. And if that was not a 'gory detail', figuratively speaking, I did not know what was. Or perhaps Ewell did not count incineration as being gory but even quite the opposite.

'You won't want to lose that time,' Beth said. 'Is it true that the longer a case drags on, the less chance there is of solving it?'

'So they say, and it seems likely. I've not been in CID long enough to speak from personal experience. But that's why I'm looking to you for help, Miss Hopewell. You knew the deceased—Mr Webb, I mean—better than anyone.'

'You're sure that it's Dougal Webb, aren't you?' Beth said.

Ewell had flushed. He hurried to correct himself, speaking directly to Hannah. 'Put it down as a slip of the tongue, please. I'm thinking along those lines, of course I am, and so are you. As Mrs Cunningham pointed out, the longer a case goes on the less chance of solving it there's said to be. So we've got to make the best start we can even though we don't have a positive identification. That means that we've got to start from the likeliest assumption. But I've no way of knowing for sure yet, one way or the other. With the young man's next of kin not known . . .'

Hannah frowned. 'What? But I can tell you that,' she said.

Ewell tried to hide his surprise. 'You can?'

'I think I can,' Hannah said cautiously. 'I nearly said something when you told us about him appearing out of nowhere. I don't know if he was still being—what did you call it?—a *model of truthfulness*. He sometimes says what he doesn't really mean, just to build himself up a bit. Romanticizing, sort of. But, for what it's worth, I'll tell you. I was at Ardrossie one time, and we could see Gifford House sitting up on the hill and sticking up out of the trees. I said how I'd like to live in a house like that some day, or like this one, a house built when there was space and quality and with country round about it, not jammed in between neighbours on either side and front and back and a garden the size of a blanket. And he said something like, "Stick with me and you'll live in that house some day. My aunt lives there and neither of them has any relatives closer than me." '

'Mrs Macevoy?' Beth exclaimed.

'It would have to be, wouldn't it?'

It happened that the Sergeant was sitting in my field of vision, at a corner table that usually only sported back numbers of magazines, and I saw her look up and frown. Beth must have caught the same look. She said, 'Mrs Macevoy didn't tell you? Surely you asked her about Saturday?'

'Of course. She didn't give you a very good press, by the way,' Ewell added in my direction. 'But Mr Webb's name wasn't mentioned and she might not have known that he was missing. She seems to live a rather isolated existence. We've been trying to trace Webb's origins. This is the first indication we've had that he was local.'

'He probably wasn't,' Beth said. 'According to Daffy, the Macevoys had only lived here a very few years before the big scandal. Dougal Webb may have moved here to be near them. He may even have heard about the job vacancy from his aunt. But, of course, after his uncle was sent to prison, he wouldn't have boasted about the connection.'

'That's true.' The Detective Inspector seemed relieved by Beth's reasoning. He returned his attention to Hannah. 'You don't know where he grew up? Or whether his parents are still alive?' Hannah shook her head. 'Never mind. One other thing. It would help if you could provide some photographs of

125

him. As many as possible.'

'I only have one or two snapshots. I'll get them back in the end?'

'I promise.'

Hannah got up. When she was out of earshot, Beth asked, 'Are you still in charge of the case?'

'For practical purposes,' Ewell said slowly. I guessed that it hurt his dignity to admit that he was no longer the top dog, but in the presence of his Sergeant he would have to be truthful. 'Superintendent Aicheson is in nominal charge but he has other things on his plate.'

Beth pounced. 'So it's being treated as a case of murder?' An inspector might deal with an unexplained disappearance but murder would usually be the province of a more senior officer.

Ewell very nearly smiled. 'I would have come to that as soon as the lassie was out of the room. There was no need to creep up on it obliquely. Likely, I'll have to take a further statement from her. But take a look at this, which has just reached us.' He stretched out a hand. The Sergeant rose and handed him a large photograph. Evidently there were no concessions to gender in the Fife CID.

Ewell passed it to me. The single transparency had been made up from four X-rays. On a reduced scale it showed a slim knife-blade which had been snapped off. It was still in place among what looked like human organs. Alongside it had been drawn a scale, according to which the blade was some twenty centimetres long. 'Do you have a knife like that?' he asked.

'Probably,' I said.

'Do you still have it?'

'If we ever had one, I expect it's still around. You're welcome to look.'

He took back the photograph. 'You're very casual about a lethal weapon.'

'Potentially lethal,' I said.

'What do you mean?'

'It wasn't designed for use as a weapon.'

Ewell blinked at me. 'I've asked for a report on the knife-blade,' he said, 'but I won't get it until the postmortem is finished and the blade can be examined. What can you suggest?'

'You called it a lethal weapon. So is a teapot, if you brain somebody with it. This wasn't made as a weapon. A stabbing knife can be one of several different shapes altogether, quite unlike this. The point is usually in line with the handle. It would be made from heavier stock, a quarter of an inch or so thick, not steel that would snap off. It can be a plain dagger shape or a clip-point "bowie" with the clip sharpened. The blade would usually be dull or darkened—blued—which I don't think is what you'll find when you do get your hands on it. And the blade would usually be tapered or grooved to let air go past. A plain, flat blade like this with parallel edges would be gripped

127

by suction. Stab somebody with this and you might not be able to pull it out again, though you might need to use it again in a hurry.'

Beth made a little sound of protest. She had never quite come to terms with the violence of my earlier career.

'I bow to your experience of weaponry,' Ewell said slowly, 'even if I wouldn't want to have had it myself. So it's a hunting knife? Or a kitchen knife?'

'Probably not a hunting knife.' I took back the photograph. 'This has a curved sharp edge and a straight blunt edge. You do get hunting knives of that shape, but they're not easy to use. The main purpose of a hunting knife is to open up a dead animal neatly. The knife in the X-rays would slit the skin but it would dig in and perforate the guts or the meat. That may be acceptable, depending on your technique and what the meat is, but not to me. A hunting knife usually has a blade shaped like this.' I dug my lock-knife out of my pocket and opened it to show him the blade. 'A curved cutting edge. A straight back edge but angled down by about ten degrees near the point—that's the "clip" I referred to earlier. It gives a blunt edge to ride along on the meat without cutting into it. When you get it out, if the clip turns out to have been sharpened I'll take back most of what I've told you.'

From Ewell's expression, he was suffering from an excess of information and needed to boil it down. 'So this would be . . . what? A kitchen knife?'

'I suppose so,' I said. 'Or a badly designed general-purpose sheath-knife. It's longer than a stalker's knife or a combat knife, and of thinner steel.'

'For use around the farm?'

'Possibly. But my first guess would be kitchen knife,' I said.

Beth had possessed herself of the X-rays. 'It's not one of ours,' she said. 'And if he was stabbed in the back, like this—'

Ewell jumped as though he had been stung. 'How do you know he was stabbed in the back?' he demanded.

'Both my parents are doctors,' Beth said. 'X-rays are always being passed across the breakfast table. I think that that was what turned me off following in their footsteps. But at least I know what a human heart looks like and which way round it is. I was only going to say that some force must have been used to get between the ribs.'

The Detective Inspector relaxed. 'You had me going there for a moment, Mrs Cunningham.' There were footsteps in the hall. Ewell recovered his transparency and put it away quickly.

'But you'd agree?' Beth asked.

'Oh, yes. The pathologist's opinion is that it jammed and was broken in an attempt to pull it out again.'

129

Hannah came back. She offered three or four small photographs to the Inspector. 'I've remembered something else,' she said. 'While I was waiting in Mr Cove's house I was sitting at the window overlooking the yard. There was a small lamp on the table beside me. At about two in the morning a car came into the yard. I think the driver saw me at the window, because he turned in a circle and drove away again.'

'You didn't see him?'

'Inspector,' Hannah said, 'I didn't even look at the car. I was waiting for Dougal. I knew from the sound of the car before it appeared that it wasn't his Lotus. It wasn't even his style of driving. So I didn't bother.'

The Detective Inspector said nothing but from the look of exasperation on his face I knew exactly what he thought of a witness who 'didn't bother to look'. Then he firmed his jaw and persevered. 'Miss Hopewell,' he said, 'if you could tell without looking that it wasn't Mr Webb's car or style of driving, then you must have some idea what sort of car and style of driving it was.'

Hannah took a few seconds to think back, and when she spoke it was less certainly than before. 'It wasn't a sporty sort of car like the Lotus. Something heavier, but not a diesel, I think I'd have known one of those. And Dougal had to pay for his own petrol unless he was doing an errand for Mr Cove, so he used

130

to keep his engine speed down.'

'I noticed the same thing,' I said. 'He changed up as soon as he could and delayed changing down until he had to. Not the right technique for a sports car.'

'That's what I was getting at,' Hannah said, relieved. 'But whoever was driving, that night, came up the farm road in a fairly low gear, changed further down to slow the car and then braked quite hard. Dougal tried not to use his brakes much. He always said that brake linings were expensive.'

*   *   *

We discussed among ourselves the mysterious corpse, the missing farm manager and every conceivable connection between the two. That was inevitable. But the subject was best avoided whenever Hannah was within earshot and when, after a day or two, it was clear that she was too distraught to pull her weight and she was packed off to have her megrims in her father's house, we were too busy and too short-handed to manage more than a snatched word or two between more pressing topics.

To make matters worse, Isobel then went down with the 'flu. For her own sake and to prevent her from spreading it to the rest of us, we declined her offer to come in and carry on with the paperwork from a cosy fireside chair.

She was banished to her bed a safe couple of miles away. The very idea of the whole complement of staff and partners being bedridden simultaneously was not to be contemplated.

Ash had been entered for a novice stake in the Lothians that Saturday. With Isobel *hors de combat*, the sensible thing would have been to withdraw, but the season would be over all too soon and Ash needed a win if he was to go forward into open stakes and pursue what we hoped was his destiny as a Field Trial Champion with a lucrative and voluptuous career at stud to follow. A whole sackful of second places would count for nothing. Daffy did not yet have a tenth of the required experience. Handling our entrants in field trials had been my responsibility until one of my relapses had pitchforked Isobel into the job with unexpectedly happy results. Obviously I would have to take over again.

Beth's immediate reaction verged on panic. Rex had returned offshore. She and Daffy, assisted as ever by Sam, could cope with the kennel routine. But Henry would be too fully engaged with Isobel either to help with the dogs or to come as my companion and bodyguard. Beth could already visualize me having one of my blackouts among strangers who would then empty my pockets and leave me to expire, alone and unidentified. I was torn between irritation at the disruption of our

132

plans and a warm glow that somebody loved me enough to worry about me.

The argument had reached stalemate when a phone call threw a mesh weight into the scales. Earlier in the season, a sporting journalist had been much impressed by one of our bitches and had written glowingly of her performance, using her exclusion from the top honour to illustrate his contention that judges could sometimes be struck with blindness or insanity. A businessman in Bristol was in the market for a trained spaniel and had made up his mind that only one of our breeding would suit. When I told him that a son of that bitch was trained and ready to go, he was willing to do a deal over the phone. It happened that he would be in Edinburgh on the Friday but would have to be back in Bristol by Saturday afternoon to prepare for a major meeting on the Monday. Could I bring the dog to meet him in Edinburgh on Friday? As a clincher he decided, while still on the phone, to buy a puppy as a present for his son.

Beth did not want to let me out of her protective custody, but there was serious money involved and she would have hated to pass up two good sales. Her resistance began to crumble. She phoned Joe Little, who was to judge on both days. She made him promise to keep an eye on me for as long as our programmes coincided and to call out the emergency services the moment that I failed to show up at an appointed time. And so I was ready, with a car full of three dogs, all the accompanying paraphernalia and my overnight bag, when Joe sounded his horn outside the gate early on the Friday morning. None of my fainting spells had ever occurred while I was sitting down but Beth had still insisted that we travel in convoy. We had a peaceful journey. A puppy may be forgiven for protesting shrilly when being transported away from home and siblings, but the presence of his uncle seemed to give him reassurance.

Beth had furnished me with a list of shopping which she considered to be essential for her future well-being. I left the list with one of the largest stores while I did the rounds of my favourite gunshops. After a quick lunch in a pub, I collected Beth's parcel and met my client in his hotel. He fell for the pup immediately and when I worked the other dog for him, in and out of the bushes at Hermitage Park, to indoctrinate him into the commands to which the dog had been trained, he expressed himself more than satisfied. I handed over the necessary papers and most of my cargo of dog-food, said a fond farewell to the two dogs and an even fonder hello to a very substantial cheque and drove out of the city through the falling darkness to the hotel where rooms had been booked.

That day's competition, a novice trial for retrievers, had gone well. Joe was already in the bar, buying his own drinks as was right and proper but lapping up the sycophancy of those who hoped to be remembered kindly next time around. When the crush began to melt away he joined me at a corner table.

'Still living and breathing, I see,' he said.

'If you can call it living,' I retorted. 'Beth does fuss rather.'

'Don't knock it,' he told me severely. 'She's quite right. I was with you the second or third time you flaked out, remember? Gave me the fright of my life. I had to lug you to the nearest quack.'

'Letting me lie flat for a while would have been enough,' I told him. 'According to the doc, it's much the same as a common faint.'

'Except that people don't always come round when it's vagal inhibition.'

'That's how you tell the difference. All the same, I owe you for that. What a pity I'm not supposed to buy you a drink. There's nothing to stop you buying me one,' I pointed out.

'Nice try,' he said. 'But if I bought a drink for one competitor I'd have to buy them for all the others or there'd be complaints about favouritism.'

We ordered another round of drinks and meticulously paid for our own. 'Are you ready for tomorrow?' Joe asked me.

'The dog's ready,' I said. 'I'm not sure about me. I'm out of practice and I haven't had time to get myself into the right state of mind. But I was working the dog not long ago. I think we'll get by.'

'I'm sure you will.' But Joe's mind was not really on my state of readiness. 'It's a bugger finding somewhere to train these days, isn't it? I've never known such a bad year for rabbits. Are you dependent on picking-up?'

'Mostly.'

'I met Quentin Cove in the Drookit Dug the other day,' Joe said. 'He told me that I could come onto Ardrossie. I thought that that was one of your patches.'

'It was,' I said. 'That's odd! He told me that he'd let the rough shooting and I'd have to stay away.'

'You must have put his back up somehow. You didn't leave a gate open that should have been closed, or close one that he wanted left open?'

'I hadn't been there for weeks. Last time I was there he walked round with me, taking turnabout to work one of his own dogs. He expressed himself as suitably obliged to me.'

'Then it beats me,' Joe said. 'Unless that chap Webb was the rough-shooting tenant. Did he shoot?'

'I don't know,' I said. As I spoke I remembered Webb's desire for my Dickson but I kept my mouth shut. The subject was fraught with danger.

'He certainly went beating,' Joe mused. 'Beaters usually shoot, though I suppose he could just have been beating to curry favour with Sir Ian and other landowners. But if Webb really had rented the shooting from his boss, now that Webb's dead Cove might feel free to hand out permissions again.'

It seemed to be the general assumption but all the same I pricked up my ears. 'Dead? Have you heard something I haven't?'

Joe shrugged. 'Shouldn't think so. It's just the word that's going around. You probably know more than I do.'

'Webb's certainly gone missing,' I said. 'And there's a body. But as far as I know there's no proven connection yet.'

'The police think there's a connection,' Joe said. 'They took an interminable statement from me about the last time that I saw Webb. I may have been the last person to see him alive,' he added with a certain pride. 'Other than his murderer, of course.'

'Murderer?' I said.

'Assuming that he's dead and assuming that he fetched up in the bonfire, it's not easy to think up any explanation other than what they call *foul play*. I was running short of feed for a nursing bitch so I drove over to Ardrossie that Sunday evening, around seven. Webb and his boss were talking in the big yard. They broke off as I pulled up. I didn't hear what they were saying but they sounded a bit heated. Then Webb got into his Lotus and drove off with an uncharacteristic burst of wheelspin. He was usually too canny to waste tyre rubber. Damn silly car for a farmer,' Joe added. 'Or for a dog trainer. All the same, if it's coming on the market . . .'

A waiter came to tell us that our table was ready in the dining room. When the conversation found its way back to Quentin Cove, somewhere about the sweet course, it was by way of a long gossip about dogs in training. 'Quentin turned up with his bitch Mimulus at an open stake last weekend,' Joe said. 'He was hoping to get a run if somebody dropped out, but he was out of luck.'

'He must be getting keen,' I said with my mouth full of *crème caramel*.

'Get a good dog and neglect him, or else work him to death,' Joe said. 'That's always been the amateur's way.'

CHAPTER SEVEN

I left an early call and was the first guest to breakfast.

The previous night, I had noted near the hotel a stretch of rough ground which had been left to gorse and weeds, the sort of ground beloved by environmentalists and dog trainers. After breakfast, I settled my bill and went out to the car. Ash came eagerly out into the cold air from his cosy bed in the back of the car, relieved himself in a cloud of steam against somebody else's rear wheel and came reluctantly to heel. A spaniel, and especially one as high-spirited as Ash, must blow off steam and I was determined that any steam-blowing would be done before we came under the judges. I took him onto the waste ground and let him race around for a few minutes. When he began to show signs of wanting to hunt I brought him back under control, worked him to a pattern through the bushes and then gave him two retrieves with a canvas dummy. That, I hoped, would be enough and not too much.

At the trial ground I felt again the almost forgotten surge of excitement as the once familiar scene took shape. Competitors, openly nervous or hiding their nerves. The two judges in a solemn huddle. The Guns, happy with their role but nervous of shooting badly before so many critical eyes. Officials fussing. And the pickers-up, who would linger to look for any birds on which the competing dogs had failed, secure in the knowledge that they in their turn could fail unseen but could play a game of one-upmanship by coming back with a bird. It was 'not done' for a picker-up to display the bird from a successful retrieve, but it had been known for one of them to allow a bird from that or even from a previous retrieve to be glimpsed as though by accident. The pickers-up liked to consider themselves the only true professionals present.

The cumbersome line moved off across a field of stubble, with a tail of onlookers and competitors awaiting the call. Conditions were difficult. In the sharp air and rising breeze, some dogs were hot to handle and threw points to the wind. The sky was dark and the air very cold. I would have expected scenting to be adequate but it was very bad. And many birds seemed determined to sit tight instead of flushing. Dog after dog pegged a squatting bird and was eliminated.

First time 'up', I knew that things were going my way. Ash, having already worked off his excess energy, was nicely in hand and working a perfect pattern but he retained enough of his innate manners to disdain pegging sitting game. He flushed several birds and pulled off a good retrieve. We went through to the next round.

By mid-afternoon, Ash was among the four dogs called for a run-off. One of the first brace, I thought, performed indifferently but each managed a flush and a retrieve. Then we were called. I reminded myself, for the umpteenth time, to stay calm and, if in doubt, *trust the dog*—always good advice but not so easy to follow in the heat of the moment.

The line was struggling through a field of turnips, thinned by winter. Despite a frosted surface over which dogs could run, the mud beneath took hold of a boot and made walking a penance. No bird with a grain of sense, I thought, would be out of the woods on such a day and looking among the roots for insects which must have died out weeks before. But Ash homed in on a small cock pheasant and kicked it into the air. The nearest Gun fumbled his shot and the bird spiralled down, a strong runner, beyond the boundary hedge and ditch.

The judge, Joe's colleague, nodded to me.

Ash had been unsighted. I pushed him, with hand signals, through the hedge and out to the fall and he picked up a scent. I wondered whether to curse or bless my luck. A difficult runner may lead to failure, or to a successful retrieve and impressed judges. I had lost sight of the bird. Ash followed his nose, plunged into the hedge and vanished. I kept my hand away from the whistle and reminded myself over and over again, *The dog knows more than you do*. When movement drew my eye to Ash again he had crossed a narrow field, hurdled another fence and was entering an area of broken ground where rocky outcrops alternated with broom and dead bracken. Surely he must have overrun his bird and picked up the scent of another? On the other hand, it was just the sort of cover for which a strong runner would head. Anyway, if I called him off now we would have failed. I waited.

Time went by. There was some chatting among the onlookers. The judge began to fidget. He was going to tell me to call my dog.

I saw movement at the edge of the cover. Ash returned over the first fence. His chin was up. He was holding a kicking pheasant clear of the ground. He cleared the nearer ditch and struggled through the hedge. There was a spontaneous round of applause as he delivered the bird into my hand, sitting. The judge, properly cautious, took the bird and parted the feathers until he found the marks of pellets.

The light was fading and snowflakes were beginning to fall as we assembled in a Dutch barn. We waited while the two judges debated. Joe glanced in my direction while listening to the other judge who was being vehement. My hopes rose. Joe, I guessed, was hesitant, just because I was a friend, and wanted to be persuaded.

Then he nodded and they gave their verdict. Ash was placed first.

I shook hands all round and remembered to thank the host and his keeper. I was glad to get back to the car and gladder still when the engine's heat began to warm the interior. I went back to the hotel for my overnight bag and to call home from the payphone in the hall. As well as confirming my continued health and imminent return after a hot snack, I wanted to spread the glad tidings. But when Beth recognized my voice she said, 'Can't talk now. Tell me when you come,' and hung up.

If she could not even take time to ask how I was or even how we had got on, something had to be seriously wrong, but what? If the house had burned down, there would have been no phone for Beth to answer. I found more money and dialled again but the ringing tone went unanswered. Without waiting for a word with Joe, or even to give Ash his well-deserved dinner, I dived back into the car and set off for home.

The early dark of midwinter was aggravated by heavy clouds and before I reached the Forth Road Bridge the snow was coming down in earnest. Home-going traffic was slowed almost to a crawl but I carved my way through it with a display of downright bad manners which I hope never to have to repeat. Twice my lights seemed to be failing and I pulled off to wipe the packed snow off the glass. I saw several cars that had slid off into the countryside, one of them still surrounded by vehicles with flashing lights. My car was determined to go the same way, but I held it more or less straight by grit and willpower and turned in at the front gates of Three Oaks after a journey time which I would have considered dangerously brief on a summer Sunday afternoon. There were no emergency vehicles to be seen, the house was still standing, there was no sign of a fire and I could see movement behind the lit curtains. My worst imaginings abated.

To my further relief Beth, leading a sleepy Sam with one hand and balancing a tray on the other, met me in the hall, shook her head and said, 'Hush!'

'It isn't Sam, is it?' I whispered.

She shook her head. 'Daffy had a bit of a shake up,' she said softly. 'She's all right, more or less, but having a lie-down. Hannah came back—she hated it at home, with her father away most of the time—and she's sitting with Daffy now. Joe's been on the phone, in a tizzy because you'd vanished without a word and he didn't know whether you were unconscious in a ditch. I told him that you would be on the way home because I'd let you know that something was wrong, so it was my fault really. I was just going to brew more tea or something. Are you hungry?'

I thought about it and realized that I had got by on one sandwich and an apple since my early breakfast. 'Starving,' I said.

She nodded. 'Go and sit with Daffy. She can tell you her story, if she feels up to it. That'll let Hannah finish up.'

Hannah, drawn by our whispering or the sound of the car, emerged from the sitting room. She looked more alert and cheerful and I thought that the image of her Dougal might be slipping from reality into memory. I was still wondering why Daffy needed a sitter.

Before I could ask, Hannah said, 'How did Ash get on?' Not, you will note, how did her

144

owner, trainer and handler get on? At Three Oaks, the dog was all-important. But at least she had remembered to ask.

'He's still in the car, and unfed,' I told her. I paused before adding, 'We won.'

Hannah beamed, stood on her toes and kissed me.

Beth looked pleased but only said, 'You're not going to crow over Isobel, are you?'

'Of course I am,' I said. 'That was my only reason for trying so hard.'

Beth made a face at me. 'Daffy won't go to hospital, won't speak to the police, won't eat or drink anything and she won't even let me call the doctor.' Beth combined a sigh with blowing a strand of hair away from her face. I tucked it back for her, took the tray from her and put it down on the hall table. 'Thanks. She says she doesn't want to be a nuisance! Well, she's a damn sight more nuisance worrying everybody sick. She just lies on the settee, moaning. See what you can do with her.'

Beth had to be seriously upset to let such *doubles entendres* slip by.

The sitting room, I found, was lit only by the firelight, supplemented by one small table lamp. Even that poor illumination seemed to be too much, because Daffy was stretched on the settee with a cloth over her eyes. She was wearing a dress which I seemed to recognize as one of Hannah's. She put up a listless hand to

145

lift an edge of the cloth and peep at me. Sarda, sprawled across her lap, watched every movement with anxious eyes. 'It's you,' Daffy said hoarsely.

It was not the occasion for a funny answer, nor a pedantic one. 'It's me,' I confirmed, throwing grammar to the winds.

'How did you get on?'

'I thought nobody was going to ask. We got a first.'

'Well done! So Ash can go forward to open stakes.' The news would usually have had her on her feet. Instead, she sounded only mildly interested.

'What happened to you?' I asked her. 'Beth and Hannah are too busy to tell me anything. And I don't think that they know a lot.'

She roused slightly but remained prone. 'We packed up early because of the snow,' she said in a tired voice. 'Mrs Cunningham invited me to stay for a meal, but there was a heap of things waiting for me at home and now I had a chance to get at them at last and have the place clean and the laundry done before Rex comes home again. Am I making sense?' she asked.

'Perfect sense,' I assured her.

'I seem to be thinking through cotton wool. Mrs Cunningham offered to drive me home but conditions were rotten for driving and I thought that I'd probably be safer walking on the back road. Well, I set off to walk home. I had Sarda with me—on a lead, thank God! It was almost dark and snowing hard, but I had a good torch and good boots with plenty of tread, so we got along all right until we came to the place between the walls, you know where I mean?'

I said that I did. The cottage which Rex and Daffy shared was on a side-road that came off on the other side of the village, but an even more minor road, little more than a lane, cut the corner and would have saved her a mile. About half a mile from Three Oaks, the road squeezed between the high garden wall belonging to a farmhouse and a drystone wall to a field.

Daffy's voice was getting stronger. 'We were in the middle of that bit when a car arrived suddenly. It seemed to come out of nowhere. One moment it was dark, a moment later the world was full of blazing bright snowflakes and a pair of lamps was rushing at us. He couldn't have pulled up on the snow, even if he'd seen me in time, and you know how narrow the road is just there. The garden wall is impossibly high so I went the other way. I threw myself to the side of the road, dragging Sarda after me, couldn't stop and ended up doing a dive over the wall into the field. I don't know whether Sarda was dragged over on the lead or if she jumped but she seems all right. It was damn close, he actually hit the duffel bag which was over my shoulder. But there's a

147

drop to the field and I came down on a big stone with Sarda on top of me. I was dazed and I seemed to have cut my head and it was nearer to come back here and anyway there wouldn't have been anyone at home. You don't mind?' she asked anxiously.

'Of course not,' I said. 'Don't be an ass. We'd have minded very much if you'd done anything else. Let's have a look at you.'

She peeped out from under the cloth again and evidently discovered that the light no longer hurt her eyes. She discarded the cloth— one of my scarves, I noticed—and sat up, tucking the skirt modestly under her knees. Marriage had certainly changed her. The change was mostly for the better but sometimes I missed the old, outrageous Daffy.

During my army days I had gained some experience of injuries. I put up the top light without causing more than a frown of discomfort and examined her. A lump like half an egg was lifting her hair above her right ear, but Beth had already cleaned up the attendant cut. Several other abrasions had been plastered. She was breathing normally and comfortably and, though stiff and sore, could move all her limbs. Her eyes looked normal. She was pale but not clammy. I judged that she had had a mild concussion but was already coming out of it.

I switched off the big light again and sat down. 'You'd better stay here overnight,' I said. 'Just in case you have any after-effects.'

'Mrs Cunningham already said that. And Hannah says that I can come in with her.'

'Good arrangement,' I said with relief. The spare bedroom now doubled as a nursery. If Daffy had slept there, Sam would have had to come in with us and he was a noisy and demanding roommate.

'It's very odd that you didn't see the car coming,' I said. 'He came from in front of you?'

'No, it came from behind. And you know how falling snow muffles noise.'

'Even so, there would have been a lot of light spilling forward and illuminating the snowflakes.'

Daffy rubbed her eyes. Her mind, usually bright, was working again. 'I didn't expect a car. You hardly ever see traffic on that road except a tractor or a small herd of cows. And I was thinking of other things. Partly I was wondering how you'd got on. Then again, it wasn't quite dark. And a lot of people prefer to use dipped headlights in fog or snow, so as not to make it reflect back in their eyes. He may have undipped the moment he saw me.'

'I suppose all that's true,' I said. 'You seem to have thought it out.'

'I've had nothing else to think about, lying here.'

'All the same, why don't you want the police?'

'What could they do?' she asked petulantly. 'Anyway, I was just as much at fault as he was. I should have been paying attention. And if I did call the police and they did manage to arrest somebody, he would probably turn out to be a friend or relation of somebody I know or somebody important and I'd be in for endless hassle. Sod's Law.'

It was certainly too late for the police to accomplish anything that night. The guilty vehicle would almost certainly be home and cold by now and much snow had fallen over the whole scene. Daffy's duffel bag was on the carpet beside her. There was a rip through which her spare jeans showed. I turned the bag in my hands. There were no convenient flakes of paint to be seen. 'We'll put this away in polythene,' I said, 'just in case. I can lend you another bag for the moment.'

Beth called me to come and take my meal. I decided to sleep on the problem.

*   *   *

There were no alarms in the night, but all the same I was restless. Daffy's accident fitted too neatly together with other events, to make a pattern which I did not want to recognize. It seemed to me that somebody might mean to do Daffy harm. The thought was not conducive to sound sleep under the same roof.

Daffy herself had slept well and was up early, hobbling around like an old lady but doing her share of the work, a still worried Sarda constantly at her heel. Daffy was showing several more lumps which had developed during the night and some bruises which had hardly been visible earlier had now blossomed into Glorious Technicolor, but I judged that any danger of serious injury or concussion was now gone. I was waiting in the kitchen when she and Hannah came in for breakfast, while Beth was getting Sam up and ready for the day.

'Think back,' I told Daffy. 'I know that you weren't paying attention at the time, but try to remember. Have you any idea what sort of a car it was?'

'None at all,' said Daffy. 'Just a big blur behind bright lamps.'

'Did it sound like a big car or a small car?'

Daffy thought back. 'Big,' she said at last.

She was probably right. The tear in her duffel bag had been up near the draw-cord and, knowing how Daffy carried the bag slung over her shoulder, almost certainly out of reach of a conventional family car. But there would be little to be gained by pursuing that line any further. Memory can record very erratically in moments of emergency. Once, in my youth, I was knocked off my bicycle by a large black car but my memory still insists that the culprit was a small red van.

151

'It came at you suddenly from behind. You were on your usual way home. I'll offer you two scenarios,' I told her, 'and you can pick the one that you think most nearly fits the circumstances. One, it was on a normal journey and you didn't see it or hear it until the driver upped his headlamps and was about to overtake you. Or, two, it was waiting in the driveway to the farmhouse until you passed by and then pulled out and followed you up. Which?'

Hannah was staring at me over her cereal but Daffy looked ready to cry. 'You're suggesting that somebody tried to run me down?'

'We have to consider it. What's more,' I said with sudden insight, 'I believe you've been wondering the same yourself but haven't wanted to recognize it.'

Daffy was shaking her honey-coloured head. 'I can't, I just *can't* believe that anyone hates me that much,' she whispered.

'If it's any comfort to you, I don't think it's anything personal. You're in somebody's way, that's all. Finish your breakfast.'

'Yes, of course.' Daffy opened her boiled egg and spread butter on a slice of toast. Her movements were abstracted. 'I'll give you this much,' she said. 'Before I got as far as the village, I saw the lights of a vehicle turn into the lane ahead of me. He could have gone ahead and stopped at the farmhouse gate and waited to see me coming.'

'Right. What's more,' I added, 'he doesn't necessarily want you dead. He hit your duffel bag. You carry most of your worldly goods in that bag. He must have thought that he'd hit you. And yet he didn't come back. If he'd been innocent, or if he wanted you dead, he'd certainly have come back.'

'He could have panicked and done a hit-and-run,' Hannah piped up for the first time.

'Right again. All the same, my guess is that somebody wants Daffy out of action. We're going to have to do something. His next move might be to poison all the dogs, or something crazy like that.'

Beth came in, leading Sam. She heaved the child onto his raised chair. Our discussion dried up. Beth would have to be put in the picture but I was not expressing my worries within Sam's hearing. When Daffy had finished her breakfast, or at least had eaten as much as we thought she needed, I got to my feet. 'Come on,' I said. 'We're going to Ardrossie,' I added to Beth.

Beth, who looks so much less than her real age, often surprises me by saying very little and then proving to be far ahead of me. 'Yes, I think you'd better,' she said. 'We don't want any more nonsenses. But don't you think you'd do better to take the police along?'

'Not at this stage,' I said pulling on my coat. 'We've no proof of anything. But letting him

153

know that we know should stop him.'

Hannah was far behind but still pursuing. 'Just a minute,' she said. 'Does this have anything to do with Dougal's disappearance?'

If I told her a lie now she would never forgive me. 'It might,' I admitted.

'Then I'm coming with you.' She grabbed her coat and followed us.

Beth came to the door. 'Don't do anything silly, any of you,' she said.

'Like what?' I asked her irritably. I had not paused to change my shoes for boots and I was slithering through several inches of snow at the time. The air had turned bitterly cold.

She looked over her shoulder to check on Sam. 'I don't know like what,' she said. 'But you usually manage to find something. I wish I could come with you.'

'Somebody has to mind the place and look after Sam,' I said. I had the engine running. I slammed my door and moved off before she could think of any more arguments.

The ploughs had been busy. The main roads were clear of snow but the sparse Sunday traffic threw up a spray of mingled slush and sand and I hated to think what the salt might be doing to the underside of my car. My companions wanted to ask questions but I shook my head. I was trying to think and to drive at the same time, which was more than enough to be going on with. The secondary road that led past Ardrossie had been snowed

154

on since the plough had passed that way and the car wanted to play at being a carousel.

At Ardrossie, things were worse. I should have been warned when I saw Quentin Cove's big Shogun parked in a field gate off the farm-road, but I went on past the loading bay of the new buildings housing the dog-food factory, silent now in Sabbath calm. I pulled round the end and entered the spacious yard. On my right was the farm manager's cottage formerly occupied by Dougal Webb and to the left the back of the farmhouse.

I touched the brakes. Instantly, brakes and steering ceased to have any effect. Luckily I had entered the yard at a dead slow pace or I would have shot straight into the open front of the big barn ahead of me and collided with a van or one of Quentin Cove's tractors, but at the last moment two wheels of the car passed from ice onto a narrow strip of frosted snow and we slewed to a halt and stalled. There was a silence, broken only by the sound of barking from the kennels behind the barn, before we began breathing again.

I found my voice. 'You two stay in the car,' I said firmly as I opened my door.

The source of all the ice was immediately evident. Quentin Cove, engulfed in oilskins, was crouched at the corner of the house, attempting a short-term repair with tape to a burst water-pipe. Onto the snow, which was already compacted by the passage of vehicles, water from the pipe was spraying and running across the surface, freezing as it went. The yard could well have doubled as a skating rink.

Forgetting that I was wearing smooth-soled shoes instead of my heavily treaded boots, I stepped out and almost went flat on my back. Somehow I managed to retain my balance. I had once been a moderately proficient skater and that half-forgotten skill, I think, saved me from going down. I remained upright, delicately poised, while without conscious effort or movement on my part I slithered slowly across the yard. I came to a halt somewhere near the centre and stood still, hardly daring to breathe.

Quentin Cove had been watching my antics, in and out of the car. He heaved himself to his feet, scowling. 'What is it?' he asked me roughly. 'You can see I'm busy.'

'I want a word with you.'

'What word? I didn't think you came for the sight of my pretty face.'

I felt my temper beginning to slip. The farmer was acting as though he was the injured party. 'If I did,' I said, 'I'm doomed to bloody disappointment because you haven't got one.'

CHAPTER EIGHT

Quentin Cove hesitated. He took a second or two to decide whether to respond to my insult with amusement or aggression. His face had always been easy to read. I saw him review his options, make a conscious decision and summon up the adrenaline. I wondered for a moment whether, in my anger, I had gone too far. I was in no state to exchange blows with a doughty farmer. My only defence would be the unarmed combat that I had learned in the army. But nobody had taught me how not to kill. My mouth went dry.

He moved towards me with clenched fists and stepped straight onto the ice. But he did not have the knack of keeping still and staying balanced. Arms flailing and legs pedalling in all directions, he approached me so directly that I was sure disaster was imminent. But I managed to skate half a pace to the side and he passed me by so close that I had to duck under one of his flying arms. He slowed and came to a halt.

We were standing almost back to back a few yards apart. Cautiously, we both turned around.

It was not a propitious time to start a serious discussion, poised as it was on the very brink of farce, but I had to have a stab at it. I said, 'I came to pay a call on Mim. I like to assure myself that any dogs of my breeding are being well cared for. They're like family to me. May I see her, please?'

He pushed back the hood of his oilskin jacket. He was both surprised and perturbed. He had been expecting anything but that. 'No, you can't,' he snapped.

'That's what I thought,' I said. 'What I really came for was to tell you that we know what's been going on. So if Daffy—Mrs Mearns— meets with any more mishaps, we'll know who to blame and so will the police a few minutes later.'

His face flamed. 'I dinna ken whit you're on aboot,' he said, but I could see that my words had hit him hard. The one thing the lawbreaker fears is being found out. In his perturbation his speech had slipped back to its roots.

'Yes you do,' I said. 'You spiked Mrs Mearns' soft drink with vodka and then called the police to report her for drink-driving. But that didn't work and you knew that if she went on showing up at field trials she was bound to meet Mim at close quarters sooner or later. So last night, you callous bastard, you tried to run her down.'

He tried to look innocent and wronged but the expression did not sit well on his harsh features. 'Whit way would I dae a thing like that?' he demanded.

158

'If you want me to spell it out,' I said, 'you didn't want any of us to see Mim again, or at least not until memories had faded. That's why you let my tyres down, to put me off coming to Lincraigs. But you particularly didn't want to go on bumping into Daffy at field trials, because she was the one person who would have realized that the dog you were running as Mim wasn't Mim at all.'

As I spoke, more and more facts and fragments of gossip fitted together and I was no longer guessing. Suddenly, I *knew*. 'You only acquired Mim,' I said, 'to get a legitimate pedigree and registration to switch to your own very similar and very talented bitch, daughter of the unplanned mating by Dorothy Hatton's dog. You couldn't even get the Hattons to acknowledge the breeding because their dog isn't registered and anyway other dogs had mated with yours before you got her back. On the other hand, assuming that it was Dorothy's dog that fathered your pup, Champion Clunie of Netherbrae figures in both pedigrees. You had a throwback to Clunie, very talented, strongly resembling Mim but ineligible to compete.'

'That means nothing,' he said. 'Nothing.'

'If you want to argue about it, we can always ask the police who tipped them off about Daffy—they don't usually act on anonymous tips. And although the breeding of Mim and of your bitch is similar it isn't identical. I still have a full sister of Mim. A DNA test would soon prove whether your bitch is one of that litter or not.'

As I finished speaking I suddenly saw the shape of another piece of the puzzle and I spoke out without giving myself time to think. 'What's more, I've only just figured out that that's what Dougal Webb was trying to blackmail me about. He thought that I was your partner in the fraud.' Another thought hit me. 'I bet he tried to blackmail you too, and that's why . . .' I left the remainder of the thought unspoken. It was beyond utterance. It might also be actionable.

He jerked, nearly slipped and only caught his balance by a wild wave of his arms. The fight went out of him and he looked ten years older. 'No,' he said hoarsely.

'You mean, that's not why?'

'I mean, I didn't! God, when you jump to conclusions you fairly cover the ground! We'll hae to enter you for the Grand National.'

I had forgotten the presence of Daffy and Hannah, and Quentin Cove had his back to them, but what I had been saying had not passed them by. While Hannah was still digesting my words, Daffy was out of the car. 'What did he do with Mim?' she cried. 'What did he do with poor Mim?' Something in her voice stabbed me through. I knew what it was like to love a dog.

'Can you produce her?' I asked him. He

160

stood, silent. I think that he was too aware of his guilt, now that he was seeing it through the eyes of others, to protest any more. 'I'm sorry,' I said to Daffy.

'He put her down? My darling Mim?'

At the same moment, Hannah erupted from the other side of the car. 'He killed Dougal, isn't that what you're saying?'

Quentin Cove's voice went up an octave. 'Chrissake no! You can't land me with that!'

But his voice went unheeded. Whatever tension there might have been between the two kennel-maids at first, that had been years earlier when they were late teenagers. They were now friends and they had become used to working as a team. Their relationship had become almost telepathic. At this moment, it was as if they were a single organism with but one thought between them. Hannah had brought a heavy walking stick out of the car with her. Daffy, her stiffness marvellously cured for the moment, had emerged on the side nearer to the workbench in the barn and she grabbed a jack-handle out of the rack. They came at him together and they had the advantage of pushing off from the less slippery fringe of the yard. Gone were my two gentle helpers, who would brood over a sick puppy like mothers. These were two furies, hellbent on revenge and caring for nobody.

Once they were on the ice they had to wave their arms for balance, adding menace to their

161

advance. Seeing the weapons brandished by the advancing Valkyries, Quentin Cove paled. 'They've gone bloody mad,' he gasped. He tried to run, made no forward progress and ended up on his hands and knees. The tumble saved him for the moment. A swipe from Hannah passed over his head. The swing removed the last of her balance and she sat down heavily, still tobogganing on her rounded backside, while Daffy slid by, still upright but beyond swiping range.

Cove was right, of course. They had gone mad. I could hardly blame them. Each believed that he had killed their loved one. But a successful blow from either weapon, especially the jack-handle, would result in endless complications and possibly the loss of a good kennel-maid. As Cove and Hannah struggled back to their feet I tried to place myself between him and the avenging harpies at whatever personal risk.

How long the dance, macabre yet farcical, went on I cannot guess. Probably only a matter of seconds although it seemed to be for an age that Cove was trying for his own front door, Hannah and Daffy were aiming to outflank him and I was struggling to stay between. I took a crack on the elbow from the jack-handle. Cove's luck held until the last second. A wild leap to avoid a swing from Daffy cost him his balance and he went down. As he struggled to rise, he took a great swipe from

162

Hannah across his rounded bottom. The crack of it and his roar echoed around the farmyard and set the dogs barking again.

The mad pursuit was interrupted by the arrival of a small blue-and-white police car which crossed the yard in a well-controlled slide. The driver, I saw, was highly skilled. The car was nursed, at the very brink of control, into slowing and turning until it fetched up, parked neatly between my car and the mouth of the barn, without quite making contact with anything solid.

The driver's door opened and out stepped DCI Ewell's Sergeant, still immaculate in uniform and still looking far too young and pretty to be an officer. She needed only a glance to see who were the aggressors, who the defender and who was the intended victim and she launched herself valiantly in our direction. Some day I must find out what her shoes were soled with, because she kept her feet until the very last moment. Arriving and almost going past, she managed to grab Daffy's sleeve and the hood of Hannah's duffel coat. The jerk acted as the last straw to her balance and the three of them fell in a heap. Quentin Cove stood dumbstruck and so did I. Neither of us had seen quite so much leg before, except on a beach or in a chorus line.

The three began to pick themselves up while making themselves respectable and at the same time nursing bruised limbs. We were all breathing heavily. At some point the sun had come out and I found that I was sweating.

The Sergeant was the first to make it to her feet. With her hair flying, her cravat adrift and dark patches of wet marking her uniform, she looked less pretty and yet somehow much more desirable. 'You,' she said to Quentin Cove, 'had better go into your house and stay there.'

While the rest of us concentrated on catching our breaths, Cove nodded and set off for his door, adopting a skating action which seemed to meet the conditions. The burst pipe, I noticed, was still making its contribution to the water and ice. When he opened the door I could hear the drone of a vacuum cleaner. The door slammed and I heard the sound of the lock followed by two bolts. He was taking no risk of being followed inside by the kennel-maids from hell.

'Now,' said the Sergeant through clenched teeth, 'you three can come and sit in my car and explain yourselves.'

The idea of being cooped up in a very small car with so much angry young womanhood had no appeal for me. 'We'd have more room in my car,' I suggested. 'At least we would be in my own territory.'

The Sergeant nodded. 'Very well. But I'll take the driver's seat.'

'I was not going to drive off with you,' I said mildly.

The Sergeant was neither amused nor insulted. 'I like a steering-wheel to rest my notebook,' she said.

We slipped and slithered our ways back across the yard without disaster. Daffy and Hannah scurried into the rear, leaving me the front passenger seat. The Sergeant placed a small tape-recorder on the dash and pressed two keys. A tiny needle began to jump whenever we spoke. The Sergeant told the tape-recorder the date, time and place and who was present while repeating the information in her notebook. She also told the machine her name. She was, it seemed, Sergeant Bremner. 'Now,' she said, 'tell me what this was about.'

I decided that I had an equally interesting question to ask. 'Do you mind telling me how you come to be here?'

'I don't mind in the least. I'll even answer you. Mrs Cunningham phoned in. She felt that you might be under a misapprehension and that any possibility of hasty action should be nipped in the bud.'

The mention of misapprehension was interesting but I decided to withhold comment until I knew a little more. 'Very sensible of her,' I said. Hannah and Daffy listened in silence while I explained the events of the last couple of days. The Sergeant listened intently while making an occasional note.

'There does seem to have been some

165

jumping to conclusions,' the Sergeant said when I had finished. 'You make an interesting point about the substitution of dogs. You may be right in what you surmise about blackmail. But motive never makes a case. To leap from there to an assumption of murder—'

Hannah spoke up from behind me. 'Mr Cunningham never said anything about Mr Cove having murdered Dougal,' she said. 'I was the one who jumped to that conclusion.'

'I was going to say it, Hannah,' I said. 'But it seems that I was probably wrong. Mr Cove wasn't the only man your Dougal put the bite on.'

'I see.' Sergeant Bremner thought for a moment. 'I think I should tell you that your conclusions were as you say, almost certainly wrong. We have not, as you seem to suppose, been sitting on our hands waiting for somebody like yourselves to do our jobs for us. Mr Little made a statement about witnessing the quarrel between Mr Cove and Mr Webb. He also stated that Mr Webb then drove off in a hurry. Mr Cove remained and supplied him with a bag of dog-meal. The transaction was hurried because Mr Cove was leaving to keep an appointment. That appointment was with six other men for drinks and a meal. They then went to a performance at the Byre Theatre. All this is heavily vouched for. By the time that Mr Cove left his friends and returned home, Miss Hopewell was already worried about the disappearance of Mr Webb and was actually waiting right here, where she remained until around four a.m.'

'But—' Hannah began.

'It's my turn to jump to conclusions,' the Sergeant said firmly, 'because I can guess what you want to say. And yes, it's possible to come up with several scenarios in which Mr Cove might have done mischief to Mr Webb. It's possible, for instance, that Mr Webb had gone off on some errand of his own about which we know nothing, forgetting his date with Miss Hopewell or else just plain standing her up. He could then have returned after she left here, roused his employer from his bed—just before dawn—resumed the quarrel and the rest followed. But that all seems very improbable and since we don't yet have confirmation that the body in the bonfire was that of Mr Webb, there seems little point discussing it.'

'I accept that,' Hannah said in a very small voice. 'But there's one thing I must know. Was Dougal really a blackmailer?'

Glancing sideways I saw that the Sergeant had written the word *was* in longhand and capitals and put a box round it. 'I'm afraid so,' she said. 'We've come across several instances that fall within the definition. He was too cautious to make a direct demand for money or money's-worth with menaces, but we now know that when he took a fancy to some

167

valuable personal item he was not above making oblique threats in order to drive home a very hard bargain. He may even have convinced himself that using knowledge to gain better terms was an acceptable business practice. That, I suppose, could have furnished any number of motives for his murder. On the other hand, it would equally give Mr Webb a motive for disappearing, if he knew that his misdeeds were coming to light.'

'Is that how he acquired the Lotus?' I asked her.

'You can't seriously expect me to tell you that. But, Miss Hopewell,' she added over her shoulder, 'if you are now thinking of blaming yourself on the grounds that he took to blackmail in order to finance his courtship of you and your possible future together, you can put it firmly out of your mind. He set out on that path before you and he had even met.'

I decided that Sergeant Bremner was a perceptive and humane young woman, undoubtedly destined for high rank. I added those labels to several others which I had mentally attached to her.

'Thank you,' Hannah whispered. 'I'll remember that.'

'That's all very well,' Daffy said suddenly, 'but we haven't dealt with the matter of the dog.'

'We're going to deal with it now,' said the Sergeant. She used the driving mirror to tidy herself further. 'Come with me, Mr Cunningham. You two, wait there, please.'

We made our way cautiously around the edge of the yard. As we did so, the spray of water leaking past the bandage on the fractured pipe diminished and stopped. The Sergeant knocked on the door. After some clattering of locks and bolts, it was opened by Mrs Dundee. She was very businesslike in a floral pinny and plastic gloves, with a large duster in her hand and a smell of polish wafting around her. 'He's below,' she said with great formality. 'Who'll I say is after him?'

'The police,' said the Sergeant. Then, noticing the unfortunate combination of phrasing, she added quickly, 'I'm not after him, I just want a quick word with him.'

Mrs Dundee stood aside as Quentin Cove came up through a trapdoor, rather like a pantomime Demon King in slow motion. He had removed his waterproofs and was in dusty overalls. 'Hell of a place to put a stopcock,' he said angrily. 'But that'll have to stay off until the plumber comes. And God knows when that'll be—half the pipes in the kingdom have burst. You'd better come in. You can carry on upstairs,' he added to Mrs Dundee. 'Don't run any water without speaking to me first.'

He led us into a shabby sitting room which smelt of mingled dust and polish. We took stuffed chairs which had sagged over the years into comfortable shapes. It was warm in the central heating and I took off my coat.

Cove shrugged out of his bib-and-braces dungarees and took his own chair. 'I don't know what this bugger's been saying,' he began.

'Then we'll let him go over it again,' the Sergeant said. She went through the same drill of briefing her tape-recorder and simultaneously making notes. Then she glanced at me. 'Now.'

'Your farm manager, Dougal Webb,' I told Cove, 'made an attempt to blackmail me. At the time I couldn't think what he was hinting at, but he seemed to think that mention of the Kennel Club would put the fear of God into me.' For the sake of the record, I decided to spell it out clearly. 'Then other things began to add up. You were very keen to buy Mim, a seriously gun-shy pup, from Mrs Daffodil Mearns, one of my kennel-maids, but when she encountered you with Mim at a novice trial, which you won, there was no sign of gun-shyness. As far as I know, there's no cure for gun-shyness.'

Cove sneered. 'That only goes to show that I'm a better trainer than you are.'

I refused to be needled. 'Maybe,' I said. 'But you were very careful to keep Mim away from Daffy at the time. On her way home, Daffy went into a pub with Mrs Kitts. You arrived on their heels and bought Daffy the soft drink that she wanted. That drink was spiked and

170

somebody phoned the police to say that she was drinking and driving. They were stopped and Daffy was breathalysed, but she was just within the legal limit. Last night, Daffy was nearly run down by a vehicle in the dark and snow. To top it all, you stopped me coming to your farm after the rabbits, on the grounds that you'd let the rough-shooting to somebody else although there's no sign of a shooting tenant and you told Joe Little that he could come onto your land. While I was at the farm next door, my tyres were let down. It all adds up to the fact that you don't want anybody who knew Mim to meet up with her again.

'You may be able to suggest any number of explanations for this combination of facts. I can think of only one. I know that your neighbour's springer covered one of your bitches some time ago. His dog isn't registered, so none of the pups could be registered nor any of their descendants to infinity. You were giving the pups away for peanuts. But I think you kept one to train as a worker and that she turned out to be brilliant. You're a well-to-do farmer without many worlds left to conquer. Your one unfulfilled ambition has been to make a name for yourself in field trials. So you were desperate to go trialling with your bitch, but only pedigreed pups can be registered and only registered dogs can be entered.

'Then you saw Mim. She was brindled, a

throwback to Champion Clunie of Netherbrae, as was your young bitch. They looked identical. The difference was that Mim was registered and had a good pedigree. You tried to buy Mim. A little later when she turned out to be gun-shy, Daffy sold her to you on the understanding that she would be going to a good home. But that isn't Mim that you won the novice stake with and were so desperate to enter in an open stake last week. That's your own bitch.'

Quentin Cove had listened in silence but with a growing expression of injured innocence. When I halted, he stared at me for a few seconds and then said, 'You're daft as a brush. And you canna prove a word of it.'

'But can you disprove a word of it?' I asked him. 'Bring out your bitch and see if she recognizes Daffy. Give us a clump of hair for DNA testing.'

'I've no need to disprove a damn thing,' he retorted. 'It's your story, it's for you to prove it. What's more, there's no law against changing a dog's name.'

'Fraud and false pretences,' I told him.

Sergeant Bremner looked up and frowned. 'I don't see the Procurator Fiscal making a case out of it,' she said. 'There's no big money involved.'

'It runs to big money in the long run,' I told her. 'And I've no need to prove it,' I said to Cove. 'I've done what I came to do, which was

172

to make sure that if anything else happened to Daffy or to us you'd find yourself being looked at damned hard by the police. And if you attempt to enter that bitch in competition again I'll make a report to the Kennel Club. They'll certainly insist on DNA testing.'

That threat shook him as nothing else had. 'Ah, now, there's no call for the likes of that,' he said quickly. 'You've said yourself, many a time, that the Kennel Club rules were a to hell!'

'I don't think I put it quite like that,' I said.

'Damn near it. I've heard you tell a committee member to his face that if their closed gene-pool policy had been in force in the old days we'd never have had half our present breeds. You said—and I remember it well—that the German shorthaired pointer was virtually the only breed to produce dual champions, show-bench and field trial, in the last twenty years and that the breed came about as a mishmash of Spanish pointer, German pointer and the foxhound.'

'And the Hanoverian Schweisshund. Don't forget that one,' I said mildly. I was rather flattered that he should have remembered my words so accurately. I pulled myself together. 'All this has damn all to do with the case. Under the rules as they are, however little I agree with them, you've been robbing other competitors of the rewards they're entitled to. In fact, come to think of it, you've robbed me.

And because my dog did not get the award it had earned, its value and the value of its progeny to infinity may be diminished. You're an amateur, but competition success is my bread and butter and you stole it from me.'

'I'll fight you. I'll fight every inch o the way,' he said furiously.

'You can try,' I said. 'I think you'll find that the odds are against you. And there's one other thing. We'll have to buy our dog-food somewhere else from now on.'

He thought it over for some seconds before it sank in. 'Damn it to hell, there's nae need for that,' he exploded. 'I'd not do sic a thing, ye ken that fine.'

'I'm sorry, Quentin,' I said. 'But you *did* do something *just* like that. Or can you still produce Mim alive?'

His eyes slid away from mine. I got to my feet and picked up my coat. 'You won't be proceeding against the girls?' I asked the Sergeant.

'I must make a report. I won't recommend action.'

'Hey!' Cove said. 'Those wee buggers laid into me, in my own yard!'

'Then you'd better show the Sergeant your bruises,' I told him. I left the room, fairly confident that, protected as he had been by his oilskins, his only bruises would be to his ego.

174

*   *   *

In the hall, Mrs Dundee's small bottom was presented to me as she worked her way backwards down the stairs, dusting and polishing the exposed woodwork as she came. I only recognized her when she straightened up, glad of any excuse to stop for a rest and a chat. 'It's yourself,' she informed me. She looked more cheerful than when I had seen her last. She was no more beautiful a sight but at least her hollow cheeks seemed to have filled out a little and her cheery grin somehow seemed to justify her over-large mouth.

'Hello,' I said. 'I didn't know that you worked for Mr Cove.'

She seated herself comfortably on the fifth or sixth tread, her gnarled face on a level with mine. 'Och, for years he was asking me to come, but I was well enough, doing half days for Mrs Macevoy and efterneens up at the Big Hoose. I couldna come here while yon skellum Dougal Webb was around the place. But then Mrs Macevoy turned me awa, just acause she couldna put her hand on a wee bit jewellery I dinna mind ever seeing. And just then Mr Webb disappears like snow off a dyke. Then Jack Gilchrist told Mr Cove I was free an he asked me again. And no afore time. Goad, the dust that was in the place!'

'What did you have against Dougal Webb?' I asked her. Surely he could never have been

175

blackmailing such a poor creature.

'He had a way wi him but I found he wisna suithfast. There was a thing he wheedled out o me, in confidence like, and then let oot the poother. But it wasna just that. Sir Ian Bewlay hissel telled me to steer clear of Mr Webb. I get my wee cottage from Sir Ian in return for my two hours in the efterneen and I'd no want to be put oot in the road for bein gran billies wi the likes of Dougal Webb.'

'Sir Ian wouldn't put you out just for that, would he?' I asked.

'He seemed awfu positive when he spoke to me. "You stay clear of yon man Webb," he said to me. "There's bad blood there," he said, "and if you want to keep what's yours," he said, "you'll gie him a wide berth."' Mrs Dundee paused. Something was missing. 'He said,' she added suddenly.

'It was good advice,' I said, 'though he may not have meant it quite the way you took it. Would you come out to my car for a minute? There's something I want to ask you and I don't want to be interrupted.' I nodded towards the sitting room door. Voices were being raised. I gathered that the Sergeant was giving Quentin Cove a hard time on the subject of where he and his car had been, around dusk of the previous day.

She looked doubtfully at me and then shrugged and came along. 'My time's amost up,' she said. It was like walking with a child,

176

but she might have taken it amiss if I had held her hand to steady her until we were on a good surface. Instead, I stooped and let her take my arm. She hopped cheerfully up into the front passenger's seat and exchanged greetings with the two in the back. Daffy and she seemed to know each other of old. I got into the driver's seat—with some difficulty because the Sergeant had parked uncomfortably close to my door. I started the engine to put a little warmth into the heater.

'You know that we found a body, just after you spoke to us that Saturday?' I said. 'And you know that the body may have been Dougal Webb?'

She nodded in answer to each question.

'It's important to find out who had a reason to dislike Mr Webb. I think you should tell us why Sir Ian had a grudge against him. Unless you've already told the police?' Mrs Dundee paled. 'I'll see that you don't suffer for it,' I added, 'and if it turns out to be irrelevant, neither the police nor Sir Ian need never know.'

'I canna be sure,' she said.

'But it began just after Dougal Webb betrayed your trust?'

She nodded again.

Daffy leaned forward so that her hair tickled my cheek. 'Mrs Dundee,' she said, 'was it anything to do with your Jimmy?'

The car moved slightly on its springs as Mrs

Dundee jerked. 'Maybe,' she said. 'It might.'

'There have been whispers going around for years,' Daffy said. 'Mrs Dundee, is Sir Ian Jimmy's dad?'

Mrs Dundee uttered a pained cry. I could feel her small frame shaking in the seat next to me. There were tears on her sallow cheeks. Then the dam burst and the story came tumbling out.

*   *   *

The sun was melting the surface of the ice, giving it a fresh polish and doing away with the last traces of grip. When Mrs Dundee had finished I got out of the car with some difficulty and escorted her back to the house, although she had less far to fall than any of us. Returning, I was faced again with the task of squeezing in through a narrow gap. In a moment of frustration I put my bottom against the Sergeant's car and pushed. On that melting ice and aided by a distinct slope, the car slid easily. Without further help from me, it travelled several yards sideways. I flinched, expecting at any moment to hear the crumpling sound as the front hit a stanchion supporting the head of the open front of the barn or the back struck the workbench. But the car, as though guided by a mighty hand, arrived between the two with an inch to spare at either end. And there it stopped.

The Sergeant was going to need help, and a lot of it, to get her car out of there and I doubted whether she would get it from Quentin Cove. But I had rather modified my favourable view of Sergeant Bremner since she and I had failed to see eye to eye on the subject of whether blocking the advancement of one of my dogs by deception had constituted a fraud. I coaxed my car gently across the yard and hurried away.

CHAPTER NINE

If, as I said earlier, God created spaniels and sponges on the same day, He knocked off after that and played snowballs. A short-haired dog like a Labrador can come in out of the snow almost bone dry, but take a small spaniel out in deep, fresh snow and it will come home like the makings for a Christmas tree, with a snowball dangling from each lock of hair. Any attempt to remove those snowballs by hand turns them into chunks of ice locked fast to the hairs.

Dogs need free-running exercise. That is one of the few incontrovertible facts in the canine world. As the snow continued, novice and open stakes were being cancelled or postponed all around; but, when the thaw came, honours would go to those who had

179

managed to keep their dogs fit and up to the mark. Training and walking had to continue. We tried hard to stick mainly to a long strip of field which a dense wood of pine and Scots fir had sheltered from the prevailing wind, but a fresh fall of snow came in on a different wind and after that each spaniel (and other hairy breeds residing with us as boarders) had to be thawed as well as dried in the blow-drying chamber which had been created from what had once been a lean-to privy, then brushed into an unmatted state and with luck returned to its kennel without picking up a fresh cargo of Christmas decorations.

Isobel was still confined to her bed—or else, knowing what life would be like at Three Oaks, she had decided to hibernate until the spring. Henry spared us what time he could, but he had his own life to lead in addition to tending a 'flu-ridden wife.

All this is merely to explain that for the next few days we were very busy indeed. I managed to give Beth a detailed account of our visit to Ardrossie, but we never seemed able to sit down at the same time long enough for a serious discussion and, to be honest, I was thoroughly sick of the subject anyway. Even Hannah seemed to have put it out of her mind. The revelation of defects in her lover's character seemed to have turned a grand tragedy into a passing disappointment. She was pulling her weight again and even singing occasionally. The church saw much less of her.

It was Beth's custom to go into Cupar on a Thursday morning to do the week's shopping, accompanied by any of us who was in need of a visit to the shops, the library or the dentist. That week, Jenny had stepped on a fragment of broken glass and cut one of her pads. Despite my ministrations, the cut was slow to heal. Isobel would certainly have got out of bed to attend to it, possibly ruining her own health in the process, so we kept the news from her, swearing Henry to secrecy, and Jenny and I joined the trip to Cupar. At the last moment Henry, whose car had gone in for servicing, decided to leave Isobel's care to a helpful neighbour and come with us.

It was Beth's journey, so she drove. She parked behind the big supermarket. She and Henry hurried inside while I led Jenny, limping bravely, through the store and along the pavement to the surgery.

The vet and Isobel had at one time been colleagues. He was a born gossip and the disinfecting and stitching of Jenny's pad was accompanied by enquiries after Isobel's health and the recitation of many recipes for the relief of 'flu symptoms, ranging from herbal through homoeopathy to folk remedies verging on witchcraft and totally unsuitable for a man of science. He replaced my amateurish bandage with a more professional version and charged me an arm and a leg.

Jenny, always a good patient, was quite unmoved by all the attention but by the time we neared our car again her better foreleg had tired and she was limping pathetically. But that fact cut no ice with a big man who arrived from behind us and thrust past to reach the door of his Isuzu Trooper, so nearly treading on Jenny's bad foot that she yipped in fear.

Instead of looking round, the man back-heeled viciously, catching her in the ribs. 'Bloody dogs!' he said.

Then he turned and I saw that he was Sir Ian Bewlay.

I had no wish to quarrel with one of the larger landowners in the area and thereby lose a valuable outlet for dog-training. Jenny was hurt but not injured. On the other hand, although I am not aggressive by nature, nobody, but nobody, kicks one of my dogs without repercussions. I began to seethe.

'Don't you dare to do that again,' I said. I was further annoyed to find that my voice was hoarse.

He turned and looked down at me from his considerable height. I saw him recognize me and decide that I was a person of no account, dust beneath his wheels. Large though he was, I thought that he looked soft. My training in unarmed combat had been years earlier but it had been thorough. There were witnesses not far away. If I could provoke him into lashing out, I was sure that I could damage him with impunity.

'Do what?' he sneered.

I pointed down at Jenny, who had retired behind my legs and was peering past, wondering what was going on. People, in her experience, just did not behave like that. 'You kicked my dog,' I said.

'So I did. What do you want me to do? Kiss it better?'

'You could start by apologizing. Tell the dog you're sorry. Give her a pat. Then we'll take it from there.'

Timothy Pratt, Sir Ian's shadow and sycophant, pushed forward. 'Who do you think you're talking to?' he demanded.

'I think I'm talking to the mannerless boor who kicked my dog,' I retorted, 'and I'm still waiting for him to say that he's sorry.' I shifted my weight onto the balls of my feet, ready to counter any sudden moves.

Sir Ian glanced around the car park, then weighed me up. My appearance may be fragile but my readiness must have shown. He broke off eye contact. 'But I'm not sorry,' he mumbled. He turned away quickly and climbed into his vehicle—leaving me frustrated but taking with him, I was pleased to note, most of a large dog-turd which Jenny had deposited in the excitement of the confrontation.

'But you will be sorry,' I promised him silently as he pulled away.

I put Jenny into the car. The rush of adrenaline had left my mouth dry and I needed a drink. But first, while my dander was still up, I wanted to fire the first shot in my battle against Sir Ian Bewlay. I needed to commit myself before my temper cooled.

The nearest public telephones were inside the supermarket. As I placed my call, I could see Beth and Henry working their way towards the checkout. Kirkcaldy answered. I asked for Detective Inspector Ewell but he was out, of course. Then, unexpectedly, the voice became helpful. Where was I calling from? It turned out that DI Ewell was not far away. I suggested that he might care to join me for coffee in one of the local hotels. There was a pause while Ewell was consulted over the radio, during which I spotted another familiar face. Then the voice told me that he would be there in ten minutes.

Beth and Henry were emerging from the checkout, putting away their credit cards. At the long worktop provided by a thoughtful management (and why can't others follow suit?) I helped Beth to transfer her shopping from a trolley into several cardboard cartons. Henry trans-shipped his own more modest purchases. I could feel Beth glancing at me. She knew that something was wrong. As much to distract her as for any other reason, I said, 'That was Mrs Macevoy behind you in the queue.'

Beth turned and stared at Mrs Macevoy's departing back. 'The fat ginger-headed tart? I wondered who she was.'

'Do you fancy coffee?' I asked her. 'Because I've made a date to meet Mr Ewell for coffee in a few minutes.'

'Yes,' Beth said slowly, 'I think that's a very good idea.'

Mrs Macevoy, as we reached the car park, was driving off in a nearly new BMW, custom-painted an unusual colour which I can only liken to that of a nearly ripe plum or the underside of a red snooker ball which is reflecting the green cloth.

We loaded the cartons of shopping onto the back seat of our car, well out of Jenny's reach but still managing to leave room for Henry. Jenny was not given to stealing food, but the habit is easily learned and difficult to eradicate. For the moment, we left the car where it was, the supermarket being better provided with parking than the hotel. It was a five-minute walk between the two and Beth said not a word. Either she was coming down with Isobel's 'flu or something that she had seen or heard had set her thinking. I wondered whether to interrupt her thoughts by telling them both about Sir Ian's arrogance and my determination to hit back; but Beth would either have told me to cool off or else she would have gone to war on my behalf.

The Detective Inspector joined us as the

185

waitress brought coffee. I had asked for a pot and five cups, but I was relieved to see that he was not for once accompanied by the alluring Sergeant Bremner. If the Sergeant was not aware that I had helped her car into its absurd predicament, she would certainly have guessed that I had had a quiet laugh at her expense.

Ewell accepted a cup (black, no sugar) and then looked at me with eyebrows raised. I glanced round but we had the lounge to ourselves except for a group of middle-aged women in the furthest corner, all talking shrilly and simultaneously. There was no danger of being overheard.

'Has the identity of the body been confirmed?' I asked.

Ewell hesitated and then shrugged. 'In confidence? It has and it hasn't. We have the report on the DNA tests. Of course, the body was partially cooked over a long period. The lab did what they could. They found a partial match with DNA obtained from hairs out of his hairbrush, but not enough for a court of law. They say that discrepancies were only to be expected. Now, what were you going to tell me?'

'I don't know how many of Dougal Webb's blackmail victims you've traced—' I began.

'One or two,' he said. 'One or two.'

'—but do you know about Sir Ian Bewlay?'

His eyebrows, which had come down, shot straight up again and stayed there. 'What about Sir Ian?'

'Do you know Mrs Dundee?'

'What does she have to do with anything?'

I decided that we had asked each other enough questions for the moment. 'She can tell you a story.'

'You tell me,' he said. 'Mrs Dundee—if you mean the old lady in the cottage near Gifford Hill—has been interviewed but she told us nothing of interest. I'd rather know what you make of her.'

'All right,' I said. 'Here goes. About twenty years ago, Mrs Dundee was housemaid at Marksmuir House. Sir Ian seduced her—or, if you credit her story, forced himself on her. When it comes to lairds and housemaids, the dividing line can be nebulous. She bore him a son.'

'A common enough story,' Ewell said.

'Here comes the uncommon bit. He never denied paternity. He couldn't. Apparently there were several witnesses to the deed because it happened on the dining table just after a boozy lunch party.'

I paused and for a moment there was silence between us. Then Beth said, 'That's awful!'

'You may—or may not—think that what followed was worse. While she was unable to work, believe it or not, he stopped her wages. Afterwards, he paid her the minimum required by law for child maintenance until the boy

187

came of age and he let her stay in the cottage in return for two hours' work every afternoon. She had to go out cleaning in the mornings to make ends meet and even so she must have had a thin time. After she lost her other job with Mrs Macevoy she was almost starving. When we saw her, the day we found the body, she was picking over the fields for forgotten vegetables in order to stay alive while she waited for her son to come home. He's an apprentice in the merchant navy. She begged a few rabbits off us, that day. She won't take Assistance—she thinks of it as charity.'

Beth was looking astonished, as well she might, but not for the reason I expected. 'Mrs Macevoy sacked her?' she exclaimed.

'Yes. Apparently Mrs Macevoy suspected her of stealing some piece of jewellery. My own impression is that Mrs Dundee would be the more honest of the two of them. I suspect that her only deception in her life was in assuming the title of Mrs when she had the child. She's never been married. But that's by the way.

'A year or so ago, Webb pretended to be very sympathetic and coaxed her story out of her. Soon afterwards, Sir Ian told her to stay well away from Webb, on pain of losing her cottage. Around that time, Webb suddenly sported a very expensive wrist-watch resembling one which I had seen and envied on Sir Ian, who still wears a Rolex but of a slightly different pattern. That would make Sir Ian very unhappy. He's a man who prefers every penny to work for him and nobody else.

'I think we can take it that Webb wasted no time before putting the bite on him and acquiring Sir Ian's Rolex at a bargain price. You can imagine how the story would have looked in the gutter press. She must be twenty years older than he is and she can never have been a beauty, besides hardly coming up to his navel. Imagine their photographs side by side along with the story of how shabbily he's treated the mother of his son. His parliamentary ambitions would have gone right up in smoke.'

'I'm surprised she accepted it,' Ewell said. 'The days are past when a landlord can behave like that. The law would have protected her. For one thing, it would never have allowed him to turn her out of her cottage.'

Henry had been listening attentively. 'She's feudal,' he said. 'I thought so when we met her on the hill. To her, he's the laird and therefore omnipotent. His whims are acts of God. If she falls on hard times, that's fate. You find them like that sometimes in the country.'

Ewell shook his head unhappily. 'That's so. The attitude gets handed down from generation to generation. He was very high-and-mighty when we interviewed him. He didn't know a thing and seemed to be insulted that we thought he might. I'll tell you this

189

much—I'm not looking forward to confronting him again.'

'Then don't,' said Beth.

'I must.' Ewell smiled grimly. 'Of all the people with a connection to Dougal Webb, he's the only one we've spoken to who has refused to account for his whereabouts between the time when Webb was last seen alive and the latest probable time of death.'

'In your shoes,' Henry said, 'I would leave that interview to your superintendent. It's more his job than yours.'

Ewell looked a little happier.

'You haven't exhausted the other possibilities yet,' I said. 'Did you ever find out where the Lotus came from?'

'Miles away,' Ewell said. 'Tracing ownership was easy. Apparently it was a cash deal and the previous owner, a Mr Pratt, claims to have received a satisfactory price.'

'Well I, for one, do not believe it,' said Henry. 'I can't see a salaried farm manager, especially one as thrifty as Dougal Webb, forking out the going price of a nearly new, expensive car totally unsuited to life on the farm. I take it that the seller was "Sanctimonious" Pratt?'

Ewell's mouth fell open. 'You mean Mr Timothy Pratt, the would be councillor? I never connected the names. He lives outside Fife and Kinross, so the enquiry was conducted for us by the Tayside Force.'

190

'And is buddies with Sir Ian,' Henry said.

'He gets up on his soapbox for animal welfare,' I said. 'But he shot his own dog up the backside quite deliberately, to teach it a lesson. He only meant it to sting but he hopelessly misjudged the range. That was on one of Sir Ian's shoots, where Webb was commonly a beater.'

'You've stolen my thunder as usual,' Henry grumbled. 'I intended to spill those particular beans myself. I was at Three Oaks when he brought the poor beast to my wife, howling miserably—the dog, Inspector, not the Pratt. The damage was so bad that she had to castrate the poor beast. Imagine how that would look to the animal lovers whose votes he's canvassing.'

Detective Inspector Ewell sighed heavily. 'That will be another uncomfortable interview. If I land Superintendent Aicheson with the interrogation of two members of the Establishment, I will not be popular.'

Beth had an anxious expression, which gave her the look of a pretty teenager. 'Accepting that,' she said, 'there's somewhere else you should look first. Why do you suppose Mrs Macevoy suddenly dispensed with the services of Mrs Dundee?'

'According to Mrs Dundee, Mrs Macevoy said that a piece of jewellery had gone missing,' I reminded her.

'And you said that you didn't believe it.'

'I did and I don't.'

'Well, then.'

Detective Inspector Ewell frowned. 'She never reported any such thing to the police.'

'Because it never happened,' Beth said firmly. 'John pointed Mrs Macevoy out to me in the supermarket just now. I've seen her in there in the past, without knowing who she was. She was always doing the typical shopping of a woman living alone. I rather envied her.'

I was startled. 'You envied her living alone?'

Beth laughed and patted my hand. 'No, you idiot! I envied her being able to do her shopping in a basket instead of a trolley, buying convenience foods instead of joints and sausages and eggs and bacon and vegetables by the ton and . . . and . . .'

'All right,' I said. 'I get the message.'

'But I get the messages. Today, her shopping wasn't as big as mine but it was much bigger than usual.'

'Maybe she was doing two weeks' shopping in one. Or stocking up for a visitor.'

'She was shopping for a man,' Beth said. 'Steaks and things. And beer and cigars. I've never seen her buy any of those before.'

Detective Inspector Ewell had literally jumped in his chair. 'She touched a nerve?' I asked him.

'She certainly did.' Ewell looked from Beth

to me and back again. 'This is no secret—it just hasn't hit the media up here yet. Mrs Macevoy's husband was jailed in England, because that's where the rape took place. He was sent to Parkhurst. For some stupid administrative reason, the only address they had for him was the hotel where he'd been staying when it happened. So word has only just reached us.

'Apparently he lost his remission because he took part—a small part—in a riot in which a prison officer was injured. He was going to have to serve out his time, which would mean several more years. So he absconded from a working party. They thought that they had him bottled in the Isle of Wight. Then he was supposed to have been seen in Kent and again on a Channel ferry. Only when that lead turned out to be false were all Forces circulated and even then it took us a few days to make the connection with a local resident.'

'Now they tell you,' I said.

'Exactly.'

The group of women seemed to have left. We had the lounge to ourselves. There was a silence while we assimilated the addition of a new character into the shifting scene.

'In that case, there's something else you should be thinking about,' Beth said at last. She looked bashfully at the Detective Inspector. 'You don't mind my making these suggestions?'

Ewell shook his head dumbly.

'It's nothing very hard and fast, just a pointer. When John was telling me about going to Ardrossie last Sunday, he said that Mr Cove was hunting under the floor for the stopcock.'

'Nothing very odd about that,' Henry said. 'In an old house, floors get relaid and the access hatch ends up in a different place, miles from the stopcock, which may not be needed for years at a time.'

'I know all that,' Beth said impatiently. 'I do know about old houses. I've never lived in any other kind. But John said that when he came up from under the floor he was all dusty with dried earth.'

I wondered where on earth (or in it) she was leading us. 'In an old house, the solum—the ground under the hung floor—isn't usually covered. It's just bare earth,' I explained. 'It gets very dry.'

'I wish you'd both stop interrupting,' Beth snapped. 'You keep telling me things I've known for years and making me forget what I was going to say next. Where was I?'

'You were saying that Mr Cove was dusty,' said Ewell. He still did not quite smile but there was a glint of amusement in his eye.

'Yes. And when John told me that, I had a sudden sense of—what do you call it?—déjà vu. I remembered Dougal Webb coming to deliver dog-food and standing in our doorway.

194

For once, he'd come in his farming clothes instead of dressing up for Hannah's benefit, and his clothes were dusty with dry earth.'

'Farmers do get dirty,' I said.

'You're interrupting again,' Beth said severely. 'It had just thawed and the ground was very wet and muddy. But it was definitely earth, not barn dust or chaff. I thought he must have been digging in an outbuilding or something like that. But Mr Macevoy, when he was jailed, was also under suspicion of embezzling from the firm he worked for. None of the money ever turned up. And Dougal always seemed more flush with money than he should have been. He dropped hints about a legacy but nobody seems to know of any other relatives than the Macevoys.' She glared at me. 'And before you think you have to remind me that he was a blackmailer, let me point out that we don't know of a single occasion when he asked for money.'

'He was too careful for that,' Ewell said. 'He preferred to force people to sell him valuable things at silly prices. Very difficult to argue about afterwards—a bargain being a bargain under Scots law, silly or not. He probably saw nothing wrong in what he was doing, using leverage to get a better bargain. He may have felt that it was no more than an extension of normal business practice.'

'Which it is, of course,' said Henry.

'Not a defence which would stand up in

court,' the Detective Inspector said. 'Adding it all together, what Mrs Cunningham is suggesting is that Mr Macevoy had hidden his hoard under the floorboards at Gifford House and his nephew found it or knew that it was there.'

Beth was nodding. 'He was good at wheedling secrets out of people.'

'But it fits very well,' Ewell said. He sounded slightly indignant, as though Beth had no right to precede him to logical conclusions. 'It even fits with some bits and pieces that you don't know. I'll set it out and you can tell me if I'm assembling it wrongly.

'We've been watching for Mr Macevoy at roads and railway stations. He may have been home before we knew that he was loose. When Mrs Macevoy was interviewed, after the body was found, she gave the officers a tour of the house. They really only wanted to visit the kitchen to see whether any knives were obviously missing, but she had non-matching knives collected over the years, not a matching set. She swore that none was missing and it was impossible to be sure, one way or the other. She almost dragged the officers round the whole place. She said that the finding of a body had made her nervous and she wanted them to make sure that no villains were lurking ready to jump out at her, would you believe? She put on a good show. They reported that there was no sign of a visitor. He was probably under the floorboards all the time. That's what threw us off the scent. If she put down the carpet after he hid, the officers would ignore the underfloor space. They were looking for an unwelcome intruder who couldn't have pulled the carpet back once he was under the floor.

'So it would seem that Macevoy arrived home, found that his nephew had been dipping into his hoard, killed him and put the body under the bonfire, ready for cremation when the foresters cleared up and lit the fire. I must go. This must be followed up immediately, before he can bolt abroad. Thank you, Mrs Cunningham. Thank you very much.' The Detective Inspector's voice was steeped in sincerity. He jumped to his feet. 'We'd have got there in the end, but you've been an enormous help. How much was the coffee?'

'Have it on me,' I said.

He nodded and hurried out of the lounge. There was a fresh spring in his step.

'You men are all so impetuous,' Beth said peevishly. 'I hadn't finished, not by a mile. And if he thinks that he's going to find Mr Macevoy lurking under the floorboards he's got another think coming.'

'How do you make that out?' I asked her. 'I thought that that was exactly what you were predicting.'

'Think about it a little more,' Beth said. 'For

197

years, Mrs Macevoy's been living in that house in some style, paying her taxes, running a swish car and going for cruises. I don't see any scandal-rag paying so much for "My Life With A Sex Fiend" that it would support that kind of lifestyle indefinitely.'

'She seems to have been pally with Sir Ian,' Henry suggested. 'He may have been keeping her.'

'That man wouldn't keep her in tampons,' Beth snapped.

I was struggling to catch up. 'You think that she was sharing the hoard with the nephew?'

'She's hardly the type to let him collar the lot. And then, can you see Mr Macevoy arriving home, finding that the nest-egg that I suppose he was counting on to take him abroad had been frittered away by his two nearest relatives and then killing one of them and settling down happily with the other one— the one who shopped him years before?'

'Now that you mention it,' I said thoughtfully, 'no.'

'She didn't seem to have any lumps on her,' Henry said reflectively. 'Nor did she have the air of one who is acting under duress.'

'Well now,' said Beth, 'from what Daffy told us, Dougal was his nephew not hers. Dougal's mother was Mr Macevoy's sister.'

'Now you're losing me again,' I grumbled.

'Well, hang on to this. I don't know much about DNA and genetic fingerprints and all

198

that stuff, but it does seem to me that if Dougal was Mr Macevoy's nephew they'd have enough bits of DNA in common to give the partial result that Inspector Ewell says the lab found.'

I had an uncomfortable feeling that Beth was going too fast. For one thing, Mr Macevoy would have needed to remain on the sweetest of terms with his wife if she was to give him food and shelter and not run to the police the first time that she went out to do the shopping. 'Let me see if I understand,' I said. 'You think that there was a fight and Dougal killed his uncle? And then decided to go into hiding? Why would he do that, rather than stay put and bluff it out?'

'You do want miracles, don't you?' Beth thought for about half a second. 'It seems to me that Mr Macevoy was the one with good reason to be angry. Or, at least, he would see it that way. My guess—and of course it *is* only a guess—is that there was a furious quarrel and he grabbed up the knife and Dougal got cut before he could get hold of it and stab his uncle. If a body turned up with a knife-blade or a stab-wound in it and Dougal was walking around with an obvious knife-slash, somebody would make the connection. So Dougal decided to vanish. If they managed to get rid of the body successfully, he could always surface again with a story about an accident and loss of memory, which would explain both

199

the scar and his disappearance. Maybe he intended to do that anyway after the cut had healed.'

'And you think,' said Henry, 'that Inspector Ewell will surround the place with cries of, "Come out of there, Mr Macevoy, with your hands up," and out will come Dougal Webb?'

'Now you're making it sound silly. But yes. And if you still think I'm wrong, think about this. Mrs Macevoy was buying courgettes and pork chops. You know how Dougal drooled at the thought of either of those foods. And now,' Beth said, 'we must move. There are dogs to walk and a ravenous mouth to feed—'

'You mean Sam?' I asked.

'Who else? A ravenous mouth to feed and Isobel will be wondering if she's lost a husband.'

'My goodness, yes!' said Henry.

CHAPTER TEN

Whatever might be the outcome of Detective Inspector Ewell's activities, we could be assured of a visit from the police within the next day or two. We waited through the next day, but the only tidings to filter through to us came from a neighbour who had been told that somebody else had caught a mention on local radio of the arrest of some unspecified person on an unspecified charge.

The expected visit came on the afternoon of the following day. What was unexpected was that this time DS Bremner was not dancing attendance on DI Ewell but on Detective Superintendent Aicheson. The Superintendent was a stout man. His colour was high, his ears and nose almost scarlet. I guessed that there was a race on between retirement and a coronary. And they wished to interview Beth and Hannah and me, one at a time. Daffy was away in my car, fetching a supply of feed from a new source and some of the dried ewes' milk which we swear by for pregnant bitches, nursing mothers and puppies. Henry had gone down with Isobel's 'flu and Isobel was at home attending to him. Our resources were seriously stretched.

I jumped to the conclusion that their mission was concerned with Beth's advice to Mr Ewell. 'Do you really need me as well as Mrs Cunningham?' I asked peevishly. 'I was just going to take a couple of dogs to the Moss.'

'We'll see you first,' said Mr Aicheson in tones which suggested that he was doing me a great favour.

Before I had time to think, I was whisked into my own sitting room. I met Beth's startled eyes over the Sergeant's shoulder and then the door closed between us.

When I had met Superintendent Aicheson

201

on a previous occasion I had gained the impression that he was the political and administrative guru rather than an involved member of the crime detection teams. It was soon clear that he was present mainly to lend authority to the Sergeant. Most of the questions were hers.

Her line of questioning took me by surprise. She was brisk and businesslike and her manner was hostile. Evidently she was not yet willing to forgive and forget the incident in the farmyard involving her car. Instead of concentrating on the events leading up to our meeting with DI Ewell, she took me back to the evening of Dougal Webb's disappearance. Had Beth and I been together for the whole evening? What corroborating details could I remember? I told her that we had watched the video of a film, hired in Cupar. What film? I had to outline the plot for her. Unfortunately, the film had proved a disappointment and my memory of it was patchy.

She switched to the subject of Hannah. What did we really know of her movements that night? How could we be sure that her phone call had come from Ardrossie? Did she have access to Henry's mobile phone, or any other? Had the sound of the connection been consistent with a public call-box? The questions seemed to follow a path of logic which was unmistakable yet not on my mental map. I gave up trying to orient myself and

202

concentrated on recalling the truth. We were innocent and therefore had nothing to fear, that was my simple philosophy, and I hoped that Beth would be wise enough to follow it.

We came back to the attempted blackmail. How had I really felt about Dougal Webb prior to that attempt? What grounds had I had for thinking him untrustworthy? I had rejected his first approach, that much was confirmed by the barmaid, but if he had not vanished, if he had come back with more specific threats, would I not have sacrificed my Dickson rather than have him approach the Kennel Club?

At that point I got a little heated. When the Sergeant uttered the word 'gun', her tone made it clear that she considered my Dickson to be a trivial but antisocial toy. I explained in forceful terms that, firstly, there was no substance in Webb's allegations and, secondly, that the chance to acquire a Dickson Round Action in mint condition comes but once in a lifetime to a man of limited means and it would have taken considerably more than Dougal Webb's threats to part me from it. Even as I spoke I realized that I must be giving the impression that I would have killed to keep the gun, but I was still relying on truth and justice. Others have done the same and lived to regret it.

The Sergeant brought us round to the story of Mim. Surely there must have been conspiracy with Quentin Cove? How else could he have hoped to get away with such a fraud? Had money changed hands? Or favours? Had the quarrel in the farmyard occurred because I was trying to deny my part in the conspiracy and leave Mr Cove to face the music alone? I pointed out that I had signed Mim's registration over to Daffy long before Quentin Cove expressed any interest in the little bitch, but the Sergeant waved that aside as a palpable smokescreen.

Part of my mind could see where the questions were leading while the rest of it was refusing to see anything of the sort. But one thing both parts of my mind were agreed on. No detective sergeant, even one as alluring as Detective Sergeant Bremner and supported by no less than a detective superintendent, was going to badger me with untrue and unsupported allegations. 'I have one question of my own,' I said. 'Who or what did Detective Inspector Ewell find yesterday?'

The Sergeant tilted her head back in order to look down her nose at me. 'You'll know soon enough,' she said ominously. 'For now, we'll ask the questions.'

I had had enough. I explained clearly and almost politely that, failing any questions which did not presuppose that I was guilty of something, I would only be prepared to continue in the presence of my solicitor. Beth, I said, could make up her own mind and usually did. And with that I made what I hoped was a dignified exit, no doubt leaving the two officers with the worst possible impression.

Beth was somewhere upstairs. I could hear her clattering around angrily. Hannah, with Sam's help, was washing puppy dishes in the kitchen but the Sergeant steered me past and I had the feeling of being watched until I had left the gate with two of the dogs.

The weather gods had relented and given us one of those days that delude us into thinking that winter in Scotland isn't so bad after all. Even the Moss was not quite as barren as usual. The dogs were enjoying it as much as I was and they wanted to romp, so I kept my mind on controlling them and saw no reason to hurry back.

We returned to Three Oaks as dusk was falling, pleasantly tired and with three wood pigeon in the bag, taken on the flight-line to the pond for their evening's drink before going to roost. Both dogs had pleased me by retrieving the pigeon—the loose-feathered birds are not to every dog's taste. Quentin Cove's car was parked beside the police Range Rover in front of the house but the man himself was waiting at the gate. My interlude of escape was over and reality came pouring in.

'I must speak to you,' he said. 'Whatever you think of me, it's high time that we compared notes.'

'Hold on a minute longer,' I told him. Hannah came out of the house to meet me. The dogs were wet and smelly but she took them over without demur while avoiding any glance in the direction of the farmer.

I turned back. He met me beside his car. 'You've got a bloody nerve,' I said.

He looked shamefaced and I noticed that he seemed to have lost weight, but he managed a shrug. 'All right, so I've sinned. And I'm regretting it, every moment. I thought I could get away with it. Then I thought that I could live with it. But I can't.'

He had surprised and partially disarmed me by not being defiant, but I had no intention of allowing him to emulate the Prodigal Son. 'I'm not talking about the fiddle. But Daffy,' I said. 'You failed to get her banned from driving so you drove your car at her.'

He rubbed a hand over his face. 'I must have been born daft. But—can you understand this? Something grand was disintegrating in my hands. I'll make it up to Mrs Mearns if ever I can.' The evening was cooling fast. He saw me shiver and remorse turned to compassion. 'Come into the car,' he said. We got in and he started the engine and turned up the heat. He sat looking out of the windscreen at nothing for a long moment. 'I've had it easy for most of my life,' he said. 'Hard physical work, but you can take that if your health's good and you've got security. My granddad was a thrifty farmer.

206

He bought Ardrossie outright and worked it up. My dad added to it. It came to me as a going concern at a time when a farmer couldn't lose money if he tried. I never faced a challenge, never achieved anything on my own.'

I was damned if I was going to feel sorry for him. 'There was the dog-food,' I said.

He shook his head. He was not to be coaxed out of his self-pity. Poor little rich boy, I thought. 'That was no challenge. It was as if the set-up was there already, waiting to happen. The right men gave me the right advice and it worked. But all my life I've had dogs. I might've gone in for sheepdog trialling, but Ardrossie's never been a sheep farm and gun dogs are the dogs I know. You heard of the man who said, "I'd give my right arm to be ambidextrous"?'

'I have now.'

'Well, that's how I felt. It was over the top, I can see that now. From here on, if I hear the word "obsession" I'll ken just what it means. But I found myself with a dog that could win. I've had some good dogs in the past, but aye with some fault—sometimes an inherent fault but often because, when I was young and inexperienced, I tried to hurry the dog along too quickly. But this time the bitch and I were in tune. You know what I mean?'

'Of course I do,' I said. I had experienced that supreme harmony perhaps a dozen times and lesser likenesses of it with two dogs out of three.

He sighed. 'Just for once, I could have gone in and matched myself against you and all the others. It drove me frantic that I couldn't run my wee bitch because of some rule that you said was nonsense and even I could see was doing nothing but prevent improvement of the working breeds. For a while, that was all I could think of. When I came to my senses, I gave thanks that I hadn't done more damage than I have. But I didn't want to do Mrs Mearns any real harm. And I didn't mean to land you in it.'

I felt a prickling of my scalp. 'Have you landed me—us—in it?'

'I hope no, but I'm feared I have. Yon Inspector Ewell arrived this afternoon with a sergeant mannie I'd not seen before. He was polite as ever, the Inspector, but under the politeness he was rock-hard. He wouldn't tell me a damn thing—'

'I know the feeling,' I said.

'—but, reading between the lines, they've decided that no one person did the deed.'

'But which deed?' I asked. 'I might be able and willing to help them if I knew what the crime was.'

'Do you not know? I found out that much— no thanks to Mr Detective Inspector Ewell,' he added bitterly. 'I had it from Elsie Dundee. They went to Gifford House yesterday and found Mr Macevoy in a hidey-hole under the floor. She saw them taking him away. So it seems that the body must have been Dougal's.'

So Beth had been wrong for once. I must remember to crow over her. 'Then what's all this fuss about?' I asked. 'If Mr Macevoy killed his nephew . . .'

'But he didn't. They seem quite sure of that, I don't know why.' The light was almost gone. Quentin Cove's voice was coming out of darkness but he sounded both plaintive and indignant. 'They seem to have eliminated every individual—so far as they know of them—with any reason to resent Dougal. Likely they're looking for other blackmail victims. But they've also decided that more than one person must have been involved.'

I thought that over, liking it less and less. The field was wide open again.

'It's a bugger,' he resumed suddenly. 'They must have decided that either I killed him over the blackmail or your Miss Hopewell stabbed him in a fit of jealous rage. The fact that I have a rock-solid alibi up to the wee small hours seems to strike them as the most suspicious factor of all. Even if young Hannah was guilty, she could never have moved the body to Gifford Hill on her own. She'd have had to have help.'

For a moment I considered myself as a suspect. Apart from the fact that I knew myself to be innocent, it made a tenable theory. 'Goddamn!' I said.

'Takes a wheen of getting used to, doesn't it?'

I let that pass as irrelevant. 'Do you know whether they've found where he was killed? Or where the knife came from? Or where the handle ended up?'

'It doesn't seem like it. I left them rummaging around the farm. I'll tell you this— if I come across a knife-handle around the place, it goes in the bottom of the midden. That's the one place they've shied away from. And they kept me away from the phone, so I decided the damage was done and I might just as well come here.'

'They'll have seen us comparing notes,' I pointed out.

'Guilty or innocent, they'd expect that.'

We fell silent again. My mouth had dried and I could feel tension in my stomach and in my neck muscles. Bad events were in the wind. My mind wanted to rush off in all directions but I held it, by effort of will, to a pattern of logic.

Could Hannah be guilty? It was physically possible. Would she kill a faithless lover? Unlikely. I would have expected her reaction to be hysteria rather than violence, but who knew the reaction of a woman scorned? Would Quentin Cove have helped her to dispose of a body? Very unlikely—unless, of course, she had inherited his secret from Dougal or deduced it for herself. She might have threatened to incriminate him with the murder. If they had been acting in concert . . . Immediately, the conundrum began to resemble the old riddle about two brothers, one of whom always tells lies while the other tells the truth. You have one question to determine which is which. The answer to the riddle, of course, is to ask one of them, 'What would your brother answer, if I asked him whether he was the liar?' Except that on this merry-go-round there was no brother who could be trusted to tell the truth.

But again, Hannah had never been a competent liar. Her few attempts at pulling the wool over our eyes had been accompanied by so much blushing, hesitation, finger-twisting and contradiction as to be wholly transparent. As I remembered her voice on the phone and her behaviour the next morning, each had been more in accordance with puzzlement than with a terrible secret.

Quentin Cove, now, was speaking from the standpoint of one who is innocent; but then, what else would he do? His story was confirmed by his friends and then by Hannah . . . up to around four in the morning. By then, time would be short. Dawn would still be several hours away but it had been a clear night and I recalled a rising moon. The sky had still been clear in the morning. In the country, even in winter, people are up and about early. Postmen, milkmen, lorry drivers, wildfowlers and others would have been on the roads. Elsie Dundee lived nearby. Easy enough, perhaps, to stop a vehicle for a few seconds and tuck the body away behind the hedge, to walk back after hiding the vehicle ... but I could not visualize any murderer daring to carry a body up a hill that was overlooked by a road and several houses, except perhaps in the dead hours just after midnight or after waiting for an overcast night. Even then, the task would be impossible without torches which might attract the attention of passers-by.

Suppose that Cove had killed Dougal Webb before leaving home, or that there had been another confrontation over the attempted blackmail when Webb returned home, after Hannah gave up and left. The factory would have been standing empty. I had been shown round it by the proud farmer. Most of the raw materials went up by conveyor into the silos and from there to top of the square tower. Nearly all the processing took place in the tower as the product progressed downwards under gravity, untouched by hand and usually unseen by eye. The ground floor was given over mainly to storage and packing, and most of the human activity was on this level. A body, wrapped in polythene, could be hidden in the tower for a day or two in safety, especially if the proprietor was on hand to allocate duties.

212

The polythene could then be used to wrap a large order, thus to disappear for ever.

Also on the ground floor was an area given over to the preparation of animal products, in machinery derived from the fast-food industry. Originally, Quentin Cove had bought his animal products already prepared but later he had decided that he was being ripped off. Dog feeds are subject to scrutiny at least as stringent as that given to human food, and sudden trouble with the inspectorate had been the last straw. Cove had struck a deal with a large concern specializing in poultry for the human market, to buy their leftovers. To these were added a steady stream of rabbit meat. At first glance, an hour spent feeding the parts of a body through those machines would have seemed a safer means of disposal than moving it to the bonfire on Gifford Hill. But the police had not missed the point. They had checked for human tissue and Cove might well have anticipated their action. He was not a fool.

'What did Inspector Ewell want to know?' I asked.

I felt Quentin Cove jump and thought that he might have been on the point of falling asleep. Stress often has that effect. The car was becoming hot. He turned the fan down. 'Nothing very much,' he said. 'What I was doing every bloody minute since I reached puberty and who could bear me out. How I got

213

on with you and those girls of yours. And then he was wanting to know about the blackmail.'

'You didn't give in to young Webb, did you?' I asked.

He grunted in annoyance. 'It was all very well for you,' he said. 'Dougal was barking up the wrong tree. You really kenned damn-all about it. But he had me by the short and curlies and he knew it fine. He could get my trialling stopped dead before it had hardly started. But he was dashed queer about it,' Quentin added. 'It was as if he didn't expect it to make a difference between us. He seemed to think that things could go on just as before.'

'Just like you do, in fact,' I said.

'Nah,' he said glumly after a moment's thought. 'I don't think anything like that. I've made an idiot of myself and I know it.'

I decided to dangle a little bait. 'What did he want from you? Money?'

'I don't know that he ever asked anyone for money. No, when he came to the point it was little enough. He wanted my video recorder. It was a good one, mind, top of the range, but it had been playing me up now and again and I'd been looking at a newer model. Living on my own, I like having a quality video machine and watching the things I want to see when I want to see them, not when some clown of a programmer thinks it's time I sat down. But I wouldn't kill to keep it, even if I couldn't have afforded another dozen of the things.'

It certainly seemed an inadequate motive for murder—if true. But there is no way to predict what a man will do in a sudden fit of rage. Quentin Cove had never been one to go around looking for a fight, but he had a temper . . .

I was wondering how to probe a little further without testing that temper too far, when the static scene began to shift. The outside light sprang to life. Sergeant Bremner and Superintendent Aicheson came out of the house. They got into the Range Rover and the Sergeant drove off without, apparently, even a glance in our direction.

The Range Rover was hardly out of the drive before the door opened again and Beth emerged, wrapped in a tartan shawl. We got out of the car to meet her but she hopped up into the back seat of the big car. 'We have to talk,' she told the farmer, 'but you are not crossing my threshold again.'

I heard the farmer make a small sound. I had heard him make the same sound when he caught his finger in a gate.

We got back into the front. While the courtesy light was still on I saw that Quentin Cove had flushed dark red and his square face looked haggard. 'I was just telling John how much I regret—'

'No time for that now,' Beth snapped. 'Tell Daffy all about it later. She may forgive you. I certainly wouldn't. I saw you out here ages

215

ago, John, but I wasn't going to let Sam join in with us so I had to wait until they'd finished with Hannah. She came out of there in tears, so she and Sam can look after each other for a while.'

'They found Mr Macevoy at Gifford House,' I told her. 'But they've cleared him of the murder somehow.'

'I got that much out of them. They told me about it, just to shut me up. They've found the lorry driver who gave him a lift from York to Kirkcaldy on the Monday, the day after Dougal disappeared.'

I began to repeat our discussion but Beth cut me off. She was in her overdrive. 'All right. So I was wrong. You can crow about it later. They've made up their minds that there had to be a conspiracy. They're probably right. Dougal was no lightweight. I don't see any one man carrying him up that hill and over that sort of ground single-handed. And in their minds a conspiracy means us.'

'There's one other possibility,' Quentin Cove said. 'Jim Macevoy could have reached home and found his wife wondering what to do with the body of his nephew.'

'Do you think she'd be much help, carrying a body across that broken ground by night?' Beth asked.

'At least it wouldn't be uphill,' Cove pointed out.

'The police wouldn't have missed that

216

option,' I said, 'but they seem to have discounted it. We never met Macevoy. How old was he when he went inside?'

'In his fifties.'

'He must be sixty or more by now,' Beth said. 'Could you picture him managing the body with no help except for his wife? She looked like a flabby lump to me, the one time I saw her.'

'You're right,' Cove said gloomily.

'I may not be. People can perform amazing feats when they're desperate. But we can't bank on it. Our problem,' Beth said firmly, 'is that while the police are looking at us they may not be looking at anybody else. They can't bring a case against any of us because there isn't any real evidence and there never will be. The fiscal hasn't yet called for an inquiry in front of the sheriff, but when it happens the facts will come out. And we'll be smeared, for ever. Not openly but by implication. If they don't make an arrest, we'll have this around our necks for years. Hannah, in particular, may go down in folklore as the girl who got away with murdering her lover. We've got to do something.'

'Definitely,' I said. 'But what?'

Beth thought it over for all of ten seconds. 'We only have long shots,' she said, 'so we'd better . . . what does one do with long shots?'

'Back them,' Cove said.

'Right. Mr Cove, can you get us into

Dougal's cottage? Or have the police sealed it?'

'No problem. But you're probably too late. The seals have been broken. Somebody went through the place—probably more than one person. The police know, but they haven't bothered to seal it again. I took a look inside for myself. Nothing seems to have been stolen, so I jalouse it was somebody looking for whatever Dougal had been holding over them.'

'They probably found it,' I said. 'It's hopeless, isn't it? If somebody already got screwed for a car or a watch—or a video—his motive's gone. He never seems to have bitten the same person twice.'

'Thanks very much,' Cove said.

Beth leaned forward. 'But we don't know that,' she said. 'Mr Cove, what was the next demand he made on you? What was the next guilty secret? Did he find some trace of Daffy on the bull-bars at the front of this car? Was he going to turn you in for attempted murder?'

'Nothing of the sort!' Quentin Cove's voice went up through the roof. I could sense his outrage. It was as unmistakable as a fart in the confined space. 'I'd been daft for a while, I admit it. I did three things I'll be bitterly ashamed of for the rest of my days.'

'Four,' I said. 'You let my tyres down.'

'All right, four. Dougal spotted the switch of dogs and he took my video off me and that's

218

all. Damn it, Dougal was already dead when . . . when I . . .'

'When you tried to injure Daffy. All right,' Beth said. 'Keep your socks on. I wanted to be sure. Who else is there? Mr Cove, you were closer to him, geographically, than anyone else. What expensive toys did he have? The car, the watch, the video. What else?'

'Clothes,' I said.

'You can't blackmail somebody for clothes,' Beth snapped. 'At least you could, but there's nobody I can think of whose clothes would have fitted Dougal. What else did he covet?'

'I've no idea,' Cove said. 'We didn't let our hair down and have heart-to-heart blethers.'

'I must ask Hannah,' Beth said musingly. 'Yes, I think we definitely want a look inside his cottage.'

'Whatever you're after, it's probably gone,' I told her. 'The victim took it back. Or the police have it. We might get a solicitor to ask for disclosure of what they've found.'

'Later,' Beth said. 'First, let's be sure that it's gone. You'll be at home in the morning?'

'I'll watch for you,' said Quentin Cove.

'Right,' Beth said. 'And until then, you bastard, behave yourself, you hear me?' As she got out of the car and the courtesy light came on, her elbow gave him an accidental crack over the head that made his eyes water.

219

CHAPTER ELEVEN

I was in no doubt that Beth's view of our predicament was the right one. We had seen other instances in which the law and justice had failed to coincide. A verdict of *not guilty* was often taken to mean *got away with it. Not proven* was worse. And if no charge was brought against anybody, that could be the worst of all because there would not even be the cold comfort of either of the other verdicts. The odium would stick. Hannah would be tainted for ever and—God help us!—the whisper might go round that she and I had conspired to kill her lover in order to further an affair of our own. Such a rumour would be no more unreasonable than many that had circulated on the local gossip-vine.

When I mentioned the danger to Beth, she only nodded. I realized then that she was, as so often, ahead of me and that this had been one of the reasons for her call to arms. My ambition to drop Sir Ian Bewlay into the mire up to and over his balding head would have to take second place for the moment.

I was in a fever to dash around and do something, anything, to upset the *status quo*, but Beth calmed me down and set me to clearing the decks for the morning. I spent the rest of the day walking dogs in the darkness and helping with the last feed and clean. Beth, meanwhile, was in her hyperactive mode, pulling more than her weight around the kennels, comforting Hannah until Daffy's return relieved her of that necessity, attending to Sam and between times making phone call after phone call. And somehow during all this frenzy a meal made it onto the table.

Sam, protesting loudly that he wanted to see his favourite video for the thousandth time, was soon banished to bed and we settled in the kitchen with Hannah and Daffy—not in order to enjoy our knocking-off drinks, long after our usual time, but to take them anyway as a comfort and a lubricant to serious discussion.

Hannah was still red-eyed and bemused by being pitched suddenly into a strange new world, but when Beth pressed her for details of what Detective Sergeant Bremner had asked her she pulled herself together. She told us that the Sergeant, after the now customary minute-by-minute dissection of Hannah's activities over what seemed to be an unnecessarily prolonged period, had suddenly changed tack. Had Hannah quarrelled with Dougal? Had she been jealous? Or had he tried to blackmail her? Into sleeping with him, perhaps? What threat had he held over her? 'And then,' Hannah said indignantly, 'she up and asked me whether I fancied Mr Cunningham.'

221

'What did you tell her?' Daffy asked, enthralled.

'I told her that she had a mind like a cesspool and that if she made any more suggestions like those I'd tell Mr Cunningham.'

The others laughed. I cringed. The idea that my wrath could constitute a threat to be held over the police was a new one to me, but it seemed that, rather than fancying me, Hannah still regarded me with awe. I was uncertain whether to be flattered or insulted.

Beth was trying, not very successfully, to hide a smile. 'What else?' she asked.

'Sergeant Bremner said that there were a carving knife and two smaller kitchen knives in Dougal's kitchen and she wanted to know if there should have been any other ones. I said that I didn't know. And was I sure that Mr Cunningham hadn't come to meet me that night? I said definitely not and anyway I had your car so he'd have had to walk about ten miles or take a taxi. Then she wanted to know if you'd ever seen that film before and I said that I knew for a fact that you hadn't. But she went on and on, suggesting things you'd hardly believe.'

'We'd believe them all right,' Beth said. 'But I'm afraid we may have to go on and on, like Sergeant Bremner. First ... Daffy, Mrs Kitts may be back tomorrow if Mr Kitts is still improving. Either way, can you manage the

222

place if Hannah comes with us tomorrow morning? We need to look through Dougal's cottage.'

'No problem,' said Daffy.

'But do you really need me?' Hannah asked nervously.

Beth paused for a moment, wondering whether to be brisk or motherly and deciding to attempt a compromise. 'We do need you,' she said. 'It may be difficult for you and bring back all sorts of memories you'd rather put aside but you'll have to be brave. We have to untangle this horrible mess if you're not to be bothered again and again, so in a way it's for your own good. Mr Cove says that Dougal's cottage had been entered. You're the one person who may be able to give us a fresh lead by telling us whether anything's missing. Or if anything's there that wasn't there before. Or if there's anything there that he wouldn't have paid for but might have got by . . . by putting pressure on people.'

'By blackmail,' Hannah said stoutly. 'It's all right. I didn't know anything about it at the time and I didn't believe it at first, but thinking it over since then I've been remembering how he could set his heart on things. Not money, just things. And most of the time he did care about how people felt, but when he wanted something he changed completely and was ready to ride roughshod over anybody. I can easily believe that he'd use threats.'

Hannah had been pressed to accept a vodka and tonic instead of her usual shandy. Beth caught Daffy's eye and Daffy surreptitiously topped up Hannah's glass. The unaccustomed alcohol was having the desired effect of loosening her tongue, but what came out in response to Beth's probing was mostly negative. Did Dougal have any enemies? Not to say enemies but he didn't seem to get on with people. Then who were his friends? Hannah could only think of Elsie Dundee's son Jimmy, who on his visits home had usually gone for a pint with Dougal. Who else might he have been blackmailing? Hannah had no idea.

Beth sighed and held out her own glass for a refill. 'We have to get a starting point,' she said. 'And you're not being very helpful. Hannah, Dougal coveted things. Did he ever say, "I wish I had a such-and-such"?'

'Sometimes.' Hannah carefully suppressed a ladylike burp. 'In fact, quite often. It was his way. Mostly it was cars. He'd see a four-by-four, much more suitable for a farmer than the Lotus, and he'd say, "I could be doing with one of those." Once it was a real pearl necklace and he said, "I wish I could give you something like that," and I said that he didn't have to worry about it, I wasn't the sort to wear pearls, pearls would look silly on me.' Hannah blinked and hurried on. 'Sometimes, when we saw something happening, like an accident or a really weird car or once it was a girl with her skirt tucked into the back of her knickers, he'd say, "God, I wish I had a video camera!" And I remember him watching one of Mr Hatton's dogs working sheep and saying that about a camera and also saying, "I wish I owned that dog."'

'That's interesting,' Beth said. 'John, just suppose that he'd had something serious on you, something that you'd really hate for anyone to know, and he demanded that you hand over your favourite dog—which would that be?'

'I don't know,' I said. 'Probably Ash.'

'Well then, would you have killed him in order to keep the dog?'

I considered the question seriously. 'It would depend on circumstances,' I said. 'It's too easy to sit here and say "no". I'm not a killing sort of person except in the way of duty, but I'm no different from other men. If the demand came at the height of a furious quarrel I suppose it might prove to be the last straw.'

Beth looked at me speculatively and then decided on a change of subject. 'Hannah, can you think of anyone who'll be better off with Dougal dead?'

'I suppose his uncle . . .'

'Who was still hitch-hiking northward at the time. Did Dougal have any insurance policies?'

225

To my surprise, Hannah's glow was not just the firelight but a definite blush. 'That was another thing he said he wished he had. He said that he was going to start one for me. And once, when I admired his Lotus, he said that he was going to make out a will in my favour. But I don't know that he did either of those things.'

'Surely,' I said, 'if the police had found either a will or an insurance policy with you as the beneficiary, they'd have said something?'

'Well, I'm not sure,' Hannah said. 'Sergeant Bremner kept asking me things like what difference was Dougal's death going to make to me. I said that losing a boyfriend was bound to make a big change. Obviously. I wasn't going to give the impression that I'd been expecting to be better off. But I think she knew.'

'Oh, my dear!' Beth said.

*   *   *

Isobel arrived on time in the morning. Henry, she said, was back on his feet, shaky but self-sufficient, and she was glad to get back to Three Oaks and less demanding patients. After a quick rush at the more demanding chores we were able to leave Three Oaks, confident that Daffy and Isobel could at least keep things ticking over. The morning was dank. We settled Sam in front of his favourite

226

video, fobbed off Isobel's questions with a very brief résumé of events and made our escape.

At Ardrossie I turned into the farmyard. Quentin Cove was standing on the now exposed tarmac. He was talking to Detective Inspector Ewell.

'Oh, hell!' I said.

'I left a message for him,' Beth said firmly, 'asking him to meet us here. But I didn't think that he'd come. I just wanted to be able to show, afterwards, that we hadn't done anything behind his back.'

'He won't want us sifting through Dougal's home.'

'We'll see,' Beth retorted.

I drew up beside the two-year-old Allegro which I assumed had brought the Inspector. He seemed to be unaccompanied. 'He's become the enemy,' I said.

'I don't think so. But that's why I didn't tell you sooner,' she said obscurely.

We disembarked. Ewell walked to meet us while Quentin Cove kept his distance and looked ready to take to his heels. I could guess that Ewell had not been offering words of comfort.

'If you've abandoned us to the wolves . . .' I began.

Ewell shook his head sadly. 'None of my doing,' he said. 'I suspect that the Super gained the impression from Sergeant Bremner that I was going easy on you.' He saw my eyebrows go up. I was always a believer in loyalty to my immediate superior. 'I'm not blaming the lassie,' he added quickly. 'She wouldn't run with tales. But if the Super asked her a direct question, she'd have to give an honest opinion.'

'Maybe,' I said. I had a suspicion that the knives might be out for Detective Inspector Ewell, who was too unsophisticated a man to realize it. What I was much more certain of was that Ewell was not above moderating his own opinions for the sake of a pretty face; but I had already known that from his fatherly attitude to Beth over the years.

Ewell ignored the doubt in my voice and nodded. 'They're checking over the possibilities of conspiracy while I'm relegated to searching for the murder scene. If we find that, we'll have the case cracked, I'm thinking. If not, then it may hang over us for years.'

'You don't have a lot to go on,' I agreed.

'We've nothing,' he said disgustedly. 'A body largely cremated. Its immediate vicinity also burned. A knife-blade that could have come from anywhere. A victim who has been practising extortion by menaces, which means that damn near anyone might have a motive for killing him, but who's to know? And to cap it all, men and dogs were scampering round and around the body,' Ewell said bitterly, 'before we got there and even afterwards. Not a footprint to be found that didn't belong to one of you men or Mrs Dundee or the foresters or your damn dogs. Or the rabbits, of course.'

'They surely can't blame you for that,' said Beth. 'The night's rain would have washed any older footprints away.'

Anyone but Beth would have received a sharp retort. 'I'd like to think so,' the Detective Inspector told her. 'But when your message said that you could give us a fresh lead . . .'

'I only said that I hoped that I could make a contribution,' Beth said. 'Mr Aicheson won't find the truth by looking at us. And that's all we want, the same as yourself—the truth. And we have a right to make our own investigation in order to establish our innocence, don't we?'

'As early as this, I doubt it,' Ewell said. 'It may depend what you had in mind.'

Beth smiled at him winningly. 'Nothing outrageous. But it's our only starting-point. You'll have searched Mr Webb's cottage up, down and sideways. But would you have known if something had been removed or shifted or put back? Or even added? You didn't ask Hannah, and she'd be more likely to know than anyone.'

'Well, it's a thought,' Ewell said doubtfully.

'So I phoned you. The seals are already broken. If Hannah says that something isn't where it belongs, you can tell us whether the

229

police took it or moved it. And if we find something useful, we'd rather find it in your presence. Otherwise somebody could say that we'd put it there.'

Ewell raised a tired eyebrow. 'They could say that anyway. As you remind me, the seals were broken.'

'We'll worry about that if it happens,' Beth said firmly. 'First, let's try to find something, if it's there to be found.' As she led the way imperiously to the cottage door she beckoned to Quentin Cove, who followed obediently in her train, producing a large old-fashioned key. The door opened directly into a compact living room.

At first glance the cottage seemed to have been the habitation of an untidy man leading a slovenly, bachelor existence; but I heard Hannah draw in breath in a disapproving hiss and when I looked again I could see an underlying orderliness. I realized then that a police search followed by any number of more amateurish searches could have disarranged even the British Museum. If everything was not in its place, at least there was a place for everything. Cupboards and shelves had been made or adapted by a loving hand to suit the intended contents which had now been replaced higgledy-piggledy or dropped on the floor.

Inspector Ewell had been carrying a large envelope. 'I was coming here anyway, one of these days,' he said. 'We took away his video cassettes for study.' He produced four cassettes and set them on a shelf which had evidently been made for them under the video recorder. There was room for many more. It seemed that Dougal Webb had intended to tape whatever took his fancy.

'Did they hold any interest?' I asked the Inspector.

He grunted and shook his head. 'They didn't interest me. Sitcoms, and I'd seen most of them.'

Beth decided to begin at the top and work down. The small cottage would only have had one small bedroom and possibly a boxroom tucked under the slates. Beth, Inspector Ewell and Hannah would have filled the available space. I could hear Hannah protesting that she had never seen Dougal's bedroom but to no avail. Quentin Cove stayed with me.

Most of the furnishings were utilitarian and slightly shabby, as befitted a young and newly qualified farm manager, but one exception stood out. I drew Quentin Cove's attention to a small but handsome Victorian dining table which took up more than its share of the limited floor-space. I stroked its deep gloss and it seemed to purr. 'This is a bit up-market compared to the rest,' I said. 'The product of blackmail? Or was there a legacy?'

Cove shook his head. 'The product of a roup. We were at a farm sale together. I bought some calves and he paid about a fiver for the table. It was in a barn, covered with chicken-shit. It took him a month of evenings and weekends to clean it up and restore the finish.'

So another promising lead was a dead end. I decided that if the table came to Hannah I would make her an offer for it. The cottage was very cold. The electric heating had been turned off by some frugal busybody. Even through my favourite sheepskin coat I was becoming chilled. Between that and the nervous tension, I was soon in dire need of a pee.

I could have stepped outside but I would have been under the windows of the house or the cottage, possibly both. 'Is the bathroom working?' I asked the farmer.

He shook his head. 'Water's drained down in case of frost. Go over to the house. It's open and the water's on again.'

'Thanks.'

I hurried across to the house. I could hear voices. But Beth always insists on my drinking several mugs of tea with my breakfast in order to 'keep my fluids up', whatever that may mean, and I was in too much of a hurry to worry about visitors or even intruders in the farmhouse.

When I emerged some little while later Mrs Dundee, complete with pinny and duster, was in the hall together with a large young man in jeans and several heavy sweaters. He was bronzed and looked fit.

'It's Mr Cunningham, Jimmy,' she said delightedly. 'You can tell him. He'll ken fine what you should dae.'

The young man—Jimmy—shuffled his feet. 'I don't know, Ma,' he said.

'Weel,' said his mother, 'ye maun clype to somebody some time. Ye canna gang back tae your boat and leave us a wanrestfu. And it'll a be waur, gin they airt it oot an ye've no said.'

Ordinarily, I would have made an excuse and my escape. But the farmhouse was warm while the world outside was not. I unbuttoned my coat, to let some more of the delicious warmth inside, and waited.

Evidently his mother's words were not only comprehensible but convincing to the young man. 'Maybe you're right,' he said at last. 'Mr Cunningham, can you spare a few minutes?'

I said that I could. But I had no intention of receiving his confidences while standing in a hallway which, for all its warmth, was distinctly draughty. I led the way into Quentin's sitting room, shed my heavy coat and got us comfortably seated.

It was a relief that Jimmy was a much clearer speaker than his mother. Dialects in Scotland change radically over comparatively short distances and my Edinburgh upbringing had not prepared me for Elsie Dundee. I had no doubt that when the two were alone he

233

would go a long way towards matching his mother's unspoiled rural dialect, but school followed by work away from home had taught him the sort of English that passes muster anywhere. Looking at him, I could understand why there had been rumours about his parentage. I could see in him the image of a slimmer Sir Ian Bewlay but without a trace of the expressions of arrogance and guile.

'First,' he said, 'my mother tells me you were good to her while I was at sea. I want to pay you back and perhaps you'd square with Mr Kitts?'

He produced a healthy little roll of notes and pushed a Clydesdale tenner into my hand before falling silent. I guessed that he would be offended if I refused the money so I put it in my pocket, with the mental reservation that it would be available for Mrs Dundee if she should fall on hard times again.

'What did you want to tell me?' I prompted him.

He was silent for so long that I thought that he must have changed his mind, but eventually he stirred. 'The last time I was home, about two months ago, I was broke. I'd been cleaned out.'

'By a lassie. The leddies was aye taen up wi him,' his mother said proudly.

'Well, whatever,' said her son, avoiding my eye. 'I reached home in the afternoon. Mum wasn't in but I knew she'd be up at the Big

234

House so I walked up there. Mrs Wartle, the housekeeper—she's the only steady staff Sir Ian keeps—she gave us a cup of tea in the kitchen. When she left the room with a tray, Mum asked if I had any money for her and I had to tell her that I was skint.

'I left soon after that and I walked along the front of the house, on the grass. As I came to a partly open window at the corner of the house I heard voices, and what they were saying stopped me as if I'd walked into a wall. "I'm sorry I made you show it to me now," Sir Ian's voice said. "And I certainly wouldn't want anyone else to see it. I hope you were damn careful with the editing." And another man asked him what he thought—just being sarcastic, you understand? And Sir Ian said that he'd better chuck the master tape away, and the unedited copy, because they could be worth money in the wrong quarter.

'I managed a peep in at the window without being seen. The two of them were watching the TV screen. The other man was that wee feller that hangs around with Sir Ian.'

'Timothy Pratt?' I suggested.

'That's the one. Just then there was a knock on the door and Sir Ian switched off the video and the telly damn quick. It was Mrs Wartle, telling them that their afternoon tea was set in the drawing room. She stood holding the door, so they upped and went, leaving things as they were.

'Well, Mr Cunningham, I'm not a dishonest man. But it seemed to me that Sir Ian had been taking advantage of my mother for years and not paying her a proper wage. And I was needing a wee bit of cash to leave with her. So I pushed up the window and hopped over the sill. They had to have been talking about the video. I ejected the cassette—we have one on the ship, so I knew how to work it. Sir Ian had a whole shelf of cassettes, some of them unused, so I put one of those in the video recorder instead and put the real one in my pocket and slid back out of the window and pulled it down after me. My heart was knocking so's I thought they'd hear it in the drawing room.

'I was away back to the road before I thought how I was going to get my hands on any of the money Sir Ian had talked about.

'It would be some little while before Ma got home. The other person I always saw on my leaves was Dougal Webb, so I walked to Ardrossie. Dougal was ready to finish for the day, and he took me in and gave me a dram.'

Jimmy Dundee paused in his tale and looked me in the eye. 'They tell me that Dougal was going in for a bit of blackmail. I can't say I'm as surprised as I might have been. I'd thought about borrowing some money from him to give to Ma, but I put that out of my mind. He could be good company, but when it came to money he was hard as stone. And he was impatient. He was ready to work for what he wanted, but he wanted a hell of a lot and he expected it to drop into his lap straight away instead of after years of sweat. But I never knew that he was a wrong 'un. I thought that he was just clever at driving a deal. That's how he explained away his car to me and he seemed to believe it himself.'

'I think he probably did,' I said.

'Likely. He certainly had me convinced. And he seemed just the sort to give me the advice I was needing. So I told him the story and he said to leave the tape with him and he'd take a look at it.

'I saw him again just before I went back to sea. He slipped me fifteen quid and told me that he was going to give Sir Ian a fright. He wouldn't say what was on the tape. I left it at that and off I went, but first I made him promise to do nothing for a while, so's nobody could guess that it was me that took it.' Jimmy looked at me anxiously. 'Mr Cunningham, I'm in no hurry to go and tell the police that I nicked something out of Marksmuir House. But Dougal's been killed and if this has any relevance they'll have to know. Right?'

'Absolutely right,' I said. All of a sudden my head, from being a vessel filled only with despondency, was buzzing with ideas. 'Leave it with me. I'll keep you out of it if I can.'

'There now!' said Mrs Dundee.

I hurried back across the yard. Was it too

237

much to hope that the compromising video cassette was still around? That it had been missed by the police and by other searchers? Probably, yes, much too much. But at least we had the possible starting-point that we had lacked.

The whole party was again crammed into the small sitting room. Hannah looked at me as I entered. 'His new jacket's missing,' she said sadly. 'So he did mean to come and meet me.' She seemed to take some comfort from the thought that her lover had not deliberately stood her up.

Beth resumed questioning a now peevish Hannah about the source of every object of any value, about most of which Hannah had not the least idea. I drew Detective Inspector Ewell aside. 'Are you sure that there was nothing missed on those video tapes?'

'Positive. I watched them myself, every inch, even the blank bits.'

I approached the video recorder, studied the switches for a moment and turned it on. There was no little symbol to indicate that a cassette was in place but I pressed the Eject button anyway. Nothing happened. My new-found optimism sagged. The compromising cassette had either been recovered or it was too well hidden even for a police search.

'Try it again,' said Quentin Cove. 'There's a fault. That's why I didn't mind parting with it. The little symbol doesn't light and it usually takes three or four tries before it'll eject.'

'You never mentioned that to our officers,' Ewell said bitterly.

'They wouldn't let me be present during the search,' said Quentin Cove.

I tried the rewind button and got leftward arrow symbols and a whirring sound. I switched on the television set and picked up the remote control. Usually the highest numbered channel is tuned to a video recorder. As the tape clunked to a halt, I tried Channel 9 and pressed 'Play' on the machine. A series of images flashed and vanished. Then the screen steadied. There was no soundtrack.

The others gathered round.

We were looking through the windscreen of a car just coming to a halt. Then the camera was carried out of the car and set down carefully on the bonnet, looking ahead. It showed a motorbike, damaged and lying on its side in the road, close beside a stone wall. The rider, still helmeted, lay pinned beneath it. He seemed to be unconscious. From the marks on the verge and the positions of bike and rider it seemed that the rider had lost control and slammed at speed into the wall.

The picture moved slightly as another person got out of the car. Then into the frame came Sir Ian Bewlay and Timothy Pratt. Sir Ian was already speaking into his mobile phone.

The two men examined the unconscious

rider and gently felt his limbs for fractures. Their faces were always in sight and I had no doubt that a show was being put on for the camera. Sir Ian took off his coat and spread it over the rider. Pratt, in his turn, folded his own coat and slipped it under the man's head. He checked that the man's tongue was forward. They stood back, satisfied. Pratt glanced at his watch.

Sir Ian took out a cigar, lit it and dropped the match.

The motorbike must have been spilling its fuel. Immediately, the rider was enveloped in a spectacular ball of flames.

Sir Ian jumped back, out of the frame, and was not seen again.

To do him justice, Pratt did what he could. The flames were rising as more fuel leaked from the motorbike. Pratt grabbed the man by his clothing and pulled him away from the pool of burning fuel, but the man's leathers must have been soaked with the petrol. Pratt ran out of the picture. He returned in a few seconds carrying a rug with which he tried to smother the flames that still enveloped the man. This was the sequence that had appeared on television and attracted to Pratt such favourable publicity. The film ran on until the arrival of the ambulance and the fire brigade. By then, I was in no doubt that the man was as good as dead. Pratt, who had himself been burned, had behaved with courage; but he would undoubtedly be damned when it was known that he had suppressed the part of the film showing the origin of the fire.

The sequence gave way to a dark frame with white speckles, indicating no signal.

There was absolute silence except for the faintest whisper from the machinery. Nobody wanted to be the first to speak. I stopped the machine. At the third try, it ejected the tape. I handed it to the Detective Inspector. He nodded.

'Wow!' Beth said at last under her breath.

The moment passed. Suddenly, everyone wanted to talk at the same time.

'It's a powerful motive,' I said. 'It doesn't prove that either of them killed him.'

'Of course not,' Ewell said. 'Whenever you get a miscarriage of justice it's because a motive has been mistaken for real evidence. But it gives us what we badly needed, a new direction. It gives us grounds for enquiry. We applied for a search warrant but it was turned down. Sir Ian Bewlay has a lot of clout and some powerful friends. What goes for him goes for Mr Pratt too. With this, we can move ahead.'

'So it was all right to search our house,' Beth said scathingly, 'but not the houses of those two pompous . . .' Her voice tailed away for lack of the *mot juste*.

Hannah furnished it. 'Arseholes,' she said, amazing herself as well as the rest of us. She covered her mouth. I guessed that she had spoken from the heart.

'That's not a nice way to speak about anybody,' Beth warned. 'But you're close,' she added.

'There was a direct and immediate connection between you and Mr Webb,' said Ewell, reverting to where our discussion had been side-tracked. 'His only connection with Sir Ian and Mr Pratt was that each admitted to having sold him something at a bargain price, some time in the past.'

Beth was ready with a sharp answer, but I had had enough. 'We have a business to run,' I said. And, as we moved towards the door, I added, 'You should be able to manage without us now.' It was unfair of me, perhaps, but I had had a bellyful of the police and it would have taken a more angelic man than me not to crow, just a little.

CHAPTER TWELVE

For several days, nothing whatever was to be learned except for guarded statements from the police to the media that they were following up a fresh line of enquiry and that an arrest was expected daily. It was the statement which comes off the rubber stamp during every murder case, but this time we knew that it could be true.

Then a letter arrived for Hannah from a solicitor. True to his type, Dougal Webb had never got around to taking out an insurance policy, which would have cost him serious money. But he had made out a valid will, using a will form from the Post Office, and had deposited it with the solicitor named as his executor. He had kept his word and left his car to Hannah along with a modest legacy in cash. So, eventually, the Lotus came to lend a little class to our gravel and Hannah, who had been taught to drive in our car by Daffy but had never before driven anything much faster than a bicycle, began collecting speeding tickets as though they were trading stamps and motor-minded boy-friends as though they were given away with a pound of tea.

Detective Inspector Ewell called to see us while we were still agog at the news of Hannah's good fortune. He was accompanied by Detective Sergeant Bremner, who seemed strangely unwilling to make eye contact with any of us. They accepted tea in the sitting room with Hannah and Beth and me.

'This is in confidence for another day or two,' Ewell said. 'But we know fine that you can keep a confidence and you've never been noted for talking to the press. We owe it to you to let you know how it worked out. The signs are that it's all over.'

'You got your search warrant, then?' Beth

said.

'With that videotape, there was no doubt of it. And it paid off handsomely. I'll let Sergeant Bremner tell you about it.'

He looked benignly at the Sergeant, who flushed. I realized suddenly that this visit was no mere courtesy but was intended to rub the Sergeant's delicate nose in the mess that had been in the making.

'Blood was found between the tiles in the kitchen at Marksmuir House and also in Sir Ian's vehicle,' said the Sergeant. She spoke woodenly and if her teeth were not gritted they were very close to it. 'The same blood group as Mr Webb and we're in no doubt that it will prove to have been his when the DNA tests are finished. Fibres found in Webb's car match the cloth of Mr Pratt's coat. An examination of some disturbed ground resulted in the unearthing of a knife-handle belonging to the blade found in Mr Webb's body.'

She paused. 'Go on,' said Ewell. The Sergeant sighed.

'Sir Ian and Mr Pratt made formal statements after cautioning. Each was adamant that he had not been on Gifford Hill for years or, in Mr Pratt's case, ever. But the soil, seeds and pollen on Gifford Hill are a unique mix and we have a soil scientist prepared to prove in court that that's where the dirt we found in the welts of Mr Pratt's shoes and Sir Ian's shooting boots came from.

'Faced with this evidence, each changed his story and tried to blame the other. Between the two versions, we can put together the truth. Mr Webb came up to Marksmuir House. It was Sunday, the housekeeper's day off, and the two men were catering for themselves in the kitchen. Webb said that he had the videotape. He then offered to buy Mr Pratt's camcorder and Sir Ian's big four-by-four, for sums which we can assume were paltry. Both men had been bitten once before. Tempers flared. What was being asked from Mr Pratt was the lesser demand, but he was less able than Sir Ian to foot the bill.'

'If he'd paused for a moment,' said Detective Inspector Ewell, 'he might have realized that the videotape would be far more damaging to Sir Ian, who could well have afforded to foot both bills. In fact, Mr Pratt's only sin had been to distribute the tape showing his own heroism and suppress that part showing Sir Ian's appalling carelessness. But Pratt realized that if his patron was knocked off his pedestal he too would suffer. He became furious and struck the fatal blow. We know it from the spots of blood on the sleeve of his coat. Go on, Sergeant.'

'When they realized that Webb was dead,' Sergeant Bremner resumed, 'they put the body in Sir Ian's car, the one that Webb fancied so much, and scrubbed out the kitchen. Around one in the morning, they went out together, Sir

245

Ian conveying the body and Mr Pratt driving Mr Webb's Lotus. They left the Lotus at Cupar station, then drove to Gifford Hill and carried the body up to the bonfire site.'

'And they broke into Dougal Webb's cottage hoping to recover the tape,' I said.

Ewell nodded. 'Probably both of them, but we're sure of Sir Ian. We already had a fingerprint which now proves to be his.' The Detective Inspector got to his feet, so the Sergeant followed suit. 'I felt that we owed you a word of thanks,' he said briskly, 'and also an apology. I'm afraid that we gave you a hard time.'

'None of your doing, I'm sure, Mr Ewell,' Beth said.

I glanced at the Sergeant. She looked as though she had bitten into a wormy apple. The Inspector had noted it too but he was merciless. 'We're very grateful,' he said warmly.

'And no doubt you've had pats on the back from upstairs,' I suggested.

He managed a faint smile. 'Some of us have,' he said. 'Come, Sergeant.'

*　　　*　　　*

When the case came to the High Court, it was over almost before it had begun. In the eyes of the jury, the evidence was conclusive. Defence counsel struggled to argue that blackmailers

246

were fair game and in season, but the fact that money, however little, had been offered rather than demanded rather clouded the issue with the jury. Pratt, the dealer of the blow, was sent to where he would have a captive audience for his pontificating. Sir Ian, as an accomplice after the fact, received a lesser sentence; but his ambitions were in tatters and he was disgraced.

In the meantime, more events had overtaken some of the other participants.

A second case was dealt with in a lower court by the sheriff. Mrs Macevoy was charged with harbouring a prisoner on the run, or some such wording. Her plea that she went in terror of her husband and had acted under duress held little water, since she had continued to deny his presence until the moment the officers lifted the hatch in the floor, but it must have had some effect with the judge because she was treated leniently. She was sentenced to do a hundred hours of Community Service, ministering to the residents in a home for the elderly and the mentally handicapped. It was generally believed that she would much rather have gone to prison.

When he went back to his ship, Jimmy Dundee left his mother better provided for. He also gave her a wad of tickets in the National Lottery and only a month later one of them brought her a one-third share in a roll-over jackpot. She continues to live quite happily in her cottage, but as soon as it became clear that Sir Ian would never return to Fife she bought Marksmuir Estate for a price which must have had the thrifty gentleman grinding his teeth. But long-standing habits are hard to break. Every afternoon she spends at work in the big house, although her Jimmy has left the sea and now, as well as living in the house, runs a business in garden supplies from the gardens and outbuildings. He is often to be seen with Hannah, driving the Lotus at a rather more sober pace than hers.

Quentin Cove's misdeeds were never brought home to him, except that Rex paid him a visit after which the two men, both somewhat battered, adjourned to the nearest pub and got drunk together. Daffy never quite forgave Quentin for the death of Mim, but we never found another supply of dog-food as good and as convenient as his and with Daffy's agreement we became his customers again. When Hebe produced another throwback to Champion Clunie of Netherbrae, Quentin was on the doorstep long before the pup was weaned, brandishing a fistful of twenty-pound notes. The two get on well together. So far, he has not managed to make her up to Champion, but at least having a goal is good for him.

Quentin has one other ambition. He would dearly love to add the Marksmuir land to

Ardrossie and with that in mind pays court to Elsie Dundee. But he does not have it all his own way. Jack Gilchrist, among others, is a rival for her hand. She has not been such an object of desire since Sir Ian first tumbled her on the dining room table.

Mrs Dundee and her son have never forgotten what little help I was able to give them. Or perhaps they think that they are buying my silence. But the sporting rights to Marksmuir land are let to me for a peppercorn rent. And that is what I call a happy ending.